TED WILLIAMS

The Pursuit of Perfection

Jim Prime
and
Bill Nowlin

SPORTS PUBLISHING, L.L.C.

02 03 04 05 06   10 9 8 7 6 5 4 3 2 1

Ted Williams: The Pursuit of Perfection/Jim Prime and Bill Nowlin.

p. cm.
Includes biographical references and index.
ISBN 1-58261-495-4

1. Williams, Ted, 1918–   2. Baseball players—United States—Anecdotes.
3. Baseball players—United States—Biography. 4. Boston Red Sox (Baseball team)
I. Prime, Jim.   II. Nowlin, Bill, 1945–

Unless otherwise noted, all photographs are from the collection of Bill Nowlin, taken by Tom Miller Photography.

All Arthur Griffin photography made available through arrangement with The Arthur Griffin Center for Photographic Art.

The 1960 Ted Williams photographs by Dr. David L. Pressman were taken on July 27, 1960 and are the only color photographs known to exist of Williams hitting a home run (it was #509, off Bob Shaw of the Chicago White Sox.) Luis Aparicio appears at shortstop in the photos.

These and other of Dr. Pressman's baseball photographs have been on display at the National Baseball Hall of Fame, the Sports Museum of New England, the John F. Kennedy Library and Museum, the 1999 M.L.B. All-Star Fanfest (Boston) and the Ted Williams Museum and Hitters Hall of Fame.

While the great majority of entries in this book were gathered by the editors in personal, original interviews, we have also gleaned comments from previously published sources. The late Tris Speaker, for example, had fascinating comments about Williams and these comments were duly recorded by George Sullivan, who graciously allowed us to reprint them. We have made every reasonable effort to contact and give due credit to all such secondary sources. If there has been an error, please notify the publisher. We will gladly correct any inadvertent errors or omissions in subsequent editions.

SPORTS PUBLISHING, L.L.C.
Visit us on the web at www.SportsPublishingLLC.com

For Glenna, Catherine and Jeffrey
For Yleana and Emmet
And for Ted

Acknowledgments

The success of this project was wholly dependent upon the cooperation of those who graciously shared their memories of Ted with us. We thank them all most sincerely. Their words are sometimes analytical, sometimes personal, often candid—but always eloquent and heartfelt. That any man could inspire such a range and depth of emotion in so varied a group of people, is indeed a tribute.

Thanks also goes to the following:

Hank Aaron
Ron Amidon
Neil Anderson
Jerrold Andrews
Frank Anicetti
Donna Bagni
Sy Berger
John T. Bird
Mark Blumenthal
John Boggs
Sue Bond, The Trevlin Collection
Bob Boynton
Charlie Bradford
Rex Bradley, Hillerich & Bradsby
Harvey Brandwein,
    The National Pastime
Bob Breitbard
Dick Bresciani, Boston Red Sox
Frank Brothers
Kathy Burns, MCAS El Toro
George Bush
Victor Campos
Linda Cann
Bill Churchman
Jim Clapper
George Dargati
Sarah Diaz
Peter Dirsa
Dennis Donley
Lib Dooley
Joe Dulak
Howard Elson
Phil Elson
Roy and Ann Engle
Joe Falls
Bobby Jo Williams Ferrell
Dick Fickert
Dick Flavin
Nomar Garciaparra
Larry Gerlach
Wayne Gilson
Paul Gleason
Dick Gordon
Curt Gowdy
Arthur Griffin
Arthur "Buzz" Hamon
Peter Haggert, Telegraph-Journal

Dean Harris
Mark Harris
Bob Harrison
Manuel Herrera
Eileen and Terry Higgins
Phil Hinkley
Henry Horenstein
Louisa Hufstader
Gina Iancherro, The Jimmy Fund
    (also Christina Zwart, Alison
    Taylor and Matt Curran)
Ken Irwin
Allison Janse
Ted Janse
Donna Kail
Jim Kaklamanos
Don King, San Diego Hall of
    Champions
Larry Knapp
Loretta Knapp
Bobby Knight
John D. Knowlton
Ellen Kolton
John Kriston
Armand LaMontagne
Max Lanier
Jean Leonard (Mrs. Buck Leonard)
Marian Leighton Levy
Howard C. Ligon
Dorothy Lindia
Bob Lobel
Anita Lovely
Lee Lowenfish
Brian Luscomb
Yleana Martinez
Debbie Matson, Boston Red Sox
"Major" Dave McCarthy
Chris McKeown
Jerry McKinnis
Ray Medeiros
Lawrie Mifflin
Dr. Clifford Muse
Gerald Nash
Donald, Jessica and Mary Nicoll
Jay Nissen
William Nowlin, Sr.
Brian O'Connor

Dick O'Connell
Buck O'Neil
Eugene Orza
David Pietrusza
Dr. David Pressman
Millie Rahn
Robert Redford
Susan Reynolds
Ben Robicheau
Ann-Cathrin S. Rosenburg
Mike Ross
Ruth Ruiz
Ed Runge
Jack Selzer
Mike Shatzkin
Mike Sheehan
Jim Shellenback
Katherine Shriver
Morris "Moose" Siraton
Mary Sit
Leland Stein
George Steinbrenner
George Sullivan
Bill Swank
Mr. & Mrs. Vin Swazey
Ellen Taintor
Maj. Gen. Larry S. Taylor
Ted Taylor
Alex Theroux
Stew Thornley
Jill Tiger
Dennis Tuttle
John Underwood
Esther Vela
Charles Venzor
Frank Venzor
John Virant
G. Jay Walker
David Warsh
Lewis Watkins
Brooke Wentz
Linda Wick
John-Henry Williams
Mark Winegardner
Harold Zats
Dick Zitzmann

We owe a great debt to Tom Bast, who gave us the opportunity to create the first incarnation of this book, along with generous support and encouragement, and to Chad Woolums, our editor, who shared and shaped our vision of Ted Williams. We are thankful that Mike Pearson and Joe Bannon, Jr. of Sports Publishing believed in the importance of a new and expanded Ted Williams classic, and we have enjoyed working with editor Erin Linden-Levy and senior project manager and designer Jennifer Polson on this labor of love. Everyone at Sports Publishing has been wonderful in allowing us to create the new edition as we envisioned it, and we look forward to working with them all to help spread the word in the months and years to come.

Finally, we would be remiss if we did not offer our thanks to our very supportive families and friends:

Thanks to my friend and co-author Bill Nowlin, a meticulous chronicler of Ted Williams and a perfectionist in his own right. And thanks again to Ted Williams for living a life that is so intriguing, meaningful, and valuable to so many.

Thank you Mom, Dad, Glenna, Catherine, Jeffrey, Margaret, Ray, Matthew, Andrew, Ben, Randi, Bill, Karen, Gary, Laurel, Gerry, Marcia, Ann, Mary, Chris, and all of the people who inspired me in my own life.

—J.P.

♦ ♦ ♦

Further appreciation to my wife Yleana Martinez, my son Emmet, and my partners and colleagues at Rounder Records, who excused my dedication to the keyboard and telephone.

Jim, from the time we first met at Ted's place, it's been a pleasure. Ted has a true friend in you who has helped produce two Ted Williams books now, one with the man himself. You have a real feeling for language as you do for Ted. We worked mostly at a distance, though linked by e-mail virtually every day, but it was a true collaboration, partner.

—B.N.

Ted with Red Sox owner Tom Yawkey.
(Photo by Arthur Griffin)

(Photo by Arthur Griffin)

Contents

Foreword

Any heroes I had when I was a kid were pretty much born out of reading Greek mythology. In real life, in real time, there was only one. It was Ted Williams. I suppose if I searched the ground for something familiar it was that he was left-handed. I was left-handed. He was from Southern California, as was I. He was a baseball player. I wanted to be one when I grew up. I never achieved this objective.

But in truth, it was something more. In those days, I had no access to television or major league ball (Los Angeles was then in the Pacific Coast League). The sport magazines and the radio were my only connection to the grander ballparks, which meant I had to create my own images of each inning. Communication was by pictures. It was these pictures of Williams—relaxing, waiting effortlessly, wrists compensating for the delay in motion and, at the last second, exploding in graceful rhythm, bat to ball—that were my inspiration.

I imagined being there. I imagined hitting the same ball from the same side in the same way. I admired his reticence to joining the Big Parade of publicity, hype and show, which has become so tiresomely prevalent in today's sporting world. He had only disdain for that. He just hit—and did it better than possibly any left-handed batter before or since.

I feel much the same way now as I did then, and I still look on with admiration. Uncompromising behavior both in and out of the park. Years later, when I made "The Natural", I dedicated my number to him. It was the least I could do.

Robert Redford

Introduction

Perfection and baseball do not mix. We would guess that if a perfectionist dies and goes to Hell, it will quickly be discovered that the national sport is baseball.

Occasionally pitchers throw what is called a perfect game—the pitcher did not yield a hit, run or walk over the entire span of the game. Surely this fits the definition of perfection. Well, not quite. Even then, it's never an individual accomplishment. A perfect game requires not only exceptional pitching skills, it requires a constellation of defensive stars, a degree of offensive ineptitude by the other team, and a lot of good luck. Since baseball's modern era began in 1903, only fourteen pitchers have thrown perfect games. Of those fourteen, only four won as many as 60% of the games they pitched during their careers.

Baseball is a game of percentages and those percentages mark the level of perfection that the player has attained. A .300 batting average suggests that you have failed seven out of 10 times at the plate. That is considered good enough to merit millions of dollars on today's diamond exchange. If a hitter goes 4-for-4 one day, he can lay very temporary claim to being perfect at the plate. The next day he may be a very imperfect 0-4. Even the perfect day at the plate does not mean he had a flawless performance. One or more of his hits may have been "tainted." In the field, he may have erred, or committed a base-running blunder.

Ted Williams came as close to hitting perfection as anyone ever has. Baseball may be known by the benign phrase "national pastime" but hitting, for Ted Williams, was a natural passion. Ted fought with writers and fans because he was not satisfied with his own performance or theirs and loudly proclaimed that he wanted to be "the greatest hitter who ever lived." He discussed the science of hitting *ad nauseam* with teammates and opposing players. He sought out the great hitters of the game—Hornsby, Cobb, and others—and grilled them about their techniques. What he liked, he used, what he disagreed with, he dismissed. He weighed his bats to the tenth of an ounce; he boned them to increase their potency. He once told Jim Prime: "I never saw a hitter in my life, myself included, who I thought got the 100 percent best performance out of his capabilities—and I probably never will." Ted also added: "Let's face it. There has never been a per-fect hitter. Ruth and Mantle struck out too much, and Cobb was a push hitter with no power . . . I could point to every hitter I saw, including Ted Williams, and tell you where they fell short of their potential."

Hitting perfection is an elusive goal. Hitters who hit for average and power are rare. In the entire history of baseball, only 10 batters have won baseball's Triple Crown (leading the league in average, home runs and runs batted in, all in the same year.) Ted Williams did it twice, and missed by .0001557 doing it a third time in 1949.

Ted Williams was not a perfect baseball player. He wasn't even a perfect hitter. He was not a perfect fly-fisherman, either. Or a perfect pilot, photographer, breakfast chef or anything else. He did succeed, however, in becoming the best hitter who ever lived, and one of the best fly-fishermen. Everything that Ted did, he strived for Best Ever. He could never settle for second best, and seeing another name ahead of him in the American League batting stats was like a red flag to Ted Williams. He had to be number one. A fierce pride drove him to greatness.

Of course, there's no such thing as perfection in life, either, but that never means it's not worth striving for. The people we most admire are those who never stop trying. It's what sets them apart from others who are content with mediocrity. Ted Williams chose difficult areas in which to pursue perfection. His odyssey was of epic proportions; he chose pursuits on land, on sea and in the air.

On land, of course, his challenge was baseball, and specifically hitting. He called it the "toughest single thing to do in sports," and then went out and did it better than anyone before or since. He didn't just want to play and wouldn't be content being a mere star in the game. As a kid, The Kid was almost never without a baseball bat in his hands. Childhood friends tell of seeing Ted take batting practice until he literally tore the covers off the available baseball. Frank Shellenback, Ted's first minor league manager, visited the teenage Ted in his neighborhood one evening after practice and reported, "Blood was trickling from Williams' hands as he gripped a chipped bat. But he kept swinging. And hitting."

Teddy Ballgame lived and breathed hitting, thought about it day and night. Ted quickly became known for his refusal to swing at a bad pitch. He was sometimes criticized for this by Ty Cobb and others. But why should

Ted Williams compromise his hitting principles by swinging at sub-standard offerings? When you do that, he said years later, "pretty soon you're just ordinary." Coming from Ted Williams, the word "ordinary" sounded like a profanity.

Ted Williams was also known for his brash self-confidence. Billy Werber knew both Ted and Babe Ruth and he observed in both men a deep and abiding faith in their own abilities. Ted, he said, was arrogant, a bit insufferable. "He believed his bat was the best, his fishing was the best, his hunting was the best, his everything. But that helped him. He believed he was a great hitter, and that made him a great hitter." Any number of players will tell how when Ted stepped into the box during batting practice, a silence descended as all the other players—on both teams—stopped to watch.

In the minor leagues, Ted was once hit in the head by a pitched baseball. Such a traumatic event can make many hitters gun-shy at the plate, often beginning a downward career spiral. For Ted, it was just another challenge. "All I kept thinking was, 'This ain't gonna stop me! This ain't gonna stop me! This ain't gonna stop me!' I kept saying it and saying it. I wasn't going to let anything stop me from being the hitter I hoped to be. Looking back . . . it was pretty near storybook devotion to the goal I had set for myself—to become the best hitter I could be."

Not surprisingly, Ted admires others for their dedication to perfection. And yet his definition of greatness goes well beyond the dictionary version. He always wanted to see every ballplayer extract the maximum potential from their ability and, to the consternation of owner Tom Yawkey, constantly dispensed advice even to opposing batters.

From an early age, Ted also pursued the sport of fishing. He was considered one of the greatest sport fishermen of all time. He carved out time whenever he could and, like his hero Zane Gray, traveled the world—to Canada, Cuba, Peru, Mexico, Russia and various rivers and salt water flats in the United States in pursuit of the bonefish, the tarpon, and the salmon. He developed the skill of fly-casting and cast thousands upon thousands of lines, striving always for the perfect approach, the perfect placement of the hook to the fish. He spent hours tying his own flies and debating with fellow anglers the best fly for a given situation. Sportsman and writer Bud Leavitt once commented, "He's absolutely demanding when it comes to perfection. For example, every single knot, every leader of his fishing tackle has to be the ultimate in perfection. He can't stand a bad knot. And he was the same way with bats."

When he enlisted for military service during World War II, Ted didn't seek out some lightweight desk job or simple home-based work in P.R. efforts on behalf of the military. He signed up for combat service, and the most technically challenging one there was: flying an airplane. He had no flight experience. The challenge intrigued him, though, and he sailed through classroom work and set a gunnery record that may still stand in Pensacola. He became an accomplished pilot, so much so he was made an instructor.

When recalled to duty in the Korean War, he took up jet flight—a new challenge at age 34—and became so proficient as a fighter-bomber pilot that he served several missions as fellow Marine Corps pilot John Glenn's wingman. Ted came back to baseball and won a couple more batting championships.

Ted's flight instructor at Willow Grove, preparing for Korean War service, was Bill Churchman, who firmly believes that Ted's native intelligence and his single-minded determination to learn created a man who could conquer anything. "If you were to say to Ted, 'We're going to give you two years off from your present duties, and we want you to become a Shakespearean scholar,' he'd be the best in the world. You could use that same theory in any field—computers, law, whatever. He'd master it."

Former New York Yankee Tommy Henrich agrees. Ted had natural ability but his superiority came because he kept developing, kept pushing himself to new levels. "He did more than out-practice everyone. He out-thought the rest of us, too. His brain, which made him a respected fighter pilot in two wars and might have made him the world's leading brain surgeon or nuclear scientist, told him that hitting a baseball is an inexact art form that requires the artist—the hitter—to pursue his work with unwavering diligence." Teammate Johnny Pesky recalls Ted saying, "If you do well today, you gotta do better tomorrow."

This attitude inspired those around him. Curt Gowdy says that Ted's work ethic inspired him to better preparation, and that made him a better broadcaster. Countless others, from various and unrelated walks of life, were simply fans, but inspired by Ted's example. We meet a few of them in this book.

Ted Williams always pursued perfection. This impressed Ernie Banks, who sees Ted as one who would not accept mediocrity: "He continually searches for better ways to do things, always challenging minds and questioning what people say and do." His first roommate with the Red Sox, Charlie Wagner, put it simply, "Anything he attempted, he wanted to be the best."

Ted's achievements have been widely recognized and

heralded. Not only is he a member of the National Baseball Hall of Fame, but he's also in three different Halls of Fame dedicated to fishing and he's honored in the United States Marine Corps Sports Hall of Fame. That says a lot.

There may be something almost otherworldly about someone who can succeed in so many fields of unrelated endeavor, prompting Maureen Cronin, daughter of Ted's former manager and friend, Joe Cronin, to quip: "What he needs is another planet."

As demanding as Ted was of himself and others, he could be the most compassionate of men. He knew he was blessed with a number of talents—though none of his achievements came easily. All that he accomplished came only as the result of those long, long hours of practice—practice with thought, dedication and determination. He understood, though—a lesson learned from his mother—that there were others who would never have the opportunity to pursue their dreams. Ted saw the unfairness of this. He really felt for sick children—those who suffered debilitating or deadly diseases such as cancer. He spent many long hours, privately visiting children who were afflicted, perhaps having lost a limb, or dying from leukemia.

When Ted took over as manager of the Washington Senators—soon to become the Texas Rangers—skeptics predicted dire consequences. How could the great Ted Williams accept anything but perfection from hitters in his anemic lineup? How could this immortal relate to mere mortals? Well, it turns out that Ted was able to inspire every single member of that team to improve their batting average. Why? Because Ted is not obsessed with perfection; he is obsessed with the pursuit of perfection. He frequently characterizes even Hall of Fame caliber players—from Mickey Mantle to Carl Yastrzemski to Wade Boggs—as hitters who "should have been better."

The people who talk about Ted Williams in this book have either observed his pursuit of perfection, been inspired by it, or both. Seeing Ted Williams hit .400 can apparently inspire you not only to be a better hitter, but a better actor, a better writer, a better contender with life's countless challenges.

Even skeptics were impressed by Ted. David Halberstam wrote a piece for the *Boston Globe* in 1986 entitled "The Fan Divided." He had strong memories of seeing Ted Williams play. "The memory of Williams and that special grace lingers. I now think often of him; we live in a nation which seeks heroes and cites as its heroes—the kings of celluloid like John Wayne and Sylvester Stallone, each of whom managed to stay out of his generation's war. I am wary of heroes in general, but as I grow older, I have become more and more intrigued by Williams, the man apart. Perhaps it is that wonderfully leathery face, for Ted Williams even looked like what he was and what he did with that William Holden cragginess. Perhaps it is the deeds, that prolonged exquisite career, the willingness to go for it on the last day of the .400 season. But finally it is as well the ability to stand apart—crusty, independent, outspoken, true to himself, living to his own specifications, and rules, the frontier man of the modern age. I have a sense of a life lived without regret and I hope that that is true."

Boating business executive Sammy Lee summed it up: "Ted Williams has always strived for perfection in both his professional and his personal life and it's my opinion that he has very little time for individuals that don't strive for the same. If he thinks you're someone that's satisfied with the status quo, he doesn't have time for you. But if you're striving to be your best, then he will thrive on that."

Through the uncompromising way he lived his life, Ted Williams continually challenged himself and he challenged others as well—even countless thousands who never met him. Ted has always said he was a lucky guy and we can feel reasonably confident he has few regrets—except, well, maybe that curve he almost hit squarely, or that one elusive fish he just couldn't land.

Like many things in life, ultimately it is not the attainment of perfection but its pursuit that separates the great from the near great. Fittingly, one of Roget's synonyms for perfect is "splendid" and although the appellation Perfect Splinter doesn't quite resonate, the nickname Splendid Splinter says it all. It is, in fact, the perfect nickname.

Ted admires others for striving against all odds. And yet his definition of greatness goes well beyond the dictionary version. He would like to see ballplayers get the greatest potential out of their ability. This is what he asked of himself and what he admired in others. He has a young friend named Tricia Miranti who has a severe physical disability. Ted has helped this young lady in her pursuit of an education and a career. Her courageous pursuit makes her a hero in Ted's eyes. And vice versa. When you prepare yourself mentally and physically for the job at hand; when your effort is the culmination of sacrifice and hard work, when you give your all in pursuit of a goal, then you are deserving of Ted's highest accolades.

—Jim Prime & Bill Nowlin

TED WILLIAMS

The Pursuit of Perfection

1

The Kid from California

Every night at 9 PM the lights at the North Park playground finally shut off and young Teddy Williams reluctantly ceased swinging at baseballs, making his way a short block and a half to the small bungalow on Utah Street that was his home. It was during the Depression, but San Diego kept the lights on late, and this helped Ted get in more swings. Years later he would claim that as his secret to becoming a great hitter—thousands upon thousands of swings.

His mother May, immersed in the good works of the Salvation Army, was often not home when he arrived and so young Ted would continue to swing the bat in the back yard—imagining the ball coming in and hitting it hard.

From his earliest teenage years, the skinny Williams kid was consumed by his interest in hitting a baseball and his proficiency grew as the years passed. He played various positions at Hoover High; school newspaper boxscores list him as a right fielder, first baseman, and third baseman—but most often as a pitcher. The papers describe him variously as "limber-armed hurler" or "lanky mound ace." Coach Wofford "Wos" Caldwell wanted Ted in the lineup every day, however. Even in these formative years the coach had no doubt about Ted's destiny. Even then Caldwell knew Ted was a hitter.

A little practice was never enough. Ted showed a fierce ambition and developed the good work habits needed to harness and cultivate his passion to succeed. Even before he'd finished high school, he'd set out on the path that would carry him to the major leagues. Well before he was 18 years old, there was no doubt that he was going to make it in professional baseball. At 19, he was a "can't miss" prospect who arguably already had the skills to play in the big leagues. The year he turned twenty, Ted Williams won the Triple Crown in the American Association. The fans in Boston had been reading about him for a year and they were primed and ready for the kid from California.

Opposite: Ted during his tenure with the San Diego Padres.
(Photo courtesy of the San Diego Hall of Champions)

WILBERT WILEY, Boyhood Friend

"Wilbert Wiley was my first real boyhood pal."
—*Ted Williams,* My Turn At Bat

Even in grammar school, we had ball teams. Before the schoolhouse opened to take the kids in, there'd be a game or work-up. When Ted would go home from school he'd have to walk by my house. That's when we were quite young, and we became friendly.

Ted would help me sometimes, go on my paper route with me, throw papers and things like that. He'd borrow someone else's bike. We'd get through and he'd say, "Let's go over to the playground and hit a few."

I can't tell you why, but his hits always seemed to carry. When he hit them flush they just kept going. I saw him hit one or two over at that North Park playground—I thought they were titanic for a kid. For anybody.

We'd tape the balls up with black tape to make them hold a little longer and then we'd pitch to one another, hit 'em and go shag 'em. I'd say this: pitching to that fella, if you tried to throw one by him, or break one off on him, or pull the string on him—that was a waste of time. Regardless of what it would be, unless you had it in there really good, he'd put it out of the park on you. And he had a ruling to himself that if a pitch wasn't in there, he'd let it go by. He wouldn't swing at that pitch. All the way up the line he was more or less like that.

I always had the feeling that Ted would have made the majors as a pitcher. There's a lot of people who don't realize, but the guy had good stuff. When you got up to bat, he'd throw you that breaking stuff and I'll tell you, it did break. And he had the best . . . he called it a palm ball. A few players still remember that. It'd come out of his hand like a knuckler. He'd give all the motions of throwing a fastball and that thing would slip out, and if you weren't watching yourself you'd swing when the ball was halfway there. Sometimes made guys feel kinda foolish.

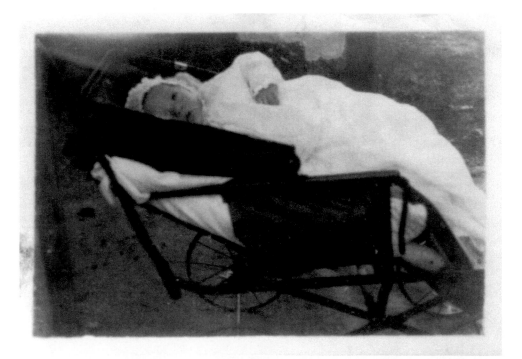

The earliest known photo of Ted, taken in San Diego October 20, 1918. Ted was seven weeks old.
(Courtesy of Bill Nowlin)

I always admired him, how he achieved and got ahead. I think Ted Williams did that himself. I can't think of anybody else I could give the credit to, because he had that determination to make it.

◆ ◆ ◆

I remember my first home run. Came against a guy named Hunt in a Sunday game in North Park. Just a poopy little fly ball to center, but it made it over the fence. There I was, a little 15-year-old standing in against guys 25 to 30 and this guy could really throw hard. I could barely get the bat around on it, and I hit that homer.
—*Ted Williams, 1988*

It was 280 feet, or something. Maybe 250 feet. It was just a fly ball, but it was a big thing for me. Now the last I heard is that I hit it over the street, or maybe over those houses.
—*Ted Williams, 1992*

JOE VILLARINO, Boyhood Friend

Ted Williams to Joe Villarino:

"I remember when you were picking sides and I was the second pick.
Do you remember who you picked first?" Joe did, and so did Williams.
"You didn't pick me, you picked Marsh. And I didn't blame you," he said.
*"He could hit." (*San Diego Union, *July 1992)*

I knew Ted better than anybody, I think, even better than Roy, because Roy Engle and them guys just knew him through high school, but I went all the way up with Ted.

We used to play marbles all the time, when we were seven or eight years old. Ted loved to play marbles. We'd run around with dungarees on, or knee pants with holes in them. His shoes were so split open from kneeling on the ground that you could see his toes. We used to have a game they called "Boston." We'd make a big circle in the dirt and put all the marbles on a little peak, and we'd shoot from the line—do that all day long.

About third grade, Ted and I used to run like the devil to the box where they had the softballs. First thing in the morning, around 7:30, they'd have a box set out with the bats and balls in it. When we were eight or nine years old, we played ball with kids 16 or 17 years of age. They didn't have Little League or organized ball for the kids in them days. We used to just get a bunch of kids up and play.

We had a game they called "Big League." We played it in a kind of handball court. There were pipes going all around it—uprights and one going across—and about an eight foot area where you could hit the ball inside the pipes and it would be a single. If you hit that pipe going across and the guy didn't catch it when it came down, it'd be a home run. Ted was good at that.

He could do anything, Ted. He liked to hunt and was a good boxer. He never did do any boxing in school, as far as I know, but he got in fights a couple of times, beat the hell out of the guys.

We'd go hunting rabbits down by where Jack Murphy Stadium is now. There used to be a swimming hole down there called Dobie Pond. I remember one time we were walking along and a big rattlesnake come slithering out right in front of Ted, and Ted just pulled out the rifle and shot it right in the head. He picked it up, wrapped it around his neck and took it home. Probably skinned it, I don't know.

I remember on Halloween, we used to raise Cain. Used to grease the streetcar tracks so they'd just skid. Then we'd steal fruit on the way home. We used to steal loquats. They had a lot of loquat trees around that neighborhood. Oh, we had a lot of fun.

◆ ◆ ◆

ROY ENGLE, Boyhood Friend

Ted Williams on Roy: "He was the guy I admired. He was so strong. Everything he hit was a line drive, bam!" (San Diego Union, November 1977)

Ted lived at the playground. I think the only reason he went to high school was to play ball. There was nobody else to play with, so he went to school.

TED WILLIAMS: THE PURSUIT OF PERFECTION

We had a pretty good baseball team. Ted was a pitcher and he was winning the ball games because of his pitching. Of course he could hit, too. One of the bad features of Hoover High School was that we played on the football field, and the right field fence was beyond the running track and there were no bleachers on the right side of the field. So I guess two or three hundred feet was only a double. A handicap with Ted. Most teams walked Ted when the score was close—there was no pitching to him when things were tough.

You know, it's kinda strange. I don't want to take anything away from Wos Caldwell, he was a good high school coach. But Ted was a student! I don't know where he got his information, but he always had that bat in his hand. He taught himself all the fundamentals that he needed to become a good baseball player. And when he makes up his mind to do something, he's going to do it or know the reason why . . . which is why he became a great ballplayer, I think.

Ted even carried a bat to his high school classes, wrote veteran San Diego sportswriter Earl Keller.

◆ ◆ ◆

LES CASSIE, JR., Boyhood Friend

I can still see him the day that he came up to Hoover for the first time. He was in junior high school getting finished with the 9th grade, which he completed in midyear. We had started baseball practice at Hoover a couple of days before the fall semester ended. It wasn't a ballpark, just a big old open space. In right field was a lunch arbor, a roof over a bunch of benches.

He came walking up right by the shops, which were close by where we were having batting practice, and he hollered out, "Coach, let me hit!" Coach Caldwell didn't pay much attention to him. We must have had a hundred guys out there trying out for baseball. He sat there on the steps of the print shop. Finally, he said again, "Coach, let me hit!" By this time, we'd run out of pitchers and coach Caldwell was pitching batting practice. So he said, "All right. Get up there and hit." The first ball went up on top of that lunch arbor, and no one had ever hit one anywhere near there. That was our introduction to Ted.

◆ ◆ ◆

WOFFORD "WOS" CALDWELL, High School Coach

Even before he came to Hoover, I had heard how loud he was! He was supposed to go to San Diego High School, but his mother didn't want him to go there. She wanted him to come to Hoover. This particular afternoon, we were out practicing baseball on the girls' side of the field, before the season started. I could hear him and two other boys approaching, about a block away. That's how loud he was.

When he arrived on the field, he shouted to me, "How about me taking a couple of cuts, coach?" I said, "Okay, get your bat and get up here and hit a couple." He proceeded to hit two of them out. I decided right then that he was really serious about hitting.

The teachers either loved him or hated him. He had one thought in mind and he always followed it. He was going to play professional baseball and the only thing he thought of was baseball. Period. He made his mind up before he got into professional baseball that he was going to be the greatest hitter that ever lived. That was an obsession with him.

He pitched in high school because he had the strongest arm. He was a skinny bastard but he could rear back and really throw that ball in there. In high school that's all he had to do, pitch them high and hard. They wanted him to pitch once later, when he was

Rod Luscomb, ca. 1925. Luscomb was the director at the North Park playground in San Diego, and worked with Ted for years.
(Photo courtesy of Brian Luscomb)

playing in Los Angeles. I don't remember what team was playing, but they put him in to pitch. The other team knocked him out of the box within about 4 or 5 pitches so that high fast ball didn't go very far.

He tells the story about the way I used to try to teach him how to run. I would put him on first base and somebody would holler "Go" and he had to be able to beat me around three bases while I had to go four. And I would always catch up with him.

I helped him get his first job with the San Diego Padres. From there, he went on up the line.

◆ ◆ ◆

"EARLY INDUCTION"
by Thomas Michael McDade

My friend Billy
Donnelly knew all
the Sox batting stances,
and he often did Williams
when hitting rocks
with a makeshift bat
from the dump
by the Cott soda plant.
One day I found
a '56 Baseball
Register
that just missed
fueling the fire
we built to blow up
aerosol cans.
As I read Ted's
stats like I was
inducting him
into the Hall,
Billy got in the stance
and I pitched him
a Reddi Wip can that
he lined into the blaze
to explode
like a season
of green Fenway doubles.

WILBERT WILEY, Boyhood Friend

Ted was a loud, good-natured kid, but witty—he liked to needle people. If you'd get around somebody who was kind of a wise guy, he could always think of an answer. If he liked anybody, he'd try to do everything in the world for them. I could see a lot of good in Ted even though . . . I'll tell you one thing with that fellow, no one would ever want to tangle with him. That guy could really fight. I mean, he was good. He got into scrapes

8

around that playground every once in a while, and I'll tell you he was a pretty good guy to stay away from. He could throw those fists and they were fast. But when he liked you, he was ready to go to bat for you anytime, speak up for you.

He came to my house a lot. I had things there that were kind of noticeable—guns and fishing tackle. Stuff like that appealed to him. Ted's dad, he was a good-natured fellow, but I only knew him to go to one game that the guy played. And most men, if you had a kid as good as that, you'd be wanting to bust the buttons on your shirt. My dad was a dry-witted guy and they seemed to get along good together. They could kid one another kinda rough and it seemed to go over pretty well with the both of them. I think you have an idea what kind of ribbing that would be. "Hi, there, jerk. How the heck are you?"

Ted and I were together often. I used to hunt when I was 12 or 13 years old and even though we were kids, we were always careful and had respect for one another—I emphasized that and he was that way, too. Once in a while, there'd be a third, but not often. We'd go out there and hunt the rabbits, quail, doves and such. Ted had amazing endurance. I did, too, at that time. Never seemed to get tired. One time we took his brother Danny with us. I'll never forget, we went about a hundred yards, and Danny began to breathe kinda hard. "Boy," he says, "I'm starting to get tired," and I remember Ted says, "Gee whiz, man. What's the matter with you? I haven't even taken a deep breath yet."

◆ ◆ ◆

JOE VILLARINO, Boyhood Friend

Ted was always kind of a—well, like they say, a Splendid Splinter—kind of a rangy kid. He was pretty close to six feet in his senior year. Gosh, he used to like to eat! Across the street from Hoover High, right on El Cajon Boulevard, there was a place we'd go to eat. On a Saturday afternoon we'd see a matinee there at the old North Park theatre. Ted didn't go to too many movies—afraid of hurting his eyes, I guess—but he liked them. He liked Olivia DeHavilland. That's the only time he'd go, when she was playing.

Ted's mother was a pretty popular woman around town. She used to ride the old streetcars and get people cornered on the Salvation Army deal. At Christmas time, she'd get her tambourine out. Ted didn't like it too well. I don't know why he held it against her, but he did seem to. She'd be out trying to make money for the Salvation Army, out hustling, late at night. She wasn't home for dinner most of the time. Usually they just left Ted money, and he'd go down and buy a hamburger or something.

His mother was Mexican. I'm a Mexican—my dad was Mexican and my mother Spanish. Once in a while somebody will ask me about Ted's mother, and if she was Mexican. They didn't believe it, because Ted, you know, he had no signs of being a Mexican at all.

Ted had a brother named Danny who had problems all through his life, always got in trouble. Danny and I got along pretty good but he and Ted used to fight like the devil—you know brothers. Ted would get real mad at him. I think one night Danny even threw a knife at Ted. They used to get into some bouts. It wasn't that Danny followed Ted around, he never did. He didn't hang around the playground much because he never got along with the kids too well. But Ted was around there all the time.

Ted Williams and Wilbert Wiley, circa 1937.
(Photo courtesy of Wilbert Wiley)

Ted's uncles and grand-mother: Pete Venzor, Saul Venzor, Natalia Venzor, Paul Venzor

The playground director was Rod Luscomb, a ballplayer himself who used to play Sunday semipro ball. He was a nice guy, a wonderful guy. Alongside the ballpark, if you fouled off the ball, it'd go in the reservoir. He'd pay a kid 35 cents to retrieve it. Then at 9 o'clock, he'd close up and go home. This would be after he had thrown Ted batting practice for hours. Ted used to get blisters. He would hit for an hour, hour and a half, and then he would pitch to Luscomb. Rod knew Ted had it, and he went out of his way to help him.

I didn't see too much of Ted when he was playing with the Red Sox. I never did try to keep in touch because he was so darn busy—all these guys around him all the time. I figured he wouldn't care about me anyway. But after he retired, every time he came to town he called me up. He'd say, "Come on, Joe, we're going to go out to dinner. Let's go have a couple of beers." He usually liked Mexican food.

◆ ◆ ◆

Where Ted benefited from the dedication of a Rod Luscomb, Ted's younger brother Danny had no such figure in his life. "It was tough enough for Ted to grow up mostly on his own," wrote Joe Hamelin. "It was tougher still for Danny, always in his brother's shadow. Daniel Arthur Williams ran with a different crowd from Ted. A tougher crowd . . . he was in trouble all the time. Rarely was the trouble so severe that May couldn't extricate him. Stealing a bicycle, ducking out on a debt, that sort of thing. Once, Ted wrote, Luscomb took a loaded gun away from Danny. Once, after Ted had stocked his mother's house with new furniture from his baseball earnings, he told friends Danny backed up a truck to the door, took it all and sold it." Another story has Ted coming home in a new Buick, parking it around the corner from the house, and finding the next morning that Danny had, in the night, taken its tires. "Just about the time Danny was getting his life together," one acquaintance remembers, "he got cancer." He died of leukemia in March 1960, before he'd turned 40, despite Ted's assistance in financing medical treatment for him.

ROY ENGLE, Boyhood Friend

We all looked forward to the day when we would go out for baseball in high school. We didn't think about the pros. There was no "pros" in San Diego. Most of us had never seen a big league game, had only heard about the big leagues. They used to have a big Easter vacation baseball program. In those days, there weren't so many teams. San Diego High and Hoover would go up to Pomona. Once the governor [Merriam] was there for something or other. I can still see Ted going up to him and saying, "Hi Guv!"

There just aren't many people like Ted. His whole life was hitting the ball. He went to school so he could do it. He played pro ball so he could do it. If he couldn't hit, he would have been a fireman or something. Probably the second most important thing in Ted's life was fishing—something to do when the baseball season was over.

It's kind of a miracle that he got so far, because his home life was horrible. His mother was a real dedicated Salvation Army person. All that she did for those two kids was to make a house. I don't know whether she was ever there much because she was really busy. She was to the Salvation Army like Ted was to baseball.

◆ ◆ ◆

Ted's mother May Venzor Williams, originally from El Paso, gave Ted his Mexican blood. Her parents came to El Paso from El Parral, Chihuahua. In the words of Joe Hamelin of the San Diego Union, *she "patrolled the streets in the '20s and '30s, collecting for the poor." Some thought her almost saintly, others considered her eccentric. Whatever adjective is more accurate, she passed along to Ted her drive and her concern for those less fortunate than herself. May Williams was once chosen as Woman of the Year in San Diego. She'd met husband Sam Williams, a photographer, when he was stationed in Honolulu during World War I.*

As Ted's fame spread, his mother would use his name to help raise funds. Barry Lorge wrote in a 1991 San Diego Union *article, "Mel Powers recalled how May Williams, a tireless crusader for the Salvation Army, would trade on her son's name for the cause, coming into the bank where he was a young teller and convincing everyone to put whatever coins they could into her tambourine. A teetotaler, she would then canvass the bars along University Avenue, telling patrons, 'I'm Ted Williams' mother. Empty your pockets.'"*

"She was VERY proud of Ted," recalled Anita Rasmussen, one of May's co-workers, in a 1980 story in the same newspaper. "It's relatively common, where one member of a family is a Salvationist and another is not, for problems to crop up, and she was very upset when he dropped out of Sunday school. But she talked about him all the time. And everything ever written about him, she'd clip it out, and put it in a scrapbook."

Grandmother Natalia Venzor, great-grandmother Catarina Hernandez, aunt Mary Cordero and baby John Cordero. Taken on Chino Street, Santa Barbara.
(Courtesy of Bill Nowlin)

LES CASSIE, JR., Boyhood Friend

My folks really treated Ted like mother and dad. He came over for dinner a lot. He knew he didn't need an invitation, all he had to do was come over and my mother would put another plate on the table.

One of the things Ted was interested in was surf fishing. He and my dad used to go out and fish the ocean in Coronado, right on the beach. God, they'd fish all night long. I went one time and thought it was the most boring thing in my life. But Ted loved fishing.

4121 Utah Street.
Ted's boyhood
home.
(Photo by Bill Nowlin)

He signed [with the Padres] before he graduated from high school in the summer of '36. I went to Lane Field with him almost every day. In '37 I went with him again, but not as much because I was working at the gas company. I started back to college in February of '37 and became a school teacher and baseball coach. I couldn't hit the curve ball, so I had to be a coach.

When Ted went to the Red Sox in '39, he asked my dad if he'd go with him and my dad said, "Sure, I'll go with you" and so they got on the bus. This was the way the Red Sox had their players travel to spring training in those days. Ted got sick in New Orleans, and they had to get off the bus and get a hotel room. My dad had to kind of nurse him back to health, go on to Florida when Ted got well.

In '46, when he got out of the service, he came over to the house and he told my folks, "I think we're going to be in the Series at least once in the next five years. When we are, I want you and Mrs. Cassie to be my guests at the World Series." My dad said, "Well, you get in the Series and we'll be there." The phone rang the night they clinched it, and Ted says, "You comin' back?" My dad says, "I told you we'd be there."

He and my mother went to Boston and Ted treated them so great. He introduced my dad to everyone in the ballpark—from Tom Yawkey to the ushers, all the players, the managers, everybody. I think it was one of the highlights of my dad's life.

◆ ◆ ◆

CEDRIC DURST, Ballplayer
(Taken from San Diego Union *article by Phil Collier, 10-17-60)*

I was Ted's first roommate in pro ball. He was a big, good-natured kid and full of confidence. He woke me up one morning—he was jumping on his bed, beating his chest, and he said, "Christ, Ced, it's great to be young and full of vinegar." I said, "Sure, Ted, but not at six o'clock in the morning."

I've seen hundreds of young ballplayers breaking in as professionals, and all of them have had one thing in common. They might hit pretty well the first time around the league, but then the pitchers learn their weaknesses. Williams wasn't like that at all. He was 17 when he joined the Padres, but he already knew more about hitting than the veterans on the club.

Two of the best pitchers in the Coast League then were Tony Freitas and Jack Salveson. They gave everybody a fit, even the older hitters. But instead of them figuring Ted out, he figured them out. The first time Ted saw Freitas pitch, we were sitting side by side on the bench and Ted said, "This guy won't give me a fast ball I can hit. I know he won't. He'll waste the fast ball and try to make me hit the curve. He'll get behind on the count, then throw me the curve, and when he does, I'll be ready." And that's exactly what happened. Nobody had ever taught him that thing. It was something he was born with, or had figured out by himself.

♦ ♦ ♦

EARL KELLER, Sportswriter
(Taken from Baseball Gold, "Padre Gold! Ted Williams" *by Earl Keller)*

As a sportswriter for the *San Diego Union-Tribune*, I was there for Williams' debut with the Padres. Much had been expected of this 18-year-old. Many said he was a natural and couldn't miss becoming a great of the game. They were so right. I had seen Ted slam baseballs so far over the right field fence for Hoover High that they landed in the front yards of houses and on roofs far from home plate. The eyes of some major league scouts looked like saucers after they saw Ted drive home runs so far.

The Padres had their troubles with Williams when he broke into the game. All he wanted to do was take his turn at bat and not learn how to play the outfield. After taking his cuts at the plate, he would go to the outfield and lean against the fence, waiting anxiously for his next turn to swing the bat. "You must learn there is more to playing baseball than just hitting," Cedric Durst told Williams as he took him in tow.

I stood at his side for hours in hotels on the road while he poured money into pinball machines. His mother had that stopped because he was using up his meal money. Ted was told to sign for his meals.

Never will I forget the towering smashes he blasted over the right field fence in San Diego's old Lane Field, as well as in other parks. I saw him hit the longest home run in history—anywhere. It was a 130-mile blast! One of his long home runs landed in a freight car which was pulling out of the yards across from the San Diego ball park and headed for Los Angeles. That home run made Ripley's Believe It Or Not!

♦ ♦ ♦

GEORGE MYATT, Ballplayer

When he was a young kid still going to Hoover School, I was playing with San Diego in the Coast League. Ted was excited about hitting, that's all he thought about in baseball was hitting. Just to see him pick up his bats was something. On the sidelines, he'd swing them. That's the first thing he'd do is come up out of the clubhouse dressing room and pick up a half dozen bats or so and start swinging them. He never grabbed a glove.

Williams is a very slow lad, not a good outfielder now and just an average arm. There is big doubt whether Williams will ever be fast enough to get by in the majors as an outfielder. His best feature now is that he shows promise as a hitter, but good pitching so far has stopped him cold.

—Joe Devine, New York Yankee Scout from 1936 scouting report

I was the captain of our team and I was playing shortstop. I'd see the signs—what the pitches were, you know. I'd give the signs to the outfielders, a certain way I stood or with my hands behind my back some way—let them know fast ball or breaking ball, help them to get a jump on balls. Once, right after the sign had been given, I don't know why but I turned around real fast. There Ted is, standing with his back to the hitter. He had his glove in his hands and he was swinging his glove like it was a bat. I called time and went out and called him a few names, told him there was something else to this game besides swinging a bat. He worked his fanny off all the time at fielding after that. It turned out that when he went to Boston, of all the Red Sox outfielders that I played against, he played that left field better than anyone I ever saw.

◆ ◆ ◆

ARTHUR SAMPSON, Author
(Taken from Ted Williams by Arthur Sampson)

"[Padres manager] Frank Shellenback," Arthur Sampson writes, "was the first baseball man who noticed that Williams had more determination to succeed than anyone else. He wasn't surprised when the 17-year-old kid he had taken on at San Diego in the middle of the 1936 season would put in an appearance at the ball park at 10 o'clock in the morning. He figured the regular attendance of Williams was the natural enthusiasm of youth which would disappear after a few days. But it didn't.

It wasn't until this gangling kid kept coming to him each night after a game had been played and everybody was hurrying home for supper to ask him for a couple of old baseballs that Frank became inquisitive enough to give Williams some attention. "What do you do with all these baseballs, sell them to kids around the neighborhood?" Shelly inquired finally. "No, sir," replied Williams. "I use them for a little extra hitting practice after supper."

This seemed like a tall story to Shellenback. Having noticed that this skinny kid would get in plenty of batting practice every morning in addition to pitching to batters for about a half hour and then take his regular pregame workout which included plenty of running in the afternoon, Frank didn't think it likely that the kid was doing much hitting after supper. And even if he was, it didn't seem possible that he could have time to knock the covers off two baseballs every night.

But he found this to be true. In fact he saw the covers battered off the two baseballs he handed Williams following the questioning that very evening. "I decided I would do a little investigating," Shelly told me one day while telling this story of Ted's unusual determination and untiring energy. "So I piled into my car after supper and rode around to Williams' neighborhood. There was a playground near his home and sure enough I saw The Kid himself driving those two battered baseballs all over the field.

"Ted was standing close to a rock which served as a plate. One kid was pitching to him. A half dozen others were shagging his drives. The field was rough and stony. The baseballs I had given him after the game were already showing signs of wear. The stitching was falling apart. The covers were as rough as sandpaper. Blood was trickling from Williams' hands as he gripped a chipped bat. But he kept swinging. And hitting."

◆ ◆ ◆

Hoover High Cardinals team at Pomona tournament. Ted is at rear in the center.
(Photo courtesy of San Diego Hall of Champions)

BOBBY DOERR, Ballplayer, Hall of Fame

1936 was my last year of playing in the Coast League. I broke in '34, '35 in Hollywood. Then in the winter of '35, they moved the franchise to San Diego. We were playing there in '36 and in June, when school was out, Ted come in for a tryout. I was standing on the right side of the batting cage, one of those old cages we used to have. All the players were standing around waiting to hit. Most players in those days were ex-major leaguers. There wasn't more than two or three real young players on our club. I remember Ted standing probably four or five feet in front of me. Nobody knew who he was. Big gangly kid. He said he was 147 pounds, six foot three. Shellenback was managing the team, and he was also a pitcher. He was pitching batting practice and he said, "Let the kid get in and hit a few." All the guys around the cage, I remember they were moaning, "Oh geez, this guy's gonna take up our time."

Ted got in and hit, I guess I'd say six or seven balls. I don't exactly remember, but he hit at least one out of the ballpark. Hit some real shots, you know? When he walked out of the cage, some guy standing on the other side of the batting cage, I wish I could remember who it was, said, "This kid's going to be signed before the week's out."

This was on a Thursday. Every Monday was an off day in the Coast League. That Monday night we were taking the train to San Francisco to play either the Seals or the Missions, two teams that played in the same ballpark. And here's Ted down at the railroad depot all excited that he was going to go on the trip, walking up and down. That was really my first experience of seeing him. He didn't really play all that much. He might have gotten in to pinch hit or something like that.

He was always talking about being a pitcher. One game in July we were playing up at Wrigley Field [in Los Angeles] and getting beat pretty good. Shellenback was trying to decide what to do—he didn't want to use one of his better pitchers in the game. Well, some way or other, whether Ted said, "Oh, I can pitch" or something, he put Ted in to pitch and they kind of roughed him up. Wes Schumerich, an ex-major leaguer who'd been with the Cubs and was then with the Los Angeles Angels, hit a home run off Ted. And that was the end of Ted's pitching. He played a little bit, a game or two now and then until the last month of the season—then we had an outfielder named Chick Shiver quit the team. Shiver was playing right field and he had a chance to get a coaching job in football somewhere back in the east. So Ted went in and played right field the rest of the season and hit pretty well.

Even at that age Ted was always asking the opinion of what he thought were the better ballplayers. He took a liking to Lefty O'Doul who was managing the San Francisco team. Lefty at that time had the reputation of being a good hitting instructor, because he had DiMaggio and Joe Marty, who he made into a real fine hitter. I remember Ted saying what O'Doul told him, "Don't ever let anybody change your style of hitting. You've got a real good style of hitting." Then of course, you've heard the stories about Rogers Hornsby. Hornsby told him to stay inside the strike zone. Ted probably had as good an idea of the strike zone as anybody in baseball.

When we were in San Diego, we'd go out every night, it seemed. We'd go together and get milkshakes. He was 147 pounds and I was skinny, and we thought we'd drink milkshakes to put on weight. That was my third year and I was playing every day by then. See, in '35 the Red Sox took an option to buy George Myatt and my contracts. Eddie Collins had come out in '35 to see us, and they took an option on the contract. Then they were coming out to decide whether they were going to take us or not in the summer of '36. You've heard the story. Collins had followed us for a week or two, up in Seattle and Portland. That's where he saw Ted just taking batting practice. He liked his swing so much

Hoover High School baseball team. "Dias Cardinales" yearbook, 1936. Standing tall, Ted is in the back row center.
(Photo courtesy of Dennis Donley, Hoover High School)

TED WILLIAMS: THE PURSUIT OF PERFECTION

that he went to the owner of the San Diego club, Bill Lane, and said he wanted to buy Ted's contract. Lane said, "No, we're not ready to even think about doing that." Collins said, "Can we have the first right to buy his contract when you're ready?" So they shook hands on it, and that's how that come about.

In '38, Eddie Collins called me and said "Get together with Ted. Have him come up and take the train together." Just as we were supposed to get together, a tremendous rainstorm washed out the tracks out of Los Angeles. Ted got a hold of a ham operator and contacted me saying, "What are we going to do?" I had to take a bus to meet the train so I just said to do the best he could. Our train stopped in El Paso and I didn't know it, but so did Ted's. When we came back that night from dinner, there was Ted prancing up and down along the train. We went to spring training together from there.

Then, of course, he's pumping Babe Herman on the train all the way across. It's just one of those open trains. There were three or four women, older women, that were in one end of the car, and Ted, Babe, and myself were down at the other end. And Ted, he's pumping Babe, and being loud like he is, he's using pillows for swinging the bat. These women finally told the porter, "Can you shut that guy up a little bit? He's too loud."

Someone once asked me to explain Ted's personality. I said that the best comparison I could make was to General Patton: Everything forward. No retreat. And no compromise. That's just about Ted's makeup and the way he operated. Everything was positive thinking all the time. No negative. Never think negative. He was just a very strong . . . well, he's one of our great people. To think of what he's done . . . in war, baseball, fishing . . . he was great in everything he's gone into. He was just that type of a fellow.

I think down deep Ted has a faith somewhat in God, but he's just so stubborn as hell that he doesn't want to openly admit it. He knew his mother did some good. Whenever we used to be with Ted and his dear friend Louise [Kaufman], every night at meal time she would say a blessing. If you weren't quite aware of it, why Ted'd say, "Come on" and he'd hold your hand and bow and he respected the fact that she was saying the blessing. I don't know. It makes you kind of wonder a little.

The year after he retired in '60, Neil Mahoney, the Red Sox farm director, wanted Ted and me to go down and look at Dave Morehead, a pitcher at Hoover High. So we went and had lunch and just a little around the corner from the hotel was where Ted's dad had his photography shop. During lunchtime, Ted says, "I want to take you over and show you where my dad's photography shop was." So after lunch, we walked over there. The building was empty at that time and we walked up this flight of stairs. Here you could just almost see Ted Williams as about a ten or 12 year old kid. Walking up the stairs, he was reminiscing, "This was where my dad had the photography shop." When we walked back he said, "On this corner is where my mother used to make me march with the Salvation Army. I used to get behind the big bass drum to try to hide." Right there, it made me feel like, well, this is where a lot of this perfectionism started with Ted. I'll always remember thinking, "I'll be darned, this is about where that started."

◆ ◆ ◆

DOMINIC "DOM" DIMAGGIO, Ballplayer

When I broke in with San Francisco, Ted was already playing with San Diego, so I did play against him in the minor leagues in 1937. I remember that well. In those days, we played seven games against each team. We played a whole week with them. In one of the earlier series that we had, our manager, Lefty O'Doul—who in my opinion was one of the finest teachers for hitting a baseball—left our dugout when Ted Williams was hitting. When he finished hitting, O'Doul took him aside and talked to him. All of us in the

North Park playground, now Ted Williams Field.
(Photos by Bill Nowlin)

dugout wondered what he was saying. Here was a competitive manager talking to a young rookie with a different ballclub. So when he got back, all the veterans on our club asked Lefty, "What did you go up and talk to him about?" "Well," he said, "he's such a natural hitter. I just told him don't let anybody mess with your swing. Don't let anybody try to change you. You've got a great swing. You're going to be a great major league hitter."

He really hit a ball unlike anybody else. He'd have kind of an up-and-over-and-down swing. Anytime he hit the ball, if he hit underneath it, the ball would soar high into the air and go great distances. If he hit the ball on top, it would just sink like a curve ball, go just over the top of the infielders' heads onto the outfield grass in front of the outfielders. I don't recall too many batters hitting the ball like Teddy did. And of course when he hit the ball on the ground, it had tremendous overspin which made it go through the infield very quickly.

Ballplayers hit balls in our day that appeared to go into the ozone, never to come down. But don't forget, I don't think there's any question that there's a difference in the ball being used. In 1946, when we came back to baseball, after serving in the armed forces, we used to be able to pick up brand new baseballs by the skin—by the horsehide—after just a few hits in batting practice. Just pick them up by the seams. That's how loose the covers were. You could hit a ball as hard as you thought was necessary to hit it against the fence or over a fence, and it would barely go to the outfield. The ball right after the war was as dead as a doornail. Today, they're like bullets.

I've told the story on occasion of when we were slaughtering the Philadelphia Athletics at Fenway Park. First, understand that there was always one leather-lunged guy out in left field giving Ted a hard time. In this particular game we were pounding Jack Wilson, who had played with the Red Sox before going to the Athletics. Connie Mack let him stay in because he was short of pitchers. Ted was kind of disgusted because he didn't want to see Jack take such a beating. So it's Ted's last time at bat and this leather-lunged guy was still on him. I think Ted had gotten three or four hits at that point. People said he couldn't hit to left field. He then proceeded to hit 14 or 15 line drives in the general direction of this guy who was sitting right by the left field foul pole. I recall saying something like, "And they say he couldn't hit to left field." He was just shooting at this guy. Finally, he halfheartedly swung at one of Jack Wilson's pitches, hit the left center field wall, and got to second base. Cronin then thought he had enough so he told Ted to come in, he was through for the day. I remember that very vividly.

◆ ◆ ◆

ARCHIE MOORE, Boxer, Hall of Fame

I met Ted at the ballpark in San Diego. It was an odd place to put a baseball park because it was in the deepest part of downtown, right next to the railway tracks. He was playing for the Padres at the time—pitching. No one could stop Ted then or later. We talked that day about the way he was pitching. He knew me as a boxer. I later heard that he came down to see some of my fights. He was one of my fans, just as I'm a fan of his.

This guy was some hitter. I followed baseball quite closely at the time Ted played and before. My heroes were mostly from before Ted's time—guys like Satchel Paige—but Ted was one of the greatest I saw. I'd agree with him that hitting a baseball is *one* of the toughest things to do in sport. There were several great boxers who were pretty hard to hit, too! Archie Moore was one . . .

Ted had a lot of self-confidence even then. He was young and when men are young they tend to be a little selfish. I was myself. Ted was a great guy though. His Hall of Fame speech opened doors. He talked about the guys like Satchel, Josh Gibson, and Buck Leonard and how great they were. He was very aware of the black issue and aware that there were lots of black players who would have loved the opportunity to play with him. Ted gave credit where it was due. He was a true sportsman.

◆ ◆ ◆

FABIAN GAFFKE, Ballplayer
(*Taken from* Fenway *by Peter Golenbock*)

Ted was my roommate at Minneapolis. He was nineteen years old and quite a hitter. The kid would shake hands with you, and you'd think he'd break your hand, that's how strong he was. He'd swing that bat like a toothpick. You had to be strong to hit that ball the way he hit it. One time in Louisville he hit one—it was 365 feet in right field and they had a light pole 70 to 80 feet up there—and Ted hit one way out of sight, over the lights and all. You couldn't see it. That's how high and far he hit that . . . .

Ted had his ways—he was a screwy kid—but he was a good Joe. He was a little hot-headed, but he would never bother nobody. He never got mad at the other ballplayers, just

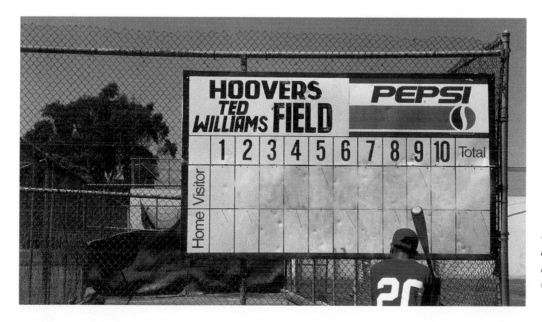

Hoover High School Field, a tribute to the school's own legend.
(Photo by Bill Nowlin)

himself. He was a ballplayer's ballplayer. One time in Minneapolis, he popped up with the bases loaded. They had these water coolers—bottle coolers upside down where you press the button for the cup of water—and he hit that SOB with the side of his fist when he came into the dugout, and the glass splattered all over the dugout. Donie Bush was the manager, and he almost threw a fit. If he had ripped a tendon, he could have been done with baseball.

◆ ◆ ◆

LEFTY LEFEBVRE, Pitcher

They had a great softball team in Minneapolis. I think that's where softball really originated, in Minneapolis, way back. The manager of the softball team decided they ought to play a game against the Millers. Well, they did. The manager said to Ted, "This guy'll strike you out." You know how Ted is. Ted said, "Like hell he will." Then the manager said, "I'll bet you five bucks he'll strike you out." First time Ted goes up, the guy did strike him out. So the next time, Ted, he must have hit the ball four hundred feet. Over the right field fence. A softball. He was going around the bases jumping like a kangaroo. Oh Jeez. He was terrific. Got a big voice, you could hear him all over the ballpark.

In Minneapolis they used to give us an appreciation day, Radio Appreciation Day. You'd get a sponsor and the sponsor would ask you what do you want? You could get a sports coat, a pair of pants, a shirt, whatever it was, you know? And when it came to Ted, he said, "I want a case of shotgun shells." He was going to go hunting.

We played in upper Minnesota and southern North Dakota, and went on this barnstorming trip after the season was over. We had an old-timer named Cohen, a second baseman, and he organized a trip driving from one town to another. Ted and I chummed around together up in Minneapolis and I used to ride with Ted in his car. We'd go from one town to the next, playing ball at twilight, because nobody had lights. We'd play from around five 'til eight. Then they always threw a big spread for us, you know, a big cookout. We'd have a few drinks and we'd go to bed late, and the next day we'd get in the car again and go to the next town, maybe a hundred miles away. A hundred miles was nothing up there.

Ted had heard that there was a lot of big jackrabbits out there, so he had got that case of shotgun shells and he put them between his legs. He had Walter Tauscher driving his car and he was sitting in the front seat with a shotgun. Christ, he was shooting at everything! We'd be going 50 miles an hour—Stan Spence and I'd be sitting in the back seat, falling asleep from the night before—and all of a sudden we'd hear BANG! We thought we had a flat tire or something. Ted thought he saw a jackrabbit. Well, in about 15 days, he emptied that whole case. He probably killed a couple of cows, I don't know. It's a wonder we never got pinched.

◆ ◆ ◆

SLINGIN' SAMMY BAUGH, Football Player, Hall of Fame
(Taken from Still Slingin': The Sammy Baugh Story by Dennis Tuttle)

Just before my rookie season with the Washington Redskins in 1937, I had signed a baseball contract with the St. Louis Cardinals. At the time, I liked baseball a little better and I still wasn't sure about a career in pro football. Being from Texas, we didn't know any-goddamn-thing about pro football. About the only thing we ever heard about (in football) was the Southwest Conference. But we sure as hell knew who the Yankees were, and the Gashouse Gang.

Well, we won the championship in Washington that year and I really didn't have to play baseball. But I had signed that contract and I'm a man who believes in his word. About a month after the football season, I went to baseball training camp in St. Petersburg. The Cardinals decided to send me to Columbus, Ohio, to get some at-bats and get into shape. My best memory of being in Columbus was seeing this 19-year-old phenom for Minneapolis named Ted Williams.

He'd go out to right field, stick his glove in his back pocket and turn his back on the pitcher and start doing jumping jacks and shit like that. He'd look over his shoulder for the pitch and do exercises in between. These old-school guys, many of them on their way back down from the majors, thought, "What a goddamned bush-leaguer." They were raising hell, saying, "Get him out of here!"

They hated Williams. Here was a young kid who didn't give a f--- about anything. Nothing bothered that cocky bastard. He'd be standing in right field in the middle of the game exercising, or practicing his swing, while the pitcher piddled around between pitches. Williams was a screwball in many ways, if you know what I mean.

But you know, that crazy sonofabitch would get up there and knock a goddamn board off the fence in the outfield. Everybody knew he was crazy. Everybody also knew he was going to be great. I always wondered how a manager would handle him. Not many would put up with that bullshit. But I guess

THE KID CLOUTER FROM THE COAST

(Cartoon from Minneapolis newspaper, 1939)

the manager was told to tolerate him by the higher-ups on the big-league team. I sat there during that series and watched this crazy kid, knowing how everyone is bad-mouthing him, and imagined what would happen if I was his manager and made the sonofabitch mad at me. If he didn't like your club, he might just leave. And how would you like to be the sonofabitch who let Ted Williams get away?

♦ ♦ ♦

HAROLD "PEE WEE" REESE, Ballplayer, Hall of Fame

I played with the Louisville Colonels in 1938 while he was playing right field with Minneapolis. I just watched him hit . . . it didn't help me a bit!

I remember a game going on and the Minneapolis ball club was out in the field. [Millers manager] Donie Bush came running out of the third base dugout. Ted was out there in right field throwing rocks at guys. There were train tracks out there and guys standing on the boxcars watching the ballgame. Ted was just throwing rocks at them. Bush shouted at him, "Ted, get in the ballgame for crying out loud and quit throwing rocks!"

♦ ♦ ♦

JOCKO CONLAN, Umpire
(Taken from Jocko by Jocko Conlan and Robert Creamer)

I met Ted Williams when he was a minor-league player with the Boston Red Sox farm team at Minneapolis. I was working in the American Association and I had been assigned to Minneapolis for spring training. That was a strange setup. Here I was an umpire, and they had me rooming with a ballplayer, a kid named Robert Robertshaw, a left-handed pitcher. This was in Daytona Beach. Williams had just been assigned to the team and he was in the next room to ours. There was a connecting door between the rooms.

I was in bed sleeping one morning, my face pushed down into the pillow, and Williams came into our room and jumped on top of me.

"Get up, Bush," he said. "Let's go!" He always called people "Bush," all through his career.

I pushed him off and rolled over and said, "Get out of here, you big skinny punk. What's the idea of jumping on me?"

"You're not Bush," he said. "You're not even a ballplayer. You're too old to be a ballplayer."

"Who are you?" I said.

"I'm Ted Williams," he said. "I hit twenty three home runs in San Diego. I'll hit forty home runs in this league."

"You better wait till the league gets started. Maybe you won't even be here."

"Is that so? You watch me. I'm a great hitter." He was. He hit forty three home runs that year.

I liked Williams right from the beginning.

They had a special promotion one night in Minneapolis. They called it Centennial Night, and they had thirteen thousand people there in that old Nicollet Field. How they got thirteen thousand in the place, I don't know. They were hanging from the eaves. Oh, it was jammed. Williams hit two home runs, and they were tremendous. They landed on the building across the street from the outfield fence. And then in the last of the ninth he came to bat with the bases loaded, two out and Minneapolis behind by a run. The count went to three and two. I was umpiring behind the plate. The crowd was yelling for another home run, or any kind of base hit, or even a walk to force in the tying run. And I ended the ball game by calling Williams out on strikes on a pitch right at his knees.

Donie Bush was coaching at third base and he came running in. "Strike?" he yelled. "It was down by his ankles. It was on the ground." A low pitch was always on the ground, and a high one is always over the head. The crowd was furious. Bush was yelling at me, and the fans were booing.

And then Williams did something I'll never forget, and it is one of the reasons I consider him a great friend of mine in baseball. He looked at Donie Bush and he shook his head.

"No, Donie," he said. "It was a good pitch. It was a perfect strike, right at the knees. I should have hit it."

I could have thrown my arms around him. I walked off the field and I thought, "What a man that is." I never had anyone else in my career do anything like that.

◆ ◆ ◆

WILLIAMS RIDES INTO CITY ON LONG HOMER; NEWCOMERS FEAST

By HALSEY HALL

Ted Williams hit one so high and fast yesterday that he rode over the city on it. He rode right into his new baseball home, into the hearts of opening day fans. That blow brought cheers for the lanky kid in right field, it helped bring in a 14-4 victory over Louisville in the debut of the 37th Association campaign at Nicollet Park.

They had been watching Williams all day. Intently. Definitely. He had come up in the first frame, missed two curve balls from Lefty Rufe Meadows. Then he slipped a liner just over Ray French's outstretched glove at third base.

He came up the second time with Meadows still hurling and the sacks drunk. This time he blasted a singing liner to center to score two tallies and knock Rufus round-legged.

Newcomers' Day

He came up a third time against Carl Boone with the singling Spence on base and did it. A terrifically towering flyball sailed like a bird over the right wall, over Nicollet avenue, over the front part of the roof across the street.

For the fans, there was your ballgame. Williams and Parmelee and Jim Galvin—the new and the old—returned as new. Williams hit the ball fast; Bud threw it that way. He only fanned three men, but he was deliciously wild with seven bases on balls; wild enough to make the boys a bit leary, keep the customers in suspense and keep his mates feeding on double plays, for they came up with three in back of him.

The Millers got into their Nicollet stride with 17 hits. Mr. Williams, how awful. Three hits. With one he nearly tore a man's glove off; with another he knocked a pitcher from the box; with the third he knocked the clouds loose.

Neverthelss, the crowd had some anxious moments as well as damp ones for Bert Niehoff's gallant visitors started to take Royalty apart in the first inning. The first three men got bingles, although they were of the scrubby garden variety, not the full-flow-cring kind that the Millers later plucked. Tony Governor beat out a roller deep to Cohen's right, took second on a wild pitch and Madura beat out a slow roller that produced a convention between Taylor, Cohen and Parmelee. Koster then bid a single to right field and Governor scored and Madura romped in as Pfleger tossed out Sturm.

That Big Third

This two wasn't erased in the Miller third. It was annihilated. Ah, sweet mystery of baschit life, listen to this rendezvous with a pitcher:

Galvin hit one over the left field wall that at no time was barely higher than the fence. Parmelee whammied a single to center. Cohen singled to the identical spot. Spence dropped a single between Koster and the right field wall. Williams bid one to center and Ray Rosebud Kolp, the famous Jockey of the Plains, ambled to the carnage. Dan Taylor splashed a solitaire to right, Pfleger singled to right, Tabor slithered a double inside third. Exit Kolp

Continued on page 10.

(Clippings from the student paper courtesy of the Les Cassie collection at Hoover High and from a Minneapolis newspaper)

DICK DURRELL, Fan, former publisher of *People* magazine

I played against him. He was in Minneapolis and I was in Columbus coming up in 1938. I remember I stopped his 26-game hitting streak. I'll tell you what he always tells people when he introduces me, he says, "Here's a guy I hated to hit against." I told him,"The feeling's mutual. I'm glad you was in the other league, too." He's one of the greatest hitters I ever saw. I told him, I'm glad you're in that other league.

—Max Lanier

Ted won the Triple Crown in Minneapolis, playing right field at Nicollet Park. I lived about three miles from there. Guys my age—12 maybe 13—we'd take our bikes and go down. We'd take our gloves and stand in back of the park.

When the other hitters were taking their five swings for batting practice, we'd scramble for the balls. If we found one, we'd bring it back and get into the game that way, because it was the Depression. When Ted came up, we'd run around the park into Nicollet Avenue, which was busy with streetcars. He'd hit one or two out with his five swings and we'd be running amongst the streetcars and cars to try and get the balls in order to get into the park. His home runs would occasionally break store windows across the street from the ballpark and the team would have to pay for the damages.

◆ ◆ ◆

DICK HOFFMAN, Fan

In 1938, Ted was breaking in with the old Minneapolis Millers. Mike Kelly was the owner of the Millers at that time, and they knew they had a personality on their hands in Ted Williams. They wanted somebody that was pretty stable, so they had Ted stay with the Tauschers. Walter Tauscher was an excellent journeyman pitcher in those days. He was a married man with a child, and they lived next door to the Beans. They had Ted live with the Tauschers because they didn't want him with the rounders—guys that smoked cigars and drank beer like Jimmy Tabor and some of those other big stars.

Jack Bean got to know Ted because he was next door to that house the Tauschers rented. Ted was four years older and he didn't know anybody else in Minneapolis. Jack used to hire dance bands and put on dances, and I worked with him on those things. Jack was heavy into music even in those days. He was a piano player. Good athlete. High IQ guy. He and Ted hit it off pretty well. So Ted would come over to Jack's from time to time and we'd play records. We'd buy records, 78 rpm type things, and we had quite a collection for those days—Tommy Dorsey, Benny Goodman, all that stuff. My older brother was quite a trumpet player, too. Ted would come over and listen to these things with us, and go to a show once in a while. He was really into it.

Jack's dad happened to be an avid hunter and, of course, Ted was into hunting and fishing so they became quite friendly—Mr. Bean, J. R. Bean, and Ted. As a result, for the next three or four years until war time, Ted came back every fall after he finished with the Red Sox. He wouldn't stay with the Beans, but they would go hunting up in northern Minnesota.

Mr. Bean said that when they'd go hunting, Ted was always working on his eyes. He'd have whoever was going hunting with him throw corn cobs at him, and he'd take a big stick, you know, and swing. Always working on his hand-eye coordination. Another little thing: he'd always be working on his wrist strength. Ted showed us some of the ways he kept his wrists strengthened. He would take a chair, just a simple dining room chair, and he would lie down on the ground and lift it by the front legs, lift it as far as he could with both of his wrists. That's a tough thing to do.

I've got a lot of respect for Ted. He was way out, there's no doubt about it—kind of nutty, off the top of his head. He'd say anything he wanted to say—never lewd or crude or anything like that—but he told it like it was. He was outspoken. It was very interesting to be around him.

His mother did social work and he would tell about different things that she'd run into with people that were really destitute. She'd find all sorts of gruesome things that they were cooking up in their ovens, when she'd go out to see them. I mean things like most of us wouldn't eat, like the family dog. He used to have a lot of stories like that.

◆ ◆ ◆

T. HOFFMAN, Fan

My dad was an outgoing guy and he had a kind of sports dinner at our house. He had guys over, like Babe LaVoir who was an All-American player on the Golden Gopher football team, Merv Dillner another Minnesota football player, the Beans, and Ted Williams. I sat next to Ted at the dinner table. It never occurred to me to get his autograph. He sat to my left. According to our family custom, the food would go counterclockwise. You'd pass the dishes. Now keep in mind he was 20 or 21 years old now and he did not speak in a talking voice, it was practically a yell when he opened his mouth. The food would come, and if it was mashed potatoes, he'd say, "No, thanks!" and then he'd take two big helpings and smack them on his plate. Then the roast beef would come around. "No, thanks!" and he'd fill his plate with the roast beef. Then the mixed nuts and he'd take about two or three spoonfuls after saying "No, thanks." Of course, we got a big kick out of that.

Ted's about 6'3", 6'3 1/2" and very outgoing, and my dad was an extrovert and loved laughing. When the evening was over, my dad was getting a little round in the stomach. Well, we got to the front door and with the back of his hand, Ted smacked my dad in the stomach, hard. He yelled, "Thanks for the dinner, Whale Belly!" And my dad, who had this roaring laughter, just filled the house with this roar. He thought it was the funniest thing in the world. And of course the rest of us just about died laughing. Ted shouted it. He smacked him with the back of his hand, and it was not a love tap. My dad Marty just thought this was the funniest thing in the whole world.

Ted came back another time, a couple of years later. I remember him coming into our den. We had an RCA Victor Victrola, the latest thing in '39. We had Artie Shaw, Benny Goodman, all this kind of stuff. We're out there playing the record, and Ted's beating on a pillow listening to these records like he's playing the drums. Just listening to the music. He loved that music! I mean, he was out there beating on that pillow!

◆ ◆ ◆

TED WILLIAMS
(Taken from San Diego Union-Tribune, *7-7-88)*

When I was 19, 20, I really came fast. I really started to show some mustard. I got a lot of great help. In the high minor leagues I was playing against guys in the game for 20, 30 years. I'd be hitting line drives to right field and the next time against me they'd be throwing crappy little curves. TURN ON THAT BALL. TURN ON IT. Those old veteran pitchers I was with would say, "Why don'tcha wait on that?" I would, and it'd be line drive, line drive, line drive. You don't think that stuck in my mind? I was just like a sponge soaking that up.

I was a good, calculating hitter at 21. Not at 27 or 30 or 32. I know I'm not a very smart guy, and Lord knows I wasn't much of a student. But baseballically, I was a cum laude.

◆ ◆ ◆

BUD TUTTLE, Teammate, San Diego Padres

When we used to go up north, we always traveled by train. Up in California, the little town on Dunsmuir up there, the train would stop and on the platform outside, there was a woman who had a cart. She had homemade ice cream—ice cream you've never tasted before. Boy, was this the best! And everybody wanted to get some. We had no air-conditioning on the train, so we'd open the windows, and when we got there, Ted would climb out the window to be the first one there to get the ice cream. He'd get about a quart of ice cream for each of us and then he'd climb back in with the ice cream while everybody else was lining up to get theirs. My favorite flavor was chocolate; his was vanilla. Coming back, we always hit it at night and she wasn't there then. He'd go right out through that window like there was somebody shooting at him.

◆ ◆ ◆

DELL OLIVER, Hoover High School Classmate

I know that he lit the trash can in the print shop on fire about once or twice a week. Just fooling around. He was just fooling around. But the teachers loved him just because of his personality and the clean-cut kid that he was. He had a goal set early in life about what he was going to do. I remember when I was in his typing class.

He was a talker, you know. He was always out to have some fun no matter where he was, and he was a great personality, but because he talked so much, he disturbed the class. So the teacher had him sit right up in front, right in front of her desk, so she could control him.

Otherwise, he'd have the whole class disrupted. I was sitting in the back, and one day I looked up there and Mrs. Hamilton, she was crying. I said to myself, "Oh, man, what did Ted say to her now to make her cry?" I heard her say, "Ted, what are you going to do with your life?" And he says, "I'm going to be the best baseball player in the world." Then she really began to bawl. She said, "Ohhhh, Ted!" [Animated moans.]

◆ ◆ ◆

SWEDE JENSEN, Hoover High School Classmate

When he was in high school, we didn't live too far apart. He used to carry a bat with him all the time. I can remember walking to school with him quite a few times, and he'd knock every flower off every bush on the way.

He was very, very adamant that he would be a big league hitter someday. I hate to say this, but none of us were great students at that time. He always said, "Don't worry about my grades. I'm going to play major league ball!"

◆ ◆ ◆

MEL SKELLEY, American Legion teammate
Why Ted Should Have Beat the Shift

The Williams Shift . . . the Boudreau Shift. Whatever you called it, it was a radical defense designed by Lou Boudreau which moved three infielders to the right side of the infield and brought the third baseman over to the shortstop hole or even closer to second base, all to defend against Ted's proclivity to pull the ball.

TED WILLIAMS: THE PURSUIT OF PERFECTION

(Cartoon from Boston Post, Saturday March 19, 1938)

At first, the only player on the entire left side of the diamond was Indians leftfielder George Case. Ted could slap the ball to left, but Boudreau was counting on Case's speed to cut any hit to a single. If Ted only got a single off you, you were doing well. Critics argue that Ted should have just bunted a few times to left and strolled to first base, and that would have ended the shift right there.

Ted never believed in compromise. Just as he wouldn't swing at bad pitches, he believed in hitting the ball the way he did best—and that was with power, not just punching the ball to left. Situationally, he'd bunt once in a while or hit to left, but as a matter of course, he hit into—and often through—the Shift.

Childhood friend Mel Skelley explains, though, how Ted truly was a good opposite-field hitter.

When he grew up, if he wanted to play ball, it was the only choice he had. Anything hit to right was ruled an automatic out. We'd hang around the North Park playground in the evening and there wasn't much to do sometimes. We'd swipe some peaches from the trees. We filled up our pockets, but Ted wanted even more and he started stuffing them down the front of his sweater. The peach fuzz rubbed off on him and he was itching all over.

Quite a few of us would go up there and play ball. I played American Legion with him one year, when Ted was 16 and I was 12 or 13, more my brother's age. We used to play pickup games there in the daytime. Ted was a star even then; he could always hit. In fact, we made special rules when we played Over the Line because he could hit better than the rest of us. You need three on each team. We'd hit to the left field side of the diamond and we'd make Ted hit to left field because he could hit better than the rest of us. You had to hit it between second and third base and then to the left side of center field.

My brother Bill and Ted were on the Padres at the same time [in 1937] and my dad used to go up and pick up his mother and take her to the ballgame with my mother. Bill had a bright red roadster with cream-colored wheels and a convertible top. They'd drive down Broadway with the top down and Ted would bang on the side.

◆ ◆ ◆

TRAVIS HATFIELD, Texas Liquor House team manager

Hatfield was a former scout for the Dodgers when he recounted this story, which ran in the Boston American *on December 14, 1950. The story said, "Ted didn't always ignore the sports fans."*

Of course, when Ted's Salvation Army mother found out the name of the team Ted had played for, that was the end of that.

Travis Hatfield paid Ted his first $5.00 to play baseball.

I had Ted with the Texas Liquor House, playing against the El Cajon team, just outside San Diego. Our pitcher, a little kid named Kettle, had a 0-0 game for eight innings when he had to leave. Kettle went to a military school, and the bus came along to pick him up.

I tried to get Kettle to stay, but he wouldn't. So Ted pipes up, "Let him go, I'll pitch the ninth." Well, the other team got a run off Ted and we came to bat, trailing by a run.

Our first batter got out, second one got on and Ted had a chance to come up.

The third batter went out and the fans started to leave. Ted looked up and waved them back to their seats. "It's not over yet," Ted was yelling at them.

And it wasn't. He poked one out for a home run and we won, 2-1. Boy, did he have a big grin galloping around the bases.

◆ ◆ ◆

RALPH THOMPSON, Ted's first batboy in San Diego

I was the first mascot for the Padres. I was also the first batboy; that was part of my job. 1936 and I was nine. They fitted me for a uniform. I had number 55. I was there from the very first day, their first year. I was there until '41.

I remember meeting Ted. A very eccentric young kid. I used to go on a road trip occasionally with the team, and the ballplayers would not associate with Ted on the road. They would not go to theaters or anything with him, because if the theater didn't start the movie on time, he'd get up on his feet and start hollering and raising hell. As a kid, I didn't care. I was happy to go. His actions didn't bother me any. He was always good to me.

He paid my way in. The other players wouldn't go anywhere with him, though. They'd be embarrassed.

(Photo by Arthur Griffin)

The Kid From California

I used to chew Mail Pouch Tobacco at the time. I picked that up from my dad. Ted didn't drink. He didn't even chew tobacco. I did, and he didn't.

I wasn't skittish. I was very mature for my age. I was much calmer than Ted; I know that. But I didn't come from a broken home. I think kids who come from broken homes where there's not a stable family life, they tend to be that way, but Ted, he wasn't introverted.

Rumor had it that he had hit a home run over the right field wall in Lane Field and they were claiming it to be the longest home run ever hit. It went over the right field wall and into an empty boxcar. It went all the way to Los Angeles. There's never been any verification of that, but I wouldn't be surprised. The train tracks were right outside the right field wall and a lot of freight cars were parked there with an open door. I wouldn't be at all surprised but what that happened.

He was a splendid hitter and just had terrific poise. He just looked beautiful up there at home plate. He was only eight or nine years older that I was.

◆ ◆ ◆

TED AND CHRISTMAS
(from a letter Ted wrote to Ed Sullivan, in the book,
Christmas With Ed Sullivan, *McGraw-Hill, 1959)*

Dear Ed,

One of my most memorable Christmases occurred in my early teens. I received my first fully electric train set with transformer and all the works. It was a great thrill for me to walk into our living room and see those beautiful trains spread out on tracks running around our Christmas tree.

One of the other family gifts that year was a new living-room rug. The very evening I received my trains I forgot to turn off the transformer and it burned out, leaking all over the rug. Boy, was I ever a popular guy around my house for a while!

MANUEL HERRERA, Cousin

Ted stayed away from the family. He was very distant. He was disappointed in his mother because she was on the street selling the Salvation Army *War Cry*. He knew that the Salvation Army took advantage of her. When she came to live with us, she was 68 years old in 1958 and just a shadow of herself.

She had worked her heart out for the Lord and there wasn't much left. But she still had a little twinkle in her eye about the Army and she still loved it. She would never say a bad word about anybody. She was a wonderful woman.

I'd say, "Where are you going, Aunt May?" and she'd say, "I'm going to see the Devil." She'd take her Bible and her Salvation Army *War Cry* and she'd head right for the Marines in the bar. There was no stopping that woman.

She would do magic tricks first. Take a cornet with her. She'd get your attention, capture you and then she'd. . . . She would do a disappearing act with a quarter and she could roll it on her fingers and get your attention with that and then ask you what hand it was in. That's the way she'd get your attention, and then she'd play a little violin or something. And then the next thing, she'd be telling about the Lord. It was always a big thing when May came.

His father called himself a Yankee. From New York. His mother was from Texas—El Paso. Ted's grandmother Natalia, who he loved immensely, grew up on a ranch in Chihuahua, Mexico. The Venzors had come across from Mexico.

They were originally Basque—"Basco"—just like Ted is, they are long and lean. Three out of his four uncles were built in that same stature. Saul, Pete, Paul and Bruno. Bruno was chunky.

Basque people are loners. They are very independent. They're serious thinkers and they do well by themselves. Remind you of anybody?

Ted did not speak Spanish, but he had a pretty good idea what was being said. I told him, "You're a damn Mexican like me and you don't even speak Spanish." He says, "Yeah, I'm a pitiful one." He understood it, though.

My great-grandmother understood English, but she spoke mostly Spanish. She even smoked Bull Durham. She learned how to smoke Bull Durham when she was a kid in Chihuahua.

Saul was his favorite. I'll tell you why. There's two reason why uncle Saul was his favorite. Number one, because Saul was a fantastic pitcher.

And he was a winner.

Saul pitched against Babe Ruth in an exhibition game when Babe Ruth and Lou Gehrig and Joe Gordon were barnstorming. He struck them all out . . . he struck them all out. In Santa Barbara. They played at Pershing Park. I think it was about 1936. They lost the game 1-0 and I think Saul got the only hit.

Ted used to play baseball right out in our front street in Santa Barbara. He played right in that driveway. When he was a little boy, he used to wear a hat and turn it sideways and say, "I want to be Babe Ruth when I grow up." He was seven or eight years old.

◆ ◆ ◆

Mr. Williams Goes to Boston

In 1939, Mr. Smith—as portrayed on the silver screen by Jimmy Stewart—went to Washington. That same year, Mr. Williams, starring as himself, went to Boston. Ted, always a master of entrances and exits, ensured his Boston debut was filled with drama. He loudly proclaimed his arrival by setting rookie marks for RBIs (145) and walks (107)—both records which haven't been matched in over six decades.

His sophomore year was at least as impressive as he raised his batting average 17 points, from .327 to .344, and topped the league in runs scored. In 1941 Ted hit his stride, batting a remarkable .406 to set the new standard for generations of hitters to come. That same year, his on-base percentage was a staggering .551. No player in baseball history has ever gotten on base more consistently. In 1942, even as he prepared for service in WW II, the first of two long intermissions from the major league stage, Ted won his first Triple Crown with 36 HR, 137 RBI, and a .356 average.

When Ted left baseball for three full years of military service, he had accumulated 127 HR's, 515 RBIs, a career .356 average, and legions of fans. Despite his baseball honors, he had also developed his detractors.

On his return to baseball after the war, Ted led the Red Sox to the 1946 AL pennant and was named league MVP. In 1947 he captured another Triple Crown. What he might have accomplished during those three prime years in between is enough to quicken any statistician's pulse.

Opposite: Ted packs for the road.
(Photo courtesy of San Diego Hall of Champions)

BILLY WERBER, Ballplayer

Ted came up in '39 and I was playing third base for Cincinnati. We played ball games against Boston in spring training and exhibitions with them in tank towns along the way coming north. We traveled in cars, on railroads, by Seaboard Airline and the Atlantic Coast Line and called on towns like Birmingham and Memphis, Florence, South Carolina and Durham and Charleston, West Virginia. I met Ted when we were making these trips.

He first drew my attention on the ballfield. Cincinnati had a very good pitching staff. We had Paul Derringer and Bucky Walters, Junior Thompson and Johnny Vander Meer, Jim Turner, Lee Grissim, and Joe Beggs. Cincinnati was an outstanding ball club at that time, and these games that we played against Boston—and we played eighteen of them in Florida and on the way north—were won by Cincinnati. Still, Ted was unmerciful in the way that he hit those pitchers—and they were good pitchers. I knew then that he would be an outstanding hitter.

Of course, Williams when he first came up was also—I don't know how to put this exactly—he was an arrogant person. He was a bit on the insufferable side. He believed that his bat was the best, his fishing was the best, his hunting was the best, his everything. But that helped him. He believed that he was a great hitter, and that made him a great hitter. Like Ruth, he had a faith in himself. As Ted developed and came out of the Marine Corps, he grew up a lot. He matured. There was a transformation.

◆ ◆ ◆

JOHNNY VANDER MEER, Pitcher

The first time I saw Ted Williams was at an exhibition game at Plant Field in Tampa. He was a rookie with the Boston club and I was with Cincinnati. He was the last man up in the game, in the ninth, and I was working the last two or three innings. Ted took a third strike.

The game was over and as I was walking off the field, he came up to me and asked, "Did you make the ball spin the other way? Did you turn it over?" The ball was low and inside; it was a sinker. "I sure did," I said. I had turned my hand over—my wrist over—and put a reverse spin on the ball. Bucky Walters was standing right close by and I said to Bucky, "That guy sees which way the stitches are turning! He ought to prove a pretty good hitter."

Hell, yeah, he saw the stitches! Or he wouldn't have asked me if I'd turned the ball over.

◆ ◆ ◆

BOBBY DOERR, Ballplayer, Hall of Fame

He should have been up in Boston in '38 after that good year at San Diego in '37. He might have been just a little bit green in some things, but he could have hit there. It probably was for the best that he played that year out—turned out he won the Triple Crown in Minneapolis. But he could have been hitting almost that good with the Red Sox. Ted just had that natural ability. He was so far ahead of everybody in that era, as far as hitting intelligence is concerned.

Any little percentage that would help him in any way, he took advantage of. He used to do fingertip pushups and work lifting chairs. He knew the extent he had to go to and didn't want to be over muscle-bound. Of course, he studied the opposing pitchers. When I was playing, you just assumed that the guy you saw last week and the week before would throw the same the next day. But Ted's feeling was that they might have a little more, and he wanted to look at a pitcher the first time up to see if the guy wasn't a little quicker or maybe not quite as good that day. If a new pitcher came into the league, he would ask somebody who had hit against him what type of stuff he had. He'd watch them warm up. He just seemed like he was ahead of everything. I'm sure that he passed on a lot of his intelligence. His theories of hitting are helping young players now.

I've seen him when he was 0 for 7 or 8, which was a hell of a slump for Ted. One day he went out and had Joe Dobson pitch to him before a regular game. He liked to have somebody pitch good stuff to him. He must have hit for 45 minutes. Dobson said, "Ted, jeez, you're going to wear yourself out before today's game." Ted said, "Well, I might not be as sharp today but I will the next day and the next day."

♦ ♦ ♦

On his way up to Boston, following spring training in 1939, Ted's final stop was in Worcester, Massachusetts for an exhibition game against Holy Cross. Ted hit his first grand slam in a Red Sox uniform in the first inning of that game at Fitton Field.

The first time Ted batted for the San Diego Padres, he had faced a pitcher by the name of Cotton Pippen and struck out on three straight pitches. Three years later, Pippen was on the mound for the Philadelphia Athletics at Fenway Park for Ted's debut in Boston. Ted got a single and a double off Pippen that day.

On April 23, 1939, it was Luther B. "Bud" Thomas who threw the ball which became the first home run Ted Williams hit in the majors. Thomas started for the A's and Ted came up in the first inning with two on and powered it out. Contemporary reports indicate it was a fastball, which Ted hit into a part of the bleachers where only Ruth, Gehrig, and Hal Trosky had ever placed one. Thomas himself remembered it somewhat differently [see sidebar].

ELDEN AUKER, Pitcher

When Ted came up in '39 there was no doubt that he was here to stay. He was really a great young ballplayer—a great eye, a great set of wrists, a student of the game. He spent the entire spring asking us fellows who had been in the league for a while how every pitcher pitched and what was his best pitch and how did he work, and where to play so-and-so in the outfield, did he pull the ball, did he hit straight away or hit to the opposite field, how fast could he run. He just drove you crazy with questions. And every time he was in the clubhouse he'd have a bat in his hands, standing before the mirror, taking swings and looking at himself—just a complete student of the game.

Of course, Ted was a real straight arrow—didn't drink, didn't smoke. I don't think he'd ever been with a woman at that particular time. Just a young kid full of ambition and highly intelligent. You didn't have to tell him the same thing twice. Ted brought enthusi-

He hit his first home run off me. The first one he ever hit. In Fenway Park, spring of 1939. He hit a sort of a change of pace, a slow ball. He pulled it hard. It was just a fair ball way down the right field line.

— Bud Thomas

Reading The Sporting News, *August 1937.*
(Photo courtesy San Diego Hall of Champions)

asm wherever he went, always laughing and joking in the clubhouse, he could hardly wait for the game to start.

We had a good bunch of veterans on the team and we all liked Ted—you couldn't help but like him. He was good friends with Jimmie Foxx and Jimmie was my roommate that year. Mrs. Auker used to have Ted and Jimmie come out to the house for Coca-Cola and fried chicken, mashed potatoes and homemade gravy. Ted loved that. He spent a lot of time with Moe Berg and Moe got quite a kick out of him because he was always asking questions. Lefty Grove and some of the veterans had been around for a while . . . Roger Cramer was there, Joe Vosmik. These were all real gentlemen and there was no hassling or anything with Ted. They understood him, and he brought a lot of life to the team.

There is one thing about Ted that I remember very well and always admired him for. When he came up that spring we got to talking once and he said, "The first money I earn, I'm going to spend it on getting my mother out of the Salvation Army." He said she'd been working there for years, and he wanted to get her out. "When I get her settled, and comfortable, and positioned in life," he said, "I'll take what's left." I know that practically everything he made that year, he sent home to her. That was his chief objective—he wanted his mother out of that work.

I hadn't seen Ted until recently [at a Hitters Hall of Fame event in 1997.] He threw his arms around me, patted me on the shoulder and said "God, it's great to see you." And he got tears in his eyes. He said, "It's been so long. Sit down here beside me. I want you to sit here with me." Such a warm gesture that you could feel it. Always so sincere.

◆ ◆ ◆

TED WILLIAMS: THE PURSUIT OF PERFECTION

Charlie Wagner, Ted Williams' longtime roommate, had the rudest of awakenings one morning. Williams was up before breakfast swinging a bat in front of the hotel room's mirror while Wagner slept. A headpost knob caught Ted's attention. So he took his stance, drew a bead on it and gave it his best home-run rip.

Bwaaaaaaanngg!

The bed collapsed, landing Wagner on the floor. "Damn, what power!" marveled Williams, his hands tingling—and Wagner's head throbbing.

"BROADWAY" CHARLIE WAGNER, Pitcher

I was his first roommate with the Red Sox and he was always an "early to bed, early to rise" type of guy. He was very consistent and thrived on good quality living every day.

I don't think he ever stayed out past 12 when I roomed with him . . . . He woke me up any number of times swinging that damn bat in the room. [Ted] was a perfectionist in everything, didn't want to be second in anything. He was baseball, baseball, baseball.

We both had the same interests in fishing and hunting and I too liked to try living right so we made good roommates. Jimmie Foxx and some of the other guys on the team teased us and called us the "milkshake guys" but that's how we were and we used to take the ribbing and give it right back.

He was a great fisherman and a great camera man; he loved to take pictures and he writes books, too. Anything he attempted, he wanted to be the best. Even defensively he did extremely well. He didn't have all the speed but he certainly wasn't slow. He always knew how much he could get in a game situation. Sure he had great ability but he worked as hard as any human being did at improving. He was hitting all the time. He was GOOD. If he had played in other ballparks, he would have cleaned house. He was almost super-human.

Probably my favorite memory of Ted is from a game in Chicago when it was the top of the ninth, the score was tied, and I was pitching. He said "If you'll tell me now that you'll hold 'em, I'll hit one out of here." I said I would, and he hit the ball over the roof and the whole works, an incredible hit. We won the game. That's the kind of player he was.

◆ ◆ ◆

MOE BERG, Ballplayer
(Taken from Kiss it Goodbye by Shelby Whitfield)

They called him screwy, but he was not any screwier than a college sophomore or any kid of twenty. The kid could hit, and it was apparent at that early time. I could tell that he would never be any DiMaggio in the field, but I knew he'd be better than the average fielder. And the thing that impressed me most was his eagerness to learn. He asked more sensible questions than most kids. I remember him asking me, "What will Ruffing throw to a left-handed batter with the count two strikes and no balls?" I knew at that point that here was a kid who had interest, and wanted to learn.

◆ ◆ ◆

It became his trademark, but it wasn't a fashion statement. He wasn't making a statement of any sort. There was all sorts of speculation about why he didn't wear a dress shirt and tie. Some people tried to say he thought he was special and thought he didn't have to follow anybody's dress codes. Like he was bigger than the game. That sort of rubbish.

Nobody on the team ever said anything about it. We knew the reason Ted wore those shirts. He didn't want to spend the money to buy dress shirts and neckties. He wanted his mother to have the money. We all admired him for that.

—Elden Auker, 1939 teammate (from the book *Sleeper Cars & Flannel Uniforms*)

DAVID THOMAS, Ballplayer

(Taken from Mudville Diaries *edited by Mike Schacht)*

One night after the 1939 season, during dinner with some friends in Minneapolis, I had occasion to ask Ted Williams two questions about his rookie season with Boston. I asked him, Who was the best pitcher you faced? And he said Ted Lyons. Then I asked him, Who was the best hitter you saw? And he said Charlie Gehringer.

Then he stood up in front of us and took a batting stance and said, "But no pitcher on earth can stop me from hitting."

◆ ◆ ◆

BOBBY DOERR, Ballplayer, Hall of Fame

We had a lot in common. We'd go to the movies—both of us enjoyed westerns. Then, of course, I liked to fish and had the place up in Oregon about the time Ted was just getting interested in fishing. We'd often walk around town. Like if the team went from Cleveland to Detroit we'd get off the train and he'd say "Come on, Bobby, we'll walk around town a little bit." So we'd walk, and he'd always be talking hitting or talking baseball. One time, one of the other players said, "Where you guys going? You mind if I go with you?" Ted said, "Oh, you guys go ahead." He didn't want a third person. He just wanted two to take a walk.

Back in 1941 or 1942, coming up from spring training, Ted says, "Let's go over to the Louisville factory." That was great. We got there, I think around 7:30 and the factory wasn't even open yet. So we set on the steps there for about a half hour. When they did open, he made a bee line back there to the old guy with the lathe and told the fellow what he wanted . . . "Any time you see those little pin knots in the wood, why, get 'em in my bats." So when he walked away from the old fellow, he handed him a twenty dollar bill. Ted says he gave him a ten dollar bill, but I know he gave him a twenty dollar bill, which at that time was a lot of money.

In '41 at the All-Star Game in Detroit, we were staying at the Book Cadillac Hotel. Mr. Hillerich, the old man, was also staying there, and Ted walked up to him, and said, "Mr. Hillerich, I want some 32 ounce bats." I remember Mr. Hillerich threw his arms up and said, "Ted, you can't get good wood in 32 ounce bats." And Ted said, "What good is wood if you can't handle it?" His theory was that quickness was the key and hitting the ball on the fat part of the barrel was more important than three or four extra ounces of wood. If you picked up Ted's bat there'd be a white spot on the fat part of that barrel where he'd hit every ball. He was the first one I knew of who went to the light bat for better control.

Ted even had a device put in the clubhouse, mounted with a big bone, and he was always boning his bats down. He was the first one to get a little postal scale which he used to weigh everything. He could pick up a bat and tell you within a quarter of an ounce what it weighed.

Something else—he always had a problem hanging onto the bat using just the resin. That's because your hands would be slimy. Ted got the idea to use olive oil with resin for a stickum. God, that olive oil and resin gave you a real firm grip with the bat. Just put a little drop of oil on your hand, then the resin. And these theories of his proved out—they eventually came to use the pine tar and nowadays they're even going to 31 ounce bats.

Opposite: *Ted selects billets at Hillerich & Bradsby, Louisville.*
(Photo courtesy San Diego Hall of Champions)

Lighter bats changed things. I feel good to know I was one of the first big guys, stronger guys, to hit a ball and use the light bat. The pitchers would want to use my bats, they were so small. Hell, Babe Ruth was swinging a big wide [bat] that weighed a ton.

—Ted Williams

Ted had everything figured out. I remember times he'd walk up to the batting cage and watch some guy pitch batting practice, and he'd say, "That guy's holding the ball with the seams" or "He's holding it across the seams." He'd pick things up that quick. Such concentration—just a very unusual person to come along.

He was as good a hitter as ever walked up to the plate. The main thing about Ted is that he was a dead pull hitter. He hit for power. How many strikeouts? That year he hit .406, I think he struck out 27 times. That's amazing for a dead pull hitter and a power hitter. I don't know how many times Ruth struck out, but it was a lot.

◆ ◆ ◆

When asked what his greatest moment in baseball was, Ted invariably replies that it was the ninth-inning home run he hit off Claude Passeau to win the 1941 All-Star game.

CLAUDE PASSEAU, Pitcher

I pitched against Ted about eight or nine times. I struck him out the first time, in the 8th inning. He got that home run the next time. One out of about eight or nine at bats, I guess, ain't too bad, but it was a good one.

To tell the truth, I'd never heard of Ted even though he was one of the better ballplayers. In a game like that, as the feller says, you already should know anything there is to know. They [American Leaguers] were asking Johnny Mize who was the toughest pitcher for him, and he said, "Passeau, because he has a sailer." My balls used to sail. A lot of pitchers, or most of them, they want a rough ball. When I was pitching, I wanted a smooth ball—kind of like a knuckleball, only much faster. That's why they accused me of cheating, because my ball was just sailing. That was my fast ball. I didn't know what I was doing. I pitched in four All-Star games and it looked like every time I was in a game, Ted Williams was there. I became used to him batting and he didn't get any hits—other than the one, the home run.

The fence, where it enclosed the outfield was only 325 feet away. Slaughter was playing right field, and he showed me it was out by about three or four inches. He said, "If it had been that much shorter, I was standing there ready to catch it, but it just nicked off." It wasn't a line drive. It was a high fly ball that landed softly. Three or four inches.

[The TV clips show Ted jumping up and down as he circles the bases.]

When he hit it, I wasn't exactly jumping for joy. But it didn't bother me a whole lot. If it had been the first home run that had ever been hit off of me, I might have been upset.

◆ ◆ ◆

Mexican baseball magazine.

ENOS SLAUGHTER, Ballplayer, Hall of Fame

Just a long stringbean swinging a bat! I know one thing he'll never forget. In the All-Star game in '41 when he hit the dramatic home run, where everybody says it cleared Briggs Stadium . . . it didn't. I was playing right field and the ball hit the upper deck, dropped back on the field, and I kept that ball 44 years. In Cooperstown when they put me in baseball's Hall of Fame, I gave Ted that ball that I had received 44 years earlier. He signed it and left it in Cooperstown.

◆ ◆ ◆

ERNIE STEWART, Umpire
(*Taken from* The Men in Blue *by Larry Gerlach*)

I have a story to tell to show what kind of guy Ted Williams was. It happened in Detroit right after the 1941 All-Star game where Williams had hit the home run in the ninth inning to win the game. Bobo Newsom was pitching for the Tigers. He had a big old "Annie Oakley" curveball that was nothing on earth but a crowd rouser. He never tried to make it a strike, and he never threw it unless he had a five-run lead or there were two out or two strikes. He threw it when he didn't want you to hit the ball. Williams was hitting. Cronin, who was playing shortstop and managing at that time, was in the on-deck circle. Newsom had two strikes on Williams and threw that big old slow curveball up there. I called it too quick. Strike three. Honestly, it was the only bad pitch I ever called in my life where it was REALLY a bad pitch. There are always marginal balls, but this was a BAD pitch. I wish it would have been strike two; then Williams would have another chance. But I took the bat out of his hands. (I couldn't change it, couldn't call it back. I could have crawled into a hole. I was sick.) Well, Cronin got on me right now. But Ted said, "Wait a minute, Joe. Do you make an error at shortstop once in a while? I play left field, and I make an error once in a while. Ernie umpires, and he makes an error once in a while. Let's go!" He trotted out to left field. Cronin said, "Ernie, what in the hell can I say now?" I said, "Nothing, Joe, it's all over now." The guy was just great.

◆ ◆ ◆

The story has often been told of how Ted came into Philadelphia the last day of the 1941 season with his average at .39955. Just the day before, his average had sunk to under .400 for the first time since late July. His .39955 mark could have been rounded up to .400, and Joe Cronin gave Ted the chance to sit it out and not risk seeing his average drop below .400. In fact, Wally Moses of the A's did sit out the doubleheader, and thus kept his average at .301. But .301 was .301 and .39955 was not quite .400 and Ted courageously met the challenge head on, not wanting to back into .400 that way.

Ed Linn points out that Ted's average technically was below .400 and both the AP and the Boston Globe reported it as such. Maybe if he'd quit the season a couple of days earlier . . . . ! But Ted actually went into that last game—a doubleheader—needing to earn the .400 mark.

Some of the old-timers were hard-nosed. Al Simmons, coaching for the A's, tried to bet Ted the day before that he couldn't do it. Hugh Duffy had told Ted, "Look, kid. Go up there and take your cuts. If you miss, you just don't deserve it."

Nothing was at stake, except Ted's immortality. The Kid went 6 for 8, and wound up with the .406 mark, unrivaled since 1941. In the first game, Ted faced Dick Fowler of the A's and got a "sizzling single" off him, bringing his average up to .402. He could have bowed out then— neither an A's victory nor a Sox victory meant anything to either team in the standings, with Boston finishing in second, but 17 games out and Philadelphia in eighth place 37 games out— but he came back to the plate. This time he smashed a home run off Fowler—number 37 for the year. Ted led both leagues in home runs in 1941, as he did in runs scored, walks, and slugging

He knew more about hitting than any man I ever talked to. He used to talk about it, talk about it all the time . . .

I said, "Let me ask you something. How old were you when you hit .400?" He said, "I was 20, I just turned 21." I said, "What did you know about hitting?" He said, "Nothing. The ball looked like a grapefruit coming up there."

—Curt Gowdy

PORTER VAUGHAN, Pitcher

Connie Mack didn't talk to the pitchers but he talked to the catcher Frank Hayes. Frank was a good catcher and when Ted came to bat, he told him that the pitchers had the word from Mr. Mack that they shouldn't let up at all, and if they did, they'd have to pay the consequences.

He didn't seem emotional at all that day, just swung the bat in a businesslike way. Whether he hit a single or a home run, he accepted it without showing any particular emotion that I recall. Ted was a great one, I'll tell you. He got two clean singles off me. The first one, he hit off a curve ball. Our second baseman Crash Davis played Ted in the hole between second and first and Ted hit the ball to his right. The second hit was off a fastball. Bob Johnson, who was a leftfielder, was playing first base and didn't get to the ball; it was between him and the base, right down the line. I felt very fortunate to hold him to two singles! Dick Fowler had started the game and Ted got a single off of him the first time up and then hit a home run in his second trip.

Obviously, I didn't fool Ted at all but it was almost impossible to fool him. He really studied pitchers and remembered everything they threw him. I'd faced Ted once before in 1940. He came up in the bottom of the ninth with the score tied and two outs, at Fenway Park. Ted singled in the game-winning run. It was a curveball—he hit it three feet over my head into center field.

I had the opportunity to meet Ted in the early 1970s when he was managing the Senators in Washington. That's the first time I had seen him since that day in 1941, a day I remember with a certain degree of pride. We joked a little bit and Ted asked me, "Why did you throw me a curve on a 2-and-1 count?" I told him, "Because it was my best pitch!"

◆ ◆ ◆

FRED CALIGIURI, Pitcher

The Red Sox held their spring training out in San Bernardino and we trained in Anaheim so we got to know Ted pretty well. We played a lot of games together, and then when we came east, we each had a railroad car on the same train. They'd pull us about 2,300 miles and we'd get off—down around El Paso and Tucson and those areas—and play exhibition games. Barnstorming until finally we got east.

I pitched that last game to Ted in 1941. I was just a young kid up there. I'll tell you something else about that game—it was the last game Lefty Grove ever pitched. He only threw one or two innings, but they had a "day" for him since that was his final game.

Everybody knew Ted was a great hitter and there were a lot of other great hitters at the time. There was a lot of excitement that day and I remember that our manager Connie Mack was saying, "Don't give him anything! Pitch to him!"

He could hit most fast balls, and the only way to get him out was to change speeds. We tried to change up on him. I know one change-up I threw him he really hit. In Shibe Park there was a kind of a megaphone that sat up on top of the wall, and that ball went as a line drive right into that megaphone and fell back into the park for a double. I suppose

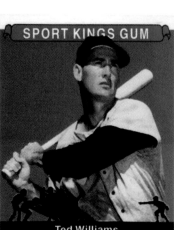

SPORT KINGS GUM

Ted Williams

that speaker was at least two feet across and he hit it pretty good. If it had been a few feet left or right, it would have gone out of the ballpark. I'd just gotten married then so I wasn't worried about Ted Williams.

◆ ◆ ◆

HUGH DUFFY, Ballplayer
(Taken from The Last .400 Hitter by John Holway)

The funny thing about it is, I never did put much store by that .438 average [Duffy holds the highest season average ever] until Rogers Hornsby threatened to better it in 1924. For more than 30 years I virtually forgot about it. Folks weren't so excited about batting averages in those days. They didn't make so much fuss over 'em. Then when Hornsby came along and hit .424, they started checking up on the old records, and there mine was.

I began to take some pride in my .438 and was kind of glad Hornsby didn't outdo it. I thought it was safe for all time, because Hornsby was just about the greatest of the modern-day hitters. I didn't think anybody would come close, but now this Williams comes along, and I don't think it's out of his reach.

I've never seen a better hitter. He's got everything to hit with. A great bead on the ball, the courage to wait up there, and the best arms and wrists I ever did see. The amazing thing is he's mostly a pull hitter. He gets a lot of home runs, but the high-average hitters are usually the fellows who hit straightaway, where there's more room for hits. That's where I made most of my hits, toward center field.

◆ ◆ ◆

JOHNNY PESKY, Ballplayer

Ted already had three years in the big leagues when I joined Boston in '42. I had first seen him around 1937 when I was just a kid, a clubhouse boy for the Portland Beavers cleaning up after the players, drying their stuff out, hanging up their sweatshirts and things like that. I watched Ted—he was 17 and only a year older than me. He was just another player on the San Diego team.

Then in Boston I lockered right near Ted, Dominic and Doerr—we could almost reach across and touch one another. That's when we became friendly. All four of us were from the Coast. We called ourselves "The Big Four" after someone hung that handle on us—Ted being born in San Diego, Bobby in Los Angeles, Dominic from San Francisco and me from Portland.

Ted was good with the players, they all liked him. He was friendly and wouldn't tell a guy what to do, but if you asked him, he was there for you. He did some joking around, not maliciously of course, just an intelligent guy who was great to be around. Ted was one of those unusual people in that he would grasp things so quickly—such a quick mind and quickness in his own body. Utterly amazing.

When he was playing, he was always in the game. "If you do well today, you gotta do better tomorrow. If you get a good ball, hit it, because out of three or four or five pitches, you may just get one good one to hit." That was his theory. He was a perfectionist, really, someone who knew what he had to do and you admired him for that. He would say, "if I strike out 50 times this year, that's a lot." He always said anybody that's a good hitter *has to hit the ball.*

Of course, the press expected him to do the utmost in a ballgame. They were tough on him, a guy with such great ability. If he didn't do it, they'd say "Oh my god. He's this.

Ted always had the reputation. Everybody in the American League talked about what a great hitter he was. I was with the Boston Braves and he had just come up as a kid with the Red Sox, in '39. We used to play exhibitions in Boston every year. Ted looked like he was going to be a great hitter even when he was a kid— one of the best hitters I ever saw.

—Al Lopez, Hall of Fame

Stephen Jay Gould, Harvard paleontologist, has demonstrated in "Entropic Homogeneity Isn't Why No One Hits .400 Any More" Discover *(August 1986)* that Ted's .406 average towers over any other hitter's accomplishments, even Hornsby's .424 mark of 1924, when considered relative to those around him. Factors such as the liveliness of the ball and the quality of the pitching are removed by taking this approach. In the decade of the 1920s when Hornsby hit .424, the average league-leading hitter batted .392 in the AL and .390 in the NL. On average, then, every year the best hitter was at .391. Hornsby's .424 was 33 points above that average top performance. Sisler's .420 in 1922 was 29 points above. When Ted hit .406 in 1941, he did so in a decade during which the top AL average was .349, and the NL best was .354. That put Ted a full 57 points above the AL's best hitters of the decade, and 52 points above the NL's best. Relative to those who hit during his time, Ted's achievement was far, far above any other .400 hitter's relative performance.

What makes the feat all the more remarkable is the fact that when Williams attained his lofty average he did so without benefit of the sacrifice fly rule. In 1941, a fly ball caught by an outfielder (which resulted in a base runner scoring after the catch) was just another out, and the batter was duly charged with a time at bat when batting averages were computed—to the detriment of the batter. [John Holway, a member of SABR] reconstructed Williams' 1941 season with a comprehensive at-bat by at-bat summary. He found that Williams hit six fly balls that scored runners from third base that year. Under present rules, therefore, Williams' average would be computed at .411.

Prior to 1888 a walk was counted as a hit. Ted would have hit .540 in 1941 had the 1887 rules been in effect.

As it was, Ted's .553 on base percentage that year remains an all-time record. Over 55 percent of the times Ted Williams stepped up to the plate, he got on base.

. . he's that." But who was any better? Sometimes players don't understand that the print media's always looking for something to write about, because that's their job. You try to be honest with a writer and sometimes there's a twist made and it makes you look like a damn fool. That happened to Ted and he resented it. He felt that what he did was his own business. We couldn't understand it either—why he sometimes got such negative press. He did what he was supposed to do and did it extremely well. Let me tell you something: baseball is not an easy game to play. It's a simple game, but it's very tough to play. Ted often said the hardest thing to do is hit a baseball thrown at you ninety miles an hour. See how you react to that. A little round ball, a little round bat. Hit it square. Ted hit them so hard, he hit them right through the wind.

◆ ◆ ◆

"THE KID"
by Gene Carney

Final day of the season
The choice is to sit it out
And go down in history with the handful
Of .400 hitters
Or play the doubleheader
The numbers that spell Ted best
May be that six-for-eight
Knocked out while on the ledge
Baseball immortality on the line
Crux of a legend
Williams accepted the dare
Too much for a single nickname
Splinter for opposing arms
Splendid for the Fenway swarms
Seemed a veteran of foreign war
Even before Korea
Triple-Crown Thumper
Who had to have the
Last turn at bat
In Teddy's Ballgame

EDDIE PELLAGRINI, Ballplayer

I joined the Red Sox in '42 and then went to the war. Ted and I were buddies in '42—that's when I first met him. He doesn't remember a lot of this stuff. When you're a ballplayer and you meet a guy like Williams who hit .406 and he asks you to pass the sugar, you remember that! And he doesn't. But I knew about him because I played in his home town of San Diego. A lot of the guys on the San Diego team had played with him when he was still a young kid, and they told me an awful lot about him. I was enthralled with a guy who's about the same age as me, in the big leagues, and hitting .406—hard things for a young kid to do. When he had that year in '41, I was still with San Diego. I said, "Whoa!" I was supposed to be a pretty good ballplayer but I said "How good is this guy to be able to do all that?"

*Ted powers one out—
the only color photos
of Ted Williams
hitting a home run
on July 27, 1960.
(Copyright David L.
Pressman, M.D.)*

Harry Kimberlin gave up the first game-winning homer of Ted's major league career. In St. Louis, the Red Sox were batting in the 10th inning, there were two on when Ted came to the plate. The Red Sox won the game 10-8.

"I remember every bit of it. I was doing a lot of relief pitching then. The ball went halfway to the Mississippi River. I always said it went to the river, but it didn't get that far. It went over Grand Avenue, though. It went over everything, son. It went over everything."

—Harry Kimberlin

The first time I really had something to do with him, I was playing shortstop. A shortstop, if he's a good shortstop, tells the outfielders where to throw the ball. I said, "Second base now with the ball, Williams." He says, "Chrissakes, I know where to throw the goddamned ball." I was only a rookie, but I said—I'll never forget it—I said, "Well, I'm remindin' you." That's about the start of it. So I went in and he says, "I like that. I like the way you did that." I said, "Well, it's just the way I play. I don't assume nothing. I know you know, but I'm gonna remind you."

One day he asked me to go fishing. "Yeah," I said, "Gee, love to go." I didn't know anything about fishing. I even hated to eat fish, for Chrissakes, in those days. I didn't like fish but I'm a little flattered. Here's Ted Williams looking for me, you know. "Where's Pelly? OK, Pelly." So I started to go with him a little bit here and there. Then one of the umpires, a guy named Red Jones, a pretty prominent umpire in those days, called me "Little Ted." Now this is before the season started, this was in Sarasota, Florida. I thought, "Oh, Jesus. I'm from Dorchester, Roxbury, we don't kiss anybody's ass and I didn't want to be one of those guys, you know, that's kissing someone's ass."

So I said to Ted, "Gee, Ted, I'm flattered that you ask me. I like you very much but everybody's starting to notice. Look, I'm trying to make this ball club. I don't want it to look like I'm following you around, and . . . " He says, "Whaddya mean, I can go anywhere I want." I said, "I know that, but I gotta make this ball club." He says, "Ah, you'll make the ball club, Dago." They call you Dago—the Californians, you know. Here they call you Guinea which wasn't a bad thing, just the way they talk. So I didn't take any offense to it. I says, "Well, I just can't do it." And he says, "Well, I was going to take you out on a date with me tonight." So I said, "Well, I'll go with you tonight!" And we went out.

Well, we went to pick up my girl. Ted says [to his girl], "Where are we going?" She says, "We're going to the theatre." So I thought we were going to the movie place, but we went the other way. I said, "Gee, I didn't know Sarasota had two movie theatres in the town." Then we came to this beautiful building, people all dressed up and everything. She was on the stage, you see. Well out comes this girl, and the closer she gets, the wider Ted's eyes get. "Jeezus, who's this?" "That's Eddie's girl friend. She's going to be with Eddie." I'll never forget her name—Heidi. She was beautiful. So she comes over and Ted's looking at her, and he says, "Well, jump in the car!" And she says, "No, I have my own car. Eddie, why don't you and I follow them?" I said, "Why not?" Honest to God, I got the prettiest girl. And Ted had a girl, she wasn't bad, but not like this one! I said, "Shit, if I'd hit .406, I wouldn't even have let your girl in my car."

◆ ◆ ◆

MACE BROWN, Pitcher
(Taken from Pen Men by Bob Cairns)

I think that Ted Williams was the greatest hitter that ever lived. Certainly the greatest one I ever saw. I was in the bullpen and saw a lot of Ted Williams' hits coming my way. I recall one in 1942. I was pitching against the old St. Louis Browns in Fenway in another of those games where I went in late, maybe the seventh. They scored a run off of me and

Arthur Griffin poses with one of his photographs of Ted.
(Photo by Bill Nowlin)

it was a tied game. Then in the top of the ninth we were behind one run and I go in and fall back on the bench. Williams comes over to get a bat and he says, "What the hell are you down about?" And I say, "I ain't down." And he said, "Well, if Pesky gets on I'm gonna hit one outta here." Then he says, "If he don't get on I'm gonna hit one outta here anyway." So lo and behold, Pesky got on and that Williams hit one nine miles, and when he come trotting down into the dugout he just looked at me and said, "I told you!"

Here's another one. We were playing in Chicago, this was 1942 at the tail end of the season. My sister and my mother, they were both in the ball park, they'd driven all the way in from Iowa to see the game. And the first time up in this ball game, it was the tail end of the season and we had second place cinched. The Yankees had first, and Williams, I think he won the Triple Crown that year and the first time up he said, "I'm gonna give them that ol' Mel Ott stance, the one with the front leg kicking, and see how high I can hit one." Well he hit one nine miles, right straight up the infield, right up the old elevator chute. And he comes into the bench kinda laughin' and he sat down on the bench beside me. And I said, "Ted, you ought be ashamed of yourself, my mother and sister have been reading about you since you started and have never had a chance to see you play. They drove all the way in from Iowa today and think about the other fans that paid just to see you today. I'd be ashamed of myself!" So he just smiled and said, "I'll hit one," and so help me, he hit one in the upper deck at Comiskey Park. When he come into the bench he said, "Mace, tell your mother that one was for her."

◆ ◆ ◆

Ted did work at hitting, though. Pitcher Ken Chase of the Senators was tough for Ted to hit. "It pained Ted," wrote Ray Robinson in his book, Ted Williams, *"that while Ken's success was rather limited against most hitters, he had extraordinary success against him. In 1942, Chase came to the Red Sox. Ted decided, then and there, that he would solve the riddle of his nemesis or perish*

(Cartoon from unidentified newspaper source, circa 1939.)

BASEBALL'S NEW BIG NAMES   PICTURE STORIES OF ROUSING MAJOR LEAGUE RECRUITS   By Art Krnz

The late Bill Lane, veteran Pacific Coast League owner, plucked tall and gawky Theodore Williams out of San Diego High School before, he was 18. Ted Williams was a pitcher and outfielder then, but the Padres signed him for his unusual power at the plate.

Boston Red Sox gave $25,000 and two players for Williams, and his mother got another $2500 for his signature.

Sent to Minneapolis, Williams topped American Association, in hitting, runs-batted-in, home runs and runs scored.

COPR. 1939 BY NEA SERVICE, INC.
Williams, not yet 21, is a bit eccentric, but smart, and a student of baseball. He calls his shots at the plate . . . sings going after fly balls. He wore a necktie for the first time when Joe Cronin bought him one on the training trip. *NEXT: Eddie Miller.*

in the effort. He asked Ken to come out to Fenway Park each morning over a period of two weeks. Chase would then throw to Ted until his arm felt like it was dropping off. 'How long does this go on?' Chase asked Ted. 'Until I can hit you with my eyes shut,' said Ted.

"One morning, after Ted had been banging the ball off the right field ramparts of Fenway, he called a halt to Chase's throwing. 'Okay, ya bum,' shouted Ted, 'I can hit you with my eyes shut now!'"

TED WILLIAMS—A MAN OF LARGE APPETITES

"I am building up strength to do a lot of slamming as we head down the stretch," Ted said in late July, 1946. "Thursday night down at Pawtucket," Mel Webb wrote in the Boston Globe, *"he did as well in the banquet league as he has been doing all along at the dish. And here's the damage Teddy did:*

At Joe McGlone's event, Ted consumed the following (noted by Boston Globe *reporter Mel Webb):*

3 shrimp cocktails
3 cups of fish chowder
1 1 1/2 inch thick steak
10 rolls
1 pound of butter
2 orders of string beans
2 2 1/2 pound broiled lobsters
1 chef's salad
3 ice creams with chocolate sauce
plus an indeterminate amount of iced tea

◆ ◆ ◆

EDWARD DONOVAN, Fellow Firefighter with Ted's Uncle John Smith

Early in Ted's career, he became so frustrated with all the attention focused on him, particularly by prying reporters, negative commentary and fickle fans, that he talked of just chucking it all and becoming a firefighter. There was a reason for Ted's choice of alternative occupation. He did have one close relative on the East Coast—his aunt Effie and her husband John C. Smith, a firefighter with Engine Company 6 in Mount Vernon, New York. When he could, he enjoyed visiting his uncle "Beanie" and maybe taking a ride on the fire truck.

"So now it's 1940," Ted wrote, "and I'm having my troubles at the plate and visiting my uncle at the fire station, seeing the firemen hang around with their shirts off, getting sun burned, playing checkers, some of them playing cards. My uncle's telling me about this $150-a-month person he's going to get, and I'm thinking, Boy, here I am, hitting .340 and having to take all this crap from the fans and writers." He told a writer in Cleveland, "Nuts to this baseball, I'd sooner be a firefighter." Ted stepped into it with that one. Around the league, the bench jockeys jumped on him, sporting fire chief's hats and ringing bells and blowing sirens.

I knew John Smith very well. I worked with him for a few years. Actually, he was John C. Smith—his middle name was Charles. His badge number was 31. My badge number was 62. I used to say to him, "You're half of me."

I met Ted. He came to the firehouse in August of 1939. My father Michael was a fireman then. We lived in the back and my father called over and said, "Brother, I want you to come over and meet a ballplayer, Ted Williams." Brother was my nickname. I was all excited, so I ran around the corner. He was standing there with a whole bunch of fellows. I couldn't begin to believe how tall he was! He wasn't heavy or anything. He was almost like an ironing board. They introduced me. I was 15 years old at that time, and Ted asked, "When are you going to get into shape?" Everybody laughed. He was just kidding around.

The fire chief was up on the third floor, so they brought him up to see the fire chief; his name was Gibson. John Smith introduced him to the fire chief.

Ted would visit the firehouse, and he used to pick up a broom on the back of the fire engine and swing it like a baseball bat. He always picked up a broom or something.

I'll tell you another thing about Ted Williams. When I worked with his uncle, he used to call up and ask how his aunt was. I never forgot that. He made a phone call no matter where he was. Chicago or Detroit, he'd call the firehouse and ask for John C. Smith, and ask how was Aunt Effie doing. I thought that was wonderful, really. You know how busy they are. He called religiously.

◆ ◆ ◆

The first time around the league, the first western trip, he might've struck out 10 times in the four towns, and his average was pretty low. But he kept saying, " Don't worry. Don't worry. I'll hit these guys." He kept his confidence. "I'll hit 'em!" He knew what he wanted, and he knew he was gonna do it. Wasn't any doubt about it.

—Joe Cronin, as quoted in *Baseball in 1939*, by Lawrence S. Katz

Terrible Ted, the Knights, and the Fenway Faithful

Ted, the media, and the fans: baseball's eternal triangle. Ted blamed the writers for poisoning his relationship with the fans. The writers wrote what they did to titillate those same fans. Ted used the media to get at the fans and used the fans to reap revenge on the media.

The three supported each other as in some primitive ecosystem. Like ravenous carnivores, the Boston newspapers competed for the juiciest Williams story; some met him head on, while the scavengers attacked from the flanks. The media fed the fans and made Ted a heroic, albeit flawed figure; Ted, reluctantly, sold record numbers of newspapers, and the fans ultimately supported both with their hard-earned dollars.

Some observers blame it on simple geography, specifically Ted's proximity—in Fenway's left field—to the fans. Certainly this exacerbated the situation. It was tantamount to being in a pit with the more rabid variety of fans baiting him from above—a Roman coliseum with emperor Egan and his cohorts in the pressbox showing thumbs down on Williams the gladiator. Yastrzemski later suffered similar abuse in that same left-field pit. Some suggest it engendered a kind of claustrophobia in a solitary man like Ted. He became a different person when surrounded by fans and media. Others point to his sensitivity, aided by those rabbit ears that could pick a single discordant boo from a chorus of cheers. More than anything, Ted hated front-runners, fickle fans who would cheer him one day and boo him the next. A man with great loyalty himself, he expected nothing less from others. When his hometown fans and media turned on him, he couldn't forgive them.

Opposite: A Williams response was seldom a predictable one.
(Fred Kaplan photo, courtesy of Lee Kaplan)

GEORGE SULLIVAN, Writer

During the first year he had a good relationship with the fans. He tipped his hat and was a very popular guy. His second year was a good year but not quite as good as the first. He didn't hit as many homers at Fenway even though they built the right field bullpen to move the fence in for him. Plus they moved him from right field to left field and even though the stands are intimate wherever you are at Fenway, in left field they're in that perch looking down, putting you more in the pit, so to speak, right in the line of the boo-birds. I don't know exactly when it started, but the writers got on his case more. Ted resented it and the fans took their cue from the media.

In 1949, when I was fifteen years old, I got the job that every kid dreams of—I was a batboy for the Red Sox. No sooner had I gotten the job than I grew six inches that summer. By the end of the season I was taller than guys like Phil Rizzuto and Bobby Shantz. Even though I did finish out the season, being taller than players was obviously not a good situation—not that they complained—so I didn't come back the following year. I then became an usher at Fenway. Eventually, I did it all over there.

Ted had a TV show in those days—on Monday nights on channel 4 —-so sometimes when I was ready he'd give me a drive back to my neighborhood because I lived a couple miles from the studio. You don't think that was a big deal, being chauffeured home by Ted Williams?

As a batboy, I was provided with some marvelous insights into Ted. It wasn't unusual for a critically ill youngster to call him from a Boston hospital. He'd come over in the middle of the night if needed. He would do this all the time and occasionally a writer would get tipped off about it. A friend of a friend or a nurse would alert a writer and a good writer would check it out. They'd grab Ted and you'd hear his booming voice in the clubhouse before a game. "Yeah, yeah, it's bleeping true! It's bleeping true you assholes but if you write one word about it, it's the last time I'll ever do it and it'll be on you. It'll be your fault." So cripes, the writer couldn't write it. That was the way Ted maintained his privacy on the thing. You know, that really impressed me as a kid—the true way of doing a good deed, not to get your name in the paper but because it's the right thing to do.

In ' 49—it was Monday, an off day—but as batboys we had to go in every day. I was walking down Jersey Street, which is now Yawkey Way and I hear something like a car backfiring, but there was nothing in sight. I heard it again and again I saw nothing. I thought it must be a beer truck backfiring underneath the stands. When I neared the Red Sox clubhouse I hear BANG, BANG and now I can tell it's coming from one of the exits and I figured something must be happening on the field and I look out and it was the damnedest sight I ever saw. There were dead pigeons completely littering the outfield and the infield. Just clumps of dead birds. I didn't know what was going on and then I see in the right-field visiting team bullpen there's somebody with a rifle out there. I squint my eyes and I say "Oh my God, that's Ted!" Ted's sitting out there in civilian clothes and he's shooting all these birds. Pigeons were always a major problem at Fenway, filthy birds leaving their droppings everywhere. Ted had shot pigeons before and I think Yawkey had even joined him on a few occasions. I watched in awe for a moment as he picked off a couple more and then I went in the clubhouse to do some chores. In a half hour I hear Ted clump, clump, clumping down the runway and he put his arm around my shoulder and said "Hey old buddy, get a couple of barrels and fill 'em up with those birds." Oh God, those stinking rotten pigeons. I think that's the day I learned to swear.

It was my batboy experiences that got me into writing. Like all college kids, I was looking to make some money. Everyone was always asking me, "What kind of a guy is Ted Williams? What kind of a guy is Bobby Doerr?" So it hit me that maybe I could write a few articles about them and sell them. I sold a series to my hometown weekly the *Cambridge Chronicle*, later became their sports columnist, and then started in with the Boston papers as a copy boy and Boston University correspondent. I was only nineteen—my first summer on the job—when the regular Red Sox writer called in sick. The sports editor looked up at the ceiling as if for inspiration. I'm sure he was thinking: *What's this world coming to? I'm going to have to send Sullivan to cover the Red Sox.*

It was an afternoon game at Fenway and when I went through the green door into the Red Sox clubhouse before the game, it was the first time I'd ever been back there since I'd been batboy four years earlier. The first fellow I ran into was Mel Parnell and he gave me a very enthusiastic greeting. He spotted Ted in the training room and yelled, "Hey Ted, look who's here!" And Ted, who can be the most cordial guy in the world when he wants to be—even in his younger days when he was more volatile—came out and gave me a royal reception, pumping my hand and putting his arm around my shoulder. Then he got to the question, "What are you doing now?" And proud as punch with my first big assignment as a newspaperman I said, "Ted, I'm a sportswriter!" He dropped my hand, looked me up and down and said, "You used to be a good kid. Where did you go wrong?" That's what Ted thought of sportswriters and that was the beginning of phase two of our relationship.

Ted was a funny guy. He certainly played the media better than any athlete of that generation. He knew how it worked. One of his favorite tricks when we went into New York was to plant a story with a New York writer. As a writer you really had to be careful. His favorite was Joe Reichler of the Associated Press. Ted would be aloof from the Boston writers but he'd go over and virtually seek Reichler out and give him some real good story. The AP story would go all around the country and you'd get a phone call in the morning from your sports editor saying, "What the hell are we sending you on the road for? How come we have to read the Associated Press to find out what's on Williams' mind?" This was Ted's revenge.

One time the Red Sox had just arrived in New York and were checking into the Hotel Commodore. At this point, Ted and Jimmy Piersall weren't speaking to each other and my first reaction was: Ted's going to pop off about this to the New York writers. I waited until Ted got his room key and started for the elevator and I cut him off at the pass and asked him about the Piersall situation. He blew up. He said, "What are you trying to do, stir up some trouble?" It didn't matter where he was, he could use some pretty foul language, but one thing I knew from watching Ted as a bat boy was that you didn't get anywhere with him by kowtowing. You had to come right back at him the same way. So here I was, a 22-year-old kid, going toe-to-toe with him in the lobby of a major New York hotel. Old ladies in tennis sneakers were clamping their hands over their ears.

One of the few instances I saw Ted screw up was once before a game when a photographer came down looking for him. Ted said "Are you ready now? Are you ready for chrissake? Where is this kid?" I think a 10-year-old kid had saved someone from drowning or done something heroic that made him worthy of meeting with Ted. The photographer said he had left him up in the boxes until Ted was ready. "Well I'm ready now, get him for chrissake." The photographer went and got him, and when the kid came around the corner of the dugout in a little league uniform, all of a sudden Ted's scowl disappeared and he

One time he spit up to the press box. Yawkey allegedly fined him five thousand dollars to mollify the press. I think Yawkey paid him five thousand dollars for doing it. He didn't fine him a nickel. He didn't like the press, either, too much.

— Bob Holbrook

Speed, an arm that makes base-runners cautious, and punch galore at the plate—that's the winning combination that prompts experts to predict great things for Ted Williams, fly chasing Red Sox rookie.

Wheaties, with plenty of milk or cream, and some fruit—that's another winning combination. It spells "Breakfast of Champions" to most of the Bosockers, Ted Williams included. "Don't take that Wheaties box away," warns Ted—"I'll be wanting more!" And that sounds like your kind of breakfast. So why not try Wheaties today?

Not yet old enough to vote, Ted nevertheless casts his breakfast ballot for Wheaties. "I'm a full-time booster for that champion cereal, Wheaties," says this youngster. (Left) Wham! Ted swings all the power of his 6 ft. 3 in. frame into that one—and away goes the ball on a homerun ride! Come out to Fenway Park and watch Williams and your other champion Bosox go to town!

When Ted Williams spoons out some fresh fruit over his "Breakfast of Champions," he's treating himself to a homerun for flavor. Try this tasty, nourishing meal today! It's great for breakfast or as a midnight snack. Ask your grocer for Wheaties!

Wheaties and advertising claims for them are accepted by the Council on Foods of the American Medical Association.

"Breakfast of Champions"
WHEATIES WITH MILK OR CREAM AND FRUIT
Wheaties and "Breakfast of Champions" are registered trade marks of General Mills, Inc.

Wheaties advertisement, circa 1939.
(Courtesy of the General Mills Archives)

was the most charming man in the world. He was wonderful with the kid and the kid's knees were just knocking and he was starry-eyed. The photographer went through the act of asking Ted if he could take a photograph even though he'd already set it up. Ted said "What did you hit last year?" And the kid said .614 or some such thing and then Ted said "Ask this kid if it's okay to have HIS picture taken with ME." Of course the kid was on a cloud. Finally he says good-bye and as the kid is walking out of the dugout someone comes up—a writer I think—and Ted forgets about the kid and starts booming obscenities at the guy. The kid snaps his head around because he's hearing words that he's never heard before. I just thought, that's too bad, it took the edge off a superb gesture. It was nothing malicious but he probably went back to his neighborhood and told people about the incident—that this was the way it was done in the major leagues.

In 1954 Ted had just announced he was retiring. The Red Sox were playing the Washington Senators and he hit a home run into the bullpen. Afterwards, we were in the clubhouse and it was the first time I'd seen him almost misty-eyed, very sentimental. The writers were all gathered around him and he said, "Hey, let's let bygones be bygones. You have jerks in your profession and I've got 'em in mine too, but there's one exception," and he pointed over to the green door of the clubhouse. "If someone came down from the press box and said 'Dave Egan has just dropped dead up in the press box,' I'd look at that son of a bitch and I'd say 'Good!'" He never forgave Egan above all others. Egan picked his shots. He always knocked the brains out of Harvard and called Boston University the "sleeping giant on the Charles." His philosophy was that there are very few giants in this world. Ninety-nine plus percent of the population are not giants—so tear down the giant and those ninety-nine plus percent will applaud. Harvard and Ted Williams were two of his favorite targets.

◆ ◆ ◆

CLEVELAND AMORY, Writer
(Taken from Fenway by Peter Golenbock)

My first article ever published was on Groton School for the *Saturday Evening Post*. The only reason I was at the *Post* was that when I applied, I told the editor I had been the editor of the *Harvard Crimson*. The editor thought to himself, "Here's a man who edited the Harvard humor magazine." The man didn't know the difference between the *Harvard Crimson* and the *Harvard Lampoon*. So naturally he needed me.

The second article was on Ted Williams. It was called, "I Want to Be an Immortal." Williams was at that time nineteen at the most. When I went to interview him at the Hotel Shoreham in Washington, he was looking out his window, and there were a lot of people by the pool. Ted said, "How would you like to be really rich?" He was so ambitious. In those days he was already a terribly highly-paid ballplayer.

I was fascinated with him, because all the time we were talking, he was taking a towel, wetting it, and swinging it as he was walking around the room. I never forgot it. He was studying everything about hitting, all day and all night in his mind, and as a result, he was by far the best hitter that baseball has ever seen. And remember, he did two war stints, during World War II and the Korean War, and they were not easy war stints.

I remember when I went to Bob Feller. I said, "How good is Williams?" He said, "I'll tell you how good he is. When I get in a tight spot and it's 3 and 2 as the bases are full and I'm one run ahead, you just do one thing: you just rear back and try to throw that ball by them, because it's the best chance you've got. But there's just one batter you can never do that to, and that's Ted Williams, because the pitcher never lived who could throw it by him."

I always liked that piece. He never liked it. I knew he wouldn't be happy with it. When you're young, you do pieces that are not as fair in view of his age as I would have done now. If I were interviewing a nineteen-year-old now, I'd make allowances for things he said. But in those days you just pounced on a rather ridiculous quote. "I would rather be a fireman."

I liked Ted because I saw him as a rebel. I was a very rebellious, liberal young man, and that appealed to me. Also I saw the mediocrity did not appeal to him. He would have rather quit than be a mediocre ballplayer, and he never went for anything but being the best.

◆ ◆ ◆

ELDEN AUKER, Pitcher

Ted's problems with the press all started with writer Bill Cunningham. In spring training, Bill Cunningham came down and wanted to interview us. That evening we'd had dinner at the Sarasota Terrace Hotel—Lefty Grove, Jimmie Foxx, Bobby Doerr and his wife, Fritz Ostermueller and his wife, someone else and Ted. There was a little mini-putt golf course down the street about 4 or 5 blocks and we were sitting in the lobby choosing up sides. We were going to have a putting match. We used to choose up sides of an evening, go down, and play a round.

Cunningham was at that time the ace sportswriter of the Boston area, had graduated from Dartmouth and let everybody know about it. Wore a porky-pie hat, and smoked a cigar all the time. Was into the liquor pretty heavy. He came down as we were getting ready to leave and Ted was sitting in his chair. Cunningham got off the elevator, walked over and just broke in—didn't say "Excuse me" or anything. He said, "Well, come on, kid, let's go upstairs and get this interview over with." He said the people in Boston are waiting with bated breath to hear all about the kid from Minneapolis. Ted looked up at him and Cunningham had been drinking, it was very obvious. Ted said, "I'm sorry, Mr. Cunningham, I don't give interviews to sportswriters that are drinking." And boy, you could have . . . this just embarrassed Cunningham terribly. In front of all of us. Well, to the day that Cunningham was taken off as a sportswriter, he never had an interview with Ted Williams. He was the guy that really started all the problems. He was the big shot. Cunningham spent the rest of his sportswriting days trying to hurt Ted and I think the rest of them kind of copied what he'd done. If he'd have been for Ted, they'd have all been for him. But Cunningham never did write one good thing about Ted. That was the beginning of it.

◆ ◆ ◆

BOBBY DOERR, Ballplayer, Hall of Fame

When they moved him from right field to left field, the fans were right over the top of him. Every little thing that happened, they'd start riding him a little bit. Ted's locker was within five or ten feet of mine and Dom's. The press was in there every night, right around him. I remember this one night he came in and said something very negative about New

Williams was an exception. He didn't like the writers, and he let them know it. When you could hit like him, you could tell the writers what to do and where to go. When you're a singles hitter, you just hope to make a living.

—Johnny Pesky

England fans. He said, "You can print that." Well, they did print it of course, and from that time on it just seemed like there was always a knock-down, drag-out battle. Dave Egan was real bad with his writing. They started to target Ted. They had so many writers that they had to write something, and certain ones would dig him about things. It got to where he was pretty belligerent with them. But it seemed like when they did start to get on him, his average would go from .325 up to .330 or .340. It would go up instead of down. Whatever they had to say was just a challenge, and it seemed like he wanted to prove to them that they weren't going to bother him. I think that was just Ted, a spur of the moment thing. He didn't hesitate to say what he felt but it wasn't predetermined. There was always some loudmouth out there, one guy that would irritate Ted. The fans as a whole were for him. Still, it didn't take much to blow up the bomb.

◆ ◆ ◆

Writer Ed Linn describes Egan in the following way: "He was a writer who could draw blood from the hide of a rhinoceros . . . a writer who sold controversy the way a butcher sells veal chops. His job was to stir up the adrenalin of his readers seven times a week and he succeeded to the extent that he was Boston's most-read, most-cursed, most-revered, most-discussed writer."

Egan seems to have seen writing and ballplaying as entertainment. Ed Linn asked Egan about his "Anti-Ted campaign" and Egan responded that he was grateful that Ted had helped him become so controversial and successful a writer, and said "he saw no reason why Ted shouldn't be grateful in return." Egan was strongly inclined toward the belief that Williams knew perfectly well that the controversy brought money into the box-office and thereby added its little weight toward keeping him the game's leading money-winner. In his later book, Hitter, *Linn suggests that Ted often orchestrated his outbursts when he had become mired in a slump. He often seemed to hit exceptionally well right after one of the storms burst.*

IRA BERKOW, Writer

Guys have different ways of getting angry so that they get motivated about things, sometimes taking it out on others. I guess McEnroe did that with referees—to get him stoked up. He didn't do that with Borg, because he couldn't afford to waste the energy. But for the most part, I think he got himself stoked up that way. I have no idea whether or not that might have been true of Ted.

Once I asked him was it true that he was a great hitter because he had these great reflexes that were tested in the upper 1/100 of the male population of the world? His reflexes were in the highest possible rank, and also his eyesight was supposed to be fabulous, able to read a license plate from a block away. He said to me, "It's all bullshit!" I said, "So what was it then?" He said, "It was all trial and f------ error, trial and f------ error, trial and f------ error, trial and f------ error!" Four times! That is a direct quote. That's exactly what he said.

◆ ◆ ◆

BOB HOLBROOK, Sportswriter

Ted had one of the finest minds I've ever encountered. Anything that interested him he pursued with a passion. How could a guy who barely got through high school . . . ? Don't tell me he was a good student, 'cause he didn't give a shit. He was always waiting to get out to hit the ball. I'm sure he was just barely getting through high school and yet he flew planes in the Second World War—flew jets, which is tremendous. I guess what I really liked about him was his intelligence. But he didn't harness his brain power. If it interested him, fine. If it didn't, frig it. He's an unforgettable person.

In the old days when I first started, reporting had evolved into something better than writing "In the fifth inning, so and so did so and so." The writers were all old timers. Mel Webb on the *Globe* was well over eighty. Burt Whitman, who was the sports editor at the *Herald*, was Ted's favorite and he was a kindly old man. They never wrote anything bad about anybody.

I had to ask Ted some pretty stiff questions along the line, about some of his dalliances that were printed in the Hearst paper. But he never was rude to me. If he didn't want to speak, I said, "Screw him, I don't care." I wouldn't chase him around. Hell, I've got my pride too. You get a very rounded education in that business and I'm glad I'm out of it, really. Now the *Record-American*—Dave Egan, Finnegan and those guys—they murdered

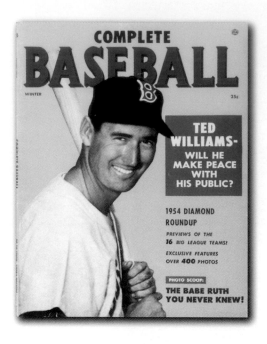

Ted. Jesus Christmas. They made a career out of it. Dave Egan was a powerful drunk in his day. He worked at the *Globe* originally but he came out of Harvard. I guess he finished Harvard in two years. He was brilliant, but a drunk and a drug addict. Every day he got on Ted and the other people thought: well, that's the thing to do! That's where you got these fellows they called "the chipmunks." They were called that because of the way they looked. They came out of New York—all these guys that were peeking in bedrooms, and what not. That kind of reporting. The chipmunks came along and started a whole new trend. They came to Boston where the tabloids were so hard on Williams. We had a few on the *Globe* who thought that was the thing to do.

If you want to know what I think, the reason that Ted Williams was the way he was comes down to this—he was smarter than most of the writers. And I think they knew it. Ted was really something, you know, and if he wasn't such a proud guy, he could have passed it off. I'm not a psychologist or a psychiatrist—I wish to hell I were—but I had enough sense to leave him alone if he was in a bad mood. When he was spitting, doing that swan dive into home plate, things like that—when he did things on the field that were public—it's one thing. And he should be chastised, or at least reported for it. But you can drive a guy crazy, especially one that's very sensitive. And don't believe he isn't very sensitive when it comes to his hitting and things like that.

With out-of-town writers, Ted was pretty cute. New York is a big town. He got along with them great except for a couple of chipmunks. He knew their strength, he was no dope. He knew everything he was doing . . . except when he went overboard. Then he'd get so incensed that I don't believe he really understood what he was saying. Jack Fadden was the Red Sox trainer and he was one of the few who could handle Ted. He was a wonderful man—the Harvard trainer—and he should have been a doctor because he really had a healing touch. Jesus, he got Ted through more ailments. Ted would say, "I'm the greatest, you son of a bee." Fadden would say, "No, there's somebody greater." "Who is that?" "The Man Upstairs." And then Ted would go into one of his tirades.

He always used to say, "I'm the greatest. Who's the greatest? I'm the greatest. Bet your ass I am, you sons of bitches." He would lose all sense of balance. Ted was scary at times. I remember being in the dugout with Mike Higgins and a couple of other guys at Detroit. It's an old field, with these stanchions in the dugout, cement posts, holding up the top of the dugout. Ted threw a bat full speed at us. I don't know what Higgins did with Ted, I never asked him. Who he was mad at, I don't know, but he almost killed Mike and he didn't miss me by much. I said, "Mike, I'm getting the frig out of here, you got a bunch of goddamned fools playing for you." It didn't hit anybody but if it had, it would've killed them. It was the only time I ever really got angry at Ted. I felt sorry for him in a lot of ways, but at that time I didn't. He knew. That son of a bitch was so strong, and that bat went by my ear. It really could have changed my whole feeling toward him. But I said, "Oh, it's Ted, what the hell?" That's the way everybody was. "Oh, it's Ted. He's just Ted, you know."

◆ ◆ ◆

PETER GAMMONS, Sports Reporter

I grew up in New England and that wonderful line John Updike wrote about Ted has always stuck with me, how on a hot meaningless Thursday afternoon in August, the team could be 18 games out of first place, but for Ted Williams the only thing at stake is the tissue-thin difference between a thing well-done and a thing done ill. He strove for excellence when most guys are coasting through. It translates to anything in any job that any of us do in life.

Ted Williams was my boyhood idol. When I was eight years old, my mother bought me a plastic statue of Ted Williams. It stayed with me. It was partially because he was my family's idol. It was what I was brought up to believe—exactly that, every day of your life you strive for excellence.

And that's what Williams did. Intellectually, physically every bit of it. And I've always had that statue of Ted. I still have it up over my desk in my office in my house, up over my computer. And that's what he represents—something for every one of us in life to strive for.

Looking at Ted from an overall perspective, in my opinion he is clearly the greatest hitter that ever lived. He gave everybody a thrill and he did so much for the game. He had a spark. He was more than a great baseball player; he was a major celebrity.

He and Joe DiMaggio were bigger than any athlete today. Ted had such a gift and a persona that if he were playing today he would lead [ESPN's] Sportscenter three times a week just by opening his car door.

◆ ◆ ◆

GEORGE SULLIVAN, Writer
(Taken from The Picture History of the Boston Red Sox *by George Sullivan)*

Throughout the fifties, the give-and-take jousts in the Red Sox training room between supreme egotist Ted Williams and master ego-deflator Jack Fadden were classics.

Typical was the summer morning Williams sat on the edge of the rubbing table and asked the trainer, "Am I the greatest ballplayer you ever saw, Jack?"

"Theodore," Fadden responded matter-of-factly, "I could name 50 guys I'd rather have."

"Fifty?" roared Williams. "Name one!"

"How about Joe DiMag?" Fadden said. "Can you field like him? Can you run as well?"

"No," Ted admitted.

"And when it comes to throwing," Fadden said, "you're the world's highest-paid shot putter."

Williams was subdued—briefly.

"Well," he persisted, "I'm still the greatest hitter—and the greatest fisherman."

"Greatest fisherman?" Fadden baited. "Listen, there was a guy who produced more fish in one minute than you could in a year."

Williams squinted. "Who the hell was that?" he demanded.

"Didn't you ever hear about the Sermon on the Mount, about the loaves and fishes?" Fadden said. "My God," Williams bellowed. "You had to go back far enough to top me, didn't you?"

◆ ◆ ◆

ROBERT B. PARKER, Author

I grew up those early years of my life in Springfield, western Massachusetts. At the time I was a young boy, the "blue laws" were still in effect, and they could neither broadcast nor play baseball on Sundays in Boston. My father, being a baseball fan, would listen to the Dodger and Yankee games that we'd pick up over what was at that time WHN in New York and WPRS in New York. Like with Ted's last at-bat, the radio broadcast was maybe better than having been there. Very vivid. Hub Fans Bid Kid Adieu. In those days, there were a number of newspapers in Boston. We had two tabloids, the *Record* and the *American*. Williams was the focus of everybody's attention from Nova Scotia to New Haven, and certainly west to Albany and thereabouts. There was nobody even approaching him, no one to compare to him.

I grew up in that anomalous position of being less a fan of the hometown team than a fan of the game. My grandparents lived in Salem, we'd come up from Springfield, or later on from New Bedford. When we'd go to visit my grandparents, my father would take me to a ballgame, whichever team was home, the Sox or the Braves. It was a thrill to go into Boston. Fenway's everything that everyone thinks it is. You walk up out of the dark stadium into the bright green field.

I know Joe Garagiola, and Joe was 20 in '46, catching behind Williams in the World Series. In '41, I would have been nine years old, and aware of Williams' .400 effort, but that was not as real as Garagiola telling me about him catching the first time Williams came to the plate. Ted said something and Garagiola replied "Yes, sir." I always kid Garagiola when I meet him; I introduce him as the fellow who outhit Ted Williams in the 1946 Series.

Being a hero in Boston is like being a politician in Boston. Those who attract attention attract controversy. This city likes to create and destroy its heroes, sometimes simultaneously. Ted Williams was detested by a vocal minority until he was old enough to be venerated. Where else could the most charismatic star of his generation come back from a war, hit a home run, and feel obligated to fire the French salute to the press box? Where but Boston?

Who but Ted Williams?

—Luke Salisbury

◆ ◆ ◆

JOE GARAGIOLA, Ballplayer
(Taken from The Picture History of the Red Sox *by George Sullivan)*

The high point of my career, at least as a hitter, had to be the fourth game of the 1946 World Series, when I was a rookie catcher with the Cardinals. I had four hits, including a double, knocked in three runs and scored another as we ripped the Red Sox 12-3, at Fenway Park to even the series at two games apiece.

That was pretty heady stuff for a 20-year-old kid. Not only was it more hits in one game than the great Ted Williams had in four games, but it tied the World Series record for most hits in a game, a record I still share with about 35 guys.

Well, I couldn't wait for the next day. Boston had a bunch of newspapers then, and my name was going to be spread all over the headlines. In the morning I rushed downstairs to the newsstand in the hotel lobby, and there it was in big black headlines: WILLIAMS BUNTS!

◆ ◆ ◆

BRIAN INTERLAND, Fan

It was July 1951, and they had the first ever Little League Day at Fenway. They invited five thousand Little Leaguers who came in full regalia, about 11 o'clock in the morning before the game started. We all jumped on a team bus, and headed into Fenway. Once got in there, we were maniacs, just trying to get as close to the field as we could. The Red Sox players put on a hitting, fielding, and pitching clinic for us.

We wound up getting in the front row, just to the left of the dugout. A photographer came and said, "You guys follow me." We didn't know what he wanted. He brought us down to the dugout and said, "Stay here." He went out, and then all of a sudden, there's . . . the Big Guy, walking towards the dugout, and he was swearing at the photographers. "What the f--- do you guys want? For chrissakes, will you leave me alone?"

It was like, "Oh my God" and they brought him down and he sat right beside me. And then Lou Boudreau came over and sat down . . . wasn't asked to, just sat down, and then the photographer started taking pictures. Ted was my hero and I was just in awe, just breathless.

Ted was great to us but he just couldn't stand the photographers. He was bigger than life and so charismatic. You know you read things but I never really took to heart that he had this running feud with the sportswriters and photographers. He just said, "Leave me alone. I want to talk to the kids." About fifteen minutes later, Mel Parnell and Dom DiMaggio came over and had their pictures taken with us. The very next day on the front page of the *Boston Globe*, there was this picture of us with Ted Williams.

Kids from Remick's Cadets meet a hero. From left to right: Ted Williams, Brian Interland, Billy Griffin, Johnny Cushing and Lou Boudreau.
(Photo courtesy of Brian Interland)

I was a huge Ted fan, lived and slept for him. I'd wake up in the morning and say "How did Ted do, Dad?" I'd never say "How did the Sox do?"

It's really true that he went to the beat of his own drummer. It's not that he had the ego. He was like everybody else. He was a sensitive guy. Some people would block the fans out, or ignore it when the sportswriters wrote something negative. But Ted would hear them out there. It affected him, but it just drove him to become even a better player, a better hitter. If he hadn't let what they wrote bother him—if he never laid any words on them as they walked in the clubhouse the next time—they probably would have just backed off. They knew that it bothered him, and that he would say something that sold newspapers. He was great copy.

How many athletes in this day and age—the great ones—the unselfish ones, would ever say "I won't go to the children's hospital if photographers are going to be there or if sportswriters know about it . . . ." They might have said "Hey, I'll deal with it. It's more important to see the kids . . . " Ted *would not go* if he knew that sportswriters would write about it, because they'd portray it in a certain way—but Ted did it because he loved kids. There's a little kid in him that never left. He's got the biggest heart of anybody that I've ever in my life seen, met, read about or heard about. People just don't know that. He always befriended little people—the cop, the firemen. He related to them better. He was never the guy who would just hustle up the politicians, the actors.

I would go down to Florida with my family and spend time with him and just continue that fascination with the man who befriended a little guy like me. It really meant a lot to my life. I don't know what would have happened to my life if he had not given me that time. It gave me a lot of confidence in myself. Music was our bond. He was and is a huge, huge jazz fan. Count Basie, Errol Garner, Oscar Peterson, Stan Kenton, Sarah

Vaughan, Ella Fitzgerald, Frank Sinatra. Dakota Staton, too. Knowing that I worked at WHDH and Channel 5, he'd talk with me about music and I'd make up a few tapes and give him a few records. Through the years I would pick up some Oscar Peterson albums, send them down to him and he'd tell me what he liked. We would always touch base and correspond. I even bought a condo a couple of blocks away in Islamorada because he lived there. It was more that just being a fan.

Ted just made everybody feel important. He made me feel important and here I was just a little guy making 75 bucks a week. There were people all over the country who Ted Williams took an interest in. He did things for people that no one ever heard about. I felt like pinching myself all the time. I'd be thinking, "Wow, ME?" And "me" could have been anybody.

I'd go down to visit him with my wife sometimes, other times we'd bring the kids along. A great cook, Captain Williams. He always called himself the Captain in the kitchen. The first time we were over there at his house, all my kids met Ted at the same time, and Ted's cooking for us, and then he's buttering my kids' bread. I was saying *Wait a second! If somebody had told me 30 years ago that my hero would be buttering my kids' bread*, I mean . . . that might not seem like much . . . but I felt like the luckiest man alive. I was pinching myself again.

◆ ◆ ◆

DAVID CATANEO, Writer
(Taken from Peanuts and Crackerjack by David Cateneo)

On April 30, 1952, the Red Sox held Ted Williams Day at Fenway Park to say goodbye to their left fielder, who was shipping out to fly jets in the Korean War. Standing on the mound and surrounded by dignitaries and photographers, Williams stepped to the microphone to deliver a short speech. The crowd cheered. Just behind him, Eddie Costello, sports editor of the *Boston Herald*, whispered, "Tip your hat."

Everyone knew Ted Williams never tipped his hat. The crowd kept cheering. Costello whispered again, "Tip your hat."

Williams tipped his cap to the right-field grandstand. The crowd went wild. Williams tipped his cap to the seats behind home plate. The crowd went wilder. Williams tipped his hat to the left-field grandstand. The crowd was in a frenzy. It was a touching moment: Williams and the Fenway fans in a warm, possibly final, embrace.

"Center field," whispered Costello. "Don't forget center field."

"Not those [expletives], too!" whined Williams.

◆ ◆ ◆

TONY LUPIEN, Ballplayer
(Taken from Fenway by Peter Golenbock)

There had been a writer on Ted's back something awful. Might have been Austen Lake. But we were in the clubhouse after the game, and the guy comes in. And Ted saw him coming. Ted was taking his clothes off, and he stood up on his stool, and in a loud voice he said, "Hey, you know this is a great world we live in today. You can get instant anything. You can get instant tea, instant coffee." He said, "You want to see instant horseshit? Give me a pail of water and let me throw it on Lake." He said that in front of everybody. Ted was wonderful.

◆ ◆ ◆

JOHN LARRABEE, Physicist

My father used to deliver laundry to the Red Sox clubhouse and so he had the chance to meet all the players. He told me that after a game Ted would shake his Coke bottle and spray it on some of the other players, things like that. He loved Lefty Grove and Jim Tabor but Ted he seemed to be neutral on. I used to say, "Oh, he's the greatest!" And my father, who admitted that Ted was always a good tipper, used to say, "Well, he's a great hitter, but you know he acts kind of childish sometimes." They used to call him The Kid, right?

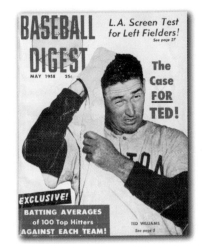

Whenever Ted was up at the plate, he used to grind that handle with his hands. Some writer said at one time, gee, he grinds it so hard and so often, I expect to see sawdust come out. I'll never forget that. I'd always watch as a kid to see if some sawdust would come out.

Another thing he did in the on deck circle, always, was time the pitcher's warmups, especially if they brought a relief pitcher in to face him. I recall that very vividly. He would stand in the on deck circle and move ahead to the edge of the circle and he would swing against the pitcher's warms just to get a little bit of edge, I think. Ted would drift out of the circle until he was almost lined up with home plate and he'd time the pitch to his swing and aggravate the heck out of the pitchers.

When I was 14 or 15, I was sitting in the bleachers one day, way up there. He came up to bat and it was a crucial situation, and I said, "Come on, Ted, if anyone can hit it out to me, you can." Well, he hit it and it was a shot that went well over the bullpen and went some twenty rows in front of me, and then bounced up over my head. Like I called it. I said, "Come on, Ted. You can do it." Bingo! He did it.

He was the greatest hitter of all time, and yet he was booed by those idiots who had the reserved grandstand seats down the left field line. A kid never booed Ted Williams — kids cheered him every time up. But these idiots would boo him, throw things at him, call him names. They were cynical adults who believed the trash in the papers. Now, Ted did do some pretty bad things out there. But I remember the ovations he got, like when he came back from Korea? I saw that game on TV. It was just unbelievable; the crowd wouldn't sit down. He's back as a hero and nobody's booing him when he came back like that.

You had a guy like Egan pointing out, every week, how Ted hit .200 in the '46 World Series. And Ted didn't do very much in the playoff game with Cleveland in '48 or in those two Yankee games at the end of '49. People basically called him a choke. Folks get riled up for many reasons, sometimes for personal reasons, sometimes as a result of the press. People always talked about Ted not being enthusiastic when they were in pennant races. But what about '55 when they made that great run? Four team race. Harry Agganis died, and they wore black armbands. They were in last place at the All-Star break and installed Billy Klaus at shortstop and then made this tremendous run from way, way down. I had never seen Ted get so excited about winning ballgames. I remember him jumping up and down at home plate and cheering when people came in to score. This from a guy the writers said lacked enthusiasm in the playoffs.

And in regard to those who called Ted a choke, let me ask this—how many times was he walked with nobody on base? Or in the late innings when the score was close? There could have been zero, one, or two outs and nobody on and often they'd walk him to lead off an inning. I remember a time he was walked intentionally with the bases loaded. As a hitter Ted was feared. He may have been stubborn hitting into that shift but he was a scientist. He was a scientist playing a sport.

♦ ♦ ♦

ROGER KAHN, Writer

(Taken from Fenway *by Peter Golenbock)*

The Red Sox were making a strong run in 1955. The articles editor of *Life* magazine was Ralph Graves, who would go on to eminence in that company called Time Inc., and he asked me to do a piece about shortstop Billy Klaus. Klaus had batted in the .270s in Triple A, and now he was hitting over .300 for the Red Sox in a very tough pennant race.

I went out with the Red Sox, and I really hadn't done that much in the American League. Klaus for those months was a hero in Boston, and writer John Gilhooley wrote in the Boston papers a story about the Klaus family called, "The Klauses and their Houses," where they had lived. Billy was a fiery player.

I went to talk to Ted Williams, who I didn't know. I walked up to Williams in the batting cage, introduced myself, and I said, "I'd like to talk to you about Billy Klaus." And Williams said, "One-fifteen at the batting cage tomorrow." I found that startling, because you don't usually have to make an appointment around a batting cage. On the other hand, he was Theodore Samuel Williams. So I said fine, and I showed up the next day, and he was there.

He was ready with a perfectly nice statement saying nothing terribly profound, that the team needed someone who could pick up ground balls and stabilize the infield, and that's what Klaus had done. I said, "I would like to get a little beyond that, that I had heard Klaus was a sparkplug."

He said, "That just sounds like writer talk. There is no such thing as a sparkplug."

I said, "Who was the sparkplug on the '46 team?"

He said, "There was none. That's just the writers."

I was at a dead end. I said. "Maybe we can look at it this way: here is somebody who was hitting in the .270s in the minors and in the .300s in the majors. You might even say that he had a bad year in the minors.

Williams growled, "Who are you asking, fella?"

I said, "I'm asking you."

He said, "You're asking me about a bad year?" He said, "Mister, I can see that you don't know very much about baseball if you're asking me about a bad year, because old T.S.W., he don't have bad years." He looked out. He said, "You see those guys?" There were the Boston writers standing in a picket line. He said, "They would give their left nut to see me have a bad year. But it doesn't happen, because old T.S.W. doesn't have bad years."

To emphasize his point, he hurled his bat to the grass, caught it, and walked away.

I went up to watch the game, and Hy Hurwitz, a small fellow, came over to me and he knew me a little bit from covering the Braves. And he said, "We all heard what Williams said. And you know Williams was putting on a show for *Life* magazine. And I just want you to know that if you ever write what Williams said about us, no Boston writer will ever speak to you again." It was absolutely crazy.

The end of it was that the Red Sox dropped out of the race, and *Life* never ran the piece.

◆ ◆ ◆

TIM HORGAN, Sportswriter

I put up with a lot of nonsense from Ted. I started covering baseball in '51 or '52. It was tough in the press box, especially when you're breaking in new. I was fresh out of college, and I ran into a buzz saw with this guy. I was kind of proud, got a job with a metropolitan newspaper, and all of a sudden this guy's telling me I'm a bum. He was tough. He was indiscriminate.

A lot of the other players resented Ted's getting all the attention. As a personality I've never seen anybody who dominated that city the way Ted did. Not Bobby Orr, not Larry Bird. Ted could do no wrong with some people, women and all. Charismatic guy. And one who produced. If we got a quote from Ted, we were golden. If you could publish the quote, you were double golden.

He was a great hitter. Not a great ballplayer, but a great hitter. He kept the Red Sox afloat, no doubt, through those years no one cared about them. People would go to the park and just leave after his last at bat. I did a column one time on a blind person, wonderful man. I met him sitting behind the screen. I said to him, "Why do you go to the game? You could just listen on the radio." He said to me, "I can visualize it all through my ears. I can tell when Ted comes out of the dugout, then when he comes to the plate, just by the crowd reaction. There's no other player like Ted."

◆ ◆ ◆

LARRY BALDASSARO, Writer
(Taken from Mudville Diaries *edited by Mike Schacht)*

I once went to a Red Sox-Yankees game with my parents and a friend of the family. I clearly remember him as a meek, quiet man nearing retirement age, someone who never showed his emotions. At some point in the game Ted Williams hit a home run and the place went wild. To my surprise, no one yelled louder or longer than our "quiet" friend. I'll never forget the sight of that stodgy old man suddenly brought to life; there he was, jumping up and down, clapping his hands, screaming with joy. At that moment he was a boy again, as young as I was. Nothing I have witnessed since has so strongly impressed upon me the ability of baseball, in its finest moments, to touch the child that survives in each of us.

◆ ◆ ◆

JOHN UNDERWOOD, Writer

Ted was the Tallulah Bankhead of sports. They were both hard to pin down. Many people consider Ted a dear friend, and others don't. He's a guy with a whole series of interesting personality traits. Above all, you've got to say his intelligence—whether he treated himself and those around him well or not—is unqualified. He's one of the smartest guys in those areas in which he has expertise that you'll ever meet. How many guys can tell you exactly why a curve ball curves and why a jet engine flies?

Ted can take cursing to a new level, can use some of the most vile and profane language you've ever heard. By the same token, he doesn't have to curse at all. He's got a wonderful vocabulary. He's a very articulate man. He can be as erudite as anybody you've ever known. He didn't write a lick of *My Turn at Bat* but he contributed everything I needed. It's not just learning how to sound like him, it's also being able to get through the hyperbole. Ted can ramble on. You just can't put down what he says. You've got to be able to write like he talks, but not write what he says.

I have some negative feelings about Ted, that have nothing to do with my respect for him. As a Christian, my feeling is to forgive and forget. I certainly don't hold any grudges. But Ted could foul a dinner party as well as anybody. I was working on the book with him . . . and my attitude was, I'll take it just so far. We were getting along well, and all of a

One time Ted got some raw meat and he threw it to the wolves out in the bleachers. That's right. They as much as called his mother a whore. I would throw something else up there to the bums like that. Don't get me wrong; it's not the Boston fans. It's the minority, the cuckoos. Good fans don't do that.

—Tim Horgan

sudden he got into one of those cranky, dark moods. We were at breakfast—I'll never forget it—and I reached for the check. He made a huge thing out of it, grabbed it out of my hand, and let loose a string of profanities. He didn't curse me. He never has cursed me or challenged me in any way like that. I know he used to say, "I wish I was as smart as you." Now, I don't think I was smarter than him, but I think he had that kind of respect for my integrity and my ability.

Then he got up and he stormed out of the place. I just sat there. In fact, I ordered another cup of coffee, I was so mad. I was seething. We were right in the middle of the research on the book. I finally mustered up enough energy to get up . . . the stream of profanities was just raw. I got up and went back to my room, for whatever I needed, then went out to the ballpark a couple hours later. I sat in the stands. When Ted saw me, he gave me one of those waves where he looks down, almost like he's saluting from the middle of his head. At this point, I'd made up my mind he wasn't going to get away with this, and I was going to abort the whole project, which would have been a disaster because I'd been working on it for a long time. I wasn't going to put up with it.

I waited until he was by himself, then I walked over to him and I said, "I want to tell you something. As big as you are, I'm not afraid of you, and if you ever do that to me again . . . As far as I'm concerned, you owe me an apology, and you're not going to ever do that to me again." And I turned around and walked away. I thought, "Well, that's it." He didn't say anything. He just turned around himself.

I was actually packing, it was now dark and there was a big knock on the door, and here's Ted. He had changed his clothes at the park, and he had kind of a whimsical look on his face. And he said, "Do you realize we're late for dinner?" And that was it. That was his apology. That was the closest he would come to saying "I'm sorry for being a horse's ass." But it endeared him to me. It showed that he did have a conscience.

I've seen him say some awful things to people. And it's hurt some very dear people. Who knows why he does that? I don't know. I've seen him being friendly to people who were total boors at restaurants. He is extraordinarily articulate with people of stature, governors of states . . . . Of course, he was close to Bush and I guess a whole variety of presidents and senators and all that. So he could talk to anybody. But he definitely has this side, his little dark side that surfaces now and then. It's almost like something pinches in his brain, and he feels the need to lash out, and he doesn't necessarily lash out at the right people. He just lashes out. Like someone with some kind of a particular malady that creates in him the need to vent his spleen. And he never forgets a slight, he admits that. And yet he could do some of the nicest things.

◆ ◆ ◆

KEN COLEMAN, Broadcaster

Ted was representing a real estate development in Citrus Hills, where he lived, in Central Florida. I had purchased a lot down there myself and Ted would come up to Boston on occasion, and we would go out and put on seminars.

One night we were at the Marriott in Newton. Ted always liked to eat early but this particular night he couldn't because we were making a presentation about Citrus Hills. I got up and spoke, and then I introduced Ted, and then we had a film. Prior to all this happening, he said to me, "Have you eaten?" And I said no. He said, "Well, are you free when this thing is over?" [chuckles] Of course you're free if Ted Williams wants to know. I said, "Yeah, I'm free." He said, "Well, listen, there's something I've wanted to talk to you about for a long time, how about if we have dinner after this is over?"

I had a boss named Eddie Costello and he knew Ted better than I did. He'd say, "we haven't heard from Williams for 10 days or so—we'll hear an explosion." Policemen could tell you that when there's a full moon, things are rougher. And most of Ted's tantrums occured when there was a full moon. Now, I don't know if this could be scientifically proven but Ted was a mooner. When there was a full moon, look out!

—Tim Horgan

We went into the restaurant at the Marriott. We were put in a corner somewhere, where people were not bothering him. We spent probably two or three hours talking about different people; we talked politics, we talked boxing, we talked about a lot of things. And then we got to talking about baseball. I asked him, if you were paying your way in today, who would you pay to see? And without hesitation, he said "Reggie." [Later on, I ran across Reggie Jackson and I told him, "You know I was out with Number Nine one night and I asked him who he'd pay to see and he brought your name up just like that." Reggie was like a kid at Christmas. He said, "You mean the man said that about me?" He was just thrilled.]

After mentioning Mr. October, Ted had to pause a little and then he came up with several other names I don't really remember right now. We had a very pleasant evening together. As I was driving home, it occurred to me that he had said he had something he wanted to talk to me about. And yet he had never brought anything up in any specific way about whatever he wanted to talk about.

I came to the realization that here he was, staying at the Marriott that night, and what he really was looking for more than anything else was company. A guy like Ted, as opposed to a guy like me, can't just walk into a restaurant and sit down and order a meal because people would be all over him. He didn't want to just go back and have room service. So we sat and we had a wonderful evening of conversation on a number of subjects. Naturally it evolved down to baseball. On the way home, I'm thinking here was a lonesome guy spending a night at a hotel in Newton, and was looking for company and didn't want to have room service, and I was there, and we knew each other, and so we spent the evening together. I think people somehow can't conceive that a man like Ted Williams might just be lonesome and tired of sitting in hotel rooms, and just want to have a conversation with someone that he knows.

◆ ◆ ◆

Ted Williams will always be loved by everyone in New England, including me, for his dedication to excellence and commitment to winning. He was a great champion and someone we can all look up to.

—Larry Bird

DORIS KEARNS GOODWIN, Historian and Biographer

The first time I met Ted was in '78 when I went down to cover the Red Sox spring training for The Real Paper. I was probably down for ten days or so. He was then the batting coach there, and he was just great. I immediately took to him. He just strode onto that field as if he were Lyndon Johnson, with whom I had worked. Just talking about hitting, never stopping, with that bat continually in his hands.

He knew I was a liberal, so he called me "Pinko." He'd just finished reading Manchester's book on Douglas MacArthur and so he said, "I'm sure you must hate him." I said, "No, I actually didn't hate him. I didn't agree with him in certain things." And we ended up arguing about MacArthur, and became somewhat friends. It really made the whole time down there fun, to be able to tease him day by day. I went down several other seasons, between '78 and '86, and he was always very friendly. When they had the Jimmy Fund 406 Club dinner for him, I was asked to speak. That was a lovely night and the last time I saw him.

I've read about the troubled relationship that he had with the press when he was a player, and even with the fans to some extent. But the fact that he's lived in his post-baseball years with such enthusiasm still for the sport of baseball—that's a reminder of what it was like when people worked so hard, as hard as he did to make himself the great hitter he was . . . and with loyalty to the team—these aspects of baseball that seem to be missing today. It's allowed many of those minor skirmishes to be totally forgotten. It's wonderful to see the way he's made his way into the permanent hearts of the people in Boston, and the media in Boston. You don't always get that in your older age.

He seemed like his stature . . . his stature was always there—I don't think anyone ever disputed how great he was . . . but the kind of emotions he generated in the fans got stronger, it seems, as time went by rather than weaker . . . I'm glad he's lived to see all that.

◆ ◆ ◆

He couldn't even eat a meal in public; he used to eat in his hotel room. Every time he walked the streets, it was like he was a movie star, only bigger. He was constantly mobbed by people and he'd get agitated and I think it's perfectly understandable that he would be upset; people would just not leave him alone ever.

—Mel Parnell

LUKE SALISBURY, Author

In 1991, when Ted Williams came back to Fenway to be honored for the 50th anniversary of his since unduplicated feat of hitting .400, I was in the press box. This was one of those remarkable moments, like the birth of my son, when the wheel had turned completely. I, who'd rooted for Williams, who'd read about his legendary confrontations with the press, was sitting with the "Knights of the keyboard." I was there because I was contributing to a biography, *Ted Williams: A Portrait in Words and Pictures*—a book Williams had ordered a hundred copies of to give to friends and former teammates.

At the press conference after the game with Texas, I got up the nerve and blurted out, "Ted, do you read any of the books written about you?"

Without missing a beat, he looked up and said, "I don't read the goddamn things, I just look at the pictures."

◆ ◆ ◆

"OPEN LETTER TO TED WILLIAMS"

By Grantland Rice
(Taken from SPORT magazine, 1957)

All you who get the cheering and the plaudits from the mob,
Who shrink because they bawl you out upon some off-day job,
Who scowl because they call you names that no one likes to hear,
Who keep the welkin ringing from the horse hoot to the cheer,
Who build you up and knock you down, from here to kingdom come,
Remember as the game goes on—they never boo a bum.

I've heard them hiss Hans Wagner and I've heard them snarl at Cobb,
I've heard them holler "Take him out," with Matty on the job.
I've heard them curse when Ruth struck out—or Speaker missed a play.
For 40 years I've heard them ride the heroes of their day.
I've heard their roaring welcome switch to something worse than hum,
But Eddie*, Ted, and Joe, get this—they never boo a bum.

[Eddie is jockey Eddie Arcaro, Joe is Joe DiMaggio]

CURT GOWDY, Broadcaster

There are three guys that people know I knew and was friendly with in my career—and they ask me about them all the time: One was Ted Williams, one was Howard Cosell, and the other was Bobby Knight, the basketball coach at Indiana. I'm always asked, "What kind of a guy is he really?" People have read all about them, their temper tantrums and so on, and they want to know. They were all friends of mine and I am very fond of them all but I've always told people this: Ted Williams is the most competent man I've ever met.

John Glenn once told me that Ted was an exceptional pilot and the perfect officer. Ted wasn't mad at the Marine Corps. He was proud to be a Marine but he was mad at the politicians. He hated politicians anyway. He thought that he was being used and that it was wrong, but he said, I'll go over and do my job, which he did. He was a great baseball player, the best all-around fisherman I've ever seen, and a great photographer. I think Ted was a good manager, too. People said he wouldn't be because he'd expect everyone to hit .400, but they were wrong. He was good with young players and was named Manager-of-the-Year once. I'd like to have seen him manage a Red Sox team with some talent. He'd have been good up there.

He had more quest for knowledge about those things he enjoyed doing than any man I ever met, and he worked harder at it, prepared more, studied. He had to know everything about whatever it might be and what made it tick. And that's why I say he was the most competent guy I ever met. In that way he always thought he'd enjoy it more.

I used to talk with him about his feud with the writers and ask him why he got so upset. He said, "Hell, you'd get upset too if they wrote some of the things about you that they wrote about me." My wife and I had a good friend in Boston named Hap Kearn. He was the publisher of the *Record American* and he was a big Red Sox fan and a Ted Williams fan. They had a columnist named Dave Egan, "The Colonel"—oh, the stuff he used to write about Williams and Rocky Marciano, the undefeated heavyweight champ. Two New England idols. He took the negative approach to them. Ted was sort of an angry young man at times during his career and he'll admit it now. Why he was angry I don't know. I guess the press and the media had something to do with it.

Some writers Ted liked. He liked Grantland Rice and he liked Frank Graham. He liked Arthur Sampson and Joe Cashman. He was friendly to certain writers, those who he thought boosted the game. He liked all the radio and TV guys because he thought they boosted the game while the other guys tore the game down. They had seven daily papers in Boston when he came up. Five of them would write how good he was and the other two would say, hey let's go the other way and we'll get some attention. That really bothered him.

They loved him in rival cities. They loved him in Detroit, which was his favorite park to hit in, and everywhere he went. In New York they cheered him or booed him but he was a star and they admired and respected him. He was big. Frank Lane, the general manager of the White Sox, did a comparison study of when Williams was in Korea and when he came back, and the attendance had increased a little over ten thousand per home game after Williams came back. He was a big draw. He was extremely popular around the league when he came back from Korea. I remember in each game where he'd come up for the first time at bat in a series, they'd give him a standing ovation. I remember seeing a picture of the jet plane he crash landed to save his life on the front page of the *New York Times* along with a big picture of Ted. He went in, did his job, and came back as a hero.

One time in the mid-fifties the Giants were coming to Fenway Park in the middle of the summer to play an exhibition game and Ted was all excited that he was going to watch Willie Mays play. Mays was the young star of baseball at that time. Ted said, "You know, Curt, the major leagues will be half black within a very few years." He was the most unbiased man I ever met. He had no feeling about religion or race. He rooted for them all. I said "Why?" He said "These black kids will go down and play in 'D' ball for a hundred and fifty bucks a month and work their way out of it. They walk everywhere, they lift things, they're stronger. They're not out playing golf and tennis like the white kid is these days. You watch, they'll dominate the major leagues." And he was right. He was a big fan of Willie Mays. He was looking forward to seeing him play. He stuck up for blacks in his Hall of Fame speech and I wasn't surprised because he was always wonderful about that.

Tom Yawkey used to talk to Ted about helping hitters from opposing teams. "Jesus, what are you doing down there? I see Mantle come up to you at the batting cage and you take him aside and help him." I was there one day when Ted told him why. He said "T.A., just remember this: if you don't have any hitting in baseball, you don't have any excitement. When you're two or three blocks from a major league ballpark and you hear the crowd roar, *someone hit the ball!* We've got to get more hitting in the game, more hitting, better backgrounds . . . " And he'd go on and on with those staccato expressions of his. "So I help them a little bit," he says. "So they come in here and maybe they'll hurt us with their hitting, but it adds excitement to the game." He was a great believer in that. He truly loved the game and that's why he used to help guys when they'd come to him.

In 1954 he reported to spring training and the first day of workouts he stumbled in the outfield, fell down and broke his collarbone. They flew him up to Boston and put a steel pin in his shoulder and so he didn't have any spring training. Then he took batting practice for a few days and joined the Red Sox on the road. In Baltimore they put him up as a pinch hitter and he flied out to center field.

The next day we went to Detroit to play a doubleheader and he put on the most amazing batting show I think I've ever seen. He went 8 for 9, with two home runs and five RBIs. Before the game I went down to the batting cage and he was up there taking batting practice and I said, "How do you feel?" and he said "Oh, I'm not swinging the bat well," and he was moaning, "I shouldn't even be playing but I'm going in." (Gowdy chuckles) And then he had one of the best days he ever had in the major leagues.

All the ballplayers were amazed. The Yankees were over in Cleveland and the next morning Casey Stengel picked up the paper and read about it and Casey said, "I'm gonna get them steel pins put in all my players' shoulders." That was probably the best day I ever saw Williams have. The day before he went to Korea he hit a home run and then he hit one on his first day back from Korea. I saw him hit the long homer into the right-field bleachers at Fenway and I saw him hit the facing at Tiger Stadium. He had a knack for the dramatic.

I remember the last day he played. I got up in the morning and went out and got the paper and came in and was going to have my breakfast before I started out to the ballpark. At this point I didn't realize it was going to be his last game. I thought we'd broadcast him in New York over the weekend. When I got to the ballpark I discovered it was to be his last game ever. And I was sort of quiet and my wife said "What's the matter, don't you feel well?" And I said "Well you know, this is Williams' last game here. I'm going to miss him. He gave me a lot of thrills in broadcasting. In fact without winning any pennants, he's kept interest alive and given me something to work with on the broadcasts."

When he hit the shot I was sure it was going to be gone. I could see it in that big high arc out toward right field and I thought to myself as he rounded first base: *My lord, he's hit a home run in his last time at bat in the major leagues.* As he was rounding the bases I thought: *What a way to go out. Wouldn't it be great if we could all go out that way, from whatever our life's work might be?* When he crossed that plate it was a great thrill to me. The only ones who knew it was his last at bat were Johnny Orlando, the clubhouse boy, the Red Sox, Tom Yawkey and Joe Cronin the general manager, the manager and me.

It was a cold, gray day. Not a very comfortable day. It was raw and there were only ten or eleven thousand people there. It was a week day but it was small crowd considering it was Ted's last game. Since then, of course, I've talked to 300,000 who were present.

◆ ◆ ◆

He didn't want to hurt the fans or the game itself. It was a very personal thing for him. He was trying to make a living, and here was a guy trying to make it tough for him to make a living. When you're doing your best and wake up one morning and read things you never dreamed of, and then have a thousand people yelling at you and calling you a dirty bum, it wasn't easy.

— Elden Auker

The Kid never turned down the kids.
(Photo by Arthur Griffin)

The Splendid Splinter Meets Shoeless Joe Jackson

By W.P. Kinsella

Spring in South Carolina, 1951. The sun casts a golden wash over the sleepy streets of Greenville, a small city that still has character. A place where the true South has not yet been pushed aside, replaced by row upon row of fast food franchises. The trees and windows appear paved with gold leaf. Ted Williams, youthful, still in his prime, strolls down the sun-dappled streets, stops in front of a small liquor store. He is on his way to spring training in Florida, has detoured out of his way in order to meet one of his baseball idols, Shoeless Joe Jackson. He checks his image in the glass of the door, touches his cheek, his hair. Ted Williams who regularly faces the best pitchers in the American League seemingly without nervousness, without rancor, with a confidence bordering on arrogance, a confidence proven again and again to be justified, for the Splendid Splinter is the best hitter in baseball, possibly the best hitter in the history of baseball, appears nervous. He takes a deep breath as if Bob Feller is about to unleash a fastball in his direction.

He pushes open the door. Joe Jackson himself is behind the counter. Joe owns two liquor stores in Greenville. His wife, Kate, has proven over the years to be a resourceful financial manager. Stories abound about the unlucky eight who were suspended for life by Commissioner Landis after the Black Sox Scandal of 1919, even though they were cleared of wrong doing by a court of law. Most of the stories are untrue. Joe Jackson, while not wealthy, does not live in poverty.

The baseball legend has not aged well. The glistening black hair is gone, his handsome cheeks sagged into jowls, what few teeth he has left are mismatched and make him look like an old man, though he is only in his early sixties.

He glances at Williams, then looks quickly back down at the counter. Williams eyes the shelves of bottles and displays of beer cartons. He makes his way to the back of the store where a soft drink cooler sits in a corner. He opens the lid and extracts a bottle of 7-Up from the tepid water, walks back to the counter and sets the bottle down. It makes a wet circle on the brown wooden counter.

"Mr. Jackson?"

"Yeah."

"I'm Ted Williams. I play for . . . ;"

"Oh, I know you all right. I didn't want to say anything," he says shyly. "I thought you might not want to talk to me. The troubles and all, you know."

"You shouldn't let that bother you after all these years. You were treated unfairly. In fact I read a few months ago that there's a movement afoot to get you into the Hall of Fame where you belong."

"It's true. There's talk about me going to New York to be on a television show, and there's been a newspaper man around asking questions for the first time in years."

"I'll be there to see you inducted into the Hall of Fame. If I make it, it'll be my proudest moment. What is it they say? Many are called but few are chosen. You know I came to Greenville especially to see you, planned my trip to spring training around this visit. I think you're the greatest pure hitter the game's ever known, and I wanted to shake your hand."

They shake with their left hands. A scene for the ages. Perhaps the two greatest left-handed hitters in the history of baseball.

"You're not such a trifling hitter yourself. I watched you hit .400 in '41. There haven't been many of us, you, me, Cobb a couple of times, Bill Terry. But I have a distinction you'll likely never equal. I hit .408 and didn't win the batting title. You reckon you'll ever do it again?"

"I'll give it all I got, but the game's changing. There's a trend afoot to bring in a hot shot to finish up the game for a starter, and I think it's gonna catch on. Hitters like us, we get a lot of hits off tired starters in the late innings."

"I thought about that, Ted. I don't know as anybody's ever gonna hit .400 again."

"Have you ever seen me play, Joe?"

"Not in person. I seen you in newsreels down in the movie theater."

"I was hoping you might have been up to Fenway . . . I'd like you to see me, you know. If you'd like to come to Boston for a home stand, I'd pay your way."

"That's mighty kind of you to offer. I don't travel much, but maybe if they send me to New York for that television show." He pauses. "I seen you play, though."

"I don't understand. You just said . . . "

"Oh, not this television. Never watched it, except on the sets they got down in the windows at Sears. A few of the rich folks in town has got one. There's this blue glow out their front windows that I see when I go walking at night after I close up the store. No, I seen you the way an old ballplayer best sees a young one. I seen you in my imagination.

"The radio's the way to watch a ball game. Sit on the porch swing of a sunny Sunday afternoon and listen with my eyes closed. But listening's best at night. Laying on the hammock on my porch, inky black, fireflies like red pepper in the air. So dark I don't have to close my eyes. Nothing but the sound of the announcer's voice, the roar of the crowd, the crack of the bat. And somewhere nearby a lonesome dog

(Photo by Arthur Griffin)

75

howls, and long gone beyond the chinaberry trees another lonesome cur howls back. I've listened to you hit, Ted. When you hit the ball square on, the crack of the bat is louder, more solid, truer. Oh, I can picture you there in the left handed batter's box, the way I used to be, my blood flowing smooth as oil. Hitter's blood, cool and calm as a soft green river about to crash over a waterfall. I could smell a hit coming, oh, the odors of the game, the grass, the grass, like a sweetheart's perfume, the leather of the ball, the fellowship of the gloves, each personally oiled and juiced, soft as a baby's cheek. The glove an extension of the arm, like a faithful pet that would give its life without a second thought.

"I lay in my hammock and listen in the red freckled blackness, the humid night wrapped around me like a comforter, and I've seen and heard you hit and run and leap after fly balls in that mean outfield at Fenway. I played right field in Fenway a couple of times; I appreciate what you go through out there, the balls slicing toward the foul line, the unpredictable caroms in the corner. You're a better fielder than you're given credit for. And as far as handling the bat, only Ty Cobb was your equal, and he was never a home run hitter."

"That's very flattering. Ty was a friend of mine, you know, cantankerous son of a gun. But he wasn't a power hitter, not like you and me, power and average, that was us. You know the Babe modeled his swing after yours?"

"I heard tell. Can't be much more flattering than that."

"I almost hate to ask, Joe, but what happened to you after? After all the troubles."

"Being cut off from baseball it was like part of me was gone, an amputation, but nothing you could see, no visible handicap. But, God, how I missed the game. No declaration from a man like Landis could keep me away from the game. I still played, you bet I did, ban or no ban. So many assumed names I can't recall most of them. One summer I was Jackson Pell, Jack Pell, another time I was Joe Jacobs, Joe Johnson. I barnstormed all across America, keeping my cap low over my eyes and my feet always enclosed in shoes. One year I played my way across the Dakotas into Saskatchewan and Alberta, I don't remember what the team was called, but I didn't even have a name, I was known as the Left-handed Farm Hand. There'd be a few whispers run through the crowd like a sudden breeze when I came to bat, and a few more after I hammered the ball for a double and stretched it into a triple, maybe knocking the ball out of the third baseman's glove with my spikes as I slid in.

"I hear you have a few 'troubles' in your own life. The press is not as kind as it might be."

"You not only speak like a poet, you're a master of understatement. The Boston press is cruel and malicious beyond belief."

"Because you're your own man."

"I suppose. I do things my way. I won't suck up to these unwashed heathens who seem to think because I'm an athlete my life belongs to them, that I'm obligated to be at their beck and call every minute of my life. I give my all when I'm on the field, but that's all I feel is required of me. Off the field I'm not obligated to the fans or the owners, the other players and especially not to the press."

"I wish I'd been my own man," says Joe Jackson. "I've wished that a million times over the years. I wish I'd had it in me to walk away completely when the idea of rigging the Series was first broached. But there were so many things I didn't understand, and those were hard men I was dealing with, hard, hard men. And there was justification. Not for me, but for Eddie Cicotte, who was cheated out of a ten thousand dollar bonus in 1918, and on a team when you cheat one player you cheat us all. At least that was the way it was put to me. While

Ted's game-used cap and glove.
(Copyright David L. Pressman, M.D.)

I couldn't go along, I couldn't find a way to back away gracefully, or of backing out of at all."

"You have nothing to be ashamed of, Joe, and I hope they clear your name and open the Hall of Fame to you."

"Since you've seen me hit, so to speak, what advice can you offer me? I've often dreamed of talking hitting with you."

"You might be a little disappointed with what I have to say, Ted. I've read, that is, Kate's read me a bit of what you have to say on the subject. I'm afraid I've never been one for theory, but one for action. Know your strike zone, is the best piece of advice I can offer. Great hitters draw walks because they know the strike zone, a pitcher wants to tempt you to go after a pitch that's an inch or two off the plate, knowing that if you do hit it you won't hit it with full power. In my day the umpires were right over 90% of the time and I don't think things have changed. Trust your judgment, and trust the umpire to confirm it. Spoil the unhittable pitches, don't go for anything outside the strike zone, and wail the devil out of the pitchers in your zone. Never let a pitcher get away with a mistake. The best pitchers in the world make mistakes, make them pay every time. And always carry a great weapon. What kind of bat do you use, Ted?"

"Finding a bat you're comfortable with is almost as important as seeing the ball clearly. They say you have to treat a bat like a sweetheart."

"Don't I know it. I had my Black Betsy carved by hand by a master, and I carried her with me personally from city to city, kept her color up with new coats of tobacco juice, polished her and comforted her just to coax an extra hit or two out of her."

"I've been known to stop by the Louisville Slugger factory and pick out the wood for my bats. I use a lot lighter bat than you did. You must have been stronger than Hercules to get round on a fastball with a 48 oz. bat."

The day is still golden as the youthful hitter strides down the street. Behind the counter of the store the veteran baseball legend smiles, stands a little taller.

From the Strike Zone to the War Zone

In the end, it was probably Ted's service in the Korean conflict that added most to his John Wayne image. Serving as a flight instructor during World War II was important militarily, but it could hardly qualify as heroic.

He joined a legendary squadron in Korea—VMF-311, based at K-3, Pohang-by-the-sea. Among its 32 members, the 311th now counted both Williams and John Glenn. One was already a nationally known sports star, and the other would later became known worldwide as an astronaut and subsequently as a respected United States Senator.

When Theodore Williams was recalled for Korea, he expressed a sense of foreboding. He didn't think he'd be coming back to baseball, if indeed he came home at all. When the Red Sox held a "Day" for him at Fenway, he thought it might be the last game he'd ever play. Already in a combative frame of mind, he hit a game-winning home run his last time up and departed the strike zone for the war zone.

Approaching 34, and furious at being recalled, Williams nevertheless turned his full attention to the job at hand, rapidly going through refamiliarization and learning to fly jet aircraft. Ever the perfectionist, and determined to do the best job he possibly could, he sharpened his skills and excelled. After several months at Cherry Point and El Toro, it was time to head to the bitterly cold Asian battle theatre. This time Ted would see his share of combat and would serve with distinction.

Ted flew 39 combat missions and took ground fire on more than one occasion. On just his third mission after arriving in Korea, his plane was hit and he limped back, crash-landing his flaming Panther jet on an Air Force base and barely escaping with his life. That was heroic, as was suiting up and heading back out the very next day. He'd become a true military hero and it certainly added to the Ted Williams lore and legend.

Opposite: Ted as a squadron duty officer with sidearm in K-3 Pohang, Korea in 1953.
(Photo courtesy of Marsh Austin)

Many articles have been written surmising how Ted might have performed had the world remained at peace. It's been estimated that had he played all five years, he would have hit at least another 150 home runs. Some statisticians claim he could even have topped Babe Ruth's then-record 714. Current home run king Hank Aaron shares that belief.

While his stats would have been embellished, his legend would almost certainly have been diminished. He would have been remembered as a great baseball player, one of the greatest ever, but Ted's military experiences have added an entire dimension and lustre to a life which hardly needed more of either.

JOHNNY SAIN, Pitcher

In '42, the draft board was pushing all of us, so I signed up with the Naval Air Corps, with Ted, Johnny Pesky, Buddy Gremp and Joe Coleman. We went to Amherst College and started our flying at the Turner's Falls airport on the Connecticut River. We flew Cubs, Wacos, and then Kitty Hawks that had these little wire struts between the two wings. Biplanes. At one point they measured our eyesight at the college and the guy doing the testing said Ted and I measured about as close as two people could. Ted's eyesight was 20-10. I had 20-15. Our depth perception was extremely good. Learning to fly, I felt we had certain similarities.

Academic work was the main reason we were at Amherst. We studied naval history, navigation, aircraft identification and meteorology. Ted & I were in the same boat as far as education went. We were both high school graduates who'd been out of school for some time so we'd kind of lost the ability to study. In other words, we had to shake ourselves a little bit.

From there we went to Chapel Hill, North Carolina which was more of an athletic program, plus academics. The academic portion was say, half a day, and the rest was body conditioning . . . learning to stay afloat for an hour and things like that. We also played all kinds of sports. They wanted to see a little blood so that's the kind of sports we were trying to play. On weekends we were able to play baseball and formed a little team there called the Cloudbusters. We played some good clubs, like Norfolk, which had a few major league players. One time in '43, they wanted to see Ted Williams in New York so we went up to Yankee Stadium on a train. The Yankees played a regular game against Cleveland, and then they picked a team from the two clubs and Babe Ruth managed it against us.

A very interesting thing happened to us while in Chapel Hill. We had a muster one day and were given a choice of the Marines or the Navy. I took the Navy just because it was a bigger outfit. I thought: Well, hell, if I go to war I want to be with the bigger outfit. But Ted chose the Marines. Now, after the war, when we got out of the service in 1945, the Navy had so many extra pilots that I was able to get completely out of the reserves. Not Ted, though—the Marines didn't have that many pilots.

◆ ◆ ◆

JOHNNY PESKY, Ballplayer

Ted and I both went into the Navy in '42, about 10 days after the season was over. Amherst, then Chapel Hill. Primary flight out of Indiana. Dominic [DiMaggio], I think was at Norfolk, and Charlie Wagner. Ted went on to Florida and got his wings. I didn't get my wings. I went into operations and got my commission in Atlanta, Georgia in '44. I was there about three or four months and then went to Pearl Harbor.

I'll tell you one thing. Ted became one of the great heroes of any era. Even fifty years later, they're still talking about him. God gave him a great body, great eyesight, great everything, and he took advantage of it. He grasped things so quickly, I know from going in the flight program with him. He went through it like a dose of salts. I was going down for extra work trying to catch up, but he just went right on through the program. As a matter of fact, he broke the gunnery record in Jacksonville. Of course, he could handle a gun. He could shoot, he was a hunter.

◆ ◆ ◆

BILL CHURCHMAN, Flight Instructor

We flew together in Pensacola. I received my wings in '43 about a year and a half before Ted arrived—he went through a longer program because he joined later. When he got his wings late in '44, he was assigned to our squadron, instructing. Everything about Ted was exemplary. He had great technique and was just an outstanding pilot—gunnery in particular. He pursued his gunnery techniques as an instructor rather than a student. Ted was older than most of the cadets. I was just 22 at the time, four years younger. Still, as far as students going through flight training and also instructing, he was in the upper tenth in the age category.

I didn't know him as well in the Second World War as I did when he was called back for Korea. There was a shortage of all pilots for Korea. They called back all the single engine Marine pilots and all the fighter pilots. I had just returned from Korea and—would you believe—I was Ted's flight instructor at Willow Grove Naval Air Station, one of the stations chosen for retread training.

Ted was only at Willow Grove for six weeks. They took all the Boston, New York, and Washington reservists. That's how Ted and I got together again. That's where I really became close to him. His daughter, Bobby Jo, who was about a year and a half or two years old then, was there at the time with her mother.

It was refresher training and Ted was adaptable as always—very adaptable. We used to horse around a lot. He hadn't flown a plane since about 1946. Still, it only took him two or three hours sitting in the back seat before he got everything right—before he soloed. We used to practice dogfighting. You go up to about 7000 feet on collision courses about 1000 feet apart and then you start scissoring and get up on the guy's tail. The technique is that you fly your airplane almost at stalling speed so you get smaller circles, then you pounce on the guy who you're fighting. I said to Williams once [on the radio] "Where the hell are you? I can't find you anywhere." He says, "Look in your goddamned mirror. I'm right behind you." He was outstanding.

I remember one of the remarks I made at Cooperstown when Ted was inducted. I was trying to explain to Ted's guests his spirit of dedication, and how bright he is despite having very little formal education. What I have always said is that he'll conquer anything. If you were to say to Ted, "We're going to give you two years off from your present duties, and we want you to become a Shakespearean scholar," he'd be the best in the world. You could use that same theory in any field—computers, law, whatever. He'd master it.

◆ ◆ ◆

Ted, pictured in Korea.
(Courtesy of Howard Ligon and the Ted Williams Museum)

FIGHTER PILOT
by Robert L. Harrison

Over Korean skies
Ted the Marine pilot flew
into a different type
of ballgame.
Where hits are few
and errors can cost
you the whole game.

JOHN GLENN, United States Senator

I think I met Ted first at Cherry Point. We were both down there going through jet refresher and he left just ahead of me. When we got to Korea, I was assigned as operations officer of the VMF-311 squadron. We assigned one of the regular Marine pilots to fly with a Reserve. I'd guess probably half the missions that Ted flew in Korea he flew as my wing man. You get to know that guy pretty well.

You fly as a two-person element. Your two people stick together and if you're going into combat, you fly together. You watch out for each other. We were doing a lot of close air support work, with napalms and bombs on the ground and rockets and so on. If somebody got hit, you stuck with that guy, and you made every effort to get him back.

The F-9F Panther was a jet but it was not as fast as the F-86, nor would it go as high as the F-86. I won't say it was more in the truck category but it was close to that in that it would haul an awful lot of bombs for a jet, and was a good platform for doing air-to-ground work. The Air Force in the Korean theater was assigned the task of flying air superiority missions with the F-86, the Sabre. We Marines would be up hitting bridges and rails, and things like that up north of the combat, of the front line area.

We did a lot of flying. Some of the more memorable missions, we were doing road reconnaissance, just two planes out on a road rec. You'd take off early in the morning, before dawn, before there was any first light even, and you flew up at altitude until you'd be way up north, oh, maybe 150 miles or so behind lines. You'd be way up there, and then you'd let down, just at first light when you could see enough to skip along on the roads flying at real low level. One plane would fly down there and the other plane would fly along about a thousand feet behind and direct the first plane on the ground to make a right over the next ridge, or whatever, make sure to keep him on the road. Then you'd shoot up any trucks and things that you found which hadn't been hidden. Usually they'd hide them in tunnels and things during the daytime but you'd try and catch them out in the open.

We were under intense anti-aircraft fire on almost every mission in Korea. They had it all over the blooming place. By the time we got out there, which was in late '52 and then into '53, it was a rare mission you went on where you didn't see anti-aircraft fire.

On his third or fourth mission, Ted had to crash-land his plane. I was not on that particular mission but I certainly knew about it. You have to understand a little bit about the old F-9 to appreciate how serious that situation was. It's one thing to get hit and another thing to have fire coming out the back in any airplane. There's a matter of some concern, needless to say, that the thing doesn't blow. Ted got hit and was coming back and there was smoke and his radio was out—he couldn't hear the radio transmissions. He knew he was on fire but he didn't want to bail out. Everybody thought he should have

John Glenn and Ted in Korea in 1953.
(Photo by Marvin Kroner, courtesy of Sylvia Kroner)

gotten out but I think Ted will tell you he was afraid he was going to knock his kneecaps off. Somebody had bailed out and came out with no legs not long before that. Ted was going to ride her in or go down with it, one or the other. He brought the thing around, couldn't get the gear down, and bellied it in. The plane slid up the runway and he jumped out of the cockpit and ran off and stood there, watched it melt down. He was just lucky the thing didn't blow.

I was with him on another mission where he got hit. Sometimes you're on a mission and you get a good hit. We were going to areas where there might be fuel dumps and ammunition dumps. And on one mission we were over of the Heaju Peninsula which is sort of the Western part of Korea and there was an area where they were building up their forces as they sent them down to the front. We were assigned an area where we thought they had ammunition stored. Well, one of the best things that ever happened on a mission like that was if you got a good hit and got it right into the bunkers, their ammunition would start going off. That's called a secondary explosion. The first explosion resulted from the bomb, the secondary explosion occurred when all the stuff on the ground started going off. I went in on this particular day and got a good hit and it was blowing up on the ground. Ted was coming right in behind me and he pulled out of his run and yelled on the radio "I've been hit! I've been hit."

I said "Head for the water" which is what we always did if you got hit—get over the ocean so if you had to bail out you didn't crack up on land. Then we'd have somebody do a Dumbo rescue—in other words, send out a seaplane to rescue you. He was heading for the water and I was going over making circles around his airplane, flying under him and looking up at the bottom to see if I could see anything—see where he'd been hit—and out under the right wing tip was a good sized hole. I went up on top and saw that the hole didn't come out on top. This was a little bit screwy. He still had the airplane under control and there weren't any problems so we flew on back and landed. What had happened was he'd had a rock blown up from the ground on a secondary explosion which had hit him in the tip tank. We always kidded him about the Williams anti-aircraft fire.

The Koreans had a word for rock which was something like "kroindyke." If you wanted to get somebody's attention at night when you were coming back from the club, you picked up a handful of gravel and threw it at a Quonset hut. You could imagine what a racket that makes inside. This was known as Kroindyking. After Ted got hit by that rock, he became known as the "Kroindyke Kid."

There's another funny story that I happened to think of. You know when you call a baseball player "bush"—well, that's the worst thing you can say to a major league player, "You're bush league." When Ted got to Korea, one day somebody referred to something about him being bush one day, joking. Ted responded like you might expect Ted to respond, sort of negatively—well, that set the pattern. He was known as "Bush" Williams from them on. Everybody liked him.

Sure. I knew about Ted Williams and his records in baseball. I used to follow baseball all the time when I was a kid. Who knows what those records might have been if he hadn't had two hitches in the Marine Corps? I always tell him what kind of a ballplayer he could have been if he'd just been a Democrat. He could have really made history. But I'll tell you—Ted isn't one who sits around and moans about what might have been. And there's nobody, I swear, there's nobody that served in the Marine Corps who is any more proud of having been a Marine than Ted Williams. He's quoted as saying that there were 75 men in the two squadrons and 99% of them did a better job than he did. I disagree with his assessment. He did a great job and he was a good pilot. He wasn't out there moaning all the time or trying to duck flights, or anything like that. He was out there to do a job and he did a helluva good job. Ted ONLY batted .406 for the Red Sox. He batted a thousand for the Marine Corps and the United States.

◆ ◆ ◆

LARRY HAWKINS,
Lieutenant Colonel, United States Marine Corps (Ret.)

I knew who he was—I'd played American Legion Junior Baseball back in the '40s when I was going to high school. I'd met Ted briefly in the ready room at Cherry Point and didn't think I'd ever see him again. Then I was in VMF-311 with Ted. I flew 111 missions there.

The day Ted crash-landed his jet, he was well ahead of me, probably about a mile and a half. As I was coming up off the target after dropping my bombs, I was pulling up and heading west, toward the Yellow Sea. That's when I spotted this aircraft going towards the north/northwest and I said to myself, "That guy's going in the wrong direction." Then I spotted the puffs of smoke coming out. At first I thought it was just hydraulic fluid. So I flew up behind and checked him over. Then I flew up alongside and looked over at him, and he looked over at me, and I still didn't know who it was.

I would have done it for anybody because in North Korea when the snow was on the ground, if you saw a guy get hit, too many times you'd see an airplane go straight toward the ground and you'd see a secondary blast and you didn't know whether he came back out or not. Once in a while we'd lose a guy and we didn't know if the guy was with us until we got home. In this case, I picked him up right after we'd come off the target.

I had turned him out over the sea and I finally turned him southward. I had taken the lead by that time and given him the signal to join up on me. He had no radio so it was just hand signals. I just patted my head and said, "I'll take the lead" and he followed me. I went out to the Yellow Sea, got him out to the

"The Kid" shooting photos in Korea.
(Photo courtesy of Marsh Austin)

TED WILLIAMS: THE PURSUIT OF PERFECTION

Ted and Larry Hawkins in Korea.
(Photo courtesy Larry Hawkins)

west side of Korea and then turned him south-southeast, following the coast line. I saw these gentle puffs of smoke coming out of the tail section. Well, I soon found out it wasn't hydraulic fluid. As we went along, it continued to stream and that's when it dawned on me that it was fuel. I thought to myself: "We've got a problem. He must have been hit either in the main fuel cell or somewhere in one of the fuel lines."

As we were flying along, I knew that I had to keep him up at high air speed, because if I let him back off from 250 or so knots, that fuel will start pooling in the bottom of that fuselage. When you slow down a Panther, you start getting a back pressure that would start pooling the fuel underneath the plenum chambers. That was a centrifugal flow engine, so you had air coming in around the engine, in addition to the air going through it. So I kept him at that pretty good high air speed—not high in relationship to today's flying, but above 250.

I set him up over the airfield—King-13—just south of Seoul. Suwon was the name of the Air Force base. So we circled around and I set him up at 7500 feet, and I pointed down to the airfield. He looked and I'm sure he caught the picture because 7500 feet at a certain spot in the air was part of the flameout pattern. Had he flamed out—by this time, I figured he's lost all that fuel—he'd have to deadstick it or eject, one of the two.

Patch worn by members of the VMF-311 squadron.

It was fortunate that I got him to that point. We had flown eastward after we went around the corner of western Korea—it was North Korea but it was a corner, and we cut back in towards Seoul. As we flew, I set him up there and started circling. Then as we got down through the first circle, I gave him the "wheels down" hand signal, which was a

He was a tremendous guy to me. He wrote my father and told him that he appreciated having a fine son like myself. I went over to his Hitters' Hall of Fame a year or two ago, and he introduced me to his son. He turned to John-Henry and said, "This is the guy that saved my ass over North Korea."

— Larry Hawkins

standard signal for that particular pattern. There's a standard pattern for a flameout. He put the wheels down and as soon as he dropped the gear, the damn wheel well doors blew open. And of course by this time we were slowing down to where we'd be under 200 knots—somewhere between 150 and 170 knots. And he broke on fire.

So I hollered over the air, forgetting that he had no radio. I said, "Eject! Eject!" Well, he didn't hear me, but he got the picture that something had gone wrong. So he slapped the gear handle back up. By this time he was burning slightly. As the gear came back up, the fire just kept smoking. There wasn't that much fire coming out of him. So we turned back to the field at about 180. He was at about 3500 feet, something around there. Then, finally, he came screaming across the end of the runway, doing about 200. I was, oh, about 150 feet in the air. His airplane had skidded to a stop, sort of pointing in a sideward position and I saw the canopy go off. By the time I was just passing the aircraft doing about 120, 130 knots, I looked over my shoulder and saw this big, tall figure scrambling out of that cockpit and running to the side of the runway. By the time I passed the other runway, and looked back, he was well out of the airplane. Must have been, I'd say a hundred yards away from it. I never saw a guy move that fast in all my life.

◆ ◆ ◆

ART MORAN, Ted's Commanding Officer in Korea

We gave the new arrivals quite a bit of indoctrination-type flying around the area before we launched them up into Indian country. The first mission they would go on is up beyond the left side of the line. There's a bit of North Korea that sticks out. Not much was going on up there, but Ted got hit up there in his third mission. It was pretty hairy.

His radio was shot out, and he was shooting flame about 25 feet behind the airplane and everybody was yelling "Eject!" and he couldn't hear them. He dove for this Air Force base. Ted didn't have any instruments, either. He slid 5600 feet and he was out and running before it stopped. And it blew.

The real punch line to the incident was that when Ted took off on his first mission to go up to Indian country [after the crash landing], the phone rang. It was the commanding general. He said, "Moran, what the hell are you doing down there?" I said, "General, is there a problem? I'm just trying to run a fighter squadron." He said, "Did you launch Ted Williams?"

Ted had been launched through the system. When he got back from the crash, I had met him and talked to him about what most of us thought about having a problem with an airplane: If you want to continue to fly, you'd better get right back in another one. He agreed with that. I said, "Well, let us know when you want to go again." He said, "What's wrong with now?"

"Great, go see the operations officer."

When the general called, and said "Did you launch Ted Williams again?" I said, "Yes, sir, I talked to him about it and told him what most of us thought about the possible reactions after having a problem with an airplane. He said he wanted to go again." "Jesus Christ! Think of the publicity!" the general said. I said, "General, down here he's just another Marine Corps captain doing his job."

I haven't talked to Ted about this one. The four people involved are dead now. My personnel officer came to me just a day or so before Ted did. He said, "Skipper, we got a problem." I said, "What the hell do you mean, we?" He said, "We. You and I." And he told me something that I'll now tell you. "You know about that big hassle that we had in the Marine Corps when Ted got ordered to active duty?" I said, "Yes." He said, "I wrote it. I

wrote the orders." He said, "Hell, I knew that Ted Williams was not supposed to be ordered to active duty. He had been promised by the Commandant of the Marine Corps at the time, at the end of World War II, that if he would let the Marine Corps use his name occasionally—always with prior permission—he would never have to serve another day of active duty. And Ted said, 'OK.'"

So here's my personnel officer telling me he wrote the orders. He said, "Hell, I knew that Ted Williams was not to be called up, but I had all the cards of the folks who hadn't been called up yet, and here was Theodore S. Williams—and he looked pretty good to me."

◆ ◆ ◆

JERRY COLEMAN,
Ballplayer and Broadcaster

We heard Ted's distress call first hand. The United States Marine Corps Air was in North Korea. We were on that mission, the whole Marine Air was up in North Korea that day. We were all listening to this as it developed. When someone says "Mayday!" it gets your attention immediately. It was all over the place. And of course, we just listened to this, listened to it, listened to it and then it ended.

We didn't know where it ended, or how it ended. And then a couple of days later we found out that it was Williams. At the time we had no idea who, just a Marine pilot. We were all on the same frequency and were listening to this unpleasant situation. We were in the air, you know. The minute someone says "Mayday!" your ears just go up about five feet.

Ted was sick when he was over there. He had an infection in his ear. Eventually it got so bad that they decided that with his persona, they should get him out of there before he ended up killing himself without the enemy contributing. So he was sent back. I was 28 or 29 and he was 6 years older than me. I would think that it was much more difficult for him at his age, with his name and his impact on the entire Marine Corps. It must have been a hellish time for him.

With the lack of Marine pilots being trained, they had to call senior first lieutenants and junior captains. Ted and I were both junior captains at that time. How many they called back I don't know, but we were in that group. Robert Ruark, who was a big writer at that time, accused the Marine Corps of trying to develop the best baseball team. All of a sudden, here's Lloyd Merriman, who played for Cincinnati, Bob Kennedy with Cleveland, I was with the Yankees and Ted with the Red Sox. Four major league baseball players called back in that group.

The last thing there was any hope of was that we would play baseball. Immediately, we were ticketed for Korea. When we got up there in December, it was damn cold—a freezing, miserable, miserable country. I don't know what they fought over that country for. Hot in the summer, blazing hot. Miserable cold in the winter. The worst part of any mission was going from the ready hut to the plane! The winds across the runway . . . I froze to death out there. You couldn't wait to get to the plane to warm up!

◆ ◆ ◆

Captain Ted Williams, USMCR, having just received his papers which placed him on inactive duty status, receives a final salute from a sentry as he leaves the Naval Gun Factory, Washington, D.C. (Photo by PFC M. Sesera, courtesy of Department of Defense [Marine Corps])

BOB HOLBROOK, Sportswriter

I'm sure Ted's very proud of his military service in serving our great country. I spent four years in the United States Navy and I'm very proud of mine. The records mean nothing. There was only one thing that counted: we won the war! That was it, as far as Ted was concerned, as far as Joe DiMaggio was concerned, as far as I'm concerned.

— Bob Feller

There's one thing that I'm correcting in my own book. They said he went peacefully to Korea. He did like hell. Ted got the notice in the New Orleans airport. Rain, mother of God, I never saw such rain in my life. We were taking a charter flight from the Coast back to Sarasota. It was the worst flight I've ever been in, or anybody else had been in, including Williams. In between stops, they stopped at New Orleans to gas up, or say their prayers or something. I'll tell you, you could hear him from there to Shreveport. His voice is very penetrating. He said, "That clapped-up son of a bitch, Taft." There were a lot of people in that place, because it was raining like you wouldn't believe. I don't blame him a bit. Four or five other big leaguers had already been called back. Jerry Coleman had already had 25 or 30 missions in the Second World War, but they called him back. It was a terrible thing to do to anybody. Taft just wanted to show them up: *These bastards aren't going to get away with anything.* A lot of people came along after those guys did their stints flying. Anyway, Ted was really . . . he wasn't suicidal, he was maniacal. It was one of those, "Give him room!" One of those "Stay away from him!" situations.

◆ ◆ ◆

CURT GOWDY, Broadcaster

Williams was furious when he was called into Korea. He thought he was being used for publicity purposes—and he was. He was 36 or 37 years old then. He didn't think at that age he should be flying a jet fighter plane, but he did and Glenn told me he was a perfect officer. He never caused any trouble, he had good morale, he followed orders perfectly. All six managers he played for said they wished they were all like him. Everybody thought that he hated authority. He didn't. He liked a strong manager, a guy that used authority. He always said that Joe McCarthy was the best manager he played for. Ted never caused any problems, never missed a plane or a train.

◆ ◆ ◆

F9F Panther jet on display at Marine Corps Air Station, El Toro.
(Photo by Bill Nowlin)

TED WILLIAMS
(Taken from My Turn at Bat *by Ted Williams with John Underwood)*

People often ask me what it would have been like if I hadn't spent those years in the service during my career. I don't know for sure, but if I had been able to play those years my statistics certainly would have been better. But so would Joe DiMaggio's, and so would Hank Greenberg's, and so would Feller's. I always said Bob Feller was the greatest pitcher I saw. Pearl Harbor hit on Sunday and on Tuesday morning Feller went down and signed up and he was in the service four full years, at the very heart of his career. And he still won 275 games.

◆ ◆ ◆

Marine Captain William T. Armagost, shows fellow pilots how he tied his shoe laces around his leg to form a tourniquet after he was hit by enemy flak during a flight over North Korea. Other pilots looking on are, left to right: Capt Conrad H. Peterson, Capt Francis Kurtz, Capt Ted Williams, Capt Jack W. Campbell, and Maj Joseph A. Mitchell.

(Photo by Sgt Curt Giese , courtesy of Department of Defense [Marine Corps])

TED WILLIAMS
(Taken from Baseball for the Love of It *by Anthony J. Conner*)

I guess my main regret was that I missed the five years to war, but I don't feel as badly about the World War II years as I do about the two years in Korea. Hell, everybody and their uncle was going into World War II, but I still don't think the Korean thing was quite right, and I think a lot of people realize that. But I guess I should be thankful I got out of there with my ass.

◆ ◆ ◆

TED WILLIAMS —STILL A MAJOR LEAGUER
by Marvin Koner

Ted Williams, one of the great hitters of all baseball time, hasn't had a bat in his hands for 14 months now. But his hands haven't been idle. He's been fingering the stick of a 500-mile-an-hour Panther jet fighter in Korea. The war-scarred countryside of that unhappy peninsula has become as familiar to him as the big-league baseball parks where he performed for cheering fans.

Ted was a member of George Bush's class at the U.S. Naval Air Station at Cherry Hill, North Carolina, in 1942. In 1991, President Bush awarded Presidential Citations both to Ted and Joe DiMaggio in a Rose Garden ceremony at the White House.

Several Marines from the Henderson Hall Guard Detachment who were guests at the baseball game between the Boston Red Sox and the Washington Senators at Griffith Stadium on August 7, 1947, are shown discussing the ball game with Ted Williams of the Red Sox. Left to right are: Sgt F.A. Cherry, Cpl M.L. Epstein, PFC J.C. Bussey, Sgt V.P. De Lorenzo, Ted Williams, and Cpl T. Ensley.
(Photo by Sgt B.A. Emerson, courtesy of Department of Defense [Marine Corps])

Where once he exploded base hits for the Boston Red Sox, he switched to blasting the North Korean and Chinese Communist armies with bombs, rockets and napalm (flaming jellied gasoline) for the United Nations. And he belly-landed a badly shot-up jet last February as skillfully as an old pro hooking a slide into third base. (Williams walked away from the wreck with only a few scratches.)

Ted was recalled to active duty as a reserve captain in the U.S. Marines in May, 1952, at the age of 33. The summons, said the sports writers, ended the Splendid Splinter's baseball career—a tremendous 10 seasons with the Red Sox during which he hit for a .347 average, won four American League batting championships and slammed 324 home runs.

Williams thought it was the end of his career, too. So far as he was concerned, the game-winning home run he struck in his last appearance at Boston's Fenway Park was his major-league farewell.

But it looks as though baseball will reclaim Thumping Theodore after all. It was reported a few weeks ago that his tour of duty will end in the fall. Asked if he'd play again, Ted smiled and said: "I'd like to get in two more seasons. But I'll quit if I can't hit at least .300"

The smile was confident.

Williams is still part of a team. But it's not the Red Sox any more, it's the V (for heavier than air) M (Marine) F (fighter) 311 squadron flying out of southeast Korea. And his fellow Marines see few signs of the terrible-tempered Ted of baseball fame who once

deliberately aimed a line drive at a heckling fan. Instead, they respect him not only as a fine pilot, but also for his evident ability to give and take a ribbing good-naturedly. The respect is deepened because they know the smiles must come hard. Williams has given up nearly five years (three in World War II) and an estimated $100,000-a-year annual salary to military service.

The kidding usually takes place in the ready room of one of the sleeping huts after flying is over for the day. The acey-deucy boards come out. And after that, maybe, there's a rugged game of pinochle—or a bull session, with Ted often in the middle.

Two or three days a week, however, Williams leaves his squadron mates early and goes to the photo lab to process photos that he has snapped himself. Photography has proved a more practical overseas hobby than his favorite stateside relaxations, hunting and fishing.

His new teammates call Williams "Bush"—short for "bush leaguer." It's all in good fun; and the nickname is not meant as a reflection on Ted's stature as a pilot or a comrade in arms. As one of his fellow pilots said: "There's nothing small about Bush. He's a big-leaguer any way you look at it."

◆ ◆ ◆

Several Marines who were guests of Griffith Stadium are shown here discussing the coming game, between the Washington Senators and Boston Red Sox on August 7, 1947, with Mickey Vernon of the Senators and Ted Williams of the Red Sox.
(Photo by Sgt B.A. Emerson, courtesy of Department of Defense [Marine Corps])

Ted with troops during World War II.
(Courtesy of Bill Nowlin)

TED WILLIAMS: THE PURSUIT OF PERFECTION

Keith Woolner created a projection for the five years missed to military service. The years 1943-45 were based on his actual stats up to that time, and 1952-53 figures were based on the actual stats plus the projections for 1943-45. All other years are Ted's actual stats. Had Ted reached 1960 with 701 home runs, one suspects he might have played another year to best the Babe.

YEAR	TM/L	G	AB	R	H	2B	3B	HR	RBI	BB	AVG	OBP	SLG
1939	Bos-A	149	565	131	185	44	11	31	145	107	.327	.435	.609
1940	Bos-A	144	561	134	193	43	14	23	113	96	.344	.440	.594
1941	Bos-A	143	456	135	185	33	3	37	120	145	.406	.549	.735
1942	Bos-A	150	522	141	186	34	5	36	137	145	.356	.496	.648
1943		153	511	157	192	34	4	40	123	163	.375	.526	.691
1944		151	511	163	196	35	5	41	126	163	.383	.532	.710
1945		156	523	164	195	35	4	47	135	157	.373	.517	.722
1946	Bos-A	150	514	142	176	37	8	38	123	156	.342	.496	.667
1947	Bos-A	156	528	125	181	40	9	32	114	162	.343	.497	.634
1948	Bos-A	137	509	124	188	44	3	25	127	126	.369	.494	.615
1949	Bos-A	155	566	150	194	39	3	43	159	162	.343	.489	.650
1950	Bos-A	89	334	82	106	24	1	28	97	82	.317	.452	.647
1951	Bos-A	148	531	109	169	28	4	30	126	144	.318	.464	.556
1952		124	592	129	194	36	3	38	120	151	.327	.464	.591
1953		136	521	101	164	29	3	29	95	125	.314	.447	.544
1954	Bos-A	117	386	93	133	23	1	29	89	136	.345	.515	.635
1955	Bos-A	198	320	77	114	21	3	28	83	91	.356	.499	.703
1956	Bos-A	136	400	71	138	28	2	24	82	102	.345	.478	.605
1957	Bos-A	132	420	96	163	28	1	38	87	119	.388	.523	.731
1958	Bos-A	129	411	81	135	23	2	26	85	98	.328	.458	.584
1959	Bos-A	103	272	32	69	15	0	10	43	52	.254	.373	.419
1960	Bos-A	113	310	56	98	15	0	29	72	75	.316	.449	.645
ACTUAL TOTALS		2292	7706	1798	2654	525	71	521	1839	2019	.344	.483	.634
PROJECTED TOTALS		2969	10264	2492	3553	688	88	701	2401	2757	.346	.485	.635

TED WILLIAMS: THE PURSUIT OF PERFECTION

The Greatest Hitter
Who Ever Lived

No man ever attacked a baseball with Ted Williams' combination of intelligence, determination and skill. That's not opinion, it's fact. If such a claim came only from Red Sox fans, you might well question it. If you heard it only from his teammates, you might think it mere loyalty. But when it comes from fellow hitters, pitchers, umpires, and writers, you have to believe it's true.

It's not just the statistics. As impressive as they are, they don't capture Williams' dominance at the plate. Ted may have thought of the process of hitting as a science, but the result was pure art. Beauty is said to be in the eye of the beholder. For fans of the Splendid Splinter, it lies in the remembered batting practice heroics, the unique sound of a Ted Williams homer, the awe in the voice of a fellow hitter or an opposing pitcher, and the respect accorded him by umpires. They remove all doubts about his superiority.

No other team athlete is more identified with a particular skill within a particular sport than Ted Williams. Serving testimony to his legacy in baseball are the recollections of those who either witnessed the art of his swing, studied the science of his approach, or admired the fulfillment of his dream. He retired from the game in typical Williams fashion, the echo of a perfectly struck ball his answer to the call of the Fenway crowd. And they, along with so many fans of baseball, continue to answer back, whether in whispers or in shouts, "There goes Ted Williams, the greatest hitter who ever lived."

Opposite: Teddy Ballgame rouses the Fenway Faithful.
(*Photo by Fred Kaplan, courtesy of Lee Kaplan*)

by *Mike Shannon*
(*taken from* The Day Satchel Paige and the
Pittsburgh Crawfords Came to Hertford, N.C.)

Rubbing their grains down tight with a bone.
Wiping them clean of moisture and dirt;
With calibrating hands, weighing them for perfect balance,
Ted Williams sat in his hotel room
And treated his bats—
Lovingly, as a venerable violinist his instrument.
Or, coldly, as an assassin his scoped-rifle.

◆ ◆ ◆

HANK AARON, Ballplayer, Hall of Fame, "Home Run King"

I've always held Ted in high esteem. As a hitter, he's above everyone else because his thinking is superior. I didn't do quite the in-depth study of hitting that Ted did, not to that extent. I studied the pitchers that I had to hit against, what their weaknesses and strengths were, but Musial and I didn't break it down like Ted did.

Will anyone ever hit .400 again? It'll be one of the toughest things for anyone to do in baseball. You might have the ability in a lot of players to do a lot of things, but whether they can keep their eyes on the prize the way Ted did is another thing. It's kind of like when you're a little kid and all you concentrate on is walking. The reason you learn to walk or talk is because that's what you concentrate on 100%.

Ted's swing was unique. When he swung the bat, the ball reacted like a tennis ball. He hit it so hard and with so much topspin. He was very, very strong—I mean unusually strong—and he had the quickest bat I ever saw. You couldn't teach the average player to swing the bat and hit the way that Ted did. It takes someone with very strong hands, very quick hands and very good eyes—someone who knows exactly what he wants to do. That was Ted. They always teach you to stay still at the plate but he had that wiggle in his bat like a nervous guy. It made the pitchers think they could get in on him and jam him but no one ever could.

I admired Ted tremendously. He was one of the greatest to ever put on a uniform, to ever pick up a bat. I talked to him and I knew his philosophy as far as hitting is concerned, but I would be fooling myself if I thought I could do some of the things that he could do. I just didn't go into the fine details of it like Ted did. Ted was a better hitter than I was, that's what I'm saying. Exactly! Let's put it this way: Ted hit .400 and some of the things that he did not accomplish were only because he lost five years to the service. He could have eclipsed Babe Ruth's home run record. He probably could have hit .400 again. The closest I ever came was .355 in 1959.

The first time I saw Ted was when I played an exhibition game against the Red Sox and I hit a home run off Ike Delock. Ted often comments about that and it's funny, when a hitter talks about hitting to a fellow hitter you can appreciate the beauty of what he's talking about. He said, "Boy, I was in the clubhouse and I heard the crack of the bat and I said 'Lord, I've gotta go look!' and I knew immediately it was one of the longest home runs that was ever hit at the Red Sox training site at Sarasota." And it was. I'd always heard about Ted Williams' baseball savvy, and right then and there I could appreciate exactly what he meant. I'd heard the crack of a bat many times. I knew the sound a ball made when someone really hit it, and knew, without looking, it was going out of the ballpark.

So I knew what Ted meant, what he was talking about. No wonder Ted's name has been synonymous with hitting in the minds of baseball people for a long time.

Sure we handled the pressures differently. Everyone does things in their own way. That's what you have to appreciate about a human being, in sports or anything else. Sinatra said, he did it his way, and Ted Williams did it his way.

I'd have to agree that 56, 755, and .406 are three of the most significant numbers in baseball history. When fans think about hitting streaks, they think DiMaggio; when they think about home runs, it's me or Ruth. But when you think about hitting, it's Ted Williams and .406.

They always claim that great hitters got a fourth strike. They said it about Ted and they said it about me and Mays and Musial. I bet that stuff came from a pitcher! Ted didn't get no fourth strike, it was just that he knew where the strike zone was and he wouldn't swing at anything outside the strike zone. Pitchers would always say, "Well, it was over the inside part of the plate or the outside part of the plate." Well, shoot, that's ridiculous!

I didn't need to ask for advice from Ted because just sitting down and talking with him was advice enough. I could hear it, I could read what was on his mind. He and I—and most good hitters—think alike, and I could tell after sitting and talking with Ted for 35-40 minutes, exactly what he was saying. There's an unwritten language between true hitters.

Always a hitter at heart.
(Photo by Fred Kaplan, courtesy of Lee Kaplan)

What made Ted so great was that he refused to think that a pitcher could get him out. I mean he just refused to buckle, and that's what it takes to be great. Somehow you've just got to feel that you are the best. That's how he played the game and that's how he left the game, as the best.

◆ ◆ ◆

BILL "SPACEMAN" LEE, Pitcher

I am the antithesis of Ted Williams. He and I were talking once during a break in spring training in Winter Haven. Now Ted thinks that pitchers are stupid and were only put on earth to serve him, and I basically argued, on behalf of pitchers everywhere, that it was only due to our good graces that we let him hit at all.

Ted questions every pitcher about what makes a curveball break. He always claimed that pitchers were dumb and didn't know anything about the mechanics of their profession, so he was trying to test me with Bernoulli's Principle of Lift. To his surprise, I spouted the whole theory of Bernoulli's Principle and the pressure between a curve ball and a fast ball, and so on.

Then it was my turn. I said, "You probably don't even know it but you were lucky to be born with a dominant right eye. Being a left-handed hitter with a dominant right eye, you weren't blocked out by the bridge of your nose and you could stay closed longer than most other hitters, and with that incredible vision you could wait until the last minute. That's why you were a .400 hitter. If you'd had a dominant left eye and hit left handed, you'd be a lousy .250 hitter like me." He said, "Yeah, yeah, whattaya mean dominant eye?" I said, "Close one eye and point at that palm tree over there." He closed his right eye and

The "Splinter" and the "Spaceman."
(Photo by Rod Clarke, courtesy of John and Stuart Savage)

pointed, then he closed his left eye and pointed. He was amazed. And the last thing I saw was Ted Williams driving away in his golf cart with one eye squinted shut pointing at palm trees and light poles far off in the distance. I loved it. It was like the revenge of the pitchers.

How would I pitch to Ted? First pitch, I'd throw him a hard fastball, inside corner. I'd start it right down the middle and run it in on his hands and try to catch him by surprise because he seemed to be a very patient-type hitter and he probably would take it—first pitch strike. Next pitch, I'd throw the same pitch but I'd start it on the inside corner and try to run it in on his hands and he would probably take it for ball one. Then I would do the same thing and I would make it borderline where he'd either have to swing or take it to go 1-and-2. Once I established that, I'd throw him sliders off the plate— sidearm sliders dropped down. Then if I got the count to 2-and-2 or 3-and-2, I'd drop down sidearm and throw a fastball right down the chute, or maybe even on the outside corner to try to back-door him. One of those that looks like a ball all the way and ends up a strike.

Next time up, I would start him off with a slow breaking ball to see if he'd take it. If he took it, that'd be strike one. I would never, never get into a pattern with him—you can't do that with good hitters. You could have thrown him nothing but hard fastballs or hard sliders and then come down to a 3-2 count and throw him a change-up—something he hadn't even seen in the sequence. That's what you do with good hitters in tough situations. If there was a base open and I wasn't afraid of walking him, I wouldn't give him a strike to swing at. Usually the vanity of the hitter makes him want to swing the bat anyway because he wants to win the ballgame himself. But Ted wasn't afraid to walk. If I could, I'd walk Ted and pitch to the next guy every time.

Bill Monbouquette used to tell me that during spring training he used to move around maybe three or four inches on the rubber just to see if Ted would pick up anything different. And Ted would step out and yell at him, "What are you doing that for? Why are you standing over there this time? You're trying to change the angle of attack!" It was that ability to observe that made him different. He knew his own pitchers as well as he knew opposing pitchers.

The most amazing thing about Ted was the number of years that he lost, the amazing stats that he put up in the years he played, the stats he put up in his later years, and the power stats that he had in a park that wasn't conducive to power for left-hand hitters. Those factors are why I consider him the greatest hitter.

If I had played in the same media environment that he did, I would have had the exact same problems with the press that he, Ted, ran into. And I did have some of those problems early in my career, but then the press became a little more liberal. I could hang around with the new guard of writers: the Shaughnessys and Gammonses and McDonoughs and those guys. I was from the age of the newer writers and we shared the same interests in music and books and movies—and we hung out together. Whereas the older writers like Clif Keane and Larry Claflin, they didn't really like me that well. But under the same atmosphere that Ted faced, I would have behaved the same way Ted did. I always gave it back as hard as they gave it to me. People asked me, "Do you read the *Herald* or the *Globe*?" and I said, "I take both papers. I read the *Globe* and I train my dog on the *Herald*."

Boston toughened Ted up, coming from California, and he gave it back in spades. In the long term, New Englanders respect people who voice their own opinions and are staunch in their views. They may not agree with you but they'll defend to the death your right to say it.

I always thought that John Wayne did a great act of impersonating Ted Williams. Ted's got that Andrew Carnegie style of up-from-the-tough-side-of-town background, and he was going to be great in spite of it all. Nothing was going to get in his way. And he did it. He was very individualistic, very Californian. The psychology of the mother-father relationship provided the perfect psychological profile for someone destined to be an over-achiever. Ted doesn't do anything nice and easy. He's kind of the "Tina Turner" of baseball.

◆ ◆ ◆

Ted couldn't wait to get up to the plate. When he was in the on-deck circle he was gripping the bat and couldn't be still. He was so eager to hit that I sometimes think he got in the batter's box before the other hitter got out.

—Virgil Trucks

STAN MUSIAL, Ballplayer, Hall of Fame

Ted is one of my good friends. Some people say we were counterparts of a sort—him in the American League and myself in the National League. I did not consider Ted a rival, though as a player you watched every opposing player in the majors and not one in particular. Ted was a scientific hitter. He studied pitchers, he studied other hitters and he studied game situations. Ted lived to hit. I've read his books and I do agree with his theories of hitting. He had a great batting stance and great eyes. I won my last batting championship at age 36 and Ted won his last one at 40, but I didn't feel old at 36—I

Ted cocked and ready, just a split-second before the release of the ball. 4:02 p.m.
(Copyright David L. Pressman, M.D.)

Ted swings at the pitch. 4:03 p.m.
(Copyright David L. Pressman, M.D.)

TED WILLIAMS: THE PURSUIT OF PERFECTION

played five more years. It did, however, become more difficult to contribute at the age of 40 or 41. Without the years of military service, Ted would have set more records than any other player. I truly admired his concentration and his great love of baseball. Ted Williams was the greatest hitter of the past century. He was the "Pavarotti" of hitting.

♦ ♦ ♦

MICKEY MANTLE, Ballplayer, Hall of Fame
(Taken from The Education of a Baseball Player *by Mickey Mantle)*

I say that I have never imitated any ballplayer, but there is one whose general attitude at the plate I have tried to acquire. That is Ted Williams, who was the best hitter I ever saw in action. Ted showed me what it means to be aggressive at the plate. When he decided to go after a ball, he really attacked it, as if he meant to demolish it entirely. There was never anything defensive about his ways at the plate, no halfhearted swings or pokes. He exploded at a ball, trying to drive it as hard and as far as he could. I know that it is not the way for every batter. But it was the right way for Ted and me.

♦ ♦ ♦

JIM BUNNING, Pitcher, Hall of Fame, United States Senator

I had more starts against the Red Sox in my years with the Tigers than any other team. I won 20 games against them and I think I lost 17. I loved pitching in Fenway Park. I guess Williams had more at-bats against me in the years we both played than any other hitter in the league. I probably was the only one who ever struck him out three times in one game. He came back the next game and hit two home runs off me. He was the greatest hitter that I ever pitched against—by as far as I can stretch my hands apart! I don't think there's anyone who came close.

I've faced so many great hitters. I was very fortunate to be able to pitch in both leagues, when there were unbelievably great hitters, from Aaron to Mays to Mantle to Musial, and all those people. But without a doubt, Ted was the best I ever faced.

♦ ♦ ♦

WILLIE MAYS, Ballplayer, Hall of Fame

He was around when I was in Birmingham. On Saturdays and Sundays we got the newspapers and the three guys that I followed were Ted Williams, Stan Musial and Joe DiMaggio, and even though all three were great, I thought Ted was the best hitter of all. Joe was the best all-around but Ted, in my mind, was the best hitter. He didn't really want to field that much. We all laugh about that, but he wasn't a bad fielder. He'd just rather hit than field.

I had a real good conversation with him at the All-Star Game in St. Louis. I remember I was in a slump. He called me over and we sat down and talked. He said, "You've got to change your stance a little bit." I said, "Why?" He went into the details of hitting—about how sometimes people go into slumps for about a week or two, and you can't just change every time that happens. If you change for change's sake, you get

Ted's legacy is that in future generations, people will drive through the Ted Williams Tunnel and go to Fenway Park and say, "The great ballplayer of all time played in this ballpark" . . . and Ty Cobb, up in heaven or down in hell, replies. "Yeah, that was me, I played there too" . . . and Babe Ruth chimes in, "I played there too."

—Bill "Spaceman" Lee

1956-Mickey with Ted Williams

worse. He suggested an adjustment. It was very impressive to me that he would watch me, as the opposition in a different league, and be able to make informed comments about my hitting.

Ted was a fanatic about hitting. He was very aware of what's going on in everybody's hitting stance.

♦ ♦ ♦

CARL YASTRZEMSKI, Ballplayer, Hall of Fame

I was just 19 years old the first time I met Ted. I went to spring training in 1960, his last year with the Red Sox. You really didn't talk to the veterans in those days unless they came to talk to you. I don't know if it's that I was nervous to meet Ted Williams—it's more that it was intimidating. He was so loud and some of the things he said! The thing is that I was in a situation where I'm trying to make the ballclub and I wasn't really worrying about other people.

In my first year I started off very slow. I actually think that was on account of Ted. I was trying to emulate him—be a home run hitter and not be myself: just an all-around player. I could never be a Ted Williams as far as hitting was concerned. He came and watched me take extra batting practice. He said, "You've got a great swing—just go out and use it." I think what dawned on me was that there can be a great swing that is not a home run swing at the same time.

We had completely different styles of hitting. I think that discipline at the plate and knowledge of the strike zone were the main things that Ted conveyed to me. You have to be yourself and maintain your concentration level. I tried to be a home run hitter at first when I wasn't one. Imagine trying to hit 40 home runs in your first year in baseball!

I read his book. He made a science out of hitting—no doubt. Just a tremendous natural talent with discipline and dedication.

♦ ♦ ♦

GEORGE STEINBRENNER, Owner, New York Yankees

Ted was a better pure hitter than Babe Ruth. He was the best left-handed hitter that baseball has ever seen. And a left-handed hitter hitting in Fenway Park, don't forget that. Not any easy deal! Day after day and year after year, I would put him at the top. If he was playing today, I wouldn't DH Ted. He was a graceful guy. To people who say he wasn't a great outfielder, I say that's baloney! I saw him play the outfield and he was better than a hell of a lot of guys we have out in outfields today. My study of baseball puts Rogers Hornsby as probably the greatest right-handed hitter. Ted and Hornsby are my two outstanding all-time hitters, left-handed and right-handed. But Joe D is probably my all-around greatest baseball player. He and Ted both had a tremendous impact on the game.

There seemed to be a lot more to the game in those days. I mean when guys hit a ball out of Yankee Stadium to left field or left center, fans say, "Boy, that's a real hitter who can get a ball out of there." Well, these guys—Ted and Joe and others—used to do it without the fences in. A home run out of Yankee Stadium in those days was unbelievable. It was juiced! And with the balls that we're throwing out there today! Ted and Joe would hit well in any era, in any game, in any circumstances.

♦ ♦ ♦

TOMMY HENRICH, Ballplayer

(Taken from Five O'clock Lightning *by Tommy Henrich)*

Ted was closer to perfection with a bat than any hitter I ever saw, then or now . . . Ted was born with uncommon ability and the keenest eyesight a human being could hope for, but the reasons behind his superiority as a hitter went beyond that . . . . He wasn't just satisfied with his natural ability as it was. He kept developing it to new levels. In other words, he worked hard.

Williams would take more batting practice than any other player. And it was never enough. He'd wait for the fans to leave after a game, drag a pitcher out with him, and go back onto the field for another half-hour or forty-five minutes of hitting. That's a long time to be hitting without interruption, but Ted would do it for periods so long that the rest of us would have dropped from exhaustion.

His brain, which made him a respected fighter pilot in two wars and might have made him the world's leading brain surgeon or nuclear scientist, told him that hitting a baseball is an inexact art form that requires the artist—the hitter—to pursue his work with unwavering diligence. That's precisely what he did.

He did more than out-practice everyone in the physical end of it. He out-thought the rest of us, too. He swung a lighter bat than most of us, 32 ounces compared with anything from 34 to 40 ounces for the rest of us, because he said bat speed was more important than a heavier bat that might give you distance. He said if you have enough bat speed, the home runs will come anyhow, and the lighter bat will give you more singles and doubles . . .

He was also more disciplined at the plate than the rest of us. Just as he did throughout his playing career . . . he insists that most hitters are simply too content to swing at balls that are not in the strike zone. He has said it a million times, maybe ten million: "Get a good pitch to hit." And when you went for something that wasn't a good pitch, you'd hear it from him, usually at the top of his voice: "Don't be so damn dumb."

He was one of those rare combinations, a man who could hit with exceptional power and for exceptional averages at the same time. People forget that in his historic season in '41, he also led both leagues in home runs with 37. As for his insistence that you have to "get a good pitch to hit," there is the amazing testimony to his greatness: while accomplishing all those things in 1941, he only struck out a total of 27 times.

That was no fluke. In this age when .240 hitters swing for the fences and strike out 125 times a year in the process, Ted's highest strikeout total was 64, and that came in his rookie season. After that, he never struck out more than 54 times—and that was the next year. In fifteen seasons after 1942, when he struck out 51 times, Ted never had 50 strikeouts again.

That's helping your team in a way that is lost on the players of today. Ted Williams was always more of a team player than he was given credit for, mainly because his individual statistics were so overpowering that people tended to overlook his contributions to his team. They never gave him credit for his skill in playing left field in Boston, but Dom DiMaggio, the man who played next to Ted, will testify to it.

Getting on base by walking was another thing Ted did better than anyone else, because of his strict self-discipline in the batter's box. He led the American League in walks six years in a row and eight times in all. The lowest number of walks in any of those seasons was 126.

◆ ◆ ◆

I'm just glad I never had to face him. I never pitched against him but the thing I'll always remember about Ted was when he hit that bloop pitch out of Fenway Park in the All-Star Game. I would have definitely kept that eephus pitch out of the repertoire after that.

—Rollie Fingers

FRED HATFIELD, Ballplayer
(*Taken from* This Side of Cooperstown *edited by Larry Moffi*)

Even at Fenway, Williams might hit for an hour before a game, three to four times a week. He'd pay someone to pitch batting practice. At home, he'd go out to the park early, religiously. He was dedicated to HITTING. During a game he'd sit and grind that sawdust out of the bat, waiting in the on-deck circle. He may have been the only hitter who a pitcher would never have to wait for. When the ball was hit while he was in the on-deck circle, by the time the ball got back to the pitcher, Ted was standing in the batter's box ready to hit. He had a chain of thought and it never got interrupted. He loved to swing that bat.

After a homer or after striking out, he had that same expression. I never saw him lose his temper, cuss, throw the bat, or break the bat. I saw him take three straight strikes one day, never taking the bat off his shoulder. And the next time up, he hit one in the upper deck, sitting on that pitch that got him out earlier.

◆ ◆ ◆

EDDIE PELLAGRINI, Ballplayer

Pitching to Ted Williams—the best way to get him out is just to pitch him right down the middle. He's going to hit everything else, going to hit .340 no matter what, there's not much else you can do. He was the best hitter I ever saw.

I played for Rogers Hornsby and one time I said to him, "You know, I know a better hitter than you, Skip." He looked at me—he was a mean bastard—and said, "Who would that be?" I said, "Ted Williams." He never played me much after that.

◆ ◆ ◆

HANK SOAR, Umpire

He was a guy who knew the difference between a strike and a ball. He never bitched a moment about it. He probably needled you about one, or we maybe needled him or something. Outside of that, never.

He didn't care what you called, as long as you stayed steady with the same pitch. If you called it a strike, stay right with it, you know. Call it the same way all the time. That's what we tried to do. Of course, every once in a while you're going to have a little trouble, you know. It'd fool him, it'd fool me sometimes. That's one of those things, but he never tried to show you up.

We never gave him an edge. That's baloney. I said to him, "You know, Ted, I'll betcha . . . you bat left-handed and I can call a ball 6" on the outside of the plate a strike and you don't know the difference. He said, "I can tell." I said, "I don't think you can." I dropped it at that. I went into Boston and did a series in there. I got in a game and the count was, I think, two balls and one strike. It didn't mean anything. They were ahead in the game, or they were way behind. It didn't make any difference. Anyway, this ball came up and it was right about 6" outside and I looked at it and I said, "Here's my chance" and I called it a strike.

And he backed out of the box, reached down and put some dirt on both hands, and out of the corner of his mouth he says, "Hank, 6" outside." Went back with the bat swinging, and that's just where the ball was.

◆ ◆ ◆

TED WILLIAMS: THE PURSUIT OF PERFECTION

Ted crouches in the on-deck circle, intently studying the opposing White Sox pitcher.
(Copyright David L. Pressman, M.D.)

TOMMY LASORDA, Baseball Manager, Hall of Fame

I remember Bob Kennedy telling me that when he got out of the service—both of them had gone into the Korean War—Bob came to Fenway Park to say hello to Ted. Ted was taking batting practice. When Ted came over to say hello to Bob Kennedy, Bob picked up the bat—he'd been hitting for 40 minutes—and there was one spot on the barrel of the bat. That's unbelievable!

◆ ◆ ◆

The Greatest Hitter Who Ever Lived

Any time anybody ever said who was the best hitter you ever faced in baseball, I never said anybody except Ted Williams.

—Whitey Ford, pitcher, Hall of Fame

CURT GOWDY, Broadcaster

In my mind, I wondered: *What really made Ted Williams great?* I think it was burning pride. The guy had a drive, a determination, a pride to really be great, and work at it. I learned how to do my job, or work at my job, from Ted Williams. I watched him. He took more batting practice and did more things to improve himself. He could have been a drunk and hit .300. But he really worked at his craft, a master craftsman. I really admired that. And one time I told Ted, I said "Ted, you made me into a better broadcaster." He said "What do you mean? I don't know anything about broadcasting."

"Well," I said, "I saw how hard you work and practice, and I decided to keep more records and files and collect everything I could on the American League ballplayers." "Well, that's good," he said. "I always want to give Tom Yawkey back $1.10 for every dollar."

◆ ◆ ◆

BOB BOYD, Ballplayer
(Taken from When the Cheering Stops *by Heiman, Weiner & Gutman)*

The best hitter I ever saw was Ted Williams. I played against the man and I know. Even when they began putting that shift on him he would still get the ball through there. I remember one game when he hit a shot right down the line. The ball hit the first base bag—the bags were held down by leather straps then—and it hit so hard that it broke the straps. The ball just died and stayed around first base, but the bag came flying out to where I was playing him in short right. So Ted got a single and I got the bag instead of the ball. I just laughed like hell on that one.

◆ ◆ ◆

PAUL RICHARDS, Ballplayer
(Taken from The Power Hitters *by Donald Honig)*

I've never seen such fierce concentration. One day in Detroit he came to bat and I was catching. I said hello to him, but he didn't answer. Now, I know Ted wasn't unfriendly; he was, in fact, a very congenial guy. I realized that his concentration in the batter's box was so deep he didn't hear me. So the next time he came up I told myself I was going to try to break in on him, just for the hell of it. I started telling him a rather spicy anecdote about a well-known player and then stopped right at the punch line. He never acknowledged a word. There's not a man alive who wouldn't have wanted to know the end of that story; so I'm convinced he never heard a word. That's how entirely into himself he was at the plate.

◆ ◆ ◆

ERNIE BANKS, Ballplayer, Hall of Fame

I first met Ted in Arizona in 1954. We played against the Red Sox. I was a rookie and my whole demeanor was this: to watch everybody, to look and learn. Some of our players pointed out Ted Williams and I came out early to watch him take batting practice. He got in the batting cage, looked at a couple of pitches, and then started swinging, hitting the ball up in the air, and then the balls started going out of the park—swinging so easy. He was telling pitchers, "Throw me one here and throw me one there, throw me inside, throw me outside." He was kind of directing where he wanted the ball, preparing for a game. What I saw was smoothness and talent. Ted was into his game. He was a professional. I would say, if giving advice to young players today: somebody's always watching you and trying to be like you. That's just what I did when it came to Ted Williams.

◆ ◆ ◆

JOE MORGAN, Former Red Sox Manager

I think he's the greatest teacher of hitting, because most people are talking about the mechanical end of hitting—which Ted does too, of course—but he teaches the mental part of hitting more than anyone I've ever heard. He tells you to study the pitcher. What does the guy throw? How is he trying to get you out? What's the situation? He always did that.

There's a thousand situations. Ted was always preaching that. I never heard another batting instructor do anything near what he did. They were all talking about mechanics. I learned more about hitting—the mental aspect—from listening to Ted than any of the other guys. How was that guy trying to get you out? The enemy. He had great natural ability, but still, he was still thinking, "How is that guy going to get me out?"

◆ ◆ ◆

YOGI BERRA, Ballplayer, Hall of Fame

Ted never wanted anyone talking to him while he was at the plate. I used to talk to him anyway, though. I'd say, "Ted, when you going fishing this year?" Stuff like that. He'd just ignore me. Today, though, if you talk to him about hitting, he'll talk all day. Back then he'd always keep his eye on the pitcher, even if he did talk to you. He'd never

Of all the hitters I ever saw, he was the greatest. My wife Bev, I'd go home, have a 2 for 4 day, and feel pretty good about it. She'd say, "Nice day, honey. You went 2 for 4, but Ted went 3 for 4." He was the greatest hitter I've ever seen. To be in his Hall of Fame is a great honor to me.

—Duke Snider

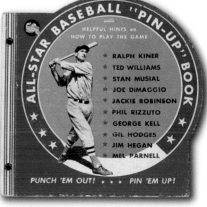

(Photo sequence by Arthur Griffin)

TED WILLIAMS:
A text-book at bat, another home run for the record books

look down either. I used to holler at him, "The balls you take, I woulda swung at!" But I never heard him complain about a pitch.

I don't have any funny stories about Ted. When you're trying to get him out, it isn't funny. He could probably tell some about me. When he first saw me when I came up in '47, he said, "Who the hell's that little guy coming up to hit, taking Bill Dickey's spot? He catches? You gotta be kidding."

Ted was the best. If he wanted to bunt, he could have hit .500. You know how they'd shift on him. All he had to do was just put the ball down and he'd have it beat.

◆ ◆ ◆

BARRY LATMAN, Pitcher
(Taken from This Side of Cooperstown *edited by Larry Moffi)*

The first game I ever appeared in was at Fenway Park and the first batter I faced was Ted Williams, who hit .388 that year. I threw three straight strikes and Nestor Chylak called three straight balls. I started hollering and screaming at him. He said, "Mr. Williams will tell you when you throw a strike." Lollar came out and made sure I kept my composure. I threw the next ball down the middle and Williams walked. And I was taken out. The next day Ted came up to me and told me I threw four straight strikes. I'm surprised he didn't swing, but I guess he wanted to see what I had.

◆ ◆ ◆

JOHN RICE, Umpire

He had his good times and his bad times. One year I was in spring training. As the camp was breaking up, he'd had a very poor spring training camp. All the rumors were he was going to quit, and it might have crossed his mind. We were in New Orleans, playing in a real small ballpark down there, really a football field turned into a baseball park. He hit a real screamer that was just foul, and he sort of stepped back out of the box and looked at me and said, "Hey, I hit that one pretty good, didn't I?" I didn't say anything. The next pitch he hit about 450 feet right over the centerfield wall. He just chuckled there, took a look at it, then started his gallop around the bases. When he got to home plate, he jumped up in the air and he said, "Looks like I'm comin' back!"

◆ ◆ ◆

JIM HONOCHICK, Umpire
(Taken from The Men in Blue *by Larry Gerlach)*

One time my intuition got me in trouble. Back in the early 1950s I was working the plate at Fenway Park. There were two men out. Billy Goodman was on first, and Teddy Williams was at bat with a count of two balls and one strike. As I waited for the pitcher to come in with the ball, it hit me that Goodman was going to steal second base. As the pitch came in I watched Goodman break for second out of the corner of my eye. That's a big no-no for an umpire, but I did it. As I watched to see if he was going to make it, I forgot I had to make the decision on the pitch. The ball was way up in Williams' eyes, but I called it strike two. I realized the mistake right away. In the meantime, they threw out Goodman to

Courtesy of Hillerich & Bradsby Co.)

end the inning. Williams never said a word. He just tossed his bat toward the dugout and trotted to the outfield. I had heard what a great guy he was, and that proved it to me. If it had been Nellie Fox or Sal Bando or Gene Tenace or one of those guys, I would have had to put them out of the ball game because they would have stood there and argued. Ballplayers today start bellyaching before they even step in the batter's box.

The next inning Williams was the leadoff hitter. As he was swinging the bat to get loose, I walked over and said, "Teddy, even if I'm not supposed to tell you, I sure blew the hell out of that pitch." He laughed and said, "No, you didn't, honey." (He always called me honey.) "I knew Goodman was going to steal, and I should have swung at the damn pitch to help him, but I didn't, so I'm more responsible for it than you." Now can you fault a guy like that?

◆ ◆ ◆

BILL McKINLEY, Umpire
(Taken from The Men in Blue *by Larry Gerlach)*

Of the hitters, Ted Williams was the greatest. He never said a word to the umpires, not one word. If he got mad, he took it to the dugout. Never said anything to me other than "Bear down, Mac, you're better than that." He'd say it while he was looking right out at the pitcher, so nobody knew he was talking. He never tried to show you up.

◆ ◆ ◆

JOE PAPARELLA, Umpire
(Taken from The Men in Blue *by Larry Gerlach)*

I worked with so many outstanding players . . . Ted Williams stood ceiling-high. He very rarely looked back at an umpire at the plate. And he would help you even to the point of getting players off your back. If you finished the season with Boston, he'd come to the dressing room, shake your hand, wish you and your family a happy winter, and thank you for being associated with the game. He was the only one ever to do that.

◆ ◆ ◆

BILL MONBOUQUETTE, Pitcher, Pitching Coach, St. Catharine's Stompers

I first met Ted in 1955 when I signed as an 18-year-old kid. I hung around for a month and had a chance to throw batting practice and be on the bench and listen to him talk. He gave me a good idea about what a hitter was thinking. When he started to talk about hitting, I was like his son, almost sitting on his lap, just listening to him. I just reversed what he said to hitters for use in pitching—how he thought, what he looked for in different situations.

He'd say, this is the first pitch he always throws me, this'll be the second pitch, this'll be the third pitch. I've heard him say on many occasions, after they got him out the first time up, "In the 7th inning, I'm going to get that third pitch slider and I'm going to hit that ball out of here." And God, if that didn't happen! There's a book called *League of Their Own* and I think he was in a league of his own. Not only is he the greatest hitter I ever saw, he's the smartest hitter I've ever known.

◆ ◆ ◆

There's no question in my mind—I've always said he was the greatest hitter in the game. I have seen some of the great hitters—Lou Gehrig, Jimmie Foxx, Al Simmons, Hank Greenberg. There are all great names but when I saw him, I said, "Hell, there's just nobody like this man."

—Joe DiMaggio, from remarks spoken at an evening with Number 9.

DON DRYSDALE, Pitcher
(Taken from Once a Bum, Always a Dodger *By Don Drysdale with Bob Verdi)*

He was a perfectionist who realized that true perfection always lies behind the next turn.

—Joe Cronin from the Introduction to *Ted Williams,* by Ray Robinson.

I was running in the outfield at Holman Stadium during spring training in 1969. The Washington Senators were in Vero Beach to play the Dodgers, and Ted Williams was the new Washington manager. Williams not only possessed one of the most picture-perfect swings ever (it's not only pitchers who can be intimidating), but he's in a dead heat with Frank Sinatra as the most magnetic person I've ever met. Talk about two men who can light up a room just by coming through the door.

That day in Vero, we got to talking about the 1959 All-Star game in Los Angeles. It was a first for the West Coast, and I got the start in the Coliseum, a nice honor. In the third inning, Williams absolutely crushed one of my pitches and hit it to the deepest part of center field. Willie Mays had to pull it in against the wall. But here it was, ten years later, and Williams' photographic memory was in vintage form.

"You know that pitch before the one I hit?" he said. "What was that? What did you throw me there?"

"Oh, that was a sinker," I answered. "The pitch you just fouled off? I threw you a sinker."

"Yeah, yeah, sinker my ass," Williams said. "I've seen some good spitters in my days, and that was one of the best goddamn spitters ever. And in a friggin' All-Star Game, you threw it!"

I just laughed and headed back to the outfield to do some more running. I couldn't tell a lie then, I cannot tell a lie now.

◆ ◆ ◆

MEL PARNELL, Pitcher

Occasionally Ted did mention that some pitchers are stupid, that they more or less threw to his power and that some just didn't know how to pitch or work the pitcher's mound. But being the great hitter that he was you can understand him ridiculing the pitching. The guy was so outstanding that it seemed rather easier for him than for many others.

As a pitcher you could pick up a lot of pointers from him. On a few occasions at Fenway Park, Ted felt he wasn't seeing enough left-handed pitching because of the short left-field wall, so during batting practice sometimes I'd throw under game conditions. By that I mean I wouldn't tell him what I was throwing to him. I would try to figure him out and he would try to figure me out. I think it helped both of us. I tried to keep the ball in tight on him. That was my theory of pitching—pitch inside and keep the hitter swinging with his elbows close to his body, make him sacrifice some of his power. If you try to hit the outside corner and miss toward the middle of the plate, then the hitter could get a strong swing with the extended arms.

Ted could pick up the spin on the ball, which certainly helped his hitting. He's the only person I've ever heard say that he could see the ball make contact with the bat. And anything Ted says about hitting, I have to believe.

Ted used to love to play against Detroit. At that time they had what they called TNT, Trucks, Newhouser and Trout. Those fellows were great pitchers and they used to challenge Ted. They wouldn't pitch around him and he loved to play in Detroit because he knew he had a challenge on his hands. He just seemed to be at his best whenever he was challenged.

I remember a game against Washington. Pedro Ramos was the pitcher for the Senators. Ted didn't know too much about Pedro at that time because he was new to the league and Ted struck out against him. After the game was over, Ramos comes into our clubhouse with the ball to get it autographed by Ted Williams. Ted told him to "Get the hell out of here! I don't sign any ball I struck out on!" He was giving Ramos a rough time. You could see tears forming in Ramos' eyes. He wanted that autograph on that baseball by all means. Then I guess Ted started feeling a little sorry for him. He said "Give me the ball and I'll sign it." So he signed the ball and with that Ramos goes out of the clubhouse full of smiles, happy as a lark with the big name on the ball he struck the man out with.

So the next time Ramos is pitching against Ted, Ted hits one about halfway up the rightfield bleachers and he hollers at Ramos: "If you find that one, I'll sign that sonofabitch too!"

Sure Ted got some preferential treatment from umpires, but so did Musial and DiMaggio and other greats. All the real outstanding hitters got it—and in many cases the outstanding pitchers got some close calls too. Over a long season, things even out.

A lot of times in the clubhouse before he went out on the field, Ted would check over his bats pretty good and he had a bone and he bone-rubbed his bats. Other than that he'd just go on out and take his cuts. He was always jolly as could be. He'd come bouncing out of the dugout like a big kid, full of pep all the time, and I think his makeup was a great part of his success. Whoever nicknamed him The Kid must have seen that enthusiasm because he did come out like a big kid. Happy-go-lucky and full of pep. I think that was an asset to his ability.

If there was a better hitter than Ted Williams ever in baseball, I'd have to see it to believe it.

◆ ◆ ◆

PEDRO RAMOS, Pitcher
(Taken from This Side of Cooperstown *edited by Larry Moffi)*

When I was pitching, I didn't want anyone to talk to me. I wanted to concentrate. I didn't like catchers to come to the mound. Clint Courtney, who was a funny guy who'd drink a lot of beer and talk about cows, didn't bother coming to the mound because all he wanted was fastballs. That was no problem except for the day he wanted me to hit Ted Williams. I didn't want to do it. He motioned for the knockdown pitch and I shook him off. Ten times! Then he walked to the mound. He said, "You goddamn yellow Cuban bastard!" Courtney and me were pretty good friends, otherwise I would have told him to get the hell away from me. He said, "Do it!" I said, "All right, get back there, I'm going to hit him." I didn't want to do it because I didn't want to hurt him. You don't hurt a Williams—you need players like that in baseball. I had a lot of respect for him. If I could get him out, why should I hit him? I don't think it's fair. But anyway, I hit him. I busted him right on the arm. The next time up, I fired one in there, and he hit one over the scoreboard. I told Courtney, "See, you woke him up!"

Ted Williams was the best hitter I ever faced. He didn't swing at bad pitches, so you had to throw him strikes. I struck him out only once in my life. I remember when Ted Abernathy, who threw submarine, struck out Williams twice in a game in Boston. He went by me to drink some water and he said, "Pete, I got the Big Man twice." I said, "You better shut up, because the Big Man has to come up at least one more time." Oh, man, in the eighth inning the bases were loaded and the Big Man came up. Abernathy got two quick strikes, but then I could hear Williams christen his bat: he rapped the ball all the

Looking at Ted from an overall perspective, in my opinion he is clearly the greatest hitter that ever lived. He gave everybody a thrill and he did so much for the game. He had a spark. He was more than a great baseball player; he was a major celebrity.

—Peter Gammons,
sports reporter

way into the bleachers. Lavagetto took Abernathy out and I reminded him of what I said. I can't repeat what Abernathy said.

◆ ◆ ◆

STEVE CARLTON, Pitcher, Hall of Fame

With Williams coming to bat during a Red Sox rally, sinker-baller Red Embree was summoned from the Cleveland bullpen. When he arrived on the mound, Embree asked Lou Boudreau if he could pitch low to Ted. "Sure you can," the Indians' shortstop-manager said. "But as soon as you throw the ball, run like hell and hide behind second base."

—George Sullivan,
Boston Herald

I used to see his name on some of the bats that we used. The first thing I remember, though, way back in the '60s when I was pitching, was Ted Williams hitting zone chart in *The Science of Hitting* showing the zones where he hit .400, .350. I figured, Hell, if Ted Williams hits .400 here and .200 there, I'll pitch to the .200 zone. I trained myself, with that type of thinking, to pitch in those zones where Ted could only hit .200 or .250. Other guys would hit much less than that. I just used it in reverse, as a pitcher. Great way to look at it, you know.

I did meet him a few times while I was active. He loves pitchers, you know! [laughter] The dumbest person on the field is the pitcher! And I always thought it was the hitter chasing that slider in the dirt. As good as you are, even if you hit .400, you're still making six outs out of ten. It's all perspective. We were enemies, you know! [more laughter]

We made some small talk a couple of years ago about the slider. The slider's a tough pitch in a couple of ways. You have to make calculations all the time while it's coming at you. We talked about how to hold a slider, what makes it spin a certain away, the aerodynamics of it, the little vacuum area that the spin creates to make the ball break. He knew all of that; he's real up on the aerodynamics of what makes a ball break, the resistance and counter-resistance.

◆ ◆ ◆

JACK BENNY AND BOB FELLER
(Heard on the Jack Benny Show [sometime between 1948 and 1951, courtesy Gregg DeNeui])

Jack is doing his show from Cleveland, Ohio this week. As a result, one of the guests he has on is Bob Feller, pitcher for the Cleveland Indians.

Bob: Well, Jack, how did you enjoy the game yesterday?
Jack: It was just wonderful. That's certainly a beautiful stadium you have there on the shore of Lake Erie. But Bob, there was one thing about the game that puzzled me.
Bob: What was that, Jack?
Jack: Well, when you played Boston yesterday, the Indians only played eight men.
Bob: No, Jack, there were nine.
Jack: No, I counted everyone on the field and there were only eight men.
Bob: Oh, well, when Ted Williams comes up we put our leftfielder in a canoe.

◆ ◆ ◆

HAL NEWHOUSER, Pitcher, Hall of Fame

I hate to lose. Ted was the same way as a hitter. Every time I ever went out to the mound, I always said to myself, "Never give in, and never give up." My idea was when I went out there to pitch, I tried to pitch a perfect game. Every time. And I just would keep talking to myself about it.

Ted was just a marvel. The first time I saw him was in Boston. At that time, we had to come through their tunnel, both teams. I wanted to see him hit. I stood behind the batting cage and tried to get an idea what pitches he had trouble with, whether it was the high ball or the low ball or inside or outside. So I'd have at least some kind of idea. It didn't make any difference!

Hitting in the third spot was just perfect for him. Pesky or Billy Goodman could bunt the ball, or single, so every time Williams came up, if either one of them got on, they had to pitch to Ted. He wouldn't swing at any bad balls. There was no set pattern how to pitch him. I'd ask around the league, as each club came into town, I would say to the pitchers, "What way do you pitch this guy?" One of them said, "No way!" He said he could hit the high ball and he could hit the fast ball.

I always wanted to pitch against the good hitters. The guys who hit .220, .230, they're the guys who hit me, because they protected the plate and they just punched the ball around. When you've got guys like Jimmie Foxx and Williams and DiMaggio—these type of guys made a game of it. I didn't care if Williams was at the plate and the bases were loaded. My standard was, "I'm not going to give up and I'm not going to give in."

◆ ◆ ◆

It was a picture swing. You don't have to be prejudiced about it. He stopped everyone in the ballpark, just with his swing. When he went to bat in batting practice, the whole park got silent as a church. Beautiful swing. Nobody's had it since.

—"Broadway" Charlie Wagner

RED SCHOENDIENST, Ballplayer, Hall of Fame

I can remember talking with Ted when the American League and National League were trading with one another. That spring when we went into Sarasota to play the Red Sox, Ted got a hold of me right away and he wanted to know about this pitcher that was traded from the National League to the American League, to see exactly just what does he throw and what does he throw with two strikes, and how is his control. He wanted to know everything about him. That's what made him such a great hitter. He had to know everything and he studied every pitcher that he ever hit against.

Baseball misses guys like him. The game needs players like him. It was always a great thrill for me to be on the same diamond.

◆ ◆ ◆

BOB HOLBROOK, Sportswriter

When Herb Score first came up, the Red Sox were training in Scottsdale. The Indians were in Tucson. They met in a night game at Tucson. The question was whether the world's fastest pitcher or the world's greatest hitter would prevail. Jesus, Ted went after that challenge like you wouldn't believe. This guy Score could throw, I mean he could really hum it. Ted worked him to 2 and 2. Then he got the next pitch, and hit it. The last time it was seen, it was going over McDill Air Force base, some place on the California border. Oh shit. All he did was chug around the bases. "How do you like that, you son of a bitch?"

◆ ◆ ◆

HERB SCORE, Pitcher

One time near the end of the '55 season, we were playing the Red Sox in Boston, and Rocky Colavito had been called up from the minor leagues. Rocky was a big Ted Williams fan. He really wanted to meet Ted. In those days, Ted had trouble coming out on the field before the games, taking batting practice. The media was always around. We were taking infield practice and I saw him and said, "Ted, there's a kid out there in right field, Rocky Colavito, who would love to meet you." So he waited until the Indians were finished taking infield and Rocky was running in, and he intercepted him halfway to the dugout saying, "Rocky, I'm Ted Williams and I'd like to meet you." That was a really nice touch.

I've never seen a ballplayer who knew Ted Williams who didn't like Ted Williams. I recall the 1955 All-Star Game in Milwaukee. I was overawed watching all these great stars coming across. When Ted Williams came in—Mantle, Berra, all those other great hitters—they all flocked over to Ted's locker to listen to him talk. About hitting.

A couple of years ago we were in Tucson before we started training in Florida and I was sitting in the stands. It was a game we weren't broadcasting and I was sitting down there watching the game. Some fellows were sitting there and one of them said, "Boy, you know the Red Sox played here one spring. You see that green board out there, way out in center field. I saw Ted Williams, he hit one way over that thing and it was still going up when it passed it. Do you remember that?" I said, "Yeah, I was standing right in the middle of that little round circle when he hit it!"

◆ ◆ ◆

ROCKY COLAVITO, Ballplayer

I learned a lot from him, and I passed a lot that I learned from him on to other hitters. The greatest hitter that I've ever seen without question. A lot of times it became a difficult situation, and I know some of the pitchers on his team would get angry because a lot of times after speaking to him, I had a pretty good day. He was helpful. He would help any young person who really asked for it. He's just a terrific guy.

I don't think race or religion ever bothered Ted. I think he took a man for what a man was. I've always felt the same way. It never bothered me what color you were; so long as you were a decent human being, you were okay with me, and I think he felt the same way. To me, he was a wonderful human being and I think that says more to me than being the greatest hitter in the world.

◆ ◆ ◆

RICHIE ASHBURN, Ballplayer, Hall of Fame

Ted Williams put a nickname on me which still has stuck to this day. I could really run, I could really fly in those days. In one of those exhibition games, he put a nickname on me: "Putt-putt." Somebody asked him why. He said, "Well, he runs like he has a motor up his ass!"

He was very good with players, with everybody. That's when he was in his element, with baseball players. He was a superstar, but he didn't act like a superstar. He treated everybody just the same and wasn't standoffish. He would get right in the mix all the time.

The first thing you really notice is the way he hit. There aren't many hitters that players watch around the batting cage. We used to do that all the time. We'd gather around and watch him hit. He had great, great ability but he also had great discipline as a hitter. When he talked about the strike zone, he knew exactly what he could do with pitches in certain parts of the strike zone. I'm sure you've read his book. To me, it's the Bible of hitting. I don't know whether everybody understands it. I think there are a lot of major league hitters who've read it and don't understand half of what he's talking about. In my own way, I knew the strike zone as well as anybody who has ever played. I can really relate

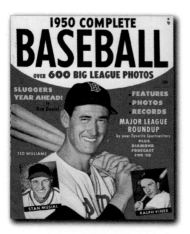

to what he's trying to say in that book. I've always been kind of a disciple of his approach. Still, to this day, it's the best thing on hitting I've seen.

There are so many hitters who swing as hard as they can, to hit the ball as hard as they can, regardless of the count, regardless of where the pitch is. I think a lot of hitters give away a lot of at-bats. I doubt if he ever gave up one! He was quite simply the best hitter I've ever seen. I haven't seen anybody close to him.

I don't know if he'd even remember this, but in the '51 All-Star Game in Detroit, both clubs got into the same room in the ballpark. It was a little early, before anything got going, before anybody could get onto the field and all that stuff. I can remember—he and Stan Musial were talking about hitting, and there were players from both clubs standing around, and you could have heard a pin drop in that room. They were talking about hitting, their approach and what they try to do. To my knowledge there was nobody there with a recorder. Just players. That was the greatest clinic on hitting I've ever heard.

◆ ◆ ◆

FERGUSON JENKINS, Pitcher, Hall of Fame

Every kid wants to watch the All-Star Game and as a kid I saw Ted on television playing in All-Star games. When I got to the major leagues, the baseball-minded people always talked about how tough Ted was on pitchers. They said he had a zone that was like, "You just can't go in there!" Pitchers just could not pitch in his hit zone—that was taboo.

I think that the dynamic thing which kept Ted playing as well as he did was that he played his entire career in Boston. As a pitcher in small ballparks myself—Wrigley Field and Fenway Park—my success was in keeping the ball down, but I know Ted could hit the low ball. Fenway was not a pitcher's ballpark but, being a left-handed power hitter, he had to take advantage of every factor he could. The ballpark was a sanctuary for him—he did his thing and pitchers had to suffer.

◆ ◆ ◆

RALPH KINER, Ballplayer, Hall of Fame

I grew up in southern California. Our high school teams were in the same league. Ted was ahead of me, and his reputation sort of preceded me. But I had heard of him and followed some of his high school feats. Back then, nobody made the jump straight from high school—to go right into Double A baseball was almost unheard of.

In 1948 I was with the Pittsburgh Pirates and we had an exhibition game during the season against the Boston Red Sox. I had built a pretty good reputation in 1947 with 51 home runs and when they came into town, the first thing he did was search me out during batting practice. Now he's pretty enthusiastic. He came charging over and said, "Where's that Kiner kid? I want to talk to him about hitting!" He was intrigued with anybody who could hit, wanted to know if they did something he didn't.

From then on, at All-Star Games and so forth, Ted would ask "What do you think about when you're hitting?" He always wanted to talk about it and he still does that today. He'll put you in situations, "Now the count's 2-and-1. What would you be looking for?" That kind of situational thinking is very unusual. I can't recall any other player ever doing that.

I'll tell you a true story. They had the winter baseball meetings in Phoenix, Arizona at the Biltmore Hotel. Now this is after I was out of playing baseball and I became the

I edged Ted out for the batting championship in 1949. The next year in spring training, some writers and photographers came over to our clubhouse and asked me if I would go over and have a picture made with Williams. I said, "I sure will." They went over and asked him. He said, "No. He led the league in hitting. I'll go over on his side and have it made." That's the kind of guy guy he is.

—George Kell, ballplayer, Hall of Fame

general manager of the San Diego Padres. Ted had just written his book, *The Science of Hitting*. I read the book, and I really enjoyed it. He was there, in I don't know what capacity, with the Red Sox or promoting his book. I was going out to play golf, and I saw him. I said, "Ted, I just read your book and I thought it was one of the greatest books I've ever read. It was *the* greatest book on hitting I've ever read."

He said, "Listen, if you find anything in there that you disagree with, just let me know." And I made the mistake of saying, "You know, Ted, there's just one thing in that book I don't agree with you on. You say in the book that you keep your weight in balance all the time." I said, basically, "Your weight shifts forward onto your front foot and your back foot almost comes up off the ground—at least the heel comes off the ground at some point where the weight has shifted." And he says, "No, no, no, you're all wrong." "No," I said, "Ted, I could show you a thousand pictures of you hitting and your back foot is on the toe, so that means your weight has shifted forward. In fact, Stan Musial and Hank Aaron actually take that back foot off the ground when they hit." He said, "Aw, no. You're all wrong. You've got to stay in balance."

By this time, we're drawing a crowd. We've got about 20 people around while we're sort of discussing this in a friendly way. He knew I played a lot of golf, and he didn't play much golf at that time. I think he was fishing or playing tennis. Anyway, the punch line of the whole thing was, he said, "Oh, you golfers are all alike!"

◆ ◆ ◆

JIMMY PIERSALL, Ballplayer

When I first started, I wasn't hitting very much. He used to say to me, "You catch the ball, I'll get the hits." And he sure did. Every day we'd see how the opposing teams would want to watch him hit. We did ourselves. The only trouble was when I got on first base and he was hitting, it was scary. He would hit those line drives. They didn't have helmets in those days. I used to get in front of Yankee first baseman Joe Collins and stay there. He didn't like that at all.

It's nice to hear people talk about Ted and I say to myself, *I had the good fortune to play alongside of him.* He did exciting things all the time with that bat. When he came back out of the service, his first time up against Early Wynn, he hit a home run. Clinched a win. Fans were coming out every day, just hoping he would pinch hit. They knew he was practicing. He was probably the most exciting hitter of all time. I don't think anybody who played against him or played with him would ever dispute that.

He'd do a good daily routine catching fly balls. He didn't want to look bad because he had pride. But hitting was the name of his game. He went 5 for 5 against Feller one day and he was unhappy because they were all ground balls. He took in extra batting practice after the game. He was such a perfectionist. To do that you have to love yourself, and Ted was in love with himself. Like all your great movie stars . . . they're hard to get along with when they're not doing what they think they should be doing. Or things are not happening the way they want it to.

◆ ◆ ◆

AL LOPEZ, Ballplayer, Hall of Fame

He was an amazing hitter. I managed in the American League 15 years. Nellie Fox, the second baseman on the White Sox, used to play practically out in right field. The shortstop was over on that side too, where the second baseman usually was. We used to

Japanese menko card, 1950s.

give him open shortstop. And we left the third baseman where he was. We didn't want to give him a two base hit, we'd rather give him a single if he hit through the shortstop. That's the shift we used to use on him. Nellie Fox robbed Ted of a lot of hits playing way out there. Nellie was in right field—deep second base—maybe about halfway between the right fielder and the first baseman . . . Boudreau put the shortstop on the side of the second baseman and the third baseman where the shortstop was. Once in a while he'd slice one to left field. I'd rather just give him a hit through the middle than to give him a double.

◆ ◆ ◆

BOB FELLER, Pitcher, Hall of Fame

There's no doubt in my mind that he was the greatest hitter baseball's ever had. There's no way you could throw a fastball by Ted.

They put in the Boudreau Shift at Fenway Park and I know Ted hit one out of the park that day. As he goes by shortstop Boudreau, our manager, he goes, "Lou, you forgot to put anybody up there in the bleachers!"

We were playing over in Cleveland a few days later and our left fielder was in centerfield. Ted purposely hit a ball right down the left field line. The ball bounced around in the bullpen and by the time the left fielder had retrieved the ball and got it back into the infield, Ted was in there at the water cooler taking a drink in the dugout.

◆ ◆ ◆

JOE CAMACHO, Coach

All minor leaguers feel they should have been big leaguers, but I didn't make it to the big leagues until I made it as a bench coach under Ted at Washington.

It's easy for sports people to say great players don't make great managers—well, there are certain exceptions to every rule. Nobody understood the game between hitter and pitcher better than Ted.

Here's something interesting about Ted regarding the shift they used against him defensively. The first year in Washington, maybe the first two, Nellie Fox, Terwilliger and Ted and I, we'd go out to the ballpark early and hit. This was about four o'clock in the afternoon. Terwilliger or I would pitch. One day Terwilliger was pitching and Ted said, "I'll hit every single ball to left field." And he did, no matter where they were pitched. He could hit to left field if he wanted to.

◆ ◆ ◆

PUMPSIE GREEN, Ballplayer
(Taken from This Side of Cooperstown *edited by Larry Moffi)*

Ted was interesting to watch at the end of his career. Even then he was probably the greatest hitter who ever stepped up to home plate. He was probably even better than his reputation. He was Ted Williams, the "best hitter in baseball." And if you didn't believe me, you could have asked him and he would have told you the same thing. He could concentrate so much harder than the average person. If the average player was going to bat four times in a game and got hits his first three times up, he'd be satisfied even if he failed

I've said this to a number of people and I truly believe this, that had Ted Williams played his entire career—uninterrupted—in Detroit, he would have hit at least a thousand home runs. Because of the difference in the distance from home plate to the outfield. It was so much more conducive to home run hitting, for the kind of hitter Ted Williams was. I'm serious! I think he probably would have hit a thousand home runs.

—Jack Harshman, pitcher
eight years in major leagues

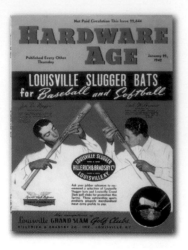

the fourth time up. He'd relax after the third hit. Ted was his most vicious his fourth time up. That's what set him apart. I wasn't surprised when he homered in his last time at bat. He would do almost anything he wanted to do. That was Ted Williams.

♦ ♦ ♦

VIRGIL TRUCKS, Pitcher

I admired Ted before I ever dreamed of coming to the major leagues. When I was playing high school, sandlot and even Class D minor league ball, I always got the sport pages to see what he had done the day before. That was over 50 years ago and after watching him and pitching against him, I haven't changed my opinion. He was the very best hitter I ever saw.

I always welcomed him back each time he returned from war duty, not so much because I liked to pitch against him, but because he was such a great hitter. I just loved to watch him hit, except when it was against me. He sure got a lot of glares from me when he would get a home run. In fact, the record books will show that he got at least 12 of my best glares as he hit that many off me during our careers together. I also called him a few choice names as he rounded the bases. He ignored my remarks.

I can never say enough about Ted, the greatest hitter and finest gentleman I've ever known. He will always be a great friend despite him being my worst enemy when I faced him.

♦ ♦ ♦

JIM PALMER, Pitcher, Hall of Fame

The first time I met Ted was when he was managing the Washington Senators. He was giving a hitting clinic and I remember him telling our second baseman, Davey Johnson—now the Orioles manager—that you need to have a six degree upswing. Davey worked hard on that. He had about 148 different batting stances for the year trying to get that six degree upswing. He'd swing and then ask me, "You think that's six degrees?" and I'd say, "No, it's only about five and a half."

♦ ♦ ♦

BROOKS ROBINSON, Ballplayer, Hall of Fame

It was a day game and there weren't that many people in the stands. I remember that no one knew it was his last game except Curt Gowdy. The time before he hit the home run, he hit a long drive to center field and I think it was Al Pilarcik who jumped up and brought the ball back into the ballpark. Then the last time up he hit the home run and he wouldn't tip his hat or anything. He wouldn't come back out to tip his hat and when the inning was over Pinky Higgins, the manager, sent him out to left field and then took him out of the game just to let everyone give him another ovation.

I was just kind of standing at third base in awe when he came around third after he hit the homer. But I didn't realize the full significance of it at the time, not really, because they still had some games left and I never thought too much about it. I've seen films of that home run and I was just sort of standing there with my arms folded, just kind of admiring it more than anything else. As soon as the game ended I ran into the clubhouse and called my dad to tell him that I'd seen Ted Williams' last home run.

I see that home run all the time, you know different shots when someone's running some old film. I see that shot and really enjoy telling that story more than anything else. When someone mentions Ted Williams, I say, "Well, you know I was playing third base when he hit the home run in his last at bat." It turned out to be one of the greatest thrills I've ever had of my baseball career.

I remember my first All-Star Game was 1960. I was seated near Williams and a fellow named Lew Fonseca, who was a good hitter in his own right.

They were sitting together and they were talking about hitting and about how Nellie Fox could be a better hitter if he stood off the plate a little and not up on top of it, and Williams was talking about how the slider broke 59.6 inches on its way to the plate, and so on . . . and they were talking about all this stuff that I didn't even know what it was. I didn't know what the hell they were talking about! And I'm saying, 'Man, if hitting's going to be this tough, I'm in deep trouble!' I remember listening to them intently even though they talked about aspects of hitting that I never even thought about.

I never took any particular pains to develop my batting. It seemed to come naturally; from the outset, I could always hit. Not like any Ted Williams, of course. I've seen them all, and he was in a class by himself.

—Tris Speaker, Hall of Fame

I think Ted Williams could talk baseball 24 hours a day. They are the only two guys I can ever think of who are in that category.

He takes his role on the veterans committee for the Hall of Fame very seriously. I heard him talking to Joe Sewell one day. Joe Sewell is a Hall of Famer who has since passed away. I heard Joe and Ted talking about players I'd never heard of before—guys with .340 lifetime batting averages. The committee has a lot of stuff to go over and Ted really enjoys that because he has studied all of the great hitters of the game and all of the great players of the game, and probably knows more about those players than anyone I know of. Of all the people on the committee he is probably more aware of what these people have done than anyone else. He knows the game and he knows the history of the game. He started playing in the late thirties (1939) and baseball was a young sport then. There weren't a lot of players before him and he's probably seen 'em all and talked to them all. That's something that I've only read about. I never got to meet all those great players—and he's seen most of them play.

◆ ◆ ◆

WADE BOGGS, Ballplayer
(Taken from The Techniques of Modern Hitting *by Wade Boggs and David Brisson)*

It happened my senior year at Plant High School in Tampa, Florida. Pitchers were pitching around me, and I was walking a lot. I didn't think that was fair, and I felt frustrated and started swinging at bad pitches. Soon, I began grounding and flying out and found myself in a terrible rut. Then, dad gave me a copy of Ted Williams' book, *The Science of Hitting*.

Ted's book was inspirational. It reinforced what Dad had always said about patience at the plate, and I got myself back on track. The second half of that season I managed 26 hits in 32 at-bats. A few weeks later, I was drafted by the Red Sox in the seventh round, I signed my first pro baseball contract, and I began a six-year journey to the big leagues.

◆ ◆ ◆

PAUL MOLITOR, Ballplayer

You can imagine my nervousness as I prepared to attend the BAT Awards dinner in New York City in January 1994 to receive the Bart Giamatti Award. After all, I'd be joining Sandy Koufax, Joe DiMaggio and Ted Williams at the head table—three distinguished men I'd never had the privilege to meet.

As I walked into the room set aside for head table guests, I noticed the three men sitting together conversing. When Ted Williams caught my eye, he leaped from his chair, headed directly toward me and began talking to me about my swing. I was so overwhelmed that I don't recall a great deal of the conversation, other than that he described my swing as a "haul-push."

I do recall thinking to myself, *Here's the greatest hitter in the history of the game and he wants to talk to me about my swing.* Needless to say, it was one of the most memorable nights of my career—and it didn't even take place on the field.

◆ ◆ ◆

BRADY ANDERSON, Ballplayer

I always wore #9 because of Ted Williams, growing up with this image in my head: thinking about him walking down the street saying that when he grows up all he wants to hear is that he was the greatest hitter who ever lived. I read his books, *My Turn at Bat* and his hitting book *The Science of Hitting* . . . I used to read *The Science of Hitting* before every game in A ball.

He was my spring training hitting coach in 1986 and '87. He asked me to swing a little bit. And he said, "Now I'd like you to swing a little more up." And I said, "But I want to swing level." And he said, "Well, look, you had 19 doubles, 12 triples and 12 homers last year"—whatever. He says, "Did you do any damage on the ground?" He goes, "All your damage was in the air."

Now, nobody will ever tell you to hit the ball in the air but Ted Williams. Nobody. And I said to him, "Mr. Williams, I've read your book a hundred times and the first thing you say is don't let anybody change you. And that was the best advice you ever got, by Lefty O'Doul." And he said, "Good. You've read my book."

◆ ◆ ◆

JENNIFER ETTINGER, Artist

Through my art I explore the mythology and need for heroes. I believe that we need to have people to emulate in order to make us better at whatever we try. I have always admired Ted Williams for his determination, his passion, and for his honesty when evaluating other ballplayers.

In my painting of Ted, I wanted to capture that moment when all his practice, passion and determination were halted momentarily until he was visually reassured of his success. I wanted to paint the moment just before the great hit: that instant when his mind and body were waiting to verify that they had worked perfectly together. That seemingly long and quiet moment for a hitter holds for me the essence of baseball.

◆ ◆ ◆

The scientist at work.
(Photo courtesy of AP/ Wide World Photos)

BOB UECKER, Ballplayer, Broadcaster

Q: Ted always says the toughest thing to do in sport is hit a baseball. Do you agree?

A: Yeah, I think it's the toughest thing to do in sports but how would a guy like Williams know how hard it is? He was one of the purest hitters in the game. It was easy for him. They oughtta ask a .200 hitter like me how hard it was. It was REALLY hard.

Q: Ted Williams batted .344 lifetime, with 521 home runs. You batted .200 with 14 homers. Explain the difference in your career stats.

A: He took time off for the war to rest. I didn't have that opportunity. I had to stay and play. I got tired.

Q: Did you ever read Ted's book, *The Science of Hitting?*

A: No, I never read any books on hitting. That's pretty obvious, isn't it? I got my hitting advice from Percy Kilbride and Marjorie Main (Ma and Pa Kettle.)

Q: Compare your hitting style with Ted's.

A: Our hitting styles were similar in that we both used a bat, we both wore spikes, and we were both in uniform—most of the time. I was more of a choke hitter—Ted was down at the end of the bat and I choked every time I was up there.

Q: As a young ballplayer, Ted's goal was to walk down the street and have people say, "There goes the greatest hitter who ever lived." Did you realize your baseball dreams?

A: After my career, I didn't walk down streets. I walked down alleys.

◆ ◆ ◆

One time I was on the mound and there was a two-strike pitch where I thought I had him. I told the umpire, "This guy doesn't need four strikes. He only needs two." He got a kick out of that. He knew more about it than the umpires did. He knew the strike zone well.

—Bob Lemon

PHIL SILVERS, Comedian

Phil Silvers once saw Ted walking down street.

"Hey Ted," he yelled, "I hope you get a couple of hits off Whitey Ford today." Ted kept walking.

"Hey, Ted, I think you're the best hitter there is in baseball today." Ted kept walking.

"Hey, Ted, I made more money than you last year."

Ted then turned around to see who it was.

[True story, told by Jeffrey Lyons' dad.]

♦ ♦ ♦

WILLIE McCOVEY, Ballplayer, Hall of Fame

Sparky Anderson, he always walked me. He would pass the dugout before the game and put four fingers up, to indicate to me that he was going to walk me. And one game in Cincinnati, he actually proceeded to do that. The first two times up he put me on intentionally. Third time up he ordered the pitcher to kind of pitch around me but I knew it was an intentional walk, and as a matter of fact on the fourth pitch I kind of reached across the plate and hit a weak ground ball to third base because I didn't want to walk. My fourth time up, I came up in the top of the ninth inning and he gets up on the top of the dugout steps and hollered "Put him on!" Of course I'm the type of guy, I never really got angry, but that was the one day, I got so frustrated and I yelled over in the dugout and said, "Who in the hell do you think I am, Ted Williams?"

♦ ♦ ♦

ALVIN DARK, Ballplayer
(From When in Doubt, Fire the Manager *by Alvin Dark and John Underwood, p. 39)*

. . . . there really were guys who would have played for nothing, and not just the ones who deserved nothing. I went to watch Ted Williams take extra batting practice at Fenway Park one day . . . I watched him hit, that beautiful textbook swing come to life, then went inside and chatted with him while they were working on his arm. You could tell he loved to talk hitting. He had nothing but a towel around his waist, and all of a sudden he jumped off the table and started demonstrating. It wasn't play acting, he was THERE, in the batter's box, really grinding. He said, "You know, I HATE THAT PITCHER. THAT NO-GOOD S.O.B. ISN'T GOING TO GET ME OUT. I'll KILL HIM FIRST." That's the way he talked, and that's the way he played.

♦ ♦ ♦

BOBBY DOERR, Ballplayer
(From The Storytellers, *pp. 66, 67, about an event in 1939)*

We were in St. Louis (Sportsman's Park) to play the Browns. Their manager was Fred Haney, who I played for in the PCL in 1934, and we was tough, really tough. The Brownies dugout was on the third-base side and you had to walk through their clubhouse to get to ours.

I saw Fred and came over to talk to him, but he saw Ted, too. Without saying anything to me, he stared Ted in the eye and said, "I've seen how well you hit. Let's see how you hit sittin' on your ass."

When the game started, the first pitch to Ted was right near his ear and knocked the big guy down. Ted got up, didn't even dust off his uniform, took his stance and on the next pitch, drove it against the right field screen for a double.

The next time up, the first pitch knocked him down and on pitch two, Ted drove it onto Grand Boulevard for a home run. That was that, and it epitomizes Ted's career; he did that countless times. He was the greatest performer in the game and no one ever got the better of him on the battlefield.

◆ ◆ ◆

JIMMY PIERSALL, Ballplayer
(Why were Boston fans so tough on Ted?
From A Bittersweet Journey *by Rick Phelan)*

Jimmy Piersall explained: They were tough on him, but you know why? They sort of sensed that when they got on him, he played better. He hit better. Ted used to say to me when I got mad about something, "I'll take care of it, kid. Don't worry." He used to talk through his teeth when he got mad. I said, "Ted, why are you getting so mad all the time." And he said, "You know why? Because I've got to be good every day. You don't."

◆ ◆ ◆

BIRDIE TEBBETTS, Ballplayer

Now I love Ted Williams. We played against each other before the war, and after the war we found ourselves teammates on the Red Sox. This one day after a game with Cleveland when Lou Boudreau had hit us pretty good, Ted Williams walked by my locker and said, "You're a nice guy, Birdie, but you're a dumb catcher." I just looked at him, wondering what was coming next. He just kept walking. Now on that afternoon Lou Boudreau hit line drives that had sent Ted Williams chasing all over left field, and Ted must have thought it was my fault for calling the wrong pitches. He brought it up the next day while we were standing by the batting cage and I said, "OK, Ted, if you're so damn smart, you call the pitches." Right there we worked out some signs so that when Boudreau came up to bat I would look out to left field and Ted would signal me. He would put his hands on his hips to signal a fastball, or touch his cap for a curve, or hands on knees for a change-up, something like that.

Now there are two endings to this story: the one Ted Williams tells and the one I tell, which of course is what really happened. What actually happened is that the first two times Boudreau came up, Ted called the pitches and Lou hit two doubles to left, which Ted had to chase into the corner. The third time Lou came up, I looked out to Ted to get the sign but he had turned his back on me and was facing the Big Green Monster, I think out of shame. So I walked out toward the mound and yelled, "You lose your nerve, Ted?"

In his ending of the story, he claimed I crossed him up and changed every one of this calls to something else. But I honored out deal, and that's my version of the story, and I'm sticking to it.

◆ ◆ ◆

I honestly believe Williams could have hit me in the Holland Tunnel in New York at midnight with the lights out.

—Vernon "Lefty" Gomez, quoted in the *San Diego Evening Tribune*

From Brothers K

By David James Duncan

“ If a strike zone is just a shape in an ump's head, which it is, then there ought to be ways of climbing inside that head and tinkering with the shape. Which there are. Pitchers of course want to expand the zone. Hitters of course want to shrink it. Either way, this ability to reach into an ump's gray matter and distort his whole strike concept, this is what I'm calling voodoo.”

Obeying an impulse, I casually said, “I don't believe in it.” I was lying. I not only believed, I was enthralled. But listening to Peter's stories I'd often noticed that the more skeptical Everett or I pretended to be, the more powerful his stories became. So I said, “If it's real, name somebody. Name one guy who really uses it.”

“Williams,” Papa said without hesitation. “Unquestionably, Ted Williams. The greatest voodoo hitter of our time.”

After Cobb the Demon, Gehrig the Cherub and Ruth the Dumb Deity, Williams the Curmudgeon was my favorite ballplayer. But I kept playing the skeptic. “How?” I demanded. “Tell me how he does it.”

“Any big crowd-pleaser,” Papa said, “any Mantle or DiMaggio or Mays can pull off a little voodoo at home games. Ump calls a strike on the corner, hometown hero turns and gives him a disgusted look, and all hell breaks loose. Strikes called on heroes aren't what the fans pay to see. And the fans are a factor, Kade. They're scary when they're roused, believe me. Where hometown voodoo backfires, though, is when the ump is stubborn. And lots of 'em are. Fans start raggin' a muley ump, he just gets pissed at Mr. Hero for showing him up and calls 'em even meaner.”

I nodded and switch hands; I'd been stirring the Dutch Boy so long I had cramps. “Ted Williams, though,” Papa said, “was anything but a hometown hero. He had a coolness, a remoteness, that people mistook for arrogance when he first came into the league, and the fool Red Sox press, even the fans, managed to despise him for this. It was just small-minded nonsense. What they were booing was his concentration, after all. And Williams concentrated so well he didn't give a damn about the press or fans. But after a couple seasons he realized that the hometown dislike was robbing him of the ump intimidation that creates hometown voodoo. If he was ever going to enjoy the advantages of a hitting hero, he was going to have to come up with something a lot more ingenious than the Disgusted Hometown Stare, see? So now listen to what he did!”

Papa paused at this point, put his palms together in front of his nose, and rubbed them so hard and fast it looked like he was trying to generate friction and set his face on fire. It was one weird gesture. I'd no idea where this one came from. “First off,” he went on, “Williams always understood a crucial fact. He knew that it's by working with what we're given that we get really good at a thing. Our natures, our character, the way we feel at gut level, this stuff is unchanging as the color of our eyes or hair or the shapes of our bones, is what I think. And since slobbering crowds and fawning reporters only distracted Williams from his job, which was crushing baseballs, he went right on snubbin' 'em. Do you follow?”

I nodded.

“So where does following his nature get him? It makes him some nasty enemies in the stands and the press box, that's for sure. Those enemies cost him at least two MVP awards. But down on the field it keeps him loose, lets him live for his hitting, wins him a reputation as a player's player and a real no-nonsense guy. And—getting back to the voodoo potential—it also earns him nothing but respect from every ump in the league. Because, believe me, umpires hate fans as much as fans hate umps.

“Fine and good. Next Williams strings together a couple great years at the plate, so that the sportswriters, much as they detest him, have to start begging him for interviews, because the fans, much as they hate him, are dying to know what makes the arrogant creep tick. But Williams sticks to his guns: he slams doors at reporters, slams line drives at the clucks in the bleachers, and leaves it at that. But writers have to write something, don't they? That's their nature. So they start winging it. They start making things up, churning out legends—Williams the Recluse, Williams the Crank Scientist, Williams the Genius, Williams the Unsung Hero—till first thing you know he's baseball's answer to Greta Garbo. And of course once this happens the writers forget all about their old dislike: they'd cross Boston on their knees to get an exclusive with the mysterious Splinter. And seeing all this, sensing the time is ripe, Williams finally strikes . . . "

Papa tried and again failed to ignite his nose. "One bleak Boston's winter day Mr. Theodore No-Nonsense Garbo Splinter Williams finally grants some overjoyed worm of a writer an exclusive audience. Just asks the guy over, sets him down in his comfortable chair, lets him fire away with the questions. Of course the dolt starts off with the usual: 'What's your favorite breakfast cereal?' 'Who do you like for President next election?' 'What's the meaning of life?' 'How long's your weenie?' and so on. But Ted's a fisherman in the off-season. He knows how to be patient. He sincerely and scientifically answers every query but the last. Then out pops the question he's been waiting for: 'How the heck do you hit so good?'

"And it's voodoo time, folks!

"No-nonsense leans back in his chair, looks as sincere and scientific as ever, and says, 'Well, I study the pitchers very closely. My mechanics and my bat speed are good. And I've got good concentration. But listen . . .' And he suddenly swoops down and stares, like the hungry old owl he is, deep into the journalist's little mouse eyes . . . " (Papa swooped down and stared into mine.) "And he says, 'Everybody knows that there are quick wrists and slow wrists, but not many know that there are quick and slow eyes too. And my eyes . . .' (Papa did some eyebrow push-ups, to let me know that these were the voodoo words) 'are the key to my hitting, they're my secret weapon. Because my eyes are so quick that I can see any pitch, even a fastball, all the way in to where it jumps off my bat . . . '"

Papa stopped just long enough to squeeze back a laugh.

"Well, Kade, the writer is just voodooed. Nobody has ever said anything like this! Hell, Ty Cobb hit .367 lifetime, and even he admitted that a good fastball was a blur and that every swing he ever took at one was just an educated guess. But not No-Nonsense. Not Theodore. He sees the whole pitch, clear on into and off his bat! So the writer humps it home to his typewriter, bangs out his story, flashes Williams' astounding speed secret to the world. And when the umps (who already admire the dust Williams spits on) pick up their morning papers, they think Jeepers creepers, what peepers! and buy it lock, stock and barrel."

Papa shook his head, and finally let his laugh fly. "That's all it took, Kade! When the next season rolled around, Williams found his strike zone was damned near anywhere he wanted. The inside and outside corners had vanished. Every ump in the league had became his personal Wally MacCloud. Because what ump would dare contradict the baby blues that saw in a fastball not a blur, but a hundred and eight scarlet stitches on four fat white cheeks? That was voodoo, Kade. One well-placed fib, a lot of fan-snubbing, and Ted Williams puts together maybe the last .400 season we'll ever see. If World War II hadn't eaten his next three seasons, his career average and slugging percentage would've been right up there in the Next World with Tyrannosaurus Cobb and the Sultan himself. No doubt about it, Kade. Williams' eyesight was good, but his voodoo was downright splendid."

6

The Kid and the Kids

Whatever else may be said of him, Ted Williams always loved kids. To them, he was "Teddy Ballgame," the man who took time out to tousle their hair, autograph their gloves, or critique their swing.

Baseball in Ted's time, probably even more than today, was a game with a powerful hold on the young—and Ted was baseball personified. Young fans would wait for hours outside the ballpark hoping for a chance to get his signature on a scrap of paper. It was a ritual that served as a convenient excuse to confront the great man, to spend a few seconds in his company without awkwardness. Ted knew it and they knew it. Of course the autograph also accorded the recipient certain bragging rights back in the neighborhood. Resale value never entered into it.

Ted never lost touch with his feelings for kids, and even today he'll light up and make his way across a room to say hello to a youngster, no matter how many VIPs may be waiting in line to greet him. When the kids were made vulnerable by illness or physical misfortune, Ted's generosity knew no limits. Stories of his kindness to the less fortunate can be found in every corner of Boston. People all over the city seem to have one, although precious few were recorded by the media. Typically these stories involve Ted, resembling some splendid but splintery Santa Claus, complete with a duffel bag of caps, balls and bats, entering a hospital via the back doors and proceeding to the bed of a sick child.

Ted's mother worked for the Salvation Army. It was not only her life's work, it was her life. Her extended family included the unfortunates of San Diego and Tijuana and they often got more attention than sons Ted and Danny. Perhaps as a result of his mother's high-profile approach to charity work, her son took a decidedly low-profile approach. Ted demanded privacy as the one condition for his personal visits to hospitals and clinics: no photographer or reporter could be present. It's a mark of how successful Ted was at preserving the integrity of his personal relationship with these children that even his beloved Jimmy Fund, celebrating its 50th anniversary in 1997, has in its files not one photograph of Ted Williams visiting children at the Jimmy Fund clinics.

Nancy Cummings of Bangor, Maine meeting Ted outside a Providence, Rhode Island hospital in 1946.
(Photo courtesy of Nancy Cummings Carr and Tim Samway)

Although his visitations were strictly private, Ted understood that to be effective he must publicly lend his name and fame to fund-raising for children's cancer research. As a result, the Jimmy Fund could just as accurately be dubbed the Teddy Fund. Ted was that instrumental in its growth and success.

ARTHUR SAMPSON, Sportswriter, Author
(From a speech given in support of the Jimmy Fund, mid-1950s)

Theodore Samuel Williams can still remember how blood dripped from blistered hands and sweat poured from the brow of a penniless San Diego kid less than 20 years ago as he strove to overcome weaknesses to lift him over the countless roadblocks in his path.

And it is this retentive memory which drives this baseball star constantly through the hospitals, settlement houses, and playgrounds of the country brightening the eyes of kids over which a shadow has been momentarily cast for one reason or another. To these youngsters, the best possible stimulant and inspiration is Ted Williams.

◆ ◆ ◆

TED ON TED:
TRIBUTE TO THE JIMMY FUND AND TO TED WILLIAMS
by Senator Edward M. Kennedy

I still remember the excitement and the awe of meeting Ted at the 1953 Statler dinner honoring the Jimmy Fund and welcoming Ted's return to the Red Sox from his service in the Korean War. I still remember being impressed by Ted's filmed appeals for the Jimmy Fund shown just before the main feature at countless movies in Boston and on the Cape.

I know about the Jimmy Fund's miracles first hand, because the Dana–Farber Cancer Institute and their cutting-edge chemotherapy treatments saved the life of my son Teddy a quarter century ago, by preventing the recurrence of the disease after he lost his leg to cancer at the age of 12. Two out of three children now leave the Jimmy Fund free of cancer.

◆ ◆ ◆

DONALD NICOLL, Consultant

"The first kid I visited in Boston, a boy named Donald Nicoll, was dying of a stomach disease. I got a nice letter from his dad, saying they were fans of mine, asking me to visit the boy . . . . I still see the family. The boy made a great recovery . . . . An awfully nice boy."
—*Ted Williams (in* My Turn at Bat*)*

He used to call me Melon Head. He came to visit me once or twice subsequently at the hospital, and then came to our house for dinner when the Red Sox were playing at home. I had an open invitation to go to ball games. The usual routine was to meet him at the hotel and then go over to Fenway Park with him, go in and hang out and take an open seat.

One of my most vivid memories was a discussion about forearm strength when he came to the house in 1940. He took a heavy, upholstered living room chair by the front leg with one hand and lifted it off the floor. I remember being impressed by that. And I remember him doing it with a kind of boyish enthusiasm.

He kept in touch with my folks over time. He came to visit after he and Doris Soule were married. After the war and up through the late '40s they were in regular touch. Obviously his record as a ballplayer and the public attention lavished on him was larger than life but in terms of the relationship with the family, it was always as a friend. There was never an entourage, never the trappings of being a famous person. I think one of the things that probably made him enjoy keeping in touch with my folks was that they really didn't make demands on him. They treated him as an individual, unrelated to his career.

◆ ◆ ◆

THOMAS SEESSEL, Executive

I was nine years old when Ted came to call on me in Chattanooga in the spring of 1947. The major leagues were much more a remote thing back then because television wasn't widespread. So I followed through the newspaper and occasionally on the radio when we could get a game.

Back then, when the players broke spring training to come north to start the season, they would barnstorm their way up from Florida and stop along the way back to play exhibition games. The Red Sox were on their way back to start the '47 season, and they had a game scheduled in

Ted Williams with Donald Nicoll, 1939.
(Photo by Mary Nicoll, courtesy of Donald Nicoll)

Chattanooga. I'd been looking forward to this for a long time, because Ted was my hero.

It was a complete sellout but my dad had gotten tickets and we were all set to go. And then I got the flu and was told to stay in bed. It was a huge disappointment!

My father happened to see Ted Williams on the street that very day, before the game. Now my father was a salesman. He stopped, approached Ted and told him the story. He could sell anything, so he sold Ted Williams on getting into a car in a strange city, with a strange man, going God knows where.

All of a sudden, into my room walks Ted Williams! I used to get all the baseball magazines so there was no trouble recognizing him. What made it interesting was that he was regarded by some as a misanthrope who would hardly give anybody the time of day. His actions really belied that reputation. He sat down and we talked for a little while. I forget how it came up, whether he offered or whether I asked for him to hit a home run for me that day. But he did.

◆ ◆ ◆

BUD BLATTNER, Broadcaster
(Taken from The Storytellers *by Curt Smith)*

Diz[zy Dean] and I went to Boston to televise the Red Sox on Saturday and Sunday. We arrived Friday night and met at the Kenmore Hotel, where Ted lived. He learns we're there and comes down from his room. I mention to Ted that earlier in the week I'd visited a hospital in the Midwest and met one of his biggest fans, a little boy suffering from leukemia, about 10 years old. The nurses loved him. Each day in the corridor, they sat him on the floor with a little wooden bat and got on their hands and knees and rolled a ball to him. He'd hit it, and as it rolled they exclaimed, "Oh, that's a double. That's a triple. That's a home run." If it was a homer, it was hit by Ted!

The little boy's room was filled with Williams memorabilia, and he asked me to say hello to Ted. I'm leaving when the nurses corralled me in the hallway and asked if I could get the young man an autographed ball or cap from Ted. I said, "No problem," and now let me tell you about a side of Ted Williams that you don't know about. He tells me in the bar, "OK, Bud, all right, fine. I'll tell ya what I'm gonna do. I'll fly in and see this boy"— he flew his own plane—"but on two conditions, and I mean this sincerely. I want to be met at the airport by the boy's mother and father ONLY. Any media or other gathering, and I'll just touch down and then take right off again." The second condition was that we were never to mention it on the air.

One of the most heartwarming stories of my broadcasting career, and I couldn't tell it. The young boy died later in the year, but he enjoyed the greatest day of his life: a visit with his hero.

◆ ◆ ◆

ARTHUR DALEY, Sportswriter, Author
(Taken from All The Home Run Kings by Arthur Daley)

The Boston Red Sox had just lost a game they had no right to lose. They had dropped a squeaker on a couple of flukes and they were so mad that they wouldn't even talk to each other, much less to strangers. And the strangers awaited outside, a mob of fans on the sidewalk. They left a narrow lane from clubhouse door to the bus which was to take the Bosox to the airport.

The angry players were so blinded by rage that they didn't see the autograph hounds. If they saw them, they ignored them as they brushed through into the bus. And then came Ted Williams, just as mad as the rest of them. Impatiently he shook off the pesky fans and leaped for the bus door. Suddenly he stopped.

"Will you help me, Ted?" said a trembling little voice.

"What do you want, kid?" said Ted, voice harsh but eyes soft. The boy was crippled and was holding an autograph book. Williams snatched it and jumped into the bus.

"Listen, you baboons," he bellowed. "Everybody sign."

The Great Man went down the aisle, collecting autographs from every member of the squad. He walked back to the door of the bus and shoved the book at the boy.

"Here, kid," growled Ted. "Now beat it."

He waited for no thanks. But he got them nonetheless in the ecstatically happy look of the proudest and most grateful little boy in Boston.

Theodore Samuel Williams is a strange one. His personality is so complex that even high-powered psychiatrists would have trouble in finding out what makes him tick. He can charm a bird out of a tree or he can antagonize people, depending on his mood. If he had not been so stubborn, he would have won over those fans who rode him unmercifully. He wouldn't even try.

But one section of the populace which thought he was the greatest was the young. Ted never was able to resist the kids and his love of children was genuine. There's no way of calculating the good he did for the Jimmy Fund.

◆ ◆ ◆

An evening with Ted Williams! What a thrill! My memories of Ted go back many, many years. Back to the '40s when I was a kid growing up in Little Rock, Arkansas. Never had seen a big league baseball game but I knew the game of baseball. Knew the history of the game. Read the books. My idols of that time were Ted Williams and Stan Musial. Then to sign professionally in 1955 and to have the chance to play against Ted Williams. To be a teammate of Ted Williams in two All-Star games. Those were the real thrills.

—Brooks Robinson, ballplayer, Hall of Fame

TED WILLIAMS: THE PURSUIT OF PERFECTION

Campers at the Ted Williams Baseball Camp. Williams is seated in the front row center next to assistant Joe Camacho. Ted's old friend and camp coach Roy Engle appears in the back row, far right.
(Photo courtesy of Roy and Ann Engle)

SHELBY WHITFIELD, Head, ABC Radio Sports
(*Taken from* Kiss it Goodbye *by Shelby Whitfield*)

Williams has seemed so much larger than life to people around him that over the years he has accrued comic-strip name tags. Maybe it was because he was the biggest presence around. People were awed at his storybook feats as a player, but his actual six-foot-four size always seemed to stun them on a first encounter. His voice could blast out a dugout, too.

Williams has been called The Kid, The Splendid Splinter . . . and Thumpin' Theodore. The players on the Senators usually referred to him as Number Nine, his uniform number, or just plain TW. His good friend and fishing buddy, Jack Sharkey, often calls him Chowderhead, and Johnny Pesky . . . lovingly calls him Bush. And a Florida Keys pal, fishing guide Jack Brothers, pinned the name Grumpy on him.

But Teddy Ballgame is his favorite. He loves to use the term to refer to himself in the third person. He got the nickname in his playing days when a Boston photographer asked his young son which ballplayer he wanted to meet that afternoon at Fenway Park. "Why, Teddy," the kid said. "Teddy who?" the father asked. "Uh, Teddy . . . Ballgame!" the boy replied. Ted loved the youngster's inspiration and he's used Teddy Ballgame ever since.

♦ ♦ ♦

LEE KAPLAN, Lighting Technician

My dad was a freelance photographer. He worked for Black Star for most of his career and did a lot of work for *Sports Illustrated* and *SPORT*. He grew up in Boston, living fairly close to Ted. Just idolized Ted, and the Red Sox.

Little Lee Kaplan shows "Teddy Ballgame" his swing.
(Photo by Fred Kaplan, courtesy of Lee Kaplan)

Dad loved photography and started pursuing it, shooting from the stands and sending in pictures. Eventually, he got a couple of assignments here and there, and got established. He was still just a kid himself when he called out to Ted from the stands, and eventually visited him a little bit in the neighborhood, got to know him.

My dad told me about how I gave him the "Teddy Ballgame" tag. We were hanging out in Ted's Boston apartment just before a game. I was antsy. I just wanted to go to the ballpark and watch the game.

My father asked me, "What's the matter? Where do you want to go?"

"I want to go to the ballgame."

"Why?"

"I want to see Teddy play."

"Teddy who?"

I said, "Teddy Ballgame."

I read that nickname fairly frequently when I'm back east. I've always been disappointed—most people out here [California] don't even know it. "The Splendid Splinter" is his main one. I guess it happened right at the end of his career, so it wasn't really a nickname that existed during his heyday. I knew it was something special—one that he liked.

◆ ◆ ◆

DAN VALENTI, Writer
(Taken from From Florida to Fenway*)*

My first recollections of baseball came in the early to mid 1950s, through the personage of Ted Williams. He made the kind of news that even a boy of three or four couldn't help noticing. Even living in the Berkshires of Massachusetts, 130 miles west of Boston (to a child 150 light years) did not dim the colossal presence of Williams. I didn't quite know who or what he was, what he meant, or even if he was nothing more than a figment of Curt Gowdy's imagination. Ted was something like my conception of God: most loved him, others hated him, some doubted him, some seemed ready to die for him. But he existed because grown-ups talked about him. For little Dan Valenti, that was enough.

◆ ◆ ◆

RAY TEIXEIRA, Fan

Having grown up in the '50s in a Revere housing project just north of Boston, there wasn't much chance for me to go to very many baseball games. Radio and TV were the outlets to my passion for baseball. The Red Sox in those days were a 2nd division club and by July there was little hope for them. Ted gave me hope. I remember waiting until what seemed like the middle of the night to hear his last at bat coming over the radio from KC—just knowing he'd park one. And many of those nights he did. I knew every stat, the value of his next hit to his average, how many hits he had in his career with each at bat. In my eyes there's no question he was the greatest striker of the baseball that ever lived. I had all his cards memorized. Knew his height, weight, birthday, home town, minor league history, on and on.

Ted was always the guy I wanted to be in stickball. I feel very lucky to have had this bigger than life guy to cheer for back then. I feel sorry for today's kids who only have a hero for the length of his next contract.

◆ ◆ ◆

Ted and Roger Engle, Ted Williams camp, 1963.
(Photo courtesy of Roy and Ann Engle)

LOU GORMAN, Vice President, Boston Red Sox

As a youngster growing up in Providence, Rhode Island, Ted was my all-time hero. I followed him through his whole major league career. He was probably the most charismatic hitter that ever played the game. Even if the club was behind by five or six runs, if Ted had one more at bat, you didn't leave the ballpark. You wanted to stay to see him hit one more time.

I had the pleasure of playing in the Hearst All-Star Game in Fenway Park when I was a kid. Harry Agganis played with the Boston All-Stars at first base and I played on the New England All-Stars at first base. The Red Sox players came up during the game. Ted sat next to me on the bench. It was like sitting next to God. I think I was 16 at the time.

Of course, later I was with the Red Sox as the general manager for ten years and Ted worked with us during that time in the minor league camp. I had a lot of conversations with him, spent a lot of time with him talking about players. The Mike Greenwells, Ellis Burks, Brady Andersons we had coming up through the system. His knowledge of hitting is just awesome. It's almost like a scientific mind discussing hitting. He's so knowledgable about picking up flaws in hitters, or noticing things that hitters don't do well. Even, for example, of telling them they're using the wrong bat, wrong weight, wrong length, the mechanics of their swing. He had a great mind.

Ted was always close to the Yawkeys and the ballclub. John Harrington, a few years ago, got him a satellite dish down there so he can pick up all our Red Sox games. He'd call me when I ran the club and talk about the team, about the players . . . make suggestions. Now he calls Dan Duquette.

Ted at a Jimmy Fund fund-raiser in Rhode Island.
(Photo courtesy of Dorothy Lindia)

When you look back on the history of the Red Sox, nobody stands out any more than Ted Williams. You had Cy Young, Jimmie Foxx, Bobby Doerr, and Carl Yastrzemski, but Ted seems to be the most preeminent figure that ever played in Boston. He's just a legend.

He used to want to have John-Henry be a ballplayer, and he'd have John-Henry down there and put him in a uniform. I don't think John-Henry had too much interest in it, and all of sudden he'd disappear somewhere and be off. To live up to the image of his dad would be impossible, to want to be or attempt to be another Ted Williams.

◆ ◆ ◆

GEORGE MYATT, Ballplayer

I never knew Ted to turn down a kid for anything, any time. I've never seen him turn a kid down for an autograph. He'd go to a hospital or a school, help out a group of kids or just one individual.

He was a good guy. I don't know how the home and visitors dressing rooms are now at Fenway, but they used to be side by side behind first base. My oldest son thought the only ballplayer in the whole world was Ted Williams. So on his birthday, it happened we were playing up in Boston at that time and I took him in with me to see Ted play. I was with Washington at the time. Ted took him in the clubhouse and talked to him, introduced him around as his buddy and everything. First time he'd ever seen him. He gave him a bat and he gave him a glove, out of his locker, something he used. It wasn't just one out of the rack.

Another time when we were playing Boston in spring training out here, I told my young son Mike, "Bring out some of your Cub Scout friends." Try to get some of your pictures taken with Ted or Bobby Doerr or any of the guys. So I talked to Ted and asked him if he would come down to the fence to have his picture taken with my son. He said, "Oh, sure, sure." So he come out after a little while. He come over to the third base dugout where I was standing, and he looked up in the stands. Mike was sitting with his Cub Scout group, and I had pointed him out before he went over. So he looked up there and he said, "Hey, Mike, you little rascal, come here. I haven't seen you for a long time." Mike comes to the fence, and the kids, all their eyes are sticking out. All of them had cameras and were taking pictures. Ted reached over and picked up Mike in his arms and pulled him over the fence and carried him around a little while and then set him back with his friends. Boy, everybody was going crazy for Mike. Mike was a real big shot, he got to touch Ted Williams.

The first time I took Mike to Fenway Park was on a holiday or a Sunday, I don't remember which; it was a doubleheader. You know how they wash down the stands with a hose. There are still these places early in the day where the water would stand before it would dry out a little bit. Mike had a brand new white suit—first time he ever had it on, to go to the ballpark. The gate where the teams and all the employees would come in, then, was in left field. You'd come right in the stands up there. The hotel where we stayed was right across the street, a block away. All the ballplayers just walked to the ballpark. As we walked into the stands, I pointed down and I said, "Right down there is where Ted plays." It excited him so much, he lost his balance and slid right down the stairs. Slippery, dirty stands. Ted had an effect on kids.

◆ ◆ ◆

The best tipper in the game was Ted Williams, always a buck a day when few players tipped a buck for a series. He was a great guy, distorted by the press which played up and played on his anger. He was excited about history, and he'd spend afternoons at the museums, but he never forgot us.

—Scotty MacDougal, Senators batboy 1958-59

JOHN DONOVAN, Former Batboy,
later Executive Vice President and Counsel for the Red Sox
(Taken from Innocence and Wonder *by Neil Isaacs)*

When I started in the clubhouse I was elated and awestruck, being around Johnny Pesky, Bobby Doerr, Birdie Tebbetts and Ted Williams. I was too overwhelmed to let anything shock me. When the Red Sox won the pennant in '46, Filene's was giving camel's-hair coats to the team. The tailors came to the clubhouse to measure them and Williams wanted the kids taken care of. They're not on the list, the tailors said (one of them was the father of Eddie Pellagrini, by the way.) Williams said, "Take care of the kids, then you can measure me." You know, I still have that coat.

◆ ◆ ◆

JOE CARRIERI, Yankees' Batboy
(Taken from Searching for Heroes *by Joseph Carrieri)*

During my first year with the Yankees when I was the batboy for the visiting teams, Ted Williams broke his bat during a game. He left it up to me to run back to the dugout and pick another one out of the rack for him. When I brought it out in front of a big crowd at the ballpark, he looked it up and down, and then nodded his head. That's recognition. If I could do that for Ted Williams of the Boston Red Sox, I knew I could do it for Joe DiMaggio on the New York Yankees.

My recollection of Ted Williams is that he was a left-handed Joe DiMaggio. He was tall, thin, strong, quiet, and manly. My clearest memory of him was as the visiting batboy in 1949. I was playing left field in batting practice. I was 13 years of age and a ball was hit way over my head. I ran and ran with my back towards home plate and before I knew it my nose hit the left field fence and I was knocked to the ground in a daze, close to unconsciousness. The next thing I remember was a big strong man with muscular arms picking me up and saying, "Are you alright, kid? Are you alright, kid?" I was hurting real bad but I looked at him and said yes, that I was fine and then delicately continued to play left field during practice.

Ted's act of kindness will always be part of my memory.

◆ ◆ ◆

TOM MacDOUGAL, Washington Senators Batboy
(Taken from Innocence and Wonder *by Neil Isaacs)*

I liked the Red Sox because I idolized Ted Williams, the greatest ever. On their last trip in, I said to him, "I'd like to have something to remember you by." He took off his hat and handed it to me without a word. I remember sitting next to him in the dugout during the second game of a doubleheader, and he put his arm around me. He didn't like writers or fans who were always pressuring him, but there was an aura about him, and players treated him special. When he spoke, everyone listened. I'd get the key to the gate through the tunnel so Ted could leave the ballpark the back way and avoid fans, and I'd watch his silhouette walking across the field. He'd always greet me with "How're you doing, kid?" but once, instead of "kid," he said "Thanks, Tommy," and I got chills.

◆ ◆ ◆

JOHN BOGGS, Sports Agent, former Senators Ball Boy

It could be pretty intimidating for a ball boy because he was bigger than life. There were a lot of managers and players who passed through that clubhouse but he just carried himself in a different way. There was this really big kid named Chuck Boatner who they used to call Groceries. One time he was trying to look through the blinds of Ted's office and Williams came up behind him and said "Is that son of a bitch in there?" He just jumped! It was the funniest thing in the world.

I'll never forget he signed a ball for me "To John, Your pal, Ted Williams." I just read somewhere that Babe Ruth did that too. Being Tony Gwynn's agent, I've got hundreds and hundreds of baseballs signed by guys but that has always been my most prized possession just because of the "Your pal."

Ted invited Tony Gwynn to Florida to receive an award in 1995 when the Hitters Hall of Fame wing to the Ted Williams Museum was opened. When we first got the invitation, I was ecstatic, but Tony is not big on dinners or recognition so here we are flying and Tony said, "There'll probably be a million people there and I'm going to get some award and probably see Ted Williams for about two seconds." But out of respect for Ted Williams he absolutely was going to attend. That first night, there was an outdoor dinner and cocktail party, and it was freezing. There were a million people asking for autographs and everything, and Tony was just shooting me glances. He says, "Yeah, I got to see Ted, shook hands with him inside the Museum, and that was it."

The next day, the ceremony goes off and it was very nice and Tony was impressed with everything, but as we got into the limousine, he says, "Come on, let's go now. We

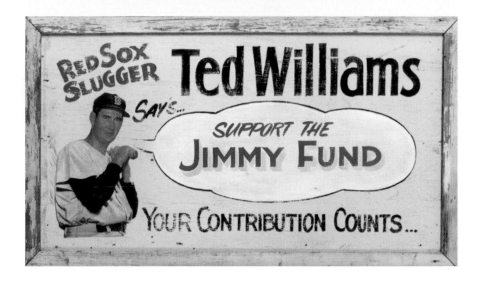

might be able to catch an earlier flight back to San Diego." "No," I said, "Come on, let's at least be seen at this luncheon to pay our respects."

The next thing we know, Bob Costas's producer called and said we'd like you to do an interview right now with Ted. We looked at each other and said, "Yeah, great." We went back there and it was Costas and his producer, the cameraman, technician, President Bush, Ted Williams and Tony. And I'm sitting there thinking, "Man, this is unbelievable." President Bush left and Tony took the President's seat, and they started talking. And I am telling you, it was like the student and the pupil. You could tell that Tony wanted to relate his batting theories when Ted was asking the questions, but always had this hesitancy that he was going to say the wrong thing. You got this sense of relief every time Ted would say, "Absolutely!" And then Tony would expound. Being a great moderator, Bob Costas would throw out a question, and then Ted would talk, and then Ted and Tony would start conversing—without even a question being posed to them, going over all kinds of different baseball scenarios.

Afterwards, Tony was absolutely bubbling. He said, "That was worth the entire trip! Just to be able to sit there and talk baseball with Ted Williams was the greatest thing in the world." We laughed and laughed. He said, "I can't believe I'm so nervous. I do this as a profession. I mean, I'm pretty confident in what I do. You just want to say the right thing." All the years I've represented Tony, I've never seen him like that. Usually he's holding court. He said, "I would have flown to the moon if I'd known I was going to have that opportunity."

And you learned a little more about Tony, too. Tony said to Ted, "Man, it's funny sitting here talking with you because I had your book (*The Science of Hitting*) when I was a kid with all the different red dots and everything, and the zones." They were laughing about that. Tony just said that he really felt he had captured a piece of history. He was still talking about it during spring training and well into the next season.

◆ ◆ ◆

JOE CAMACHO, former Baseball Director
of the Ted Williams Camp

I was always a Red Sox fan, living in this locale; I always liked Ted. Our high school team won the Tech Tournament they used to have in Boston, and we got a trip to Washington. The Red Sox were there for Opening Day, and one of our assistant principals got us tickets. Ted hit one of his longest home runs. We were up in the bleachers and he hit it over our heads about forty rows up.

I was a principal at an elementary school in New Bedford and they asked me if I would be the Baseball Director at the Camp. We had kids from all over the country who came to the camp, ages 8 to 18. And Ted naturally was actively involved. His greatest attribute was his tremendous enthusiasm. We used to take kids from camp to play the Norfolk Prison inmates, and he'd question the warden about what they liked, what they didn't like, as far as food is concerned. He thought of everyone.

♦ ♦ ♦

STEVE FERROLI, Founder of the Ted Williams Baseball League

A guy named Earl Matheson was working as director at the camp and he kind of cornered Ted and said "You've got to talk to this kid, this kid is just of out of his mind. He talks your technique hook, line and sinker. He knows you better than you do." And of course that sparked Ted's interest.

You have a staff meeting before the camp opens and Earl Matheson was going over what to do and what not to do—how a summer camp works. All the fundamentals. Then he gets to assignments, and some they handed out, and some were up for grabs.

He said, "Who wants the little league batting cage?" Everybody kind of chuckles because in a summer baseball camp, the little league batting cage is the place where the hardest thing to do in sport gets taught to little kids at 85 degrees all day long. No one wanted that. To me, as a physical education major and as a hitting guy and as somebody who was really into it, I thought that I could have died and went to Heaven. I shot my hand up to beat everyone else and there was open laughter in that room. In about three weeks, I could not go anywhere without about 20 or 30 kids following me. And they were getting results.

There's this huge cafeteria at the Ted Williams Camp, and one side holds about 300 kids, and the other about 50 coaches. So I'm 21 years old, and I had just met him the day before, and he had shook my hand and ironically said to me, "Oh, you're the hitter." I just said, "Well, I put my time in." And that was probably a good answer. I remember shaking his hand with my right hand, and then pinching myself so I wouldn't spaz out or something. So he says, "We'll talk, me and you. I've heard a lot about you and we're gonna talk." I was thrilled but I thought this will never happen.

So I come in the next day, and he says, " Alright, you wanna talk hitting, let's talk hitting, whattaya got?" I had gone back to my room and made up a list of 25 questions. I had no pockets in my cutoff sweats and I had literally put them in my underwear in case I had a chance to talk to the greatest hitter of all time. If I didn't have that paper I was dead, because I'd go blank. I had read about him so much, and I had so much respect for him. I pulled the paper out and opened it and he looked at me funny, sort of half smiling! And then he liked me. He was like: *Shit, this kid's ready, he's prepared.* I said, "Did you stride the same way on a curve ball as you did a fast ball?" He goes, "No, I did not. That's a good point." And he gets up and demonstrates. "On the breaking ball I get back here just a little bit more, just a little bit back there more." And we talk about delay things a little bit. That wasn't in his book, and I tore that book apart.

That was a good start, and I became a lot better after that comment. Then I said, and this is classic, "If the count is 3 and 1 and you're looking for the fast ball and you get it, but

Williams and Steve Ferroli, director of the newly formed Ted Williams baseball league.
(Photo courtesy of Steve Ferroli)

you get it in a tough spot, would you swing at that pitch or would you go into a two strike situation?" "Jesus!" he said, "No one's ever asked me that before . . . . that's a hell of a question, and I'll tell you the answer to that, buddy. Who's the guy out there, who am I facing? Now if it's Feller, I'm going for that three-one pitch, because I'm not going two strikes with him. But if it's somebody else who's not so tough, you know, then I'd maybe wait for something better, and go to a two-strike situation." He was impressed with that question, and that's a great question, it really is—do you give it up, do you go to another thing, or do you hit away at three and one? And I had a bunch more.

Sitting there like this, I asked him every question on the page of paper and he answered every single one. He was as excited about it as I was. And you know if they weren't good questions it would have been, "Don't waste my time." But I had him, I had his interest, he was with me, he was in it, he loved it. I knew it and that made me comfortable after those first two sentences. I was like, *Boy, this is like being out with my best buddy from the neighborhood.* And that's the feeling I had about him. Then we hit a lull and he says, "All right, I gotta go!" I get up and I'm right behind him and we pass by this classic picture there of him hitting one and the umpires looking up. He stops, and I stop behind him. And he kind of drifts off, and he's looking at it and says, "You know, I'm gonna tell you something and I don't tell very many people this. But on most of my home runs, I was three-quarters of an inch up the bat." And then, "See ya!" No dismissal, just gone. Not a half inch, not an inch—3/4 inch! That says it all, doesn't it? Who says 3/4 of an inch? Who?? You gotta love it!

Another time I'm sitting with about three or four other college players, and he comes in the cafeteria, sits down at the table and he says, "You know, Ferroli, I went to the plate X amount of times, and I hit X amount of singles, and X amount of doubles, X amount of triples, and X amount of home runs, and every goddamn time I tried to get the ball in the air—but you know, I made more outs on the ground." Now when he said that to me, of

*Emmet Nowlin, young fan
of No. 9.*

course, everybody else looked down like, *Huh? That doesn't make sense.* But I knew the answer, I knew why, and I said back to him—and God, when I think about this I can't even believe I opened my mouth, but I was a young, cocky kid, and I was a nice kid. My dad didn't raise any wimps, you know? And I said, "Well, geez, you know, I have a theory about that." Oh my God—he looks at me, and I said, "The baseball is a white sphere, and the lighting source is always above, whether it's cloudy or under the lights, or a bright sunny day and the sun is coming down—the light is coming down and therefore the top of the ball is brighter than the bottom of the ball. And when you speed that up, 80, 90 miles an hour, the bottom of the ball becomes almost invisible, and therefore you have a legitimate optical illusion.

"You attack the top of the ball and top it down. I think what you were doing was hitting the top of the ball because of a legitimate optical illusion." Now no one had ever stated that. Maybe some of the great old-timers knew it, but I was the first one to put it on paper in my book. And I said the ideal swing is a slight upswing when the hitter is think-ing under the white, 'cause that's where the middle of the ball is. I'll tell you, he looked at me—I will never forget the look he gave me—he looked at me like he loved me and like he hated me at the same time.

And he goes, "Well, that makes sense." And he didn't stay long and make conversa-tion, he left. I think he was irritated, because someone had said something that he hadn't thought about and it made perfect sense. So now, you can see how our relationship built.

Here's my thing. I'm 16 years old, and I can throw like hell, and I got a good attitude, and I got some ability, and I'm a good basketball player—I'm a decent athlete, you know? But I'm not that good a hitter—a .270 hitter. And this kid Ronnie Disbrow is better than me. We're playing on the same freshman basketball team, and he hits the ceiling in a game. This is the kind of kid I'm talking about—nice kid, great kid—but he just didn't have it. I'm the second highest scorer and he can't throw it in the ocean! And yet in baseball he's a .400 hitter and I'm a .270 hitter. I'm wondering why.

Come to find out, Ronnie Disbrow's father played double-A for Cincinnati, and Ronnie Disbrow's father is showing Ronnie Disbrow how to do some things at a young age, and he's a good hitter, technically. And right there, I said boy, *how* you do something is so important, maybe as important as what you're born with. Then I made the trip to the library, and I get *The Science of Hitting.* At that time Ted was just a name on things: Ted Williams fishing rods, tents, it was all over the place. Ted Williams, Ted Williams, Ted Williams. To me he was just a pimp, he was somebody that my grandmother said spit at the fans who loved him. I mean I was Yaz, and Tony C, Bobby Orr—not Ted. Ted was for my dad!

So that's how I saw him as a kid. But I go to the library, and I open the card catalog: Hitting, *The Science of Hitting*, Ted Williams. Oh cripes. The next card I go to, different subject. One book!

I never really knew what Ted looked like, I hadn't really registered his body type or his face, and I see that classic book with the stripes on it, and I look at him, and he's tall and big like me. Not like George Brett or Yaz but kind of big and lanky like me. So I start reading the book: *Hitting a baseball is like swinging an ax into a tree, but most players don't understand that or haven't even thought about it.* I'm not even reading it, I'm flipping through it and I'm giving him the benefit of the doubt. But remember, while I'm reading this book, I don't like him. He just wasn't cool, so to speak. He was John Wayne, not Clint Eastwood. So, I get my best buddy, Scott Mottau—I say, "Scottie, throw me a few balls." I stand nice and easy you know, I just go like this: (BOOM) Holy shit! This is the best thing about teaching—if you're good you can get a kid's ego to take over, and that's what happened to me. Out of a book! Bam! I saw that ball go and I said "Throw me another one," and I just kept hitting them. That summer I hit .355 with eight home runs. My whole life changed. Ended up being a .400 hitter in college one year. Out of a book, this guy gave me the greatest excitement in my life. Think of that—it's beautiful!

Ronnie Disbrow didn't know what a hitter I was. I caught him, passed him, and buried him, because of Ted Williams. And guys I played with on my high school team that were way more talented than me, I buried them. They never got as far, never were as good, and they'd sit right here and tell you they could never hit like Steve Ferroli, when in reality they were way better than me, they just didn't know what they were doing. They didn't have that book. And I got hooked, just like the Atlantic f------ salmon!

Think of all the kids that are losing interest in this great game because they don't know these things. It's just a shame that more people don't understand what Ted Williams did as a hitter. That's what I get upset about. I've taught so many kids. I've done some nice work and I'm proud of that. But without Ted Williams, I'm a gym teacher! Think how big he was, to say I'm going to take this mongrel kid with a lot of enthusiasm, and I'm gonna stand behind him.

Artwork by Catherine Prime

◆ ◆ ◆

BILL NOWLIN, Fan

Both my father and Ted were splendid splinters. My dad was 6'3", weighed about 139 pounds, and had this wavy black hair. He knew just about everything and, while he certainly didn't play for the Red Sox, that somehow didn't stop me from making the connection. My father was also in the war, though we weren't supposed to ask about it. Something about being in Intelligence, and North Africa, and a plane crash. I never did ask, until the 1990s.

Ted was 6'4", skinny as a kid but stronger than my father, I now realize. How the two got bound up together, I don't know. Probably a kid's need for heroes. To believe that someone has it all together. That there is something good, something excellent, something consistent, in the universe which you can rely on and emulate. I hope to be a good father to my own son Emmet. I'm not sure there are any Ted Williamses around, though, in today's world for him. Maybe that puts more of a burden on me.

◆ ◆ ◆

MORT LEDERMAN, Manager of General Services for The Jimmy Fund

In my 45 years at The Jimmy Fund, I've met everybody from Muhammad Ali to President Reagan to Prince Charles. Ted impressed me like crazy because he was a very sincere, no bullshit guy. He was really dedicated—a very bright, articulate gentleman. He didn't thrive on publicity; it didn't mean anything to him to look around to see who's watching.

I'm 6'2", and Ted Williams is 6'3". My job is to meet these people and when I got on the elevator with John Wayne, he looked like a big, towering ghost. He was the biggest man I've ever seen. I was the only one there to see John Wayne come up to Ted Williams and when Ted put out his hand and said, 'I'm Ted Williams.' John Wayne said, 'Heard about you, boy.'

◆ ◆ ◆

```
Thank you for
joining the
Jimmy Fund
team.
```

Ted

MIKE ANDREWS, Executive Director, The Jimmy Fund

No one is more synonymous with the Jimmy Fund than Ted Williams. The impact he has had is tremendous. He wasn't one of those celebrities with a lot of demands. He became the spokesperson, and it gave him something outside of baseball that he could attach himself to—and did he ever! Today he is still as interested in giving as he was as a player.

In my opinion his great accomplishment—outside of his ability to hit a baseball—is what he has meant to the Jimmy Fund.

◆ ◆ ◆

A vital, glowing Kate Shaughnessy, age 10, appeared late in the evening of December 15, 1995, at a dinner held at Boston's Park Plaza Hotel and read Ted Williams a poem he will never forget. The dinner was a "black-tie" event to honor Ted and the launching of the 406 Club for The Jimmy Fund in Boston. Each member of the 406 Club pledges $5000 to The Jimmy Fund.

After tributes from Bob Costas, Doris Kearns Goodwin, David Hartman, Larry Doby and others, Kate took the stage, introduced by her father, Boston Globe sportswriter Dan Shaughnessy. Two years earlier, Kate and her family learned that she had leukemia. When Ted began fund-raising for The Jimmy Fund in the late 1940s and early 1950s, the diagnosis would have been a near-certain death sentence. Thanks largely to research at the Dana-Farber Cancer Institute, parent organization for The Jimmy Fund, the recovery rate is now over 80%, and Kate is one of the fortunate children who have benefitted from these tremendous strides in cancer treatment.

A POEM TO TED
By Kate Shaughnessy

Ted Williams is a really, really great guy.
He really likes kids, but he hates wearing ties;
He won two Triple Crowns and was the MVP twice,
He feuded with sportswriters, but to kids he was nice.
521 homers, he's in the Hall of Fame,
He's The Kid, The Thumper, and Teddy Ballgame.
He would do anything for the Jimmy Fund,
And I'd like to say thank you, for all that he's done.

DAN SHAUGHNESSY, Sportswriter, Author

Ted's son, John-Henry, happened to be trying to reach me about a business venture, at the time my daughter was in the hospital. I returned his call and said I'm not going to be able to do anything right now, and here's why. Within 10 minutes, the phone was ringing in the hospital, in Kate's room, and it was Ted.

Kate knows nothing about old-time baseball stars. She held the phone a few inches from her ear and said, "Daddy, there's a loud man on the phone, telling me I'm going to be okay." She passed the phone to me and Ted Williams bellowed, "Dr. Farber used to tell me, 'Ted, we're going to find a way to cure these kids.' Sure enough, he did it. You tell your daughter she's going to be fine."

It's been a nice thing. *Sports Illustrated* ran the poem. She was in *SI* before I was. She loves baseball. She played on the softball team this spring.

Since then, Ted always asks me, "How's your daughter?" The Jimmy Fund had the poem, they did some sort of a plaque-type thing, where the poem was stenciled in there and she signed a note to him. He has it hanging in his house somewhere. He always tells me that he looks at it every day and he's inspired by it. He's so generous about that.

Ted with Tip O'Neill and John Glenn at a Jimmy Fund event in 1988.
(Photo courtesy of Phil Ayoub)

It always struck me what a miracle that I would devote my life to covering sports, and baseball, and this charity that we've all known about all our lives would end up having such an enormous impact on my own family.

I'm 43 and have been aware of The Jimmy Fund since my earliest days. It was just something we all knew. Ted's very humble about it and doesn't make a big deal out of his brother or any of that stuff. There was just something about it that was important to him. And if you talk to Pesky or any of them, they make a big deal out of it, about how giving he was about that. He was a real sucker about that every time.

I was just so proud of her. I was more nervous than she was. I look at the video now and I was shaking and quivering up there, and Kate just banged through it. After reading the poem, Kate left the stage and walked to the table where Ted was seated, to shake hands. Ted did most of the talking. She told him what grade she was in. He told her, "Oh, you seem like you could be in sixth grade. You seem a lot smarter than that, you know. Tell your dad, OK?"

It was just a very touching, wonderful thing. It was a real treasure for us. I'll show the video to those relatives who will sit through it. Kate and Ted Williams. Three minutes. My heart goes out to him. I'll always be indebted for what's he done, and for the cause.

Today, Kate's where they want her to be. I always knock on wood. She's in remission. The margins are so much better than when we were kids. It's really one of those deals where modern science is remarkable in saving lives. Ted, of course, was a huge player in all of that.

◆ ◆ ◆

THE DAY I MET THE SPLENDID SPLINTER
by Ted Janse
Reprinted by permission of Health Communications, Inc., © 2001

My autographed Ted Williams baseball sat in my work drawer for more than 20 years. I was quite unprepared for the day I opened my drawer and discovered that the prized possession had been defaced! There, in bright, bold indelible ink, my three adorable daughters, ages ten, eight and five respectively, had left their collective mark: "Carl Yastremskee Rules," "Your Pal Looe Tiant," "Babe Ruth Was Here," and other random scribbles.

It felt like someone had just pierced my heart. I was furious. If ever there were justification for punishment, surely defacing an autographed Ted Williams ball would qualify—especially with The Curse of the Bambino! As I tried to control my temper, I called for my daughters, and thought back to the day I met Teddy Ballgame . . . .

I was just 12 years old in 1948, but remember the event like it was yesterday. My mother mentioned that Ted Williams' wife, Doris, had her hair done at the same salon. "He lives at Lucille Place," my mother casually mentioned, as if it was no big deal.

Ted Williams was my idol. I followed his appearance in every game and could quote his daily batting averages and RBIs. I got into heated arguments with anyone who tried to tell me there was a better player, and even got into one playground fight with a kid who said that Johnny Mize was better.

I chose a Saturday morning, grabbed a clean baseball and rode my J. C. Higgins bike uphill almost all the way. I told no other kids what I was doing. I knew that Mr. Williams could be difficult with the press and his critics, but I also knew that he liked kids. I hoped he wouldn't mind the intrusion.

I parked my bike outside of his house, baseball in hand. As I stood at his front door and rang the ball, my knees were knocking. What would I say? Looking down, practicing my speech, I saw the door open. I looked, up, up, up, and there he was, standing there, a giant of a man, smiling at me, a strange kid with a baseball in hand.

"P-p-pardon me, sir. I was wondering if you could sign my baseball for me?" I stammered.

"Sure," he said. "Come on in!"

"Come on in!" He said, "Come on in!" I was in Ted Williams' hallway!

"Would you like a Coke?" he asked.

"No. No, thank you, sir," I managed to say. I was still in shock.

"How do you like the baby?" he asked, pointing to the adjacent baby carriage.

"Oh, he's alright I guess," I blurted out. (I later learned the "he" was, in fact, a "she.")

Mr. Williams laughed at my lack of gender sensitivity and signed my baseball. Then he walked me to the door and wished me good luck.

"Th-thank you, Mr. Williams," I said, still in shock.

The bike ride home that day was magical. When I reached my house I ran in to tell my parents about my adventure. They were hardly amused. Face red and arms waving, my father warned: "Don't you ever tell anyone what you did today, or they'll never give him any privacy. Do you understand me?"

"Yes, sir," I said. And I kept my promise.

My mind returned to the present as I looked down at the now-colorful baseball in my hands, and up at the sheepish faces of my three artisan-daughters who stood before me. I realized that to them, Ted Williams was an unknown. In fact, the whole mystique of baseball was void in their world of Barbie dolls and fingernail polish.

I realized then that my girls needed a lesson about baseball: the joy you feel on opening day; the exhilaration you get when you hit another player home; and the kindness shown by a baseball idol who invited a kid in for an autograph.

"Want to know who the first person was to sign this ball? . . . "

♦ ♦ ♦

I was like a kid in a candy store. When he was talking, I was like a little kid. He was the teacher, and I was a kid. But I hung in there and made a few of my points, talked about how I do it. That was clutch. That was worth the trip.

—Tony Gwynn, Ballplayer

Other Lures, Different Strikes

When Ted retired from baseball, many observers assumed he would be miserable. After all, his entire professional life was devoted to perfecting the art of hitting a baseball. For him, hitting perfection was the Holy Grail, and what, the conventional wisdom demanded, could possibly replace such an all-consuming quest? What could substitute for this grand obsession?

Fishing, that's what. Ted Williams single-handedly destroyed the popular image of the fisherman sitting dozing on the shore with a six-pack at his elbow. For Ted, fishing was no passive pursuit. He brought the intensity of the batter's box to the fishing hole. He attacked the "hobby" the way he once attacked a 3-1 fastball.

Fishing and hitting require subtlety, attention to detail, an eagerness to learn. On the surface both seem entirely inappropriate for a man of Ted's temperament. And yet Ted exhibited the same patience with a rod and reel that he once showed at the plate. Granted, it was an aggressive brand of patience.

Ted loved all kinds of fishing, but he especially loved his battles with the Atlantic salmon. For him, Salmo salar is a mystical fish which as an adversary has no equal. He pursued it for four decades with an almost religious zeal. He studied the fish, charted its moves, learned its likes, dislikes and habits; he kept records of water and air temperature. He rated the effectiveness of certain flies and tied those flies with the touch of a surgeon. He poured over his records like a monk deciphering manuscript.

Ted regularly stood for hours waist-deep in the Miramichi River, only to release his eventual catch. He became an outspoken conservationist, ruffling some political feathers in the process, and once threatened to take his own life if anything were to happen to the "fightingest fish, pound for pound, in the world."

Opposite: Ted with catch.
(Courtesy of Dorothy Lindia)

Fishing TIPS from TED

HOW TO IMPROVE YOUR CASTING
...and Other Helpful Hints

by *Ted Williams*
CHAIRMAN, TED WILLIAMS SPORTS
ADVISORY STAFF

SEARS
ROEBUCK AND CO

Courtesy of SEARS, ROEBUCK AND CO.

FRANK McKENNA, Former Premier of the Province of New Brunswick

There will never be another hitter as gifted as Ted Williams. The rock-solid concentration, picture-perfect swing and elegant style will never be cloned. He was the perfect ballplayer. Everybody knew it.

I knew it, growing up on the farm in Apohaqui, New Brunswick. Like most Maritimers we had deep roots in the "Boston States." Most of our relatives lived there and most of our interests in baseball centered around the faith of the Boston Red Sox.

I can recall spending night after night with my ear pressed to an old radio hoping that the fickle ionosphere would cooperate in getting the Red Sox game to me. Sometimes the signal was crystal clear. Other times very garbled. Nevertheless, it became a passion for me to follow the career of Ted Williams. Nothing excited my passion as much as hearing the roar of the crowd when Ted Williams, Mickey Mantle, Stan Musial and other legends of baseball came to the plate.

With Ted Williams you always knew you would get a superb performance. He had a dignity, a grace, a presence that cannot be put into words. All of the assets that make a good baseball player were captured in one uniform. He was the Boston Red Sox. He was baseball. He was my hero!

I later came to know Ted Williams as an avid salmon fisherman. It was with a sense of astonishment that I discovered his passion for fishing rivaled his passion for baseball. It was with even more astonishment that I discovered that his passion for fishing was centered on the Miramichi River in the Province of New Brunswick. The Miramichi became my home as well and I continued to enjoy the legends of Ted Williams. He was renowned as a fisherman on the Miramichi. He became a close friend of many Miramichi outdoorsmen. He was known in the fishing tackle shops and the local community. He was respected and admired—not as a great baseball player but as a great salmon fisherman.

He also became closely associated with the conservation of the species. To me that is not surprising. A mighty talent like Ted Williams would recognize the majesty and the grandeur of the proud Atlantic salmon. He would recognize that it represented perfection in its own milieu and was worthy of our respect and support.

◆ ◆ ◆

SAMMY LEE, Director of National Promotions for Ranger Boat Company

The first time I met Ted, I interviewed him for a syndicated radio show that I produce on fishing. We spent the day at his home in Hernando, Florida, talking about his fishing travels around the world. Later that same summer, I accepted an invitation to Ted's home on the Miramichi River; we fly-fished for five days.

When I went to visit him on the Miramichi, I had never fly-fished in my life. Had never held a fly rod. I went out and bought what was recommended to me and I thought it was great equipment. I thought I had everything. I went out and got a custom pair of waders, the whole deal. Then I get up there, and the first afternoon we're sitting on the front porch, and Ted says, "Well, I guess you want me to help you rig up, don't you?" I said, "Well, I would appreciate it, since I don't know what I'm doing." He looks at my equipment and says, "Oh, My God! Where'd you get this stuff? Oh Jesus! You won't catch a minnow with this stuff!" Immediately, he jumps on my equipment to see how I'm gonna rebut him, you know. I said, "Well, it was recommended to me." He says, "Well, whoever recommended it has never fished for Atlantic salmon, that's obvious! Oh, my God! I'm going to have to loan you some of my equipment!" Ted does that because if you take offense to it, you're dead. You have to throw it right back at him: "Well, I was going to catch them on bass tackle, but I was afraid I would embarrass you." You get the idea.

Anyway, the first morning that we're planning to go to the river, I head to the cabin, I get my equipment, I get my waders, and I come back over. I'm getting ready to put everything on and he says, "So where do you think you're going, kid?" I said, "I'm going fishing." He says, "Oh, no. You have not earned the *right* to get in *my* river. If you're as good as you think you are, you're going to sit on the bank and see if you can learn something. This afternoon, when we come in, I'll see if you've picked up on enough things to earn the right to get into my river." God almighty. That's a pretty bold statement. Sure enough, I spent four hours sitting on the river bank taking pictures of him. Listening to him: "You see what I'm doing here, kid? Why do I have my elbow here? Why am I casting like this?" I mean, he's constantly asking questions. Well, finally, that afternoon he lets me get in the river. And then he walks out there with me, to show me the casting technique. He spends maybe ten or 15 minutes. Then it's "Aw, I can't stand this! You're crucifying me! Oh my Gosh, you're the worst thing. Why did you spend your time to come up here? I'm going to sit on the bank. Let's see if you can practice. Listen, start casting and start working down this river."

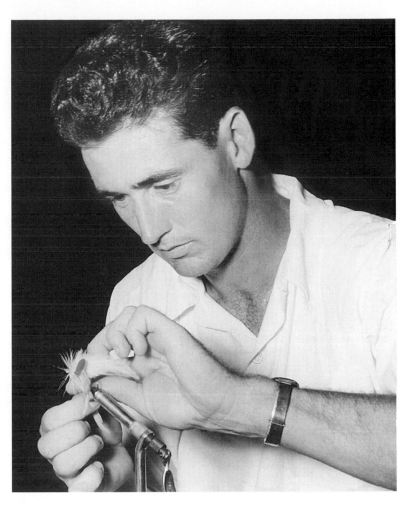

Ted enjoyed tying his own flies, and could talk for hours about the lore and mystique of fly fishing. He has written that "Half the thrill of salmon fishing for me is tying my own flies." (Photo by Fred Kaplan, courtesy of Lee Kaplan)

So in the meantime he goes back up on the bank and he's sitting up there with Clarence, a guide friend of his, and another gentleman who had driven up to visit him. The three of them are just kind of chatting amongst themselves. Mr. Williams is just constantly screaming at me, "Elbow up! Elbow in! Cast higher! Oh my God! Not so far on the back cast! Come forward!" I'm just listening to this stuff and I'm thinking, *God, it's got to be easier than this.* And I'm working down this stream bed, like he's asked me to. Remember, until that point in time I had never once fly-fished, had never even been in a free-flowing stream or river. So I get to a rock, and I think, "Well, I'll just step over it." As I raise my foot, the current catches me, and I go ass over teakettle, straight upside down. My waders fill up with water. At this point the only thought in my mind is, *I'm fishing with his rod and reel,* I'm thinking, *If I let go of this rod and reel, I'm dead meat. I will drown with this rod and reel in my hand, but I will not let go of it.* So here I am, trying to regain my balance, full of water, looking like a drowned rat. But I come up and I've still got the rod and reel in my hand. I never turned back to look at him. I just started back casting, but I could hear him in the background, "That's good for you! Everybody needs to be baptized in the Miramichi! Keep fishing!"

My times with Mr. Williams, on the Miramichi . . . . We were sitting on the front porch one afternoon. I was interviewing him for some radio show and I kind of made mention—because it's so peaceful up there—I said, "This Miramichi means a lot to you,

doesn't it?" He said, "You know, I've traveled all over the world. I've been to nicer places, I've been to better fisheries. But this place is home." It meant so much to him. Now, because of his health, he can no longer go up there. I don't know if I can relate that to the loss of a loved one, but I think it's quite similar. Even today, when we chat, he'll reminisce about the times he's had on the Miramichi, even more than the time that he spent in Islamorada. Islamorada, it seemed to me, was more like a highway of folks coming and going constantly. When Ted got to Canada each year, it was his retreat. A place where he could be left alone.

Williams takes a lunch break with a favorite fishing guide, Louis St. Germaine. (Photo courtesy of Tom Hollatz)

In the summer of '91 Ted went on a fishing trip to Russia with a few friends of mine: Bobby Knight, Charlie Hoover and Jerry McKinniss, who hosts the ESPN outdoors show called *The Fishin' Hole.* The first series I did with Ted was on this trip to Russia.

Jerry McKinniss sent me a copy of the videotape that they had done in Russia. I assumed when I sat down with Ted that he would spend the majority of the time talking about the fishing. Instead, he spent most of that interview talking about the places that he saw, and the Russian people. Everybody I've visited with—from the cameraman to Jerry McKinniss to Charlie Hoover—they all said that he got along better with the Russian people than anyone in the group. He would go out of the way to shake hands with the people, to try and have a dialogue with them and communicate. He was so in awe, I guess, and had such respect for those people to be able to survive the way they do. He really, really enjoyed that trip. I asked him a couple of years ago, if he had the time, would he do it again? He wishes now that he had spent more time touring the Russian republics than he had fishing.

Jerry McKinniss and Bobby Knight are best friends, have been for a long time. It was because of the respect and admiration Coach Knight and Jerry held for Ted Williams that they pursued getting him on the trip. Here's three of the most famous sports people in the country in their respective sports [basketball, baseball and fishing] and Jerry said they couldn't go anywhere—from New York across the Atlantic all the way to Russia—without somebody on the plane, somebody in a restaurant, somebody in the terminal, somebody knowing Ted Williams, and not knowing who these other guys were.

I want to tell you that, in the last six years, my admiration, my respect and my love for the man has grown to the point that he's like a member of my family. I go down and see him five to six times a year. He still loves to fish. A lot of people don't realize that his stroke has debilitated him to the point that it's difficult for him to function like he used to, and it's difficult for him to fish. But he will go fishing with me sometimes, in some of the pit lakes in central Florida, and he will sit there and critique me. His son likes to say that a Ted Williams critique is like getting a hot poker shoved up your backside. It's one of those things where he's saying, "You call that a cast? Aw jeez, I ought to show you how to cast, kid. Oh, my God. If you can't get any closer to bass than you're casting, I wouldn't even bother with trying to throw that."

I learned this from the first day I was with him: Ted Williams has always strived for perfection in both his professional and his personal life and it's my opinion that he has very little time for individuals that don't strive for the same. If you're around him for very long and he gets a sense that you're just there to live off him or show him admiration, or if

Ted visiting the original Sloppy Joe's in Havana in 1953, relaxing during a fishing trip.
(Photo courtesy of Bill Nowlin)

Other Lures, Different Strikes

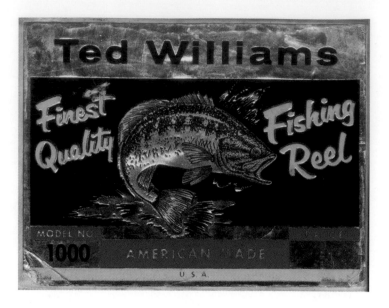

he thinks you're someone that's satisfied with the status quo, he doesn't have time for you. He'll pick up real quick on what your pursuits in life are. But if you're striving to be your best, then he will thrive on that. That's one reason that when we go fishing now, I'm constantly showing him new knots that I've learned to tie, new fishing lures, new casting techniques, new ways of working lures. And he's so inquisitive, so attentive to the little things—why you would throw a sidearm cast versus an overhand, why you use bait casting versus spinning tackle. He just sits there and even though he's lost some of his eyesight in one eye, he is so attentive to everything, whether it be wildlife, how the fish are hitting, the patterns that we're fishing, the bait that we're using—his thirst for knowledge is unquench-able.

◆ ◆ ◆

JERRY McKINNISS, Host of ESPN's *The Fishin' Hole*

The Russian trip was simply put together because I knew how much Ted liked to fish for Atlantic salmon. We went to the very northern part of Russia. It would be like us in Little Rock going fishing in Yellowknife in the Northwest Territories, that's about how far it was up there. We ended up in a town called Murmansk, about 150 miles above the Arctic Circle, and then we took a helicopter on into the camp. We fished the Umba River, on the Kola peninsula. It was still a Communist nation at that time. There was a big red star on the side of the Aeroflot helicopter.

In the States and on up in Northeast Canada, you catch very few Atlantic salmon. An Atlantic salmon fisherman doesn't expect to catch many fish. If you could average one a day, it would be a hell of a deal. Over there on a good day you can hook up maybe 25 or 30 of them. I had already been there once, and I knew what it was going to be, so I knew that Ted was going to go bananas. This was Atlantic salmon heaven.

To catch Atlantic salmon in these numbers you have to be good, you have to make the right presentation and do everything right, otherwise you won't get a strike. So the challenge is still there. Well, Ted was very good! I don't go fishing with celebrities just because they're celebrities. But I am a true baseball fan. I was a pitcher in minor league baseball with the old Kansas City A's. I was absolutely raised on baseball so the fact that I was going fishing with Ted Williams was unbelievable. Each evening after supper we'd relax and I'd be watching Ted Williams tie flies and tell stories about himself and Joe Cronin and Joe DiMaggio. Let me pinch myself right here! It was like a dream. My father had passed away by that time, but I thought a hundred times as we were going on this trip, "Jeez, if my dad could see me, going fishing with Ted Williams!" The river was treacherous. It was extremely swift, and the bottom had a great deal of moss growth. We had trouble getting Ted out to the places where we wanted to get him because he just wasn't that stable. Finally, we got the idea to take an inner tube and put Ted on one side and me on the other, and walk him out to where he needed to go. To get to the right place, you needed to get to at least belt-high water, sometimes a little deeper. We'd get Ted anchored into a really good place. I remember standing there by him, holding that inner tube while he kind of leaned up against it, watching him casting, getting some line out on the water, getting prepared, and hearing him say, "Okay, we're going to make some history now!" He was extremely good. I mean he could really shoot a line! His knowledge of the right fly and the right presentation was just as perfect as I guess his eyesight was thought to be. I've fished with great fly fishermen, and Ted would be in the top ten for sure.

Another thing—I was so impressed with how he handled fish with his rod after he hooked them. You could tell that Ted is a conservationist. He has absolutely no desire to kill fish, ever. He has no desire to prove what a great fisherman he is by showing you his big catch. If he has fooled a fish to the point of making it strike—even if he doesn't catch the fish—then that is a bit of a victory for him. Ted's challenge was just between him and the fish. I just wonder if those fish realized that they were dealing with the last man to hit .400 with a major league baseball uniform on!

◆ ◆ ◆

HOW I NEARLY KILLED TED WILLIAMS
by *John D. Knowlton*

John Knowlton grew up in Greenville, Maine, a town of 2,000 in the 1940s located on Moosehead Lake. Greenville was (and still is) a stepping-off point into the great north woods with flying services doing business out of several coves.

During the summertime, kids played with firecrackers of every sort until they were banned in 1949. Kids could practice space science with a four-inch salute which would put a Campbell's soup can into low orbit. Aerial bombs could be home-fashioned by topping a three-inch salute with the all-purpose M-80s.

Those single-engine airplanes that landed on Moosehead Lake were inviting moving targets to John and his friends. One of them was often piloted by the Maine State Fish and Game Flying Service's warden Bill Turgeon.

To us seasoned pros, a low flying airplane was a quarry more technically appealing, more worthy of plotted consideration than, say, such other opportunities as a looping bird or a slinking cat. In the heat of our pyrotechnical competitions an aerial bomb would sometimes be elevated in the general direction of a returning plane. Moosehead Lake's outgoing air traffic almost always took off up the lake away from town; the opportunist had only to wait for their return. Their gliding return to base brought them low over town, an area pockmarked with natural and man-made recesses and fringed by trees where an urban guerrilla could hide. The specialist could send up a whiz-bang and run to cover in one smooth motion. Of course we never aimed directly at a plane. Bracketing was the merit badge skill.

One soft summer evening in 1948, just after dinner and several days after the Fourth, a squad of us waited in a unused pit—the other faces and identities are have melted away

Ted's home on the Miramichi River (right). A sign near Ted's cabin (below) on the Miramichi River, New Brunswick, Canada warns trespassers and fishermen away.
(Photos by Bill Nowlin)

with time though I suspect at least one of the Diehl boys was there. They were my next-door neighbors and they were handy in things mechanical. Sure enough, we heard a plane coming, in this case the Game Warden's Stinson. Judging the moment, we fired two home-made charges and scattered. Out of the corner of my eye I could see that one had knuckled well to the right of the descending plane, but I did not stop to study any further.

Later that evening, John learned that TED WILLIAMS was said to be in Greenville!

Well, Greenville probably wouldn't see the Messiah, but Ted Williams would do nicely. Napoleon arm-wrestling George Washington at the annual High School Fair wouldn't pull half the audience of a Williams appearance. He was the stuff of deep-wood dreams.

John ran home to tell his mother, who ran Knowlton's Restaurant in town.

Before I could babble my message she said, "Ted Williams is in the dining room. Put an apron on and go wait on him."

As the waitresses scurried for cover, I peered into the dining room and there HE was sat in profile at the near table! Ted was with three others, two unknowns . . . and the new Game Warden Pilot!

Oh my God, he came in on the State Fish and Game plane! I could have killed TED WILLIAMS!

I waited until he finished his soup and went out to present the bill. I wanted to confess to Ted, plead a childish prank, beg forgiveness, and even tell him that I didn't boo his pop-up, but I could only timidly croak a request for his autograph.

Every now and again I was chilled by the thought: "What would have happened if we had hit the plane? That was too grim to contemplate. I gave up aerial bombs forever.

◆ ◆ ◆

BOB KNIGHT, Basketball Coach, Indiana University

Ted was always my favorite player. As a kid he was my favorite because of what a great hitter he was and because of the effort he put into hitting. Then as I grew older and began to understand a little bit more about a lot of things, I realized that here was a guy who absolutely stood for some things, and stood on his own. I thought he was unique, not just among players but among people. I developed a real feeling of admiration for him.

Jimmy Russo was probably the best of all the major league scouts. He was with the Orioles and had become a big Indiana basketball fan, and through our conversations, he knew how much I admired Williams. So in 1981 Jimmy made arrangements for me to meet Ted at spring training. Ted was there as a hitting coach for the Red Sox. It was the year we won the national championship.

Jimmy and I went over one afternoon and sat there all day watching Ted work with hitters and talk to kids. The Red Sox had a complex in Winter Haven with three or four fields where they had most of their minor league players working out. Ted was there watching batting practice. He was in uniform and he jumped up off the bench and I'll never forget this. We'd just won the NCAA championship and Ted was all fired up about that. He said, "What the hell did you do with that time-out that made you play so well in the second half?" And then we talked about basketball and the Indiana team. It was the first time I'd ever met him and each time since I have always been amazed and intrigued by one thing—his enthusiasm. I'm not sure I've ever been around a guy who's as enthusiastic as Ted Williams.

In '91 Ted and I went fishing in Russia with Jerry McKinniss, for a show called *The Fishin' Hole* on ESPN. Ted really loved to fish for Atlantic salmon, so I told Jerry, "You know, I think I can get Ted Williams to go with us on a trip." I called Ted and he said, "Well, where the hell are we going?" and I said, "Russia," and he said, "Russia! Goddamn! Russia? Goddamn, coach!" And then he said, "Now are YOU gonna go?" And I said "Yeah, that's what I'm calling you for, to take you along." And he said, "Well, if you go, I'll go." And that's all there was to it. It was never any of this, Well I've got to give this some thought . . .

Ted told me that based on his experience with Atlantic salmon, we were going to fish six days and if we each hooked ten fish, it'd be great. Well, he hooked 17 fish and I hooked 22. (But when you write this, put in parenthesis that I reluctantly admitted that I fished a hell of a lot more than he did. Just make sure that you get the numbers in there right, I want to stick it to him a little bit on the numbers.) He really is a great fly-caster. I've fished with a lot of guys and there's nobody that can fish a fly rod better than Ted.

Curt Gowdy loves Ted, and Curt had told me, "Now, you can't treat him like he's your idol. I mean you've got to get on his ass because he's going to get on yours." So we're about to make this trip to Russia, and I'm sitting in the Pan American lounge at Kennedy Airport. When I checked in, the guy at the FinnAir counter was a basketball fan and he recognized me and I said, "I've got a friend who's coming in here: Ted Williams." He said, "Oh, the baseball player?" and I said, "Yeah, he's a big, good looking, dark-haired guy. You'll recognize him as soon as he walks in. You send him up to the lounge."

I'll never forget this. I'm in the lounge watching the last day of the Senior Open. I go out to use the telephone and when I come back there must be over a dozen guys watching the end of the tournament and my friend Jim from Houston, who I'd just met, has saved my seat for me. As I walk in, I look the group over and I see Ted sitting there right in the middle of this group. So I sit down and I say, "Jim, how's Nicklaus doing?" I'm a big Nicklaus fan and Jim gives me an update. Then I say, "You know, there's an interesting thing about golf. There's a swing involved in both golf and baseball but I've never EVER seen a goddamn baseball player who could play this game." I said, "It's SO much harder than hitting a baseball." And I mean you could have heard a pin drop. I'm sure some of these guys recognized *me*, and I'm sure they *all* recognized Ted, and the thing that's going through their minds must be: *Jesus, these might be the two most temperamental guys in sports history, and here's one of them knocking the shit out of something that the other one does.* I'm looking at Williams out of the corner of my eye and he's just sitting there chuckling. I said, "Goddamn, I didn't see you." And he said, "Yeah, in a pig's ass you didn't see me, goddammit!"

Now how about this? Ted is a self-educated guy and yet he is probably as well-educated as most people who have a Ph.D. We get on the airplane to Russia and he says, "Okay coach, we're gonna have a little contest here. We're gonna talk about who we think the five greatest Americans of our lifetime are. And I said, "Well, goddamn, that's unfair to begin with!" And he said, "Well, you're not up to it coach? Your knowledge isn't broad enough to discuss this subject? Hell!" I said, "No, you son of a bitch, you're about 25 years older than I am. You've got more resources than I do!" Now this goes back to Curt Gowdy saying you've got to get on his ass. "Awright," he says, "goddammit we'll make a little allowance—since the turn of the century." And I say, "Which century?" And he gets to chuckling. You know, when you come back at him with some bullshit things he kind of likes it. He says, "THIS century—the turn of the 20th century." Now I know he's the staunchest Republican in the whole world so I say, "Well, if we're going to talk about this century, we have absolutely no recourse but to start talkin' about Franklin Delano Roosevelt!" *Eventually* the SOB has to agree that we have to include Roosevelt in this. We must spend two hours arguing about the five greatest Americans. I stick Truman in there and Ted wants to put Nixon in, and I say, "Nixon's got a flaw. We can't take Nixon, goddammit. I know Nixon's your buddy but leave friendship out of this!" Now I like Nixon and he made good points about Nixon opening up China, opening up foreign policy, doing this and that. But I said, "What he's gotta do is what you would have done. He's gotta stand up and say, 'We f----- up.' No one would have thought a thing about it if he had done that."

Then I mention Martin Luther King and let me tell you, Ted gave me as great an answer as a guy could give. He comes back with Joe Louis. He said, "I'm going to tell you why Joe Louis. He was the first black man that blacks across the country could listen to, and look up to, and follow and pay attention to on a national basis. Every black person in America listened to Joe Louis fight and we're talking about back in 1936 and 1937, not the sixties." He made a hell of an argument. He didn't disagree with the King choice but we were selecting people in different categories and if we we're going to pick a guy for civil rights, he thought Joe Louis was just as important as King. We went back and forth. He brought up MacArthur and I said George Marshall. Back and forth. And I'll tell you what—he had reasons and sound arguments for all his choices. We exhausted the subject without ever agreeing on each other's five.

Now here's one of the neatest things that's ever happened to me in my lifetime. We're on the plane on the way back from Russia and he and I are sitting in the back, and we had gone over there to do this TV show for McKinniss. Jerry had gone back a day before we did so Ted and I and the cameraman were coming back on our own.

There were three seats in the back and Ted sat in the middle and I sat on his right and there was a professor from Brandeis on his left. I'm reading and we're talking back and forth and then I kind of fall asleep. But I'm not *really* asleep. Ted and this guy are talking and the guy's asking about our trip to Russia. I'm dozing in and out and as the conversation proceeds the guy asks Ted, "What's coach Knight like?" And Ted pauses. Now I have my head turned away from him and he thinks I'm asleep. I just happened to catch this and as I said, it's really one of the nicest moments of my life. Ted said, "Well . . . the son of a bitch is just like me!" [emotion in Knight's voice]

TED WILLIAMS: THE PURSUIT OF PERFECTION

Ted with Joe Lindia during a fishing trip in the Florida Keys.
(Photo courtesy of Dorothy Lindia)

Ted and Coach Bobby Knight. In the words of Curt Gowdy, "Knight's a pup out of Ted Williams."
(Photo courtesy of Bobby Knight)

Ted was Manager of the Year in baseball once and he could have been a good basketball coach, too. When he decided he wanted to do something, it was like hitting a baseball or fishing. He has a real keen ability to figure things out and understand them, and he would have studied the hell out of it. He would have seen what other great coaches would do—what Iba would do, and Pete Newell, and Clare Bee—and he would have studied all that and then come to his conclusions.

Probably no one in baseball had a greater impact on the game or was freer with advice than Ted Williams. Moose Skowron, the former Yankee, is a real good buddy of mine. Moose told me one time the Yankees were playing in Boston and he was having trouble hitting. So he asked Ted what to do and Ted said, "You're trying to hit the ball to left field all the time. You've got to hit it to right field." And he talked to him about how to do that and that day Moose hits two home runs, beats the Red Sox, gets in the locker room and there's a phone call for him. It's Ted. And Ted says, "Goddamn it, don't you tell those f------ Boston writers that I told you about hitting to right field." I would bet that never in the history of baseball did a guy take more time to give of himself than he did.

I agree with Ted that hitting a baseball is the single toughest thing to do in sport. If you make thirty percent of five foot putts, you're done. If you hit the fairway 30 percent of the time, if you complete 30 percent of your passes, if you're a 30 percent field goal kicker, if you're a 30 percent field goal shooter . . . I can't think of a single thing in sport, other than hitting, where you can be 30 percent effective and be really good. But if you hit a baseball and you're 30 percent successful doing it, you're a hell of a player and you're making zillions of dollars today. When Ted played, you were a great player if you could be successful 30 percent of the time—in '41 he was successful *40* percent of the time. I'm not sure that there's anything else in the world of sport like that.

Have you read John Updike's piece on Ted's last game? The two greatest lines in the article are when Ted didn't tip his cap and Updike says that after all "Gods do not answer letters." The other one was the very ending of the piece where he said that Ted had known how to do the hardest thing of all, to quit.

◆ ◆ ◆

TED FERREE, President, Miramichi Salmon Association

My wife and I owned a camp on the Miramichi for ten years, where we spent our summers. Our place was up the river about 50 miles from Ted's. I was always impressed with his almost baseball-like technique of casting. He was a masterful caster, and could throw a great long line. If there were any salmon around, Ted would hook them. Just a fun guy to watch. If you love salmon fishing, you know what I mean.

Ted's the kind of man who's great to fish with because he's like a big kid. He loves to catch fish. He releases everything—at least I've never seen him keep a salmon. I guess it's just part of his makeup. He's a conservationist at heart and I think primarily he sees it as a great thing for future generations if conservation works.

To be honest with you, I think it was Ted's idea that the Association come up with an award for journalistic support of the Atlantic salmon. Jack Fenety, then President and for so many years a great President of the Association, probably had the idea to name it the

Ted Williams Award. Then along came a man named Bud Leavitt, Ted's dear friend, a real sweet guy. For a number of years, Bud was instrumental each year in selecting the recipient of the Award.

◆ ◆ ◆

JACK FENETY, Past President, Miramichi Salmon Association

Since 1953, when the Miramichi Salmon Association started, our fight was for conservation. We were happy to welcome Ted because he not only picked up on our ideas but he had ideas of his own. He was also a kind of magnet to draw attention to the association and promote our dinners in Boston and New York. And Ted was a true conservationist, an active conservationist. He was one of the very first to practice "hook and release" in Atlantic salmon angling in New Brunswick and he did it long before it was mandatory. Over the years he's caught hundreds of Miramichi River salmon and released almost all of them.

Ted encouraged others to conserve. One thing he always hated with a passion was double hook flies and he fought passionately to have them removed from the waters. He believed that you would catch and probably land as many fish on a single hook as you would with a double. The double hook people countered by saying that you've got two chances of grabbing the fish and if it's held by two hooks, you're more likely to land the fish. Ted's point was that we're in a conservation era now, so why not go to single hooks. Since we're not going to keep these fish anyway, why not give then a fighting chance to get away.

Ted just thought that people should be more sportsmanlike and more conservation-minded. And this had a very noticeable effect on people from south of the border who came here to fish. Here was an American who had a message and he was a real active conservationist in that he fished probably more than any of our members. He fished the whole season. When he wasn't on his own water, he was in Nova Scotia or wherever. Technically, Ted Williams would cast a fly as well as anyone who ever fished for Atlantic salmon. He was an expert. He had that great hand-eye coordination in baseball and he had that same hand-eye coordination in fishing. He just loved to fish and he called the Atlantic salmon the greatest fighting sport fish in the world.

He was more than just a figurehead. We would have been content to have him just lend his name to our cause, but he helped us greatly in recruiting new members and increasing interest in salmon conservation south of the border. The Americans were, and are, by and large, better conservationists than the Canadians. They long ago destroyed much of their heritage in the industrial age and now welcome the great privilege they have of coming to Canada to fish and hunt. Ted enhanced that desire on their part. We used to have a lot of American itinerants who came up here in the black salmon season and there were no boundaries, no limits. They would kill 30, 40, even 100 fish. There are pictures of them all laid out on the ground and the men standing around with grins on their faces and cigars in their hands and a belly full of booze. Happy days are here again! This was an image that we wanted to destroy and eventually did. Ted helped us to do that. He once threatened to cut his own throat if something wasn't done to prevent the poaching of Atlantic salmon. The presence of Ted Williams in New Brunswick from his first to his last days there was focused on conservation. He was firm in his determination. The things he said about judges being too lenient on poachers are legendary now.

◆ ◆ ◆

TELEGRAPH ✷ JOURNAL

71 CENTS   SINCE 1862   SATURDAY • SEPTEMBER 25, 1993

Ted Williams is a baseball legend and a living monument to sport fishing. But he is losing his last great love and his heart is breaking. So great is his passion, he is willing to make the ultimate sacrifice for the Atlantic salmon.

Unless New Brunswick acts...

'I'm going to cut my throat'

CANADA   THE SUNDAY DAILY NEWS, OCTOBER 3, 1993

Williams vows to end life to save Miramichi salmon

BLACKVILLE, N.B. (CP) — Baseball great Ted Williams, gruff and tempestuous as ever, has shaken up some New Brunswickers with his strange way of pleading for saving his beloved New Brunswick salmon.

"I'm going to cut my throat right here" if the federal fisheries department doesn't stop people from killing the salmon, the 75-year-old Boston Red Sox slugger said in a recent interview with the *Saint John Telegraph Journal.*

"That's his nature," president Jack Fenety responded about his fellow director of the Miramichi Salmon Association a few days later in Sussex, N.B.

"He's a John Wayne type, who steers his own course and is master of his own ship. Talking about killing himself for the salmon is how he wouldn't tip his hat to the fans at Boston. He's a lone eagle."

Williams's statement helped the cause, Fenety said.

"His passion and devotion to the Miramichi River and the Atlantic salmon are unquestionable. Ted Williams's affinity with the river and its fish borders on the spiritual."

After Williams's comment was published, people telephoned the association expressing support for more conservation, Fenety said.

"I think Ted overstates the case, but he overstates it in a way that will jolt the public."

Williams, who has been fishing the Miramichi since the 1950s and releasing the Atlantic salmon he catches long before it was mandatory, likened salmon killing to murder.

"I would almost feel like I've put a knife in my vein and bled a little bit if I ever took a salmon out of this river," he said.

Judges who only fine poachers are accomplices to the death of salmon, and a New Brunswick judge who recently fined a salmon poacher $500 should be hanged, he said.

Last month, the federal Fisheries Department closed salmon fishing in all rivers flowing into the Bay of Fundy. The move was aimed at conserving Atlantic salmon stocks, which have fallen to near-record low levels.

Williams blamed the salmon's decline on commercial fishing at the salmon's feeding grounds in the Atlantic Ocean and overfishing by local anglers and Indians. Though natives are allowed to net salmon for their own food, some of them barter the fish, he said.

Williams is mad at fishermen who keep big salmon. (To keep up breeding stock, Canada requires anglers to release all adult salmon they catch. Infants, known as parr, are also protected but fishermen can keep adolescents, known as grilse.)

"All they're thinking of is getting the big fish now," Williams says. "Screw the river, get the fish."

BILL TAYLOR, President of the Atlantic Salmon Federation

I am currently president of the Atlantic Salmon Federation, but when I got the Ted Williams Award in 1991, I was executive director of communications and public policy. I'd been a writer before joining the Federation in 1988. I've always had a very deep interest in salmon conservation.

The salmon is a barometer for a very healthy environment. It's a very sensitive species, so it's one of the first to show signs of decline when you have too much pollution, acid rain, or what have you. It's like the canary in a coal mine. If our rivers are healthy and can support salmon, it's indicative of a healthy environment. In turn, a lot of other species are benefitting from the work that we're doing.

We're strictly a conservation organization—supported by a lot of anglers who are concerned that salmon stocks are depressed and who know that we need to do a lot of work to restore them and clean up our rivers. The recreational salmon fishing industry is a $40 million dollar a year industry in the province of New Brunswick, and the Miramichi is probably responsible for at least half of that, being the largest salmon river in North America.

I met Ted in 1986 at an Atlantic Salmon Federation conclave on the Miramichi. At that time, I was a volunteer. He was always very helpful and concerned, willing to do whatever he could to help us further our salmon conservation mission. He's a huge man with a strong handshake, very confident and very outspoken. And kind of loud—the kind of person who gets your attention. I've always been fond of him. There's this sort of air about him. He commands respect, and he commands your attention when he enters a room.

When Ted's award started in 1980, there would have been approximately 7,500 commercial salmon fishing licenses, people fishing salmon in the sea with nets in eastern Canada. Today there are a couple of hundred. They have been bought out, purchased back by the Canadian government because of the advocacy efforts of the Federation. There are restrictions on the size of the netting, and very strict quotas on the number of fish that can be taken. Our efforts are making a difference, no question. A species that was teetering on the brink of extinction has been saved.

◆◆◆

JIM PRIME, Fan

Ted Williams and Roy Curtis were a latter day version of Tom Sawyer and Huck Finn. Ted, like Tom, was the one with the grandiose schemes; Roy, like Huck, went along for the ride. Their river was not the mighty Mississippi; it was New Brunswick's mystical Miramichi, the most productive Atlantic salmon fishing river in North America. Roy and Ted first met in 1958, just after the close of a baseball season in which the then 40-year old slugger had captured yet another American League batting crown. The first exchange between them was a snapshot of their personalities: Ted, abrasive, blunt, challenging; Curtis, modest, unwavering and concise. "You know anything about salmon fishing?" Williams demanded of the man whose life blood was the river. "Some," replied Roy. Some indeed, as Ted would soon discover. He eventually took to calling them "the best one-two fishing team on the Miramichi."

◆ ◆ ◆

JOHN UNDERWOOD, Author
(Taken from Fishing the Big Three, *a conversation between Underwood and Roy Curtis)*

"He was pretty cocky, uh?"

"No. Well, yes. Maybe a little. But in forty years on the river I've met an awful lot of fishermen; and most of 'em, either they can't fish a'tall or after a year or two they start telling YOU. Most of 'em you have to straighten out for sure."

"You had to straighten Ted out?"

He grinned, "Some. But don't tell him I told you that. The thing is, I liked him right off. He's such a great big kid, you know. Just a dandy fellow to be with. And, of course, now I really can't tell him anything. He likes to tell me."

"I think he believes he's the best," I said. "Is he the best?"

"The best I've seen," said Roy. "Forty years, and I ain't seen none better, no. There's days a fellow can beat him, maybe, but day in, day out, he's the best. He can do it all. He can tie the best flies, rig 'em just right. He can cast to the toughest spots. He can cover more water than anybody. He knows exactly how to play 'em, and he has a fine steady hand to release 'em, and that's an art for sure. Sometimes I sit on the bank and never lift a finger."

"I bet you like that."

Roy ignored me. "And PERSISTENT, oh, my. He'll stay out there all day, any kind of weather. Stay and stay. Another feller'd quit, but he won't. He has wonderful staying power."

Watching Ted, he hooked a salmon, fought it in, then bent down to release it.

"He's releasing it?" I asked.

"Yeah," said Roy.

"All day for one fish, and he's releasing it?"

"Yeah," said Roy Curtis. "Persistent."

From the pocket of his flannel shirt, he took out and opened what resembled a metal cigarette case. Inside, in neat little rows, like earrings in a jeweler's display, were the flies he had been tying at night in the basement.

> In good salmon flycasting, timing is everything. Normally you can see the salmon you are going after in the water. The ability to make your eye gauge exactly where that fly ought to light on a running river and then pass in the proper spot in front of the salmon to make him rise and take is an art. Ted was one of the very best.
>
> —Ted Ferree

"You know, Roy," he said, "I discovered something about tying a Conrad a couple days ago, and I think you oughta know—something that could help you a lot." But instead of showing Roy the fly, he cupped his hand over the case mysteriously.

Roy grinned and waited.

"Naw, I better not," Ted said. "I better keep this to myself. You're a big Canadian guide, up all night tying flies. These amateur efforts wouldn't interest you." He turned and held the fly out of sight, studying it. "I don't know if you're ready for this or not."

Roy waited. Finally, inevitably, Ted turned back to reveal his creation. Roy adjusted his glasses and held the fly up to the morning light.

"Yeah, that's a good one," he said.

"A good one? A good one? Boy, there IS a lot of jealousy around here. That's a peppermint stick, that fly. Even you could catch fish with that fly. I was gonna make you a little presentation, too, but now . . . . "

"Oh, I'll take it for sure," said Roy.

"Yeah, yeah, I knew you'd say that." Ted winked at me. "What do you think of Ted Williams now? What-do-you-think-of-Ted-Williams?"

◆ ◆ ◆

BEING TED WILLIAMS
by Jim Prime

Like most baseball-playing boys of my generation, I had been Ted Williams many times. Playing for the Freeport Schooners, I was always Ted Williams when I stepped to the plate against the Westport Whitecaps or the Tiverton Mohawks. When I returned to the dugout after striking out on three pitches, I felt more like Don Buddin, but I was definitely Ted when I went up there.

I even tried to emulate Ted Williams' attitude. I developed a vocabulary of profanities that would make a lobster fisherman blush. I strived to affect a certain disdain, an air of assured indifference to my surroundings coupled with an intensity of purpose. Unfortunately, the image I held of myself proved out of step with the reality of my on-field mediocrity. I came to the inescapable conclusion that nothing could be more futile than trying to be Ted Williams with a Barney Fife body.

These adolescent dreams and fantasies had been relegated to the dusty attic of my middle-aged mind—along with the Raquel Welch poster, the October 1960 *Playboy* centerfold, and the green and red kryptonite—when I received the phone call.

The caller informed me that Ted Williams was to be inducted into the Atlantic Salmon Hall of Fame. Good, I said. Well deserved. "Ted has just gotten out of hospital and his family would like for you to accept the award in his behalf."

After all these years, I was being asked to be Ted Williams for a day.

I tried to look at the issue objectively. I could never hit a baseball like Ted, and my fishing abilities fell far short of his. On the other hand, we both love the Red Sox and Ted once told me I was "the most persistent son of a bitch" he had ever met, which surely puts me on some sort of level with the Big Guy.

And like Ted I have always pursued perfection. Surely the fact that he had gained considerable ground on it while I was left in its dust was just a matter of degree.

The big day arrived. It was Friday, October 12, 2001 and that very evening Ted Williams was to be inducted into the Atlantic Salmon Hall of Fame in Doaktown, New Brunswick, Canada. Now I knew something of how Carroll Hardy felt that time he pinch-hit for Ted. I knew something of how Carl Yastrzemski felt when he took Ted's place in the shadow of the Green Monster. In preparation for the event I struggled to find the tie that binds—the one thing that Ted and I had as common ground.

As I sat at the head table, nervously awaiting my turn to speak, my fevered mind drifted back several years. At the time, I was writing a book with Ted entitled *Ted Williams' Hit List,* and I was one of several guests at Ted's fishing lodge. After a wonderful meal and a few drinks, some of us wandered outside to stretch and watch the dark, silent Miramichi River flow past. On a whim I went to my car and got an old Reggie Jackson model Adirondack bat out of the trunk. Approaching the group, I swung the bat once in the cool evening air. It was a disjointed swing and I was glad that no one — least of all Ted—had noticed.

I tentatively offered the bat to Ted and as he enveloped it in his huge palms, it suddenly resembled a wand in the hand of a wizard. He swung it once and I swear I saw the river part.

Captain Williams at sea.
(Photo by Fred Kaplan, courtesy of Lee Kaplan)

Shaking myself from my reverie, I watched the other speakers with the same intensity that Ted once used to scrutinize pitchers from the on-deck circle. The room grew warmer and somehow smaller. I was claustrophobic. The glass of wine I had drunk and the poached salmon I had eaten were not compatible. The salmon—as is that species wont—was endeavoring to swim upstream. When it came time for Ted to be inducted, my name coming from the microphoned master of ceremonies, sounded hollow and distant, like Sherm Feller, the longtime PA announcer at Fenway Park. Now batting for Ted Williams, Jim Prime. Prime, batting for Williams.

I longed to do something to prove to myself that I could be Ted Williams, if only for this one evening. I strode to the microphone, trying to exude confidence. I considered cursing at the few members of the press who were present, but just as quickly dismissed the idea. I thought of not tipping my hat to the crowd, but since I had none, it would have been an empty gesture. I thought of giving the assembled group some hitting tips: Be quick. Be patient. Get a good ball to hit! The advice would have lacked credibility coming from such a sadly surrogate Splinter. I glanced at my wife in the audience and she gave me an encouraging smile. Deciding to follow my script, I began:

"I am honored to accept this prestigious award on behalf of Ted Williams and the Williams family. The names are different but the level of excellence is the same. Members of the Atlantic Salmon Hall of Fame are the Mantles and Cobbs and Ruths of salmon fishing. Facing a top pitcher like Bob Feller was the equivalent of the challenge Ted saw in fishing the Atlantic salmon. Ted thanks you from the bottom of his heart for this honor."

God did not mean for fisher folk to wear suits. At that point in my brief speech the temperature in the crowded room had reached unbearable levels and a wild impulse mingled with a blast of heat from the air duct behind the lectern to overwhelm my senses. Recalling Ted's legendary disdain for neckties, and suffering genuine discomfort in this stifling room, I decided to do what Ted Williams would have done. I grabbed my collar and loosened what one writer has rightly called the "blunt garrote" that has shackled mankind for generations. I pulled the necktie over my head and cast it aside with obvious and theatrical contempt. People looked at me as if I had snapped. There was light buzz as the tables of five and six fashionably dressed men and women fidgeted and coughed nervously.

Before the bailiffs could come to carry me away, I gave a scowling invitation to all males in the room to join me in a tribute to Ted by doffing their neckwear. It caused an uproar not unlike the storming of the Bastille and the cry of "off with their heads." Neckties were discarded like overpaid free agents.

I wasn't exactly Terrible Ted, but I wasn't exactly Don Buddin either. It was something Ted would definitely have done. He loved to tie flies, but he hated to tie ties. As I did it, I actually did feel like Ted Williams. I had finally discovered our tie that binds.

I felt like tipping my hat, but of course I had none.

◆ ◆ ◆

GEORGE CURTIS, Proprietor of Black Rapids Salmon Club

Ted and my father had their little set-tos every now and again but they worked together as a team. When Ted first came up here, he was a little hard to get along with. He wanted to change everything, wanted to run the natives off pools that they had fished all their lives. He bought a pool in Upper Blackville and he was going to run everybody off of that. He didn't want to see the natives fishing it, even though they were across the river, on the other side. He said, "Roy, we've got to do something about these natives." My father said "Ted, the only way to get along with these natives is to let them go on about their business and fish. They're not interfering with you, they're not fishing when you're here." Ted was awful upset at first but dad said, "Ted, you're going to catch a hell of a lot more flies with honey than with vinegar." He had to learn to get along with the people. At first he thought he was going to try to run everything but that soon changed. He came around the last ten years or so that he fished for salmon here. He was a different guy and in the end everyone got along just fine with Ted Williams.

Ted had an awful love for the salmon and he accomplished a great deal for conservation. He told it like it was and smartened up a few of the politicians. We had the CBC (Canadian Broadcasting Corporation) up in 1982, a show called The Fifth Estate, and he opened up on the politicians on that show. That was when they finally smartened up and bought out the commercial fishermen. I think Ted had a lot to do with that.

Dad didn't really know anything about baseball. To him Ted was just another guy and that's why they got along so well. They were really great friends, good buddies. Ted had Jack Dempsey up one time at the camp and my father nearly went crazy over Jack because my dad was a boxing and hockey fan. Ted couldn't figure it out. Ted said, "Roy, I've got Jack Dempsey coming up here, would you like to meet him?" "Cripes," dad said, "I sure would!" Ted couldn't figure that out.

◆ ◆ ◆

VIN SWAZEY, Miramichi Guide

As a kid, I'd heard Ted and the Red Sox on the radio. But I really didn't follow baseball that much, so I didn't have a lot of baseball questions to ask Ted about. I think Ted liked not being bugged about baseball while he was trying to relax and enjoy himself in New Brunswick. My camp was next to Ted's, and visitors would often ask about Ted Williams. If I thought the visitor's interest was sincere, I'd sometimes call Ted on the phone and ask whether he would be willing to say hello. "Is it important to you?" Ted would ask. If I said yes, it would be good, then Ted would drop by.

Ted talked louder in Boston. Then when he came back to the Miramichi, he would sit and talk quietly about different people. Fishermen. Fishing talk. I'd sometimes drop by Ted's place, just to sit for a while, just to say hello. I wouldn't have any sort of agenda. After some time had passed, Ted would say, "OK, what did you come for? I know you came for

Hall of Famer hitter and . . . fisherman. Ted receiving his induction from Larry Colombo into the National Freshwater Fishing Hall of Fame.
(Photo courtesy of Ted Dzialo, National Freshwater Fishing Hall of Fame)

something." But really I hadn't come for anything at all. For someone like Ted Williams, that had to be a relief. People have always wanted things from him. But I'd always play along. "I haven't been catching anything. I thought maybe you could help me." Ted liked that.

Ted's young daughter Claudia landed a salmon one day, and Ted asked me very quietly, "Did she kill that fish?" I said, "Yes, she did." Ted said, "Is that all right with you? How do you feel about it?" I said I thought it was okay but Ted was truly disappointed. He shrugged and said, "What can you do?"

John-Henry was fishing down on the river one time. I didn't know who it was when I arrived and I said, "Who's that, Ted?" He said, "Isn't he a good fisherman? Much better than you!" I said, "Well, he throws a good line." Then I realized that it was John-Henry and added, "Well, he should be good. You taught him, and you wouldn't teach me!"

◆ ◆ ◆

FRED CORREIA, Barber

Ted used to have his hair cut all the time at my place. When he first came into town there was an old guy by the name of Rogers who used to hang around him a lot. He was a guy who kind of befriended Ted when he first came into town, an usher or something. He came in the shop and said to me, "Well, Ted doesn't get his hair cut around here. He goes to Boston." Next thing I know . . . I always cut Ted's hair. He said that he thought I was a pretty good barber.

He used to call me "Bush" and at the time I thought it was an insult. Then I found out he says that when he likes a person. I didn't get on that until somebody clued me in. I thought, why are you calling me Bush? I thought it meant minor leaguer, like I didn't know what I was doing.

Ted fly-casting on the Miramachi River, Canada.
(Photo courtesy of Sammy Lee)

Most of the time Ted and I talked about fishing, but one time there were a bunch of guys around. They knew he was around so they piled in and the conversation got turned over to baseball. He basically talked about hitting, then gave a demonstration. He was standing up against the wall to show how a lot of guys just use their arms to swing, but that hitting really involves the hips. I was thinking, gee, if I'd heard that as a kid . . . . it made a lot of sense. He said, "Put your back flat against the wall, and try to take a swing and get any power without twisting your hips." That's a pretty good demonstration.

When I first started learning how to flycast, I used to have an old wooden bamboo line, an old line, an absolutely useless line. I had it strung up in the barbershop, so that when I had a break, I could just take the rod and go out next to the building where there's plenty of space and practice flycasting. I got it down so I was pretty good, particularly with such poor gear.

I remember one day Ted was sitting in the chair and I spun the chair around, naturally, while cutting his hair, and he spotted the fly rod in the corner. He said to me, "What's that?" I said, "That's a fly rod!" Well, of course, I knew that he knew it was a fly rod, but I was saying it as if, "Oh, you don't know what it is, mister?" He said, "Well, I know that's a fly rod. But what are you doing with it?" I said, "I've been practicing doing some flycasting." And he said, "Are you any good at it?" I said, "I'll get some line out." He said, "Do you think you can beat me?" I said, "I don't know. What do you say we go out and have a contest?" He says, "I'll tell you what. If you can beat me, I'll give you my car."

So we went out and he says, "You make the first cast." So I made the first cast and I got a pretty damn good distance on it. Anyway, he got up and he made a cast and beat me by a couple of feet. He probably could have beat me by ten. I don't know.

I always thought the guy knew an awful lot about a lot of things. Some guys termed it as opinionated. They didn't like to hear it. I think many of those people felt like that because when they knew something, they didn't want to encounter somebody who probably knew as much about it as they did, somebody who wasn't supposed to. After all, he was a baseball player. But that guy would know about transmissions, he'd know about gunning—as a matter of fact, I remember one time we got talking about distances. I was a duck hunter. I can remember him saying, "From how far away are you hitting them?" I said I felt pretty good. He said, "How far are you hitting them?" I said, "Well, I don't know. I think it's about 40 or 50 yards." He says, "Look out the window. How far from here?" I said, "I think from about here to that pole out there." He said, "How far do you think that is?" I said, "I think that's about 45 yards." He said, "I think it's 55 yards." So he got up and he went out and he walked it off. You know, you can get a pretty good idea when you're walking, you get about a yard a step as long as you're not trying to jump it too far. He was right on the ball. He was pretty sharp along those lines.

He was in the shop one day getting a haircut, and I saw one of my friends drive up. My friend had just lost his wife to cancer, and I knew that he was a great fan of Ted Williams, talked about him all the time. I said, "Hey, Ted. This guy out here is a great fan of yours, and he's just lost his wife. Would you mind going out so I can introduce you to him?" Well, he took the time to do that and it was really kind of the highlight of the guy's life. It wouldn't have meant that much to me, but that's the way some people are. And it wasn't just "Hi." I thought it was pretty damn good.

◆ ◆ ◆

JIMMY ALBRIGHT, Fishing Guide

I was probably the first person who Ted fished with for tarpon and bonefish, so he probably picked up a few pointers from me. He may not be the best of everything, but he was the best all around. He's the best fly fisherman, the best sail fisherman, and the best bonefisherman, spinning flies, bait casting . . . .

He called me from Boston when he was still playing ball, that was in '46, and made arrangements to come down and fish with me for a week. That's the way we got started. He had come to Florida in '45, over to Everglades City on the west coast. He went over there to fish for snook with baitcasting rod. In the meantime, spinning had been developed, and they started to fly fish. I was the one who started that. Through word of mouth he had heard of me and then he spent most of his winters down here, after the war.

I introduced Ted and Louise Kaufman. Lou was the only woman that he ever had any respect for or loved or anything else, as far as I was concerned. She was married and had four children, two girls and two boys. I had known Lou for quite a while, and they had a little tournament going which Ted and I fished. Lou fished in the tournament on her own, in another boat, and afterward I introduced them. She was a real good fisherman.

We fished from '46 to the '80s. Forty years with time out, of course, for the Korean War. We probably fished fifty days a year. Ted was at my house when he was called back to the service. He'd been fishing with me for a week, and when we came in he left to go back to his home in Miami. Meanwhile I kept getting phone calls after he'd left asking where he might be. Well, I never told anybody anything that I knew about Ted, so I told them that I didn't know where he was. Finally his business manager, Fred Corcoran, called. I asked why everybody was looking for Ted, and he said that he'd been called back in the service. Well, Ted got home, and I guess there was a lot of media around and everything, so he got in his car and drove back down. Wanted to know if he could stay with me for a while. We kidded among ourselves because I'd had a bet with him that he'd be called back before I was. I was Navy. I never got called back. He never should have been called back either.

The two of us, we joked a lot. If Ted would make a mistake, why, I'd ride him about it, and if I'd make a mistake, he'd ride me. It was never anything more than raise your voice type of thing. Other guides would try to take him fishing and not charge him but of all the times that Ted and I fished he never once fished a free day or expected one out of me. It was all business. He was a good friend. My best. But Ted could be awful rough and intimidating. I noticed it with other people.

When he was with me, I more or less protected him. I wouldn't introduce him to people unless I thought it was somebody he wanted to meet. One day somebody brought Jack Nicklaus over to Ted's house—Jack wanted to meet him. Ted and I were sitting there watching a ball game and Jack came to the door, was introduced and they sat and talked a long time. You see, Ted said he always wanted to meet Jack. Ted was a frustrated golfer.

Sam Snead fished with us. Benny Goodman. Ted liked Benny because he enjoyed his music. They couldn't either one compare with Ted as far as fishing goes but they enjoyed it. The one thing Ted always said he wanted to do when he finished baseball was to get a trawler type boat, about 60 feet long, and he and I go all around the world in it, fishing. I wasn't much for traveling around but that was his dream for a long time—to go on a ship and take guns and fishing tackle and just hunt and fish the rest of his life.

◆ ◆ ◆

SAM SNEAD, Golfer

How good a fisherman was Ted? As we say in French, "Le Meiux," the best. In the clubhouse before a game or during a rain delay he'd pull the fly rod out and say to someone "Hey, open up that back pocket of yours." And he'd flip that thing right into your uniform pants pocket.

—Bill Monbouquette, pitcher

Once, I was in New York at a game between the Red Sox and the Yankees and Ted was telling me that his power hand was his right hand when he bats left handed. I said, "Uh-uh, it's your left hand." As a right-handed golfer, I swing it with the left and crank it with the right—the swing is similar in baseball. That day he went 4 for 4. Well, you know how he can blast off. "Oh you SOB, you and your power hand! Standing there with the ball on the ground not moving, waiting on you to hit it. I'm up at bat and here comes this ball in there ninety miles an hour and ducking." I said, "But Ted, you foul and you get another shot. Now when I foul I have to go find it and play it." Then I said, "You're hitting the ball to the whole world out there and I'm trying to get it in a 4 and a quarter inch hole. Now which is the hard one?"

He'd say things like, "Who the hell wants to go up there and tap in a two foot putt?" But he soon found out that golf is a hell of a lot tougher than baseball! We'll never know if he could have been a great golfer. A man is great in one sport and lousy in another. I never played golf with him and I wouldn't want to, either! I don't think Ted had the patience for it. There are so many little things in golf that I don't think he could have put up with. I saw him chipping and pitching once and instead of having his weight on his right foot like a left-handed swinger should, his right foot was coming up. I said, "You swing like a bloody girl!" Now . . . I played baseball, I was a pitcher. Baseball is not hard. How would I have pitched to Ted? I'd have thrown *at* him, not *to* him. He might have gotten on first but that wouldn't have been so bad.

To Ted everybody was "Bush." If he liked you, everything was okay, but if he didn't like you, you better be walking the other way. I have fished with him. I remember one time he said to me, "Now, Bush, when the tide starts to come in, I want you to pole me. Well, we didn't have a bloody pole in the boat and the wind's coming off the land and he's standing up in the boat and his jacket was bulged out like a sail. All of a sudden he sees this bonefish tail right close to the beach and he said, "Come on, Bush, pole me. Get me over there!" Well, our oar was only about two feet out of water and we had an old heavy boat anyway and you couldn't do much of anything with him standing up and only two feet to work with. "Man," he says, "Golfers! Golf, that's a hell of a game!" I said, "If you say one more word I'm going to knock your ass out of the boat with this paddle." And then he started to laugh. We had to crank the boat engine back up to get in. He was a great fisherman, a hell of a competitor, and a great friend.

◆ ◆ ◆

BOB TOSKI, Golfer

I played a lot of golf with Ted when I was the pro down at Ocean Reef in the Keys. We used to talk about the golf swing and the baseball swing and make comparisons. I always admired Ted because I thought he had the greatest eyes, and one of the greatest dynamic swings in baseball. When he hit that bat against that ball he was electricity, a bolt of lightning. But we got into some pretty heated arguments.

I always told him: "In baseball you get three strikes, in golf we only get one, and like Snead says, we have to play our foul balls. In baseball if you strike out, the next guy can come up and hit a homer and win the game. I'm one man competing against a field of 150 players—if I strike out I don't have eight other guys on the team to help me." We argued all the time. What could he say? I know that in baseball you have to hit a moving object, but the hard part of golf is that our strike zone is always at the base of our feet. I asked him, "Ted, what's the hardest pitch to hit in baseball?" He said, "A low pitch." I said, "Well, you know where the golf ball is, don't ya? We have to go down and find it and we have to find it with 14 different clubs. We have to play a lot of different shots. We have to hit it high, hit it low, hit it far, hit it short, roll it on the ground, hit it in the air. And we don't have three fields to hit it to. We always have to go to centerfield. If we go to right or left field, we're dead." I gave him all that stuff.

As a golfer, Ted shot in the low 80s. I think his best score was 82. Now I'm 5'7" and 127 pounds, but I used to outdrive him. He came down at the ball too steep, causing it to go high. His angle of approach was too great. With a driver you must strike the ball with a level-to-ascending blow but he was hitting the ball with too much descend. So his ball was floating and my ball was driven. He was hitting high pop-ups instead of line-drives into the centerfield bleachers. I'd say, "Your angle of approach is piss poor." And he'd say, "You little shit! Some day I'll get even with you."

I never went fishing with Ted but he put on a demo on the putting green once. We were always challenging each other, so he said, "You may be able to hole a thirty footer, but I can put this fly in that cup and you can't do that!" And boy, did he put on an unbelievable demonstration. He gave that rod a couple of waggles like it was a golf swing and flicked that thing right in the cup from 30 feet away. I said, "Listen, I can't put the fly in the cup and you can't put the ball in the hole, so we're even Ted."

◆ ◆ ◆

DAVID HARTMAN, Former Host, *Good Morning America*

For a few hours that day we fished for bass. Fresh water, a small lake in Florida. Ted caught some. We talked rods and line, lure presentation . . . how to catch bass in THAT pond, THAT day. And we talked about self-discipline and passion and hard work and doing what you do as well as you can do it.

That night we had dinner together. Then, about midnight we walked to our cars. In the restaurant parking lot Ted said, "Show me your stance and swing!" It was way too late in life to matter, but I took the stance, focused on an imaginary pitcher in the darkness and took a rusty, batless swing. Ted erupted. The master at work. Batting Instruction 101, as if the World Series depended on my next swing. I'm grateful for those moments with Number Nine late at night in a Florida parking lot.

◆ ◆ ◆

CLIFFORD AMBROSE, Fishing Guide

I was a guide for 43 years. Cecil Keith and I fished out of Jimmy Albright's and that's where we met Ted originally, had to be in the '40s or '50s. I fished him in the first Islamorada tarpon tournament, back in 1964, and he got the largest tarpon in the tournament. We would have won it, but he wouldn't fish like I wanted him to. He was determined he was going to win it on spinning. Of course, you can catch more tarpon on fly. At the time, he was working with Sears, and he didn't have a fly rod with his name on it. He had all these Ted Williams spinning reels and bait-casting reels with his name on them. And everybody told him he couldn't win the tournament with them, so he says, "I'm going to show them I can." I said, "Well, Ted, you probably can, but you'd do it a lot easier on fly." "Nope! I'm going to do it on spinning." And actually, we had the winning fish on, but he broke him off. Ted got impatient when he couldn't turn the fish and these are probably 150 pound fish on ten or 12 pound test line. That would have won it.

In the '60s, Ted put up money for the Ted Williams Conservation Award, which he still funds. The award is presented to a sports writer who is deemed over a 12-month period to have contributed the most to salmon conservation. It has become one of the more highly prized awards for writers to earn.

—Jack Fenety

The next year he fished the tournament with Jimmy Albright and he used nothing but his fly rod, and beat me out. He was probably the top fly fisherman in the country.

In later years, Ted mellowed out. I was a guide and I'd be out on the water and have a young fellow and his dad with me. I'd say, "There goes Ted Williams." The kid's eyes would light up, so I'd run Ted down. He'd see who it was and he'd pull over and stop and he'd be real nice to the kid. In the early days, he didn't want to be bothered at all. A lot of people gave him a fit, and so he gave it back to them. But he was getting on up where he wasn't in the limelight as much and he mellowed out. I liked him real well. Everybody says, "How'd you get along with him?" And I say, "I've got no problem with Ted. We get along fine." If he wants to yell and scream, I just let him yell and scream. It don't bother me.

◆ ◆ ◆

JOHN A. SMREKAR, Friend

John Smrekar, 84, of Ely, Minnesota, is one of Ted's oldest and dearest friends. The two men have hunted deer in Minnesota and ducks in Arkansas. They have fished for bonefish off the coral reefs of Islamorada, Florida and cast for Atlantic salmon on the Miramichi River in New Brunswick. On the surface they would seem an unlikely pair. Smrekar is a religious man with a deeply personal relationship with God; Williams, on the other hand, sometimes treats Him like an umpire who just called him out on strikes.

I'll never forget the AP headline: FAMOUS TED WILLIAMS LOST IN ELY AREA WILDERNESS. Of course I had to read it after the fact because at the time I was "lost" with Ted Williams.

My hometown of Ely is located in the northeastern corner of Minnesota. Ted and I had hunted and fished together there many times without incident. On this occasion, the late John Koschak and I had invited Ted to come up for some deer hunting. Little did we know that before we came out of the woods the eyes of the nation would be focused on our small community.

Now Ted was a great fisherman, an excellent shot and a patient and knowledgeable hunter. He wasn't cocky, was a good listener, and was easy to get along with. A great team man who followed directions. He wasn't afraid of the vast Minnesota wilderness, but he sure respected it.

We scheduled a plane with skis attached—wooden runners for landing on ice—and departed Ely early in the morning for one of our favorite secret spots on Basswood Lake. Ted shot a big buck right away and our party of nine filled up their quota by noon. We dragged the deer to the lake shore so we could load them on the planes when they returned for us at 2:30 in the afternoon.

It started to snow about 1 p.m. but we weren't too concerned. Then a severe wind came up along with more snow. We waited, but no plane came at 2:30, 3:30, or 4:30 and when it still hadn't arrived by 5:30, it was getting dark. We knew because of the bad storm that there would be no plane to pick us up this day.

We had two alternatives: find a place to build a fire or walk cross country six miles northeast to the resort. We decided to walk, reckoning that if all went well, we would be there by midnight. It was one of those bitterly cold northern Minnesota nights, and the heavy snow made it extremely tough going; however, by following the compass, we were doing okay. Williams, although a bit weary physically, led by example. He was a man of faith, patience and good judgment. A cool head in difficult situations. He proved, beyond doubt, that he was a seasoned and courageous woodsman.

It was near midnight when one of our party, Dr. Whitters, a friend of Ted's from Princeton, Minnesota, came to me and said, "I should have told you this before, John. I had back surgery about six weeks ago. My back is killing me and I can't move another step." We had no choice but to make camp, build a fire, and wait for daylight. I used my Boy Scout ax to cut firewood and soon we had a roaring eight-foot fire going. I used to take a lot of guff about bringing this hatchet with me on hunting trips but that night everybody, Ted included, kissed it several times.

As daylight approached, I went on a little reconnaissance trip and you know what I discovered? We were in the back yard of the resort—our destination! After the tough night we spent, everyone was overjoyed.

The resort was closed up and we had to break in. There were lots of stoves and dry wood and we soon had it heated up. We found lots of dry food—spaghetti, rice, beans, raisins, prunes, coffee, tea and dry milk. We chopped a hole in the ice to get water and I threw all the food in a stock pot, cooked it and served it with steaming coffee and tea and spaghetti. Everybody said it was the best spaghetti they ever had—of course, they'd had no food since noon the day before so everyone was ravenous.

Knowing that the ordeal was over, Ted Williams put his arms around John and me, in a warm friendly manner straight from the heart, and said, "I had every confidence in you. I knew the hunting party was in good hands and I had complete faith in your leadership." He was so grateful. There was a graciousness about the man that the news media never saw, or at least never reported. He cared about people both on and off the field.

The planes were out looking for us and they spotted our white distress flag. We were soon back safely in Ely. The phone lines into town were totally jammed. Just about every news source in the country, as well as the Boston Red Sox owner Tom Yawkey and Ted's teammates were placing frantic calls, desperate for information on Ted. When Ted saw the media uproar he got pretty mad. A statement went out immediately to the newspapers stating that Williams was not lost and that he had merely "spent the night in the Ely area woods with his hunting companions." People still talk about it in these parts.

Gene Tunney and Ted in New Brunswick.
(Photo courtesy of Vin Swazey)

◆ ◆ ◆

RALPH KINDER, Barber and Duck Hunter

Ted was a character, I'll tell you that. Real plainspoken. You know, he was supposed to have been the best fly fisherman in the whole United States. He loafed down at the barber shop in Mound City a few times, a real ordinary guy. It never made any difference if you had any money or not. Garth Sharp brought Ted up and introduced us and I hunted with him for about eleven years. This would have been 30 years ago. Hell, he'd come up to my house and if we'd have to wait a couple of hours or something, he'd just take a pillow, throw it down on the floor, and lay right down and take a nap. He once gave me a brand new shotgun which I've still got, and even flew me down to Kansas City to see one of his ball games when he was managing the Rangers. We got in a lot of arguments but it was always friendly.

He was a good cook you know. We'd kill those snows and blues and he'd say, "You take a couple of them in, get 'em cleaned, and I'll cook 'em. He'd have both the kitchen windows up and smoke just rolling out of them. I remember Garth said, "Goddamn, he used every pot and pan that we had to cook them damn geese, but by God he done a good job."

When Ted had that first stroke, I couldn't believe it. Well, I could, too. I told him one time, "I'm going to give you a little advice, Ted." "What's that?" he said. "By God, you'd better start backing away from the table." "You mind your own goddamned business!" Like I said, real plainspoken.

◆ ◆ ◆

DOYLE CARLTON, Businessman

Billy Goodman brought Ted. See, they trained over at Sarasota in those days and we lived in a little community about 65 miles from Sarasota. I had known Billy Goodman for several years and when Ted come over it was such an interesting experience. He stayed two days and two nights. We shot quail and dove. I learned, after he was in the dove field, what a good eye he had because he could really lay them down. He didn't miss many shots, yet he wasn't impressed with himself. I always liked that.

We had some of the cowboys there, and some of the business people, and he was just as nice to everyone as he could be. This was when he was 38 years old. That's another thing we laughed about, they wrote in some article—"that 38-year-old Ted Williams, he's getting to be an old man," you know. Still, he was such a student. I would hear him and Billy talk about hitting. He would raise the question, "Billy, if you were facing Bob Feller, and you had a man on first and second, he had two strikes on you and two balls, what would you be looking for?" He was so perceptive, and such a student of hitting. I would listen to Ted and Billy Goodman talk about hitters and hitting, and technique. I don't know how anyone could have been a better student of the hitting game than Ted Williams.

He met my son who was just a little boy at the time. I think Ted had an influence on a number of us. Here he was, the last man to ever hit over .400, THE Ted Williams and, as far as he was concerned, he was just one of us. That's how he impacted our people here. Just so kind. When you're talking about a good heart, man that heart was good. I think about the work he did with the Jimmy Fund, always thinking about others. He had a very unselfish heart. That exterior's so gruff you would think, *How can anybody be this gruff?* But his heart is just as gentle and tender as his outward appearance is gruff.

I'll tell you a story he told me one time. When he got ready to leave the first time he came here, he said, "Well, I want to tell you that I've never had a better time in my life." And he says, "This is as good a bunch of men as I've ever been around. Usually, you have one jerk in the crowd. You didn't even have one of them." Then he said, "One thing I appreciated is having the blessing before our meals." He said, "You might not believe this, but I thank the Lord every day for my blessings." Now Ted Williams told me that.

◆ ◆ ◆

BUD LEAVITT, Friend
(Taken from an interview by Dick Wimmer)

I first met Ted in 1939. I was seated in the dugout at Fenway Park talking to Bobby Doerr. Lefty Grove was the pitcher on this particular hot, muggy day, and suddenly this voice down at the end of the bench said, "Hey, Bush, come'ere, will ya." And I said, "You talkin' to me?" And he said, "Yeah." And I'd never met Williams, this tall, long-necked kid, and I said, "Hell, if you wanna talk to me, come up here." Well, you know, nobody ever talked to him like that, and he did come up. He was boning a bat, and he said, "I heard you live in Maine." And I said, "That's correct." And he said, "Boy, you must have some great fishin' there." And I said, "Yeah, we do a little fishin' there." He said, "I'll be up someday." And I said, "Great."

Well, you know, I thought that was just so much dugout talk. Those were the days when the teams traveled by train, they always had Monday off, and, goddamn, one Sunday night not long after, he called and said, "I'm comin' up." And he did. We were in the middle of a real hot spell, and I told him the fishing was pretty lousy at that time of year, but he said, "That's all right." So he spent a couple of days—and God, that was 50 years ago!—and from that time on, why, hell, we've fished together, we've gun-hunted together, we've golfed together, and he's been a very, very close friend. Though not, however, without he and I havin' sparks between us. I mean he's a perfectionist and he has a difficult time comprehending mediocrity. And I'm mediocre in whatever the hell I do, whether it's hittin' a golf ball, castin' a salmon fly, or shooting waterfowl. And he's absolutely demanding when it comes to perfection. For example, every single knot, every leader of his fishing tackle has to be the ultimate in perfection. He can't stand a bad knot when he's casting that lays down badly. And he was the same way with bats. Hell, I watched him time and time again look at 25-30 pieces of wood before he found one he wanted. And he's the same way with photography, he's the same way with whatever the hell he does. He's never just good at it, he's great at it. And he's a great fisherman, truly a great fisherman. If you rate 10 or 15 of America's best anglers, especially in fly rod fishing, you have to include him. I mean I've seen him perform some incredible stunts on an Atlantic salmon, on bonefish as well as on tarpon. He's not just good, he's expert. And I'm frequently asked to name the 10 best fishermen I ever fished with. Well I've fished with some damn good ones, but he's certainly right up there in the forefront.

And as far as hitting a baseball, I don't think anyone ever swung a bat with the beauty, with the power, with the perfection of Ted Williams.

A lot of people think he's mellowed over the years. Well, he hasn't mellowed a helluva lot. Believe me, he hasn't. He's still a very, very private person, generous to a fault, check grabber   Christ, he was the one cut Johnny Orlando in on the World Series dough when those cheap bastards wanted to cut him out. And he's still, even at this late age, probably the most charismatic sports figure in our lifetime. An example is once we had just arrived in Alaska, and a couple of the dingiest, really crummiest-lookin' Eskimos you ever saw in your life were in the airport. We're waiting to get our duffels prior to flying in to a place called King Salmon for fishing, and one of these Eskimos points to the other and he shouts, "For cryin' out loud, that's Ted Williams!" And here's a guy been out of the game for almost 40 years, two generations of kids have been born, they're gone to college and departed, and he's still remembered as vividly today, and by some of the most out of the way people.

But my favorite baseball memory of him, though, has to be his last game. And for this reason: We had a young man in town by the name of Cornelius Russell III, who sustained a broken neck in a game with Kimball Academy in Kimball, New Hampshire. And Connie was a wheelchair victim from that time until his death in recent years. He was an ardent Red Sox fan. And one night, some years before Ted retired, we were sitting in my office and I said to him, "Come on, let's take a ride." He said, "Where we going?" I said, "Never mind, let's take a ride." And you know he rarely goes anywhere without an invitation. So we stopped at this house, and he said, "What the hell are we gonna do?" So I said, "I want you to meet a friend of mine." And I introduced him to Connie. Well Christ, they became fast friends. And Ted never made a trip through Maine without seeing Con or calling him on the holidays to wish him a happy Christmas, a happy Thanksgiving, a happy birthday, whatever. And Connie had never seen a major league game and never seen

Ted Williams was really the Hemingway of Islamorada. He put it on the map an really helped develop it into what it is today. He was a perfectionist and had incredible eye-hand coordination. Because he was such a perfectionist and intolerable of anyone that couldn't execute, he really became misunderstood.

—Gary Ellis, founder,
The Redbone Journal

Williams play. So I made arrangements with the Red Sox and gathered up half a dozen of Connie's pals—he had a van that was custom-made so they could wheel his chair in and out—and we sat right behind the Red Sox dugout. Christ, there wasn't anybody in the ballpark anyway, the were only 10-11,000 people there that day, a lousy overcast day. And Ted popped one his last time up. Though he never intended, even if he'd hit nine home runs, to make the trip to New York. He said, "I'm duckin', gettin' the hell outta here. So bring Connie and all those kids back to the hotel."

And the way he celebrated his departure from major league baseball was opening up a couple of bottles of wine back at the old Somerset Hotel, while the police protected him from the crowds trying to get a last look, and spending it with this kid in a wheelchair.

◆ ◆ ◆

I don't think Ted was ever meant to be a celebrity. He just wanted to be a great hitter. Then he wanted to be a great fisherman. Those are two things he certainly achieved.

—John Underwood

BOB BREITBARD, Longtime Friend

We both started at Hoover High in February of 1934. His love was baseball. At times, he brought his bat into the classroom. He'd put it under his desk. He carried a bat and he would put it under his desk.

He did wear a tie to our graduation. When we graduated in February of '37, Principal Floyd Johnson got up and said, "Now I have two awards to present, one to Bob Breitbard and the other one to Ted Williams. These awards are for typing 32 words a minute without an error." We got typing awards. That was our claim to fame.

When we dedicated a highway after Ted here, the Ted Williams Freeway, he and John-Henry and myself and Claudia, we went down to feed the animals down in the wild animal park. We're riding around in this truck, we're feeding the animals, the giraffes were coming up and eating out of our hands. We were feeding the hippopotamus and he looks up and about 300 yards away, I would say, on the side of a hill, he said to the guide,

"Isn't that an Alaskan blah-blah-blah buck?" "Sure is," said the guide.

"How the hell did you know that?" "Well, hell, I saw them in Alaska."

"Gee, there's only three of them in captivity and we have one of them here." "Well, I saw them up there. Hell, that thing must weigh four hundred and forty pounds!" The guide looked at him and said, "I can't believe you. That weighs four hundred and forty-three pounds."

We'd go by and he'd tell us the name of this eucalyptus tree. "It sure is." And "I know what kind of bird that is." He knows all these things.

◆ ◆ ◆

CURT GOWDY, Broadcaster

His legacy will be to promote the idea of being a real student of the sport. To study the fish, study the waters and apply oneself to the sport and practice. That's what his contribution will be. He always felt that the more you put into it, the more you get out of it.

I'd have to say he's a perfectionist. Natural. Honest. Thorough. Misunderstood. Sensitive. I say misunderstood because he had a running battle with the media for most of his

Ted feeding a giraffe, while son John-Henry looks on at the San Diego Zoo.
(Photo courtesy of San Diego Hall of Champions)

career. There were some people that started looking into his past and his family history, and it really made him angry. He took all of that personally. If I strike out, boo me. If I make an error, criticize me, but why go after my family? And sensitive, because, you couldn't believe it but he could pick out one boo in a crowd of 50,000 cheering fans.

One time, when the Red Sox were in Washington to play the Senators, there was a national casting competition set up at the reflecting pool in the shadow of the Washington Monument. Ted called me up and asked me if I wanted to go over. We met in the lobby and walked over. They had platforms built over the pool and all of these casters were up there practicing. All the guys recognized him. One asked him to take a look at his equipment. He took a few practice casts, then made his presentation cast, handed the rod back to the man and told him it was all right. Later they measured the cast and it was six feet short of the mark that eventually won the national championship.

◆ ◆ ◆

The Magic Baseball Card

A children's story by Jim Prime

Playing baseball on an island in the Bay of Fundy presents some special problems. For one thing, there's the fog. It creeps slowly across the field, swallowing first the outfielders, then the second baseman, and finally the pitcher.

Bernie Lemieux hated playing ball in the fog. He heard the crack of the bat and knew the ball was coming toward center field. But he couldn't see it. Then—at the last split second—he flicked his glove towards a round white blur and grabbed it for the final out in the top of the ninth.

"We need radar out here," Bernie yelled to his friend Marc, as they jogged in for their turn at bat.

"Count your blessings," called Marc. "At least the outfield is fairly level. This infield makes the surface of the moon look like a putting green."

Bernie was first up at bat. Someone yelled, "Smack one for the Schooners, Bernie." Bernie smiled and patted his hip pocket. His good-luck piece was still there. It was only a bubblegum card—a laminated rectangle of cardboard. It had a picture of a baseball player on one side and the player's life history on the other. But this was no ordinary card. This was a 1956 Ted Williams, given to Bernie by his grandfather just a few weeks before his granddad died.

Bernie and his grandfather had spent many long hours together talking about baseball—today's baseball and the baseball of 40 years ago. They disagreed about domed stadiums, artificial turf, and the DH rule. But they both agreed that Ted Williams had been the greatest hitter of all time.

Bernie felt powerful with the bat in his hands and the card in his pocket. He stepped into the batter's box and squinted through the fog at the Westport Whitecaps' pitcher.

The first pitch was waist-high and just a little inside. Bernie jumped on it, driving it deep into right field. As he rounded first base, he could see the ball drop just beyond the outfielder's reach. Between second and third he made up his mind to try to beat the throw to the plate. The second baseman took the relay and fired homeward, but Bernie slid in under the catcher's tag for the winning run. Final score: Schooners 3—Westport Whitecaps 2. The card had come through again.

As soon as Bernie got home, he knew that something was up. His father and brother Rene were sitting at the kitchen table looking over maps and brochures. His father looked up and smiled.

"What was the score?" he asked.

"Three-two for the good guys," said Bernie. "What's going on here?"

Just then he saw a brochure with the words *Things to do in Boston* on the front. His heart beat faster.

"We're planning our vacation," said his dad, still grinning.

Without thinking, Bernie felt for the Ted Williams card and tapped it three times for luck. They were going to see some ball games. He just knew it.

His brother Rene looked up from a list he was making. "I'm going to Boston to visit Mom, and you and Dad are going fishing," he said.

Bernie looked from his brother to his father. This had to be a joke. But his dad was nodding his head.

"That's right, we're going salmon fishing on the Miramichi River in New Brunswick. What do you think of that?"

Since the news was announced like a present, Bernie tried to act pleased. But he wasn't. He wasn't pleased at all.

Rene is going to be in Boston watching Red Sox games with Mom, while I'm up the creek with Dad, thought Bernie. And Rene wouldn't know a baseball from a turnip if it hit him!

Bernie looked out the window of the log cabin his father had rented on the Miramichi. The morning sun was sending shafts of light through the pine trees. It was 6:05 a.m., and his father was standing over a pan of sizzling bacon and eggs. They sat at the table and ate in silence. Finally, his father spoke.

178

"I know you'd rather have gone to Boston, see the Red Sox play and all that. I just thought . . . Well, I know I've been on the road a lot the last few years. I thought it would be nice for the two of us to spend some time together."

Bernie was surprised. He hadn't really thought about how often his dad was traveling. Maybe because he'd had granddad. But more than that, he had thought he had been able to hide his feelings about not going to Boston.

"It's okay, Dad. Really, we'll have fun."

"I know you miss your grandfather. You two were always together. I miss him, too. He was my dad, remember. And you'll be happy to know that he taught me a little about baseball. Did you know that Ted Williams hit a home run in his last time at bat?"

Of course Bernie knew. But he had no idea that his dad knew stuff like that.

His father continued, "Did you know he was the last ballplayer to hit .400 in a season?"

Bernie smiled patiently, "Dad, I don't want to hurt your feelings, but I think I know everything there is to know about Ted Williams."

It was his father's turn to smile patiently. "Maybe so," he said, "but we'll see. Before our week is over you just might learn something new."

By 7:15 they were at the river, casting for Atlantic salmon. Bernie was surprised to see the long smooth casts his father made. As they fished, they talked baseball. Every so often there would be another Ted Williams question.

"Did you know that he hit a home run every 16 times at bat?"

"Yes, Dad, I knew that," said Bernie. But even though Bernie knew all the answers, it was great to have someone to talk baseball with again.

"Do you still have that card that your grandfather gave you?" asked his father.

Bernie was a little embarrassed. He didn't think anyone knew about the card.

"Yes, I've got it with me." He reached into his pocket, but when he pulled the card out, it slipped through his wet fingers and dropped into the fast-moving river.

Bernie made a grab for it, but he couldn't move fast enough in his clumsy hip waders.

"Get it, Dad!" He yelled, but it was too late. The plastic-coated card was bobbing wildly in the current.

"We've got it get it back!" Bernie cried desperately.

"The river narrows below here," his father said as they clambered toward the shore. "Maybe it'll snag on the rocks." He didn't sound very hopeful.

As they made their way around the river's bend, they saw a tall man bending to scoop something from the water. He examined it closely and started to laugh.

Just then the man saw Bernie and his father on the shore.

"Is this thing yours?" the man asked, wading toward the shore. There was a smile on his tanned face. Somehow the face looking familiar, Bernie thought, like a long-ago friend who had got older.

"Yes, sir," panted Bernie. His voice was ragged with relief. "It slipped out of my hand. It's my good luck card. My grandfather gave it to me." Bernie realized he was babbling and stopped abruptly.

"Is this guy your dad?" asked the tall man.

"Yes, sir." He waited for his father to introduce himself, but instead, the two men shook hands like old friends.

"Then you must be Bernie—the ballplayer."

Bernie looked puzzled.

"Maybe I'd better explain, son," said his dad. "This . . . is Ted Williams."

Bernie looked as if he had seen a ghost. The man standing on the shore who was holding his Ted Williams baseball card *was* Ted Williams. "No wonder you looked familiar, but . . . "

"I told you that you might learn something new this week," said Bernie's dad. "I'll bet you didn't know that Ted Williams has had a camp on this river since 1955."

"I sure didn't," beamed Bernie.

The rest of the day Bernie talked baseball and fishing with his dad and Ted Williams. For Bernie, a dream had come true.

That night, as they made their way back to their cabin, Bernie pulled the baseball card from his pocket. In one short day he had met his hero, Ted Williams, and discovered a new friend to talk baseball with—his dad.

The magic was still alive.

TED WILLIAMS: THE PURSUIT OF PERFECTION

Remembrances of Swings Past

There are countless people who have been influenced by Ted without ever actually having met him. For some, it is the tableau of Ted's swing frozen in their mind's eye: A kind of excellence in motion—something to strive for. Some were even more impressed by his single-minded determination to excel. This determination helped galvanize many to action along their own career paths. Still others were intrigued by his image as a rebel and a loner, as a conservative and a war hero. The precise qualities that inspire such deep admiration in everyone from Kerouac and Corso to Nixon and Bush are impossible to define.

Because Ted Williams has lived such a full and varied life, it is not surprising that he has touched the lives of a diverse array of people. Through the years, Ted has socialized with Presidents and policemen, astronauts and actors, fishermen and philanthropists.

Some had only fleeting contact with Ted: a phone call just missed, a picture on a wall, a teenage girl's crush. These, too, are close encounters of the Ted kind.

Opposite: A souvenir for a fan, Ted Williams Field, San Diego.
(*John McCutchen photo, courtesy of San Diego Hall of Champions*)

DABNEY COLEMAN, Actor

Dr. Francis Kelly, who was virtually my stepfather, introduced me to baseball in Corpus Christi, Texas in the forties. There weren't a lot of baseball fans in Texas at that time. We didn't have radio broadcasts of baseball there so it was not easy to follow the game, but I did. In 1949, when I was 17 years old, Dr. Kelly sent me up to St. Louis in a roomette on the train to see Big League baseball. I saw 12 games in 14 days. I saw the New York Yankees, the Boston Red Sox and the Philadelphia A's play the Browns. I also saw the St. Louis Cardinals play the Philadelphia Phillies—all at Sportsman's Park. This was the first time I had seen these guys in person or even seen a uniform.

When Boston came in to play the Browns, I was a total Yankee, total Joe DiMaggio fan. I had seen both DiMaggio and Musial play, but when I saw Ted Williams, I remember thinking: *This guy seems like he discovered that he has a talent that no one else in the world has. It was as if he had invented this game and said, "I think I'll call this thing baseball because I do it better than anybody else." And more to the point—with more grace and with more ease than anybody else.* From this point I was, reluctantly, a Ted Williams fan.

As time went on, I got to know more about him—how he went back to Korea and crash-landed his Panther jet, how he received medals and things like that. Somewhere along the line I put it all together and I realized that Ted Williams was probably the first rebel that I ever experienced—before the writers and the actors, the Kerouacs and the Brandos and the Jimmy Deans—that this guy went back to 1940 as a rebel. He came in as a rebel, he stayed as a rebel, and he left as a rebel—then came back and left again, and he's STILL a rebel. For those reasons—always having an affinity for that kind of personality—Ted Williams became an icon to me. For me, Ted's appeal transcended athleticism.

There was almost an animalistic grace about Ted Williams. He was like some kind of cat—a jaguar or some other smooth, long-legged, graceful-moving animal. He had a grace that not even Joe DiMaggio possessed. There was an absence of all tension in his form at the plate. I remember when I saw him I thought, *Well, this guy looks like he's in the middle of a game taking batting practice*. Other guys appeared as if they were in a crucial game, even with a DiMaggio or Musial you'd notice a discernible tension. Now those guys both got great results, but Williams—he's going to go up there, take a few swings, and then he's going to go out and shag a few flies. Ted looked like fear was the furthest thing from his mind.

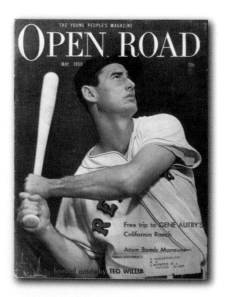

It wasn't my idea to have Slap Maxwell talk to Ted as part of his routine, but the people who wrote the show knew me. Jay Tarses wrote it and he was also a baseball fan. Then all of a sudden in Slap Maxwell, here was this character whose idol is Ted Williams. We even had a discussion about it later and I said, "How did you know about that? Did we ever discuss that?" His answer was "No." So it was a total coincidence. But long before that Ted Williams was my idol. I once asked Ted to do the show and he wrote a letter back saying, "Yes, I'd be glad to help you out next year." My biggest regret about not doing it a second year was that I was not going to have Ted Williams on the show. He had agreed to do it and unfortunately we didn't go again. It would've been fantastic.

At the time when he was playing and they were talking about a movie, I always thought that Robert Ryan would have made a good Ted Williams. There was a certain attitude that Robert Ryan had, and he also looked like Ted and was built like him. The other guy who could have done it, if he was an athlete at all, was Gregory Peck. Today, Jesus, I can't think of anybody to play Ted.

Speaking of Ted as an actor . . . I remember a story. Now I don't know how appropriate this is to say, but I didn't even like Ted Williams until I saw him. He was so good that he hurt the Yankees. And it was either DiMaggio or Williams.

You didn't like them both, it was one or the other and I liked DiMaggio. But in the winter of 1946, I read that Ted Williams signed a contract—I think with Twentieth Century Fox—to make a movie. I remember reading that and screaming out, just hollering out and bursting into tears and running to my mother and saying, "Mother, Ted Williams isn't going to play baseball anymore." I thought it meant he would never play baseball again. I was literally dissolving in tears and I couldn't even understand why, couldn't get it. But that's what happened. I don't think he ever made any movie. In those days that sort of thing happened all the time. They'd sign people to a contract and then either not make the movie or make it and shelve it. They'd give 'em X dollars and say we've got you under contract and if something happens we'll do it. Ask Ted what he thinks of Robert Ryan.

The Kid and the Duke— The Williams persona drew comparisons to another American legend. From left to right: Bruce Cabot, Patrick Wayne, John Wayne, Red Buttons, and Williams.
(Photo courtesy of The Jimmy Fund)

Could Ted have been an actor? That's a tough question to answer. If he'd wanted to be, he would have been. Something tells me that being an athlete and having the personality he possessed, he wouldn't do it. There's a great resistance with a lot of athletes because they would have to give up emotions. Now if he'd ever gotten the idea that he wanted to, I have a feeling that he could have done it because he was a passionate guy and that's very important. He certainly had the looks. Just a matter of whether he would want to cross that bridge. I'm not sure Ted would ever be prepared to do that.

Do I see the John Wayne comparison? Well . . . . yes, except that, it's a funny thing . . . Ted Williams, as tall and big as he is, has the energy of a little kid. He's athletic and energetic when he expresses himself. He conveys enthusiasm in the way he talks with his hands and body, and grace in the way he moves. I'm talking about even when he was 72 or 73 years old. He is a very passionate opinionated person and that's what makes him interesting. Ted has always had a great sense of drama.

◆ ◆ ◆

PAUL GLEASON, Actor

I was in the Cleveland chain and later played in the low minors with the Red Sox organization. I was there from '59-'62. Ted lived in Islamorada, Florida, and I lived down there and I used to talk hitting with him all the time there and up in Boston.

Back then I was kind of an arrogant little guy. Here's the thing: there's a difference between Ted Williams and all other hitters. For example, I told him one time that he screwed me up as a hitter and he really got pissed-off. "Whattaya mean I screwed you up? You're screwin' yourself up, drinkin' and runnin' around!" He used to tell me "Wait for your pitch until you got two strikes on you and then protect the plate." I was always behind the count because I was waiting for my pitch and they'd throw strikes and if it wasn't my pitch, I'd take it or I'd foul it off, so I was always 0 and 2. I went 1 for 23 one year listening to that advice. I was standing up at the plate like a statue. The difference between Ted Williams and hitters like me would be that he can wait for his pitch and when he gets it he doesn't foul it off—he hits it right on the nose. When I wait for my pitch I might miss it and strike out.

I used to good-naturedly discuss the different hitting theories with him because I used to talk with all the hitters. I'd talk with Hornsby and Waner and Williams. Paul Waner was my number one guru and he would always have you swinging down on the ball, have that bat at the top of the strike zone hitting line drives. And Williams used to ferociously argue against that. He'd say, "You've GOT to swing up. The pitcher's mound is elevated, you've got to have a slight uppercut in your swing." But when I did that I'd pop the ball up, see, so I used to say, "My way is Waner's way." Williams wanted every hitter to subscribe to his formula which he had proved successful, but what's good for one hitter isn't necessarily good for another hitter. And I certainly don't mean that as criticism of Ted.

I used to get in fierce arguments with Ted over his approach versus Waner's, and Ted would say, "Ah, f— Paul Waner! What does he know?" because that's the way Ted is—he wouldn't really mean it that way—but you know how Ted thinks. He would just fly off the handle about anything. But he's a funny guy, too. All of a sudden he'd say, "OH, OKAY! YOU'RE RIGHT! I'M WRONG! YOU'RE RIGHT! I'M WRONG!" You've gotta realize, here he was talking to a baseball bum—an out-of-work minor league wash-out talking to a Hall of Fame hitter. He's studied and broken down hitting and made it into a science that very few can argue with. And he's saying, "You're right. I'm WRONG! I've been WRONG all these years!" He just goes on and on when he gets on a tangent. "Oh no, hey, you're right! You've hit a LOT of home runs! I've been wrong all these years man! I'm glad you set me straight on that, Paul, ya f———- punk."

At the time I was a minor leaguer in Florida, I knew Jack Kerouac. I met him in 1961. He was from a suburb of Boston called Lowell and he was a Red Sox fan. Jack used to go watch them play all the time and his number one player was, as he used to call him, "Number 9." Ted was his favorite. We used to talk about Williams all the time, and since I was acquainted with Ted I would tell Kerouac stories about him.

I remember one of the stories I told Kerouac. He got a big kick out of it. I was working out at Fenway Park and we were in the dugout and I was sitting next to Williams down at the end of the bench. It was during the other team's batting practice and he was watching the other team's hitters and he and I were talking about the weather in California versus the weather in Florida—why even though San Diego has a great climate he prefers Florida's weather because of the humidity. This was 1960 and he wasn't talking to sportswriters much, if at all. In fact, after the games I would be up in the press box with the farm director and all these writers would come over and say, "What did Teddy say?, What was Teddy talkin' about?" And I'd just say "Oh, nothin' much." Anyway, this particular day there were three writers sitting way down at the other end of the bench and I saw them but I didn't notice that they were creeping and sliding and inching closer to us. They kept edging over so that they could overhear what Ted was saying. I didn't know that he was aware of it and I was barely aware of it myself.

Suddenly Ted exploded. He said, "I SEE YOU SONS OF BITCHES! GET THE HELL OUT OF HERE! I AIN'T TALKIN' TO YOU. THIS AIN'T NONE OF YOUR BUSINESS. GET THE HELL OUT OF HERE, YOU MOTHER F———! GET YOUR ASSES OUT OF HERE!" And they scurried down through the tunnel like rats out of a burning house, all three of 'em.

I think Jack really related to Ted. He loved Williams because he was outspoken and uncensored. He let things flow and that was what Kerouac looked for in everything in life—people who didn't revise their behavior, didn't conform. Kerouac was keenly grateful to see this in a guy in sports because most sports guys behave rather conservatively. They're trained to contain their emotions, but in Ted's case he just let it fly.

to see this in a guy in sports because most sports guys behave rather conservatively. They're trained to contain their emotions, but in Ted's case he just let it fly.

When Ted was young he was an exuberant, ebullient, enthusiastic fellow who loved baseball and loved life, and when he saw how fickle the fans could be he was sensitive enough that he said, *Okay I'm not giving them that part of myself. I'm not going to share my enthusiasm with them anymore. F--- 'em. I'm not tipping my hat.* He was sensitive enough to back off from that, but I don't think he ever lost his enthusiasm for the game or for developing the science of hitting.

Some fans turned on Ted. I think because he is a combative person, it fed him and he used it. Some shrinking violets would have been crushed by that but he was a courageous, stand-up guy who liked the competition, the rivalry, and loved a good argument. Kerouac used to hitchhike down to Boston from Lowell, starting in 1939, to watch Ted play and he said, "The thing I loved about Williams was his glee. He had great glee." I'll never forget that. And I thought . . . that glee subsided when the fans turned on him. He was an outgoing guy and he never lost that, but I think he just decided he wasn't going to demonstrate his glee anymore if they were going to boo him.

Kerouac admired Ted's spontaneity and the fact that he didn't seem to have any regrets about what he did. He behaved the way he wanted to behave and he didn't apologize for it. One of Jack's big things as a writer was that he was always connecting things from other walks of life to his writing. His writing was pure spontaneity—he didn't revise. He called it sketching. He wrote first thought, best thought, no revising. I think he liked the fact that Williams wasn't tentative. Let's put it this way: Ted Williams was courageous enough to be himself.

I've always said that Ted Williams would have been a natural as an actor because he had a great sense of reality. He would have been a great actor because he would have used himself well. Beneath Ted's bluster is a very sensitive person. He did things behind the scenes for people that he did NOT want known. He looked after people. He had a sensitivity toward people in less fortunate situations.

Who would he have been like as an actor? He'd have been like John Wayne. He'd have walked in and solved all your problems. Williams is very honest, very truthful. All great actors are very truthful. They have that sense of reality. Ted would have stood there like Spencer Tracy or James Cagney and told it like it was. He wouldn't have pussyfooted around like some phony. And that's the way Ted really is. He's a very loyal guy but once he thinks you've been disloyal, you're through.

Now here's the irony. We're talking about all these associations and connections. This is absolutely true and I don't know if Williams would ever remember saying this to me but I remember we were talking about heroes and I told Ted that my hero was Mickey Mantle [laughs]. Williams was never my hero but he was a guy I respected enormously. And I asked Ted, " Did you ever have any heroes?" I fully expected Williams to say, "F--- no! I don't have heroes, I'm my own hero!" Instead he said, "My hero when I was a kid coming up was John Wayne." I swear to God he told me that. I said, "Really?" He said, "Yeah, I tried to walk like him and talk like him. He was great. He was my hero." I said, "No shit?" And then I said, "TED, YOU'RE THE REAL JOHN WAYNE!!!" He said, "Naw, there was only one John Wayne." I said, "You went to war. He didn't go to war. He was AN ACTOR. HE'S AN ACTOR! His dad was a drugstore clerk in Glendale! You're the real John Wayne, you're the real Duke!" "Yeah," he said, "but I loved John Wayne. I loved the way he walked and the way he talked. I tried to imitate the way he talked." Isn't that something?

♦ ♦ ♦

It was an honor to know and witness Ted Williams as one of the most dedicated baseball players in the sport. To be a champion in any sport requires a great deal of focus and perseverance, and Ted was a true champion in every respect.

—Richard Petty, the king of stock car racing

"DREAM OF A BASEBALL STAR"
by Gregory Corso—taken from The Happy Birthday of Death

I dreamed Ted Williams
leaning at night
against the Eiffel Tower, weeping.

He was in uniform
and his bat lay at his feet
— knotted and twiggy.

'Randall Jarrell says you're a poet !' I cried
'So do I ! I say you're a poet !'

He picked up his bat with blown hands;
stood there astraddle as he would in the batter's box,
and laughed ! flinging his schoolboy wrath
toward some invisible pitcher's mound
—waiting the pitch all the way from heaven.

It came; hundreds came ! all afire !
He swung and swung and swung and connected not one
sinker curve hook or right-down-the-middle.
A hundred strikes !
The umpire dressed in strange attire
thundered his judgement: YOU'RE OUT !
And the phantom crowd's horrific boo
dispersed the gargoyles from Notre Dame.

And I screamed in my dream :
God ! throw thy merciful pitch !
Herald the crack of bats !
Hooray the sharp liner to left !
Yea the double, the triple !
Hosannah the home run !

LEONARD NIMOY, Actor

I was born in Boston's West End and I used to go to Fenway Park periodically, sit in the bleachers and watch the games. I'm talking about '40, '41, '42, during the war, some of it before the war, some of it just after the war. I saw him hit some long balls.

I read his book *My Turn at Bat,* and it told me some things that I had never before appreciated. What it takes for a guy to be a batter. Making a craft and a science out of it. Studying the pitchers, studying his own timing. Hitting as many balls as possible in order to get to the point of perfection that he attained. It wasn't something that the guy was able to walk out of his own house one day and do, just put a bat on his shoulder and start hitting balls. He worked very hard at it. I developed a real appreciation for the dedication that he put into learning how to do what he set out to do, the work that goes into the perfecting of a craft, in his case perfecting the art of hitting a baseball.

TED WILLIAMS: THE PURSUIT OF PERFECTION

Just like with actors. People think that "I could be in a movie if I'm really good looking and if I'm in the right place at the right time." Hollywood over the years has developed the myth that actors and actresses are chosen. "You, you be an actor in my movie." No training, no work involved. The myth continues.

◆ ◆ ◆

FLOYD JOHNSON, Ted's Former High School Principal
(From Ted Williams by Arthur Sampson)

Ted may have been a rebel as far as the social graces go, refusing to wear neckties or cater to the presshounds or the fickle fans, but he was not one to challenge authority. He respected strong figures like Patton and McArthur, and had no disciplinary problems in his five years of military service. He'd always had a bit of an unconventional approach, though, setting himself on an equal footing with those who might appear to be his superiors in one way or another. Perhaps this comes from his youth, when he often spent time with the fathers of some of the other kids, like Les Cassie's dad, when even Les didn't go along. Roy Engle has often told the story of how Ted, being introduced to Governor Merriam of California, simply stuck out his hand and said, "Hi, Guv!"

When Ted Williams attended Hoover High School, he habitually dropped into my office for a chat. During those chats, it never occurred to me that Ted would usually slump down into his chair and put his feet up on the principal's desk. The subject would usually be either baseball or fishing, subjects I was just as interested in as Ted. And I'd be enjoying the conversation so much I'd be completely oblivious to his posture and unconventional way of talking to the school principal. This was never impudence on Ted's part. To him all folks on the school campus were the same—faculty, principal, or kids.

◆ ◆ ◆

JORDAN RAMEN, Writer

I worked for Bill Doll who was a wonderful press agent. He handled entertainment people like Mike Todd, the producer, who did *Around the World in 80 Days*. He landed Sears Roebuck as an account, at the time when Ted had just retired. In 1961 or '62, somebody at Sears said to Bill, "Ted's not active anymore. Can you come up with any ideas to keep Ted in the public's eye?" So Bill said, "Well, why don't we get him to do a sports column? I think I can get it syndicated."

Bill Doll came up with this idea, and broached it with Ted. Ted said, "Fine, but obviously I'm not going to write it. I want to approve who the writer is." Bill got some legitimate professional sports writers to submit columns anonymously. And he said to me, knowing that I was an enormous fan, and knowing I was doing some writing, "Why don't you write a column and I'll throw it in the bundle we send off to Ted, because Ted is going to make the final pick?" So I did, and it wound up that Ted picked me out of all the professional writers. He said, "This guy writes the way I think."

That's how I got the job. I got in the picture strictly by good luck. When I was five or six growing up in Boston, I had a scrapbook. I was cutting out things from the old *Boston Post*, about Ted's exploits. When I was about five or six years old, I was just into it. I had two uncles who kept taking me to ball games. So Ted was one of my idols, along with Benny Goodman and Tarzan.

Loretta Knapp, retired pie shop proprietor, on Ted Williams: "Once he got and wrote on one of my licenses, 'Your chili was great.' He gave you a lot of respect, very gentlemanly. I always looked forward to him coming in. My maiden name was Williams and I can remember my father talking Ted W. the ballplayer. I also remember trying to claim his as an uncle but never convincing anyone that it was true."

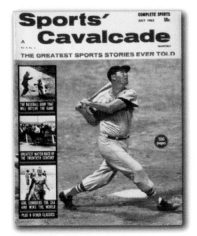

It was only supposed to run for about three months. It wound up running over three years. It was a once a week column that wound up getting syndicated in ninety newspapers. The first time it ran, we were on the front page of the *Boston Globe* and other papers throughout the country. Ted had to okay every column and I don't know if anyone believes it or not, but at one point he even corrected grammar. I don't know if anyone ever thought of Ted as a grammar maven. But he would do that.

Every column was approved except for one that involved Paul Hornung. There was a gambling scandal involving Hornung when he was playing with Green Bay. I did a column—well, rather Ted did a column—let's say I ghosted a column, sort of defending Hornung like he wasn't betting on himself or whatever. Anyway, Ted said, "We can't run this because when I got out of the service, I made three or four bets with a rookie on the Detroit Tigers named Dick Wakefield." Ted said, "I bet him some money that I'd beat him out in home runs, batting average and RBIs. And I did." He says, "So I won whatever the money was. But if the sportswriters got ahold of that, they would do me in." So that column never ran. That was the only column he never approved.

We had Ted sit down at a typewriter and took pictures as if he were writing the column. That's the one we would send out, to show it was Ted doing the column. Boy, did those Boston sportswriters jump all over him when those columns came out. I mean they CRUCIFIED him, and me. There was a guy, Gillooly or the Colonel, I forget which one, and he found out it was somebody else doing the writing and not Ted. He did a whole column called "The Splendid Splinter and the Splendid Spectre," the latter referring to me, of course.

Believe it or not, at one point we had a script to do a TV documentary on Ted. Ted had mentioned that he had all this wonderful film. So we got a first draft script written. We did two versions of a Ted Williams song, which I happened to write. One was a jazzy version, which Ted himself liked better, sung by a jazz tenor to a bossa nova rhythm. The other was a little choral group version for children, a square piece. Everybody liked the idea, and we thought we could tie it all together.

We had everything lined up, had everything written, and you remember an actor named Robert Ryan? Well, that's who we were going to have play Ted. Sears had given us ten thousand dollars to get the show started, and we hired four researchers. We sent the four researchers up to Boston and they went through all the libraries and newspapers and gathered all sorts of tremendous stuff. Then the guy who spearheaded the whole thing at Sears died, and the person who replaced him didn't care for Ted. And so it never happened.

♦ ♦ ♦

GEORGE STEINBRENNER, Owner, New York Yankees

I go back a long way with Ted Williams and he doesn't even know it. I grew up in Cleveland and was a great Indians fan and used to go to their games all the time. I can remember one night Ted was walking up East Twelfth Street. I believe he was on his way up to the Statler Hotel where the Red Sox used to stay. Well this was kind of a rainy, cold night. I wasn't at the game that night but he was obviously coming back to the hotel and so I started to walk with him and I just introduced myself. Now all I ever knew about Ted Williams was that I thought he was one of the greatest I ever saw play, and that the press was always saying that he was standoffish and that he didn't like to talk to people. Well, we walked a couple of blocks together and I just told him how much I thought of him as a player and he was utterly . . . so nice. Such a nice man! He didn't know me, I was just a nobody and he was . . . Ted Williams. All the things in the press had made such a hell of an

Chip Off the Splendid Splinter by Nova Scotian folk artist Gerry Hoare.
(*Courtesy of Jim Prime*)

impression on me as a young man. Then I just said: "Well, screw those guys that are writing that Ted Williams is this and Ted Williams is that. He's a class act." And that's exactly what he was. He was talking to me and I couldn't get over it.

I don't know that I would have handled the proposed Ted for Joe DiMaggio trade situation the way it was handled because I don't think I would have ever given up Joe DiMaggio for anybody. They were both in the same category. Ted is to the Red Sox what Joe DiMaggio is to the Yankees. I don't think that would have been the trade. I think what I probably would have done was said, "If you let me keep DiMaggio and trade me Williams, your wife will be my partner in the Yankees."

I know both men. I know Joe very well and I put him on a pedestal and I would put Ted on the same type of pedestal. Regardless of what he may have thought of the Boston press, the people of Boston really loved Ted Williams. Everybody respected both men. They had some things in common and one of those things is that they command that great level of respect. They are just those kinds of individuals.

Ted and Joe were the epitome of that great Red Sox—Yankee rivalry. And yet, I will tell you something about Ted Williams. When Phil Rizzuto—a Yankee who played against him all those years—needed a friend to get into the Hall of Fame where he belongs, nobody in baseball battled any harder for him than Ted Williams.

I remember once that I talked to Ted about coming over to work with our hitters and I think it was Sully (Haywood Sullivan) who found out and went to get him to coach hitters for the Red Sox. As a manager, who knows? I've been in coaching, I've been a coach myself, in Big Ten football, so I know. The great players don't always make great managers. More times than not it's the guy who wasn't a great player who turns out to be a hell of a manager—Casey Stengel, McCarthy, Alston, Lasorda. I've got one right now who was a damn good player and is also a damn good manager, Joe Torre. It's hard to judge.

Speaking of coaching, I think I'd have gotten along fine with Ted if he'd played for me because I don't have too much trouble with guys who can back up what they say. Ted Williams is a man who can back it up. How much would you have to pay him on today's market? You wouldn't pay him, you'd just give him half the team. He'd be your immediate partner.

◆ ◆ ◆

TOMMY LASORDA, Baseball Manager, Hall of Fame

I met Ted when I was with Kansas City and pitched against him in spring training. He was always ready to help anybody; it didn't make any difference what uniform you had on. Then, when Ted managed, I was still managing in the minor leagues. We talked at length about managing. He asked me quite a few questions. His experience of managing was that he started right in the major leagues. He played a very important part in a lot of hitters' lives and I loved talking to him about hitting. We became friends and through the years we have become even closer.

I remember a time I was speaking at a sports banquet in Toronto, and I looked in the audience and I saw Ted and Ferguson Jenkins sitting there. I was surprised to see Ted Williams at this banquet in Toronto! Of course, I introduced him when I got up to speak and he motioned for me to give him a call after the dinner was over, which I did. He invited me up to his room, ordered us a drink, and we talked about hitting.

About three o'clock in the morning, he looked at me and said, "You're a good friend of Frank Sinatra's, aren't you?" I said, "Yes, I am." He said, "Well, you know, Frank has been my guy. I have never met him, but by God, he's a great singer. I love to listen to him. Boy, what a great legend." I said, "Why don't you tell him yourself, Ted?" He said, "What do you mean?" So I picked up the phone. It was midnight in Palm Springs. And I called Frank. I said, "Somebody wants to talk to you."

So I give the phone to Ted Williams. Ted says, "Frank, I told Tommy, you're my guy. I've always enjoyed you very much—your music, your singing. You're great." He went on like that for about five minutes, and finally he handed me the phone. Sinatra said to me, "Jesus! I can't believe I was talking to Ted Williams!" It was a mutual admiration society.

When I was selected for the Hall of Fame, Ted got on the phone to me. He said to me, "You know how much I love you, Tommy. You know how much I respect you." I mean, it gave me chills when Ted Williams said that.

Ken Coleman came to me in spring training [in 1988], and he said, "Look, we're going to honor Ted Williams. But the only way he would agree to be honored would be if he could pick out the speakers and you were one of the speakers." I was honored and elated and promised Ted I'd be there. Now, we go on to win the World Series that year, and Peter O'Malley's planning to take the whole organization to Rome—not the players, but the people who worked there. I told Peter, "I already promised Ted Williams . . ." And that's where I went, to the Ted Williams tribute in Boston. I never did go to Rome. That's how much love and respect I had for the man.

Ted's my friend. I look at him and think . . . if you saw God and you said, "God, I want you to create a person of all kinds of talents—baseball player, fisherman, pilot . . ." I think He would have created Ted Williams.

◆ ◆ ◆

VINCE PIAZZA, Father of Mike Piazza, New York Mets Catcher

I met Ted Williams several times through Tommy Lasorda. Tommy and I were both born and raised in Norristown, Pennsylvania. Tommy's a little older than I am but I used to watch him play as a kid. I always admired his game and we stayed in touch as the years went by.

Tommy often gave speeches, and several times he put on clinics in Cherry Hill with Ted. Ted would talk about hitting, Tommy about motivating. After one show, Tommy invited Ted to come up to Norristown but there was the biggest snowstorm. Fortunately,

I had a car dealership and so I wound up getting a four wheel drive vehicle, and driving up with Tommy and Ted. We ended up in this dinky little place called the Gateway Diner up in Jeffersonville, Pennsylvania, and we bring Ted Williams into the place about 11 o'clock at night. We had a late breakfast there, and outside it's still snowing. We're telling baseball stories.

Tommy says to me, "Hey, is Monsignor Larkin around?" He knew Monsignor played professional baseball. So I call Monsignor on the phone to tell him that Williams is at the diner. Monsignor Larkin was sleeping but I woke him up and got him out of bed. He does not know at that time that it's Ted Williams. He just heard the word Williams. But he leaves the parish to come on over, and I see him at the door and bring him back. As he's walking in, he says to me, "Where's Ike Williams?" He's thinking it's the fighter. Then he walks in the back and sees Tommy sitting there with Ted Williams, and the guy almost passes out. I swear, it was the funniest thing you'd ever want to see, the look on this man's face when he saw Ted Williams—in this snowstorm, at one o'clock in the morning, in a neighborhood diner. He could not believe it. This was his idol.

As the discussion goes on about hitting and playing, Ed Liberatore mentions to Mr. Williams, he says, "You know, Vince has a boy, seems like he swings the bat pretty good, Ted." And Ted says, "You do?" He talks in that deep tone. I said, "Yeah, I do, Mr. Williams." He said, "Where do you live?" I said, "Over to the other side here, over to Valley Forge. It's about five minutes from here." He said, "Can I see this boy?" I said, "You gotta be kiddin' me!" I said, "Certainly." He said, "Do you have some place we could watch him hit?" I said, "Yeah, I put this old rinky-dinky batting cage in the back yard." This was in the winter but we had a real mild winter. He said, "Would you pick me up in the morning?" I said, "Would I pick you up in the morning? You gotta be kidding?"

I'm thinking to myself, *My Gosh, this guy's going to come over to the house and watch my boy hit*. And sure enough, the next morning we pick Ted up and he comes over to our home. I introduce him to Michael, and Ted's watching Michael hit, going on and on about how well he thought the kid could hit. Then he said, "My God, this kid swings the bat better than I did at his age." Michael was 15. He says, "I can guarantee, Eddie, you'll get all kinds of scouts looking at this kid." He's going off and on. He said, "I'm going to tell you something. This kid doesn't need a thing. The only thing I see that he should be doing, I'd like to see him raise the bat barrel just a little bit. Other than that, don't let anyone ever touch this kid's swing."

I show Ted that Michael can hit left-handed and he says, "Well, I think that he should hit left-handed, too. He's just a little slow in the hips, but if he can catch up, he'd be a hell of a left-handed hitter." When Michael comes out of the cage—I'll never forget this—Ted says, "Mike, I want to tell you. There's only one thing I want you to think about. What I see in that cage is about 50 percent of what's required for you to be an extremely good hitter." Then he taps him on the head, and says, "This is the other 50 percent. If you can get this—the mental aspect of the game—you'll be one hell of a hitter. You'll hit 25 home runs in the major leagues."

So now Mike, he's all beside himself. We go in and we have breakfast at the house. He says, "Mike, I want you to do one thing for me." Mike says, "Mr. Williams, what's that?" He says, "I want you to go out and get my book on hitting." Mike says, "Mr. Williams, I have your book." "You do?" he says. "Get it for me." He runs upstairs and grabs the book. He runs back down, and Ted takes the book and looks at Mike, and he opens the first page and it's blank of course, and he writes in there, "To my friend Mike. Don't forget me. I may need tickets one day to get in to see you play." And he signed it "Ted Williams."

◆ ◆ ◆

REGGIE JACKSON, Ballplayer, Hall of Fame

I first met Ted in Oakland, 1969. He was managing the Washington Senators. You heard stories, that he was a tough guy, hard to talk to—you almost became afraid of the man.

There was a photographer named Freddy Kaplan who knew Ted and he said, "Would you like to meet him?" Who wouldn't want to meet Ted Williams? I was a 21-year-old rookie and I went over with Kaplan. Ted just put his arm around me and said, "You know, I like your swing." Everyone else was telling me to cut my swing and not to uppercut, and here I've got the greatest hitter in baseball telling me "I like your swing. You've got a perfect uppercut. I think you have a chance to hit six hundred home runs.' I had a picture of him and the second time we played the Senators in California, I asked him to sign it for me. He said, "Don't ever change your swing," and he put that on the picture.

I'm a baseball fan and was a great statistician. I always thought it was an injustice that he wound up with 2,600-some odd hits and didn't get a chance to get 3,000 because of his service. Ted Williams to me is like Joe DiMaggio, Babe Ruth, Lou Gehrig, Willie Mays,

As far as his language goes, you love Ted in spite of it all. He lived through a lot. I remember Ted's anger . . . but he was a man who carried very deep feelings for people. He isn't all tough guy. He's soft as a grape underneath.

—Lib Dooley

he wound up with 2,600-some odd hits and didn't get a chance to get 3,000 because of his service. Ted Williams to me is like Joe DiMaggio, Babe Ruth, Lou Gehrig, Willie Mays, Hank Aaron—it stops pretty much there. Ted Williams was the greatest hitter that ever lived. He is an American natural resource.

◆ ◆ ◆

TITO FRANCONA, Ballplayer
(Taken from This Side of Cooperstown edited by Larry Moffi)

I always remember the first game I played in the big leagues. I went out to the ballpark early in the morning, about eight o'clock. We had a one o'clock game. It was Boston. I put my uniform on, then walked around the field to get acclimated. I was sitting in the dugout, and all of a sudden I see this big guy coming out of the Red Sox dugout. Number 9. Ted Williams.

He walks across the field and comes into our dugout and says, "Are you Tito Francona?" And then he starts telling me about hitting.

When we're done I'm wondering, "How the hell does he know who I am?"

Never mind, I found out. My roommate was Harry Dorish, who played with Boston in the '40s. He called Ted Williams up the night before and told him I was going to be there early. So *Williams* came out early. He made me feel comfortable. Gave me some tips.

I never watched many big league games before that. The Red Sox were taking batting practice, and I was off on our side of the field with my back to home plate. All of a sudden everything got quiet. I turned around, and Ted Williams was taking batting practice. Our whole team ran behind the batting cage to watch this guy hit. Sportswriters were watching him.

They hit about five minutes for each ballplayer. He'd hit five minutes, then everybody went back to doing their business. About twenty minutes later, same thing; everything got quiet. I turned around, he's hitting. Everybody runs to the cage . . . .

The sportswriters used to rag him a lot. One writer I remember in particular called out, in a heavy Boston accent, "Hey, Ted, you can't get around on the fastball anymore!"

He was hitting. He turned around and he looked at that guy and he said, "Jesus Christ couldn't throw a fastball by me."

◆ ◆ ◆

DAVID CATANEO, Writer
(Taken from Peanuts and Crackerjack by David Cataneo)

For dinner one night at spring training in 1988, two reporters from the Red Sox training camp ventured to a roadside restaurant in Auburndale, Florida, on Highway 92, about fifteen minutes west of Winter Haven. Painted in large, white letters on the rust-colored shack was the name Cafe Turtle and Catfish. A placard in the window advised, "Warning: Guarded by Trained Attack Pit Bulls with AIDS." In the entryway just inside the creaky, wooden screen door loomed a stuffed black bear. Further inside were three clean, well-lit rooms with round tables and metal chairs. Further back was an airy hootenanny hall with a bandstand. In each room, the walls, ceilings and corners were crammed with Americana, with a strong southern accent.

Among the hundreds of items were Civil War brass knuckles; an autographed photo of Tennessee Ernie Ford; a certificate of sale for one slave, dated September 9, 1840; a Remember Pearl Harbor license plate; a ball and chain; three taxidermy-preserved taran-

walking stick fashioned from a bull's penis; a Texas Ranger's badge; a stuffed bobcat head; and an Abe Lincoln campaign button.

The menu included fried whole catfish, quail, frog legs, soft-shell turtle, fried rattlesnake, shark, alligator, and armadillo. A Dixie-raised diner judged the fare authentic and tasty. Missing only from a perfect evening was a touch of "the pastime." So the tattooed waitress, Ana Samarco, was asked if there were any baseball artifacts among the memorabilia. "I don't think so," she said after some thought. "But we did used to have a baseball player hang around here all the time."

Asked his name, she replied, "Ted Williams. He'd always come in and have my mother cook him up some softshell crab. He'd bring his own. Do you know if he's been sick? He's usually come in here by now, and we've been worried about him."

Diners from Boston assured her the Splinter was okay. He was just campaigning for presidential candidate George Bush and was expected the following week.

"Good," she said. "I'll tell my mother so she can stop worrying about him."

BILL NOWLIN, Fan

While countless Red Sox fans have memories of Ted Williams silhouetted against the muted green of Fenway's leftfield wall, I grew up with Ted on my bedroom wall. In 1951, when I was six years old, I had a brief hospital stay and, unknown to me, my dad wrote to Ted—the patron saint of all sick kids—and secured a photo made out to me personally, and signed "Your pal, Ted Williams."

In 1988, when a friend and I went to the Red Sox spring training in Winter Haven, Florida, I finally had a chance to meet the man on my wall. We arrived hours before the actual game and proceeded down to the lower four fields where the prospects were working out. As we passed the dressing room, out came Ted Williams in full uniform. There were eight or ten fans present, but Ted headed straight for a boy in a wheelchair, chatted with him—and him alone. He then hopped on an electric cart and drove himself down to the lower fields. I followed on foot.

He spent brief moments offering comments and critique to the players. Remounting his cart, he signed a few items for the remaining handful of persistent souls. I hung back—in awe and respect—as the Ted-mobile sped off up the incline to yet another field. Again I followed.

There was now only me and one other person left. It was now or never. He probably just wanted to be rid of me, this 43-year-old kid who shadowed him for an autograph. But it was the first autograph this grown-up kid ever sought. And Ted took the ball from me, never glancing up. I explained how my father had given me that photo and how it had been on my wall for 37 years. "Unhhh!" he said, handing back the ball, signed, before the cart silently carried him away. The wall of silence had been broken.

♦ ♦ ♦

EVANGELISTO "GELI" GAROS,
Retired Slaughterhouse Operator

I met Ted through hunting, in the middle '50s. A friend of mine used to train his dogs up in Weare, New Hampshire and through him I became acquainted. We used to bird hunt, mainly woodcock and partridge, and fish all the time.

I stayed up at Ted's camp in New Brunswick. He was a good cook. He was also a good sport, and not just when it came to hunting. We often went out to restaurants and

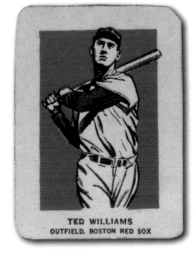

TED WILLIAMS
OUTFIELD, BOSTON RED SOX

everywhere we went, people would be asking for autographs. There was a restaurant in Columbia we stopped at one day. Somebody spotted him and brought over a whole school class of kids.

There was a turkey farmer there by the name of Blake and he said, "You're not going to sign for the whole lot?" "Oh, yeah!" Ted said, "for kids! Oh yeah?" If you were a grownup, he didn't give a damn—he'd tell you where to go. But kids? He would stay there and talk to a kid day and night. Even if we were in a hurry to go hunting, he didn't care, he'd give an autograph to the kids. If he'd see some kids playing ball, he'd go over to talk.

I remember he came down to a baseball dinner in Manchester. After the dinner he would stay at the hotel and this one time we were going up to his room and there were some kids waiting outside the door. It was three o'clock in the morning but these kids were there. A guy whose grandfather used to own the Sears Roebuck Company told the kids to go away and Ted found out about it. And, boy, did he blow his top! He sent the guy down to find the kids—at three o'clock in the morning! He said, "You so-and-so! You never send kids away! If you don't find them, you better not come back!" Anything for the kids. If it was an older person, Ted didn't give a damn.

♦ ♦ ♦

PAT WILLIAMS, Basketball Executive, Orlando Magic General Manager

I spent seven years in baseball with the Phillies organization at the start of my career. But I fell in love with baseball when I was seven years old. I grew up in the Philadelphia area as a huge A's and Phillies fan. My uncle Bill had a big influence on me and uncle Bill loved Ted Williams. My very earliest memories . . . everything related to Ted! When it came time to make me eat something, well, "Would Ted have eaten it?" "I wonder what Ted is doing now; I wonder what Ted is thinking." I mean, uncle Bill was absorbed with Ted, and so that was passed on to me. My all-time sports hero is Ted Williams.

In 1954, I went up to the games every weekend. The very first time I met Ted, I was about fourteen years old, it was at an A's—Red Sox doubleheader. I waited outside the park with the hordes of kids, trying to get autographs. The Red Sox bus was there and Ted was sitting in the front seat, with the window open signing autographs.

I remember two things. Ted, leaning out the window with this clamor of kids trying to tear the bus apart. I remember hearing him say—you know how animated he is—"If you don't get in line, I'm not signing any of them." I got him to sign his picture. I still have it. I got home that night, and the A's lost the doubleheader, and my mother who was a big baseball fan, too, said "Oh boy, what a disappointing day!" I said, "Disappointing? I got Ted Williams' autograph!!"

Now you've got to jump forward to four years ago. I'm in Florida and I make the acquaintance of Lewis Watkins who is the founder of the newly launched Ted Williams Museum. They're having the grand opening of the Hitters' Hall of Fame, and Lewis sends me an invitation as one of the celebrity guests. You talk about the thrill of a lifetime! At this point, I'm 53 years old, and I'm at this convention with Joe DiMaggio, Muhammad Ali, Stan Musial, Bob Feller . . . and Ted Williams. Like a kid at a candy store, to be in Ted's presence. I've got this huge blown up classic picture of Ted Williams and Babe Ruth in 1943. It's half as big as I am, but I lug that sucker up into the reception and I go and get Ted to sign it. It now hangs proudly on my office wall.

♦ ♦ ♦

I don't think there ever was anybody who could play Ted Williams on the big screen. He was a movie star without being a movie star. I knew John Wayne very well and I agree with that comparison—but the only one who could have played Ted Williams was Ted Williams. Both were Americans who typified what an American male should be. Both were masters at being men, the best at what they did. But the only one who could have played Ted Williams was Ted Williams.

—Eddie Fisher, entertainer

TED WILLIAMS: THE PURSUIT OF PERFECTION

BILL LEONG, President of Key Strategies

Living in New England with its rich sense of history and sports, you learn to not only look at where you are going but where you've been and I would have been remiss if I didn't educate myself about Ted Williams in the same way I did about Paul Revere.

I started reading old archives of the *Globe* and the *Record-American*. I wasn't looking at it from the perspective of baseball but just as to what made this guy tick . . . like I'd buy a book about Bill Gates, just to see what makes the guy tick. The more I read about Ted Williams, the more I realized that he transcended baseball; that's why I became a fan. His work ethic, dedication, skills and confidence could be applied to other areas of work outside of baseball. I found myself rededicating my efforts to be the best I could be in my career just as he dedicated himself to becoming the best hitter in baseball.

◆ ◆ ◆

JOE FALLS, Columnist

I remember Ted coming to Detroit near the end of his career and I'm standing at the batting cage. It's a Friday night and the Tigers drew a lot of fans back then. It was maybe 40 minutes before the game but there was a good size crowd in the ballpark watching batting practice. And Ted comes out of the dugout and walks right to the cage, gets set in the cage, and takes seven swings. I'm standing here watching this. The first one he lines down the right field line just inside the foul pole. Crash! Home run into the upper deck. The second one went a little further into the upper deck. The third one a little further. And now the crowd starts to pick up on this. The fourth one—BOOM, a little further. He did it seven times straight times—seven times in the upper deck, each one a little longer than the last one and by the time the seventh ball went out, the place was in an uproar. I'd say 25,000 people were roaring because they saw what he was doing. He turned around, went back to the dugout, went down the steps didn't say hello, good-bye, kiss my ass, tip his hat, nothing. That's a true story.

Many years ago, I was at Deerfield Beach, north of Miami, and I approached 100 people and said, "I want to give you a name and see if you know who it is: *Ted Williams!*" And 100 out of 100 knew who Ted Williams was! I wrote a column about it for *The Sporting News*. This was 20 odd years ago and Ted had been away from baseball for a long time at that point. Some of the kids said he was a fisherman—which knocked me out, really knocked me out! Who would think of Ted Williams as a fisherman?

I went to see him every year in Winter Haven. He liked me because I could talk about Phil Marchildon's arm and I could talk about Joe Coleman Sr., so I was a guy who understood where he came from. The modern guys couldn't do that. I mean I was there the day he got all those hits in Detroit after he broke his collarbone. One spring Ted took me out to a Chinese restaurant. Now you'd think after 51 years in this business, at the age of 69, that I could handle that stuff. Are you kidding me? Ted Williams buying ME dinner? Come on. I was never one of those who palled around with players. I never socialized with them, never played golf with them—never did any of that and I still don't. But this is Ted Williams. So he takes me out to dinner and he does the ordering. You've gotta eat what he eats because you don't get a chance to order. So I ate what he ate and then he says, "Okay, now we're going to finish the evening off right." The old chocoholic took me to Howard Johnson's and orders a fudge brownie with chocolate ice cream on it and chocolate sauce on top of all of that and I had to eat one, too. I was repulsed, but I had to eat it.

I can look across my room and see a six-foot tall cardboard cutout of Ted Williams in his Red Sox uniform swinging a bat. I may be the only guy in America you'll find who has a Ted Williams cardboard cut-out. My little two-year-old granddaughter gave it to me. When she was one year old she came down to the basement and said, "Hi papa!" I said, "Where's Ted Williams?" And she went right across my basement office and touched the cardboard cut-out.

◆ ◆ ◆

DAVE McKENNA, Pianist

I grew up in Woonsocket, Rhode Island. I used to get taken to games to see Ted. He was a skinny guy. From '46 on, I used to go on my own. The first time I saw him was against the Yankees. We got to the park pretty early, just as Ted was taking batting practice. What a beautiful thing it was to see him hit those line drives. Later, I wrote two instrumentals, "The Splendid Splinter" and "Theodore the Thumper" with Ted in mind. I like "Theodore the Thumper" better, just a little jazz riff.

Ted showed up at the Copley Plaza one time in the 80s. Brian Interland brought him in. You know Ted and Brian are very close. Brian would come in and say, "I'm going to bring the Thumper in one night." I'd say, "Yeah, yeah." I didn't believe him. So one night Brian came in, walked past the piano and said, "Dave, remember me?" I said, "Yeah, you're Ted Williams' friend." He said, "Right behind me!" And there's the Thumper! He said, "Now come over." I took a long intermission and talked to Ted for about 50 minutes . . . actually Ted did all the talking, but I was delighted to listen. Brian said, "Dave, Ted must like you, because he hasn't said a word. Usually he jumps all over people who are smoking." I said, "Oh, Jesus!" I put my cigarette out. I said, "For you, Ted—for nobody else, but for you, Ted—I'll put my cigarette out."

◆ ◆ ◆

OSCAR PETERSON, Jazz Pianist

Back in the mid-1950s, Ted came into Boston's Hi-Hat Club with a couple of his comrades to catch my show. I didn't know he was coming. Someone asked me, "Do you know who's standing back there?" I said, "No" and they said it was Ted Williams. I couldn't believe it. He's always been one of my favorite athletes. The manager took me back and introduced us, and he was so cordial. He told me how much he enjoyed what I was doing and I told him what a big fan of his I was. He came in several times after that.

I have always had great respect for what Ted did in the baseball world. I grew up in Montreal and the press there followed his successes quite closely. In high school, we got into sports and people talked about who they liked in each particular sport. Ruth was before my time; Gehrig followed that, but Ted was always my favorite. We were all playing baseball then. Everybody played baseball. Ted was top rank. Top drawer. He was like a god when he walked up to the plate, a man with a stature and a grace that you just don't find today.

◆ ◆ ◆

Object of fan affection, Ted motors through the street.
(Photo courtesy of The Jimmy Fund)

Ted with Yogi Berra.
(Photos courtesy of J.J. Nissen Baking)

MARIO FINOCCHIO, Nissen Bread Commercial Writer

I used to work at a television station in Worcester, Channel 27. We used to produce animated commercials for the Nissen Baking Company, and I met Ernie Bowler, who was the advertising director for Nissen.

We were just talking, and he said, "If you could have anybody you wanted to be a spokesman for Nissen, who would you want?" I thought just a moment and said, "Ted Williams." He said, "That's exactly who I was thinking of." At this time Williams was not really in the news. We didn't have much of an idea where to find him.

Ernie made a few calls but had no luck trying to reach Williams. Nissen had a box at Fenway and a couple of months later we there among several friends of the Nissen people—included among these people was Miles Baker. He must have been in his late 80s or 90s, and he said, "Ernie, do I understand that you're trying to reach Ted Williams?" Yeah, we said. "Well," he said, "He's my house guest in the summer."

The following week I got a call from Ernie. He said, "Guess where I'm going next week! I'm going to meet God." I said, "What are you talking about?" And he said, "I'm going to meet Ted Williams." I said, "You gotta be kidding me." Ernie was thinking fast on his feet, and he had talked to Bud Leavitt knowing that the way to get to Williams was through Bud. He sort of implied that if anything came of it, we wanted to include Bud, too.

Ernie flew up to New Brunswick, and found Williams' house on the Miramichi River. The day after, he called me and said, "You and I gotta get some scripts written fast." One thing we tried from the beginning was to write a script with Ted and Bud sort of joking back and

forth. We never tried to sell too much, we just tried to create humorous conversations between a couple of old friends, kidding each other.

We drove down this dirt driveway, crossed a little bridge, and came to this ranch house. I remember Williams came around the corner of the house, all pumped up, "WHERE THE HELL HAVE YOU BEEN? JESUS CHRIST!" Didn't even know us, of course. Shook everyone's hand. You just stand there thinking, "Wow, it's Ted Williams!"

We were there two days and made the first two commercials after blowing a lot of lines. Some of it was shot outside by the river, some of it was shot inside. It was windy as hell and the cue cards kept blowing away. There was this light and I thought, *Christ, it's going to fall in the water and electrocute everybody.* We were sort of feeling our way. Bud was the butt of the jokes in all the early commercials. It wasn't until we got going, sort of tested the water, that we realized we could poke a little fun at Ted, too. By the end, we were really hammering him. All the while, though, you're working with this hothead. When you'd tell him he blew a line and it had to be done over again, he couldn't understand why. Then it would have to be done over again because Bud blew the line or something went wrong with the equipment. Or the sun moved. I got a little tense at times. But Ted was very nice about it. He's a perfectionist himself, not just as a hitter, but at everything he does. He wanted to do the best job.

The first or second night, we were all having dinner, and having a few beers. It got dark, and he's still sitting out on the porch talking baseball with Bowler. People kept going in and out and suddenly I was the only one sitting there with Ted. He was talking about the time he met Babe Ruth. I was sitting there in the dark talking to Ted Williams about people I had never met, who are all in the history books, in the record books. And a shudder ran up my back. I can't really believe that I'm even sitting here talking to this guy. At his house.

The next day while we were setting up, he was down in his basement, a walk-in basement, making flies. He saw me walk by the door, and he barked out for me to come in. He was showing off these flies and wanting to know did I know anything about it. Of course, I didn't know a damn thing about it. He was showing me why some flies work and some don't, how if they stand upright on a table, they work better than flies that flop over. And he's proud of it. I don't know what he's talking about, and he's got feathers and threads and all kinds of things, working on stuff with those big hands. It was so much fun just to watch him.

◆ ◆ ◆

JEFFREY HUTT, University Student, Halifax N.S.

I first saw Ted Williams in a Nissen bread commercial when I was in grade school. I didn't even know who he was, but I soon learned the superhuman details of his career and he instantly became my favorite player.

My friends and I used to argue for hours about who was the greatest baseball player. As a young Red Sox fan in the mid-1980s, I was pretty well disarmed for these battles. Boggs didn't have enough power, Rice was too old, Greenwell too young. Since there were no rules to prevent you from adopting a retired player, I went for the heavy artillery and chose Ted. He was clearly the best. I admired Ted because even as a fifteen year old boy he had vowed to become the greatest hitter who ever lived, and then he went out and did just that.

◆ ◆ ◆

LIB DOOLEY, The Queen of Fenway Park

Ted should have had a sister and he didn't. I'm the sister he never had. I first saw him play in 1940, the year after he came to Boston. My father was quite a baseball person. He had affiliations with the Braves early on and he took me to Braves Field. "Daddy," I said, "I don't like this place. It's dusty." They didn't have any cement outside, behind the field itself and they didn't have any backs on the chairs, and I didn't like it. So I said, "I want to go to the other park." He said he'd take me there if I behaved myself and didn't ask too many questions. When I saw Fenway, I said, "Oh, this is NICE." I used to sit up in the old press box.

During those years that Ted was away at war, the games were poorly attended. After the war, going to the ballgame became like a hobby to me. I've been a season ticket holder since 1944. It's just the thing I chose to do, rather than play bridge with women who talk. Other people do other things; I chose to go to ballgames.

There were many games where the fans got on Ted—and relentlessly—often over an entire homestand. We had a group who sat in the bleachers and signalled to others in the stands betting on what Ted would do each time at bat. They were there solely to make money, and often they came down hard on Ted. It was envy and greed, regardless of what he did. Immediately after Ted's last at bat they would leave the park—settle their wins and losses and be gone. Eventually they were detected and thrown out. He just developed a variety of fans.

I'll tell you why he never wore a necktie—when he was young, he just didn't have the money. Neckties were a symbol of the times, but cost more money than he could afford. When he first arrived, he had nothing, absolutely nothing. Those were times when Hugh Duffy used to help him along with things—not financially, but advise him on how to live on what he had and not complain, just to concentrate on baseball. I know he sent money to his mother.

Ted has just celebrated his 79th birthday. I've known him for over half a century and I'm proud to be his friend. Ted was not all tough guy. I have recognized a great loneliness in his life that most people never saw. In earlier years I'd see him come home from that ballpark when it was dark. And then he'd be alone, making his flies for fishing.

◆ ◆ ◆

As far as I'm concerned, Ted Williams was one of the finest baseball players who ever played the game. Not only was Ted an outstanding athlete, he was and is a patriot and a fine American. He is the kind of man that our nation's kids can look up to. Ted Williams is a true hero in every sense of the word and I am proud to call him my friend.

—Gene Autry

MAUREEN CRONIN, Daughter of Joe Cronin

I think when I first really started having a crush on him—and I do, I have a terrible crush on him and have had my whole life—one of my neighbor's little nephews had leukemia, and it was back in the days when they really didn't have much of a cure for it. Ted used to go over to the hospital all the time to see this little boy. I can remember being impressed by this as a little girl because this little boy was my age, and I remember being very sorry this boy was dying. I must have been eight or nine.

My first recollection was knowing how nice this person was, what he was doing for this little boy and how appreciative the family was of Ted. That was the first time I realized how special he was compared to the other ballplayers. You go to a ball game when you're younger and it's kind of hard to concentrate for nine innings. But when Ted came up to the plate, there was something special. You always stopped what you were doing and paid close attention because he was just so much fun to watch when he was at the plate.

He and my dad were quite close. When my dad was really sick, he used to call just about every day and talk to him. He was really sweet about calling on the phone. Dad admired Ted for his devotion to the game and for all that he did for baseball. I think Ted kind of looked at my dad as half-brother, half-father. He was always trying to tell Ted how to deal with the press. Of course, that really didn't work. I think like all strong-minded people, Ted has his definite preferences, his likes and dislikes. He'll decide what he thinks of you very quickly after asking you very few questions and he'll ask some very direct questions. But he appreciates talent and appreciates the good in people around him. If he likes you and respects you, it's an incredible relationship. He's always looking for the good in people.

◆ ◆ ◆

SHIRLEY O'CONNOR, Fan

Nineteen forty-six, the year they were in the playoffs, I used to chase him home. It's a little embarrassing to me now. I was young then . . . it seems like a hundred years ago. We lived on Park Avenue then, just two blocks down the street from Fenway Park. My roommate Anne used to enjoy baseball, too. We'd go down and watch them get into their cars, and I think about four or five times I followed him out to his home. I don't know why; he must have thought I was stalking him. I had a bright red convertible. As soon as he turned off on his street, I turned around on Route 9 and came back. In Wellesley, off Route 9. He had a Cadillac, went like a bat out of hell.

He took an awful beating from those fans in left field. I used to fight for him, because people in that corner were so awful to him. I had what I suppose you'd call puppy love. It was more of a passing fancy. I'm 74 now. I never really followed any other player.

I belong to Winchester Country Club, and he's played golf there a couple of times. That's the only time I ever met him. I was on the 10th tee and I told him I had been in love with him. I said "Don't you love these old ladies?" He was just as pleasant as could be. There's just something about Teddy Baby.

◆ ◆ ◆

LINDA CANN, Editor

Getting a telephone interview with Ted Williams was beyond my wildest expectations as the editor of the alumni magazine at Acadia University in the small town of Wolfville, Nova Scotia. But I knew I had a big story on my hands when Acadia's sports writer, Jim Prime, collaborated with the Splendid Splinter to produce *Ted Williams' Hit List* in 1995.

The mere opportunity to see Williams would be a cherished fantasy in this region of Canada with its solid tradition of all-out Red Sox fans. And here was Jim, talking weekly with his sports hero from his nearby New Minas home to produce the definitive ranking of the all-time best hitters in baseball. What a scoop for an alumni magazine.

I had listened to telephone tapes of Williams and knew of his longstanding rapport with Jim who had pitched the idea for the book. I had seen, framed on Jim's wall, the cherished accolade sent by Williams upon finally deciding to take a swing at the project— a letter from Teddy Ballgame himself referring to his fan and coauthor as "the most persistent son-of-a-bitch I ever met."

On the spur of the moment one day, at Jim's urging, Williams decided to offer me the precious interview I sought. Jim phoned ahead. I had left only ten minutes prior. A frenzy ensued at the Alumni Hall, coworkers frantic in their attempts to track me down.

Soon after, the greatest hitter who ever lived does phone, and the interview . . . Ted Williams answers a single question, one asked by my answering machine's tape—"I'm in a meeting, would you like to leave a message?" He did. The message, "Damn!" Click.

Would he call again? Are there second chances in baseball? Imagine my excitement when after lunch the phone rang. On the line I heard the sound of a familiar voice bellowing "Hello, is this Linda?" After my opening spiel, I paused for breath, then realized it to be a familiar voice alright, just not the one I had heard on those tapes. My husband, wondering if I had heard from Ted, surprised that I hadn't recognized his well-known talent for voice impersonation after 31 years of marriage. I told him he was lucky his mother was visiting or he would be in big trouble at supper.

I never did get to interview Mr. Williams or chat with him for that matter. But I will always treasure the note left on my desk that day: "Ted Williams will be calling any minute. Please wait by the phone."

◆ ◆ ◆

STEPHEN KING, Writer
(Taken from An Evening with Number 9, Nov 10, 1988)

I was at the general aviation terminal in Bangor, Maine where I live, and there was a young guy in the terminal and I'm thinking he looks familiar, I've seen him somewhere before. He looks at me, too, but I'm kind of used to that. People look at me and sort of steer clear a little bit. They don't know what I'm going to do.

I went outside to have a cigarette, because my wife doesn't like me to smoke around her . . . and this plane lands and I'm standing by this chain link fence and the young guy goes out and meets two people getting off the plane and immediately I know why he looked familiar—because his father was Ted Williams.

He brought him over to the chain link fence where I was standing and says, "I'd like to introduce you to my dad." It was John-Henry Williams, the young man. Ted and I kind of shook our fingers through this chain link fence. Wonderful craggy face.

Now, I've got a son, he's 11 years old, never seen Ted Williams play. For some reason, baseball heroes aren't like rock stars or even movie heroes to young kids. Their legend remains very, very bright for a long time after the colors of other legends have faded. That's true for grownups, too.

I wanted to be cool, you know. I wanted to be Joe Cool. I walked until I got out of Ted Williams' sight line—and then I ran so fast I lost all the change out of my pockets, my wallet—left them all right there on the ground—and I'm in the terminal ahead of him!

My boy Owen is 11 years old. This kid is totally blase. Stephen Spielberg once gave him an E.T. clock that didn't work. Totally blase. He's met Jack Nicholson and these guys, and everything. But he's got a baseball card collection. He's a big fan. And Ted Williams walked in. My kid's reading a comic book and I grabbed him by the elbow and I brought him over and he's looking up and I said, "Owen, I'd like you to meet Ted Williams." The kid's jaw fell to his shoetops! He was totally blown away! Here's this great big hand and Owen kind of reaches up and says [King uses falsetto] "It's nice to meet you, Mr. Williams." Blew him out! Blew me out, too!

I'm a fan. To me, he was THE sports figure in the New England that I knew as a little boy growing up. There are a lot of sports figures in New England sports history. To me, he was the franchise. Literally, he was the Boston Red Sox. In '56, '57, '58, '59—you're a kid, you want your team to win, you need your team to win. We hated the Yankees. The Yankees are poison to us. To me the Yankees could drop dead in the street. Listen, when it comes to the Red Sox, I'm Johnny Most! He was very important because he was there. If

He looks like John Wayne, and when I asked him about Jackie Robinson he looked at me like Wayne would and said, "That man had tons and tons of guts."

—Ken Burns

the team wasn't that good, if the pitching wasn't that good, Williams was there. He stood up, he played, he was dedicated. He was baseball.

◆ ◆ ◆

LET THERE BE TED:
A CAREER OF BIBLICAL PROPORTIONS
by Jim Prime

In the beginning God created the Red Sox. And they were without form and void of talent and charisma.

And God said, Let there be Ted. And the three wise men, Collins, Cronin and Yawkey did travel west in search of their star and lo and behold they found Ted, called the Kid abiding there and brought him back to the Land of the Bean and the Cod, even unto that Eden called Fenway, to lead the Red Sox from bondage. And in his first year he did drive in seven score and five runs. And Yawkey the overseer did heap riches upon him and the Kid did smile and exult, for batting was his birthright and all of Boston was his kingdom. And everything he touched was golden and the fans said he had miraculous vision and could walk on water and he was the favored son.

And in his third year he did bat .3995 entering the season-ending doubleheader and still he did not sit out the games to preserve the coveted mark but did play and risk all. And he did go 6 for 8 and finish at .406 and the people did rejoice and prayed that the Kid could lead them to baseball heaven, called the World Series.

And he sought the counsel of the elders, of Cobb and Hornsby and Waner and Duffy, and he did listen well and attend their words. And he faced wicked curves and sinful sliders and hellacious fastballs and evil eephus pitches and did smite them all mightily. And he did feast mainly on fastballs and did pull them into the stands by the scores. And umpires did love him because his eyes were sharp and true and they made him to walk time and again. But verily pitchers did not love him and did devise new weapons to stop him.

Now it came to pass that the scribes did conspire against the Kid and did revile him and crucify him almost daily in the press and bear false witness against him. And the Kid did cast them from the dressing room. But the congregation did believe the scribes and many did turn against him. And the Kid did not turn the other cheek but was filled with wrath and hardened his heart and rebuked them and cursed them and spat at them and did not forgive them and called them front runners.

And a great war came and the Kid did fight mightily in defence of his land. And he and his baseball brethren wandered in this wilderness for three years and did smite their foes and earn much glory. And when their prodigal son did return, the people of Boston did rejoice once more. And he did win his second baseball trinity, the Triple Crown. And he did give succour to the unfirm through the Jimmy Fund and gave comfort to the less fortunate and did not yet herald it abroad.

And the Indians did conspire against him and did devise the Boudreau Shift to test him. And other tribes did likewise. And all manner of things were written of him by the scribes. And he was drafted to fight again and was gone from baseball for full two more years. And he returned and continued to smite the ball exceeding well.

And the scribes continued to plague the Kid throughout his career and caused him to lose at least one MVP award, though he was anointed with two others during his days among them. And when the time came for the Kid's exodus from baseball, he did verbally smite the scribes in their Tower of Babble and did ridicule them and call them Knights of the Keyboard. And the day was dark and the Kid did go out in a blaze of glory with a homer in his last at bat. And the congregation shouted hosannahs and adored him and waited for him to relent and doff his hat but he did not, for that was not his way.

And when five seasons had passed the scribes softened their hearts and voted him to the Hall of Fame and he spake eloquently about his love of baseball and did entreat the tribunal to correct past injustices and admit the deserving but oppressed to this Promised Land.

And Ted did proclaim the word to hitters far and wide, and spake of a slight upswing and preached his three commandments:

1. Thou shalt have the patience of Job (Get a good ball to hit) 2. Thou shalt have the wisdom of Solomon (Proper thinking at the plate) 3. Thou shalt have the speed of David vs. Goliath (Be quick with the bat)

And so it was written in the *Science of Hitting* and the word went forth and it was a revelation. And his disciples were many and they did heed his words and so the gospel was spread through the generations from Kaline to Yastrzemski to Boggs and even unto Piazza, Bichette and Gwynn. But false prophets tried to lead them from this righteous path with heretical teachings. And so the Waner method begat the Lau method and the Lau method begat the Hriniak method. But these false doctrines were scorned by Ted. And Ted saw some hitters swinging down on the ball and was saddened.

And he did go on to loaf and fish. And verily we shall not see his like again in this favored land.

Amen.

◆ ◆ ◆

BOB COSTAS, TV Commentator

Hitting a baseball was Ted's passion. How much did he enjoy it? Read between the lines and then you be the judge as Ted tried to explain the exact feeling during a radio interview with Bob Costas:

COSTAS: Ted, what does it feel like when you hit a baseball perfectly?

TED: Well, I could compare it to a couple of things (evil snickering in the audience), but . . . but (Ted is now laughing) it's one of the greatest things that ever happens. (Costas joins the illicit laughter) I can tell you it's a lot of fun. There are very few feelings like it" (Everyone is laughing hard). That's why they call it the national pastime.

◆ ◆ ◆

LEIGH MONTVILLE, Sportswriter
"Ted and Tide"

Spring training, Winter Haven, 1978 or 1979, the first year Ted came back. He'd been away for a number of years. I'd been a sportswriter for a while. He was my boyhood idol, Ted Williams, but I'd never run across him. So I had a little anticipation to see what this guy was like. At Winter Haven, the clubhouse was divided into a larger room and a smaller room. The smaller room had the coaches and selected veterans. They shared the space with a pair of enormous washing machines. I was in the smaller room and then all of a sudden you heard that big voice saying to Vinnie Orlando, the clubhouse guy, saying. "Vinnie! You use Tide to wash these uniforms. Why do you use Tide? Is it cheaper? All

Ted Williams stands for what is right about our great country. The desire to excel. The willingness to help other, less fortunate people—particularly the children—and the ability to be strong and independent and yet compassionate and giving.

—Ronald Reagan

"Vinnie! You use Tide to wash these uniforms. Why do you use Tide? Is it cheaper? All those soaps out there, is Tide better than the other soaps? Is there some special ingredient in there? Does it get the uniforms whiter?"

Everybody turned toward the noise because there was no alternative. There he was, Ted, himself, huge, instantly dominating his surroundings. He was wearing an Hawaiian shirt. He would have been 60 years old. Maybe 61. He was tanned and robust, looking as if he had just returned from the high seas or the deep woods. A pair of sunglasses hung from his neck on a piece of fishing line.

There was also the feeling like around this guy, there's fun all the time because he's always challenging and questioning and making you look at things that are normal things, and kind of turning them upside down.

That was my first sighting of the guy. I've always felt that I have an interest in stuff around me, but not as much as that!

◆ ◆ ◆

ERNIE JOHNSON, Ballplayer

When I was a [Braves] rookie in 1950, we played the Red Sox in a city series, and I got a chance to pitch. It's late in the game, and Williams comes to the plate. I thought I'd try to get a curveball over the outside corner. Instead, Ted hit one in the seats; it's rolled to the Kenmore Hotel by now. The game is over, and we're walking through the clubhouse. Billy Southworth was our manager, and he was trying to make me feel good, build my confidence, but that's not how it came out. He put his arm around me and said, "Don't worry, he's hit them off better pitchers than you." I'll never forget that—and I've tried.

◆ ◆ ◆

DON LEE, Pitcher
Ted Hit Homers Off Father/Son Combination

My dad Thornton told me, "When you pitch to Ted Williams, you never throw him the same pitch twice." I said, "Well, I'll remember that."

One time I threw him three changeups in a row, which Daddy said never do, and he broke his bat on home plate because he stood and took it. He looked at me and I thought to myself, "Don't you ever throw him another one!"

You tried doing these different little things—in fact, if memory serves me, that was the only hit he ever got off me. He hit this home run, though, and boy, it was a blast. It was in Fenway Park over the bullpen and it was a slider. Two balls and no strikes. I didn't get it in far enough. I'm # 518 if I've been correctly informed.

He rounded first base and he said to me as he rounded the bag—I was looking right at him—he says, "Take that, you son-of-a-bitch! One off your old man and one off you, and I'm gonna quit." That's what he said. He ran around the bases and I never forgot that.

◆ ◆ ◆

NOMAR GARCIAPARRA, Ballplayer
Why Ted Hit .400

Many people feel that Nomar Garciaparra could be the next man to bat .400. He's not so sure.

Ted's incredible desire to be the best has always been an inspiration to me. To this day, I am amazed to hear his stories, his memories vivid, recalling each pitch and each hit as if he were still in the middle of the game. One of my strengths is hitting high notes, and I know from experience that hitting a baseball is much more difficult. But there is a similarity between baseball and music: You must have hits to win in both, and each requires perseverance and hard work to ever experience success.

—Michael Bolton, singer

TED WILLIAMS: THE PURSUIT OF PERFECTION

I tell you what. It's hard to hit .400. I realized that this year. Everybody was making a big deal about me chasing it this year. I also realized something about where I play.

I know why Ted hit .406. In July, late in July, I was sitting on deck and I really didn't know what my average is. Honest to God, I don't pay attention to what I'm hitting. It really doesn't matter to me. I was sitting on deck and I hear a fan yelling at me, and he goes, "Three ninety eight? Come ON!"

I was on deck and I kind of chuckled. I turned around and the fan was dead serious. He wanted to kill me! So now I know why Ted hit .406 !

I remember going home that night and saying, "God, why did you put me in this city?" But the next thing I said was, "God, thank you"—because that's what drives you, people like that. It really does. They're awesome.

◆ ◆ ◆

TED AND LOUISVILLE SLUGGER

Talk about a craftsman knowing his tools. As we enter the 21st century, it is astonishing to reflect on the fact that Ted Williams actually knew the man who turned the first Louisville Slugger baseball bat. That bat was made some 52 years before Ted started playing with the San Diego Padres.

Thus there is a direct connection between Bud Hillerich, who turned the first bat for Pete Browning in 1884 and Ted Williams, arguably the greatest user of this tool. It is not unlike Isaac Stern knowing Stradivarius and then going on to greatness.

Ted signed with Louisville Slugger in August, 1937, but was not your average customer. He displayed tremendous interest in the primary tool of his trade and regularly visited the bat factory.

Stories abound about Ted and bats, how he could tell if a bat was a fraction of an ounce off; he regularly weighed them on post office scales. He wouldn't leave them on the grass for fear that humidity would add to the weight. One time he complained to the factory that the taper on the handles was off. Company officials checked and found that Ted was right; they were off by 5/100 of an inch! "My father told me that story," Bud's son Jack Hillerich recalls.

Poignantly, when Bud died in November 1946, it was reported by the Associated Press that the only baseball player to send a telegram of condolences to the family was Ted Williams. "I still have that telegram," Jack said in late December 2000.

◆ ◆ ◆

LEIGH MONTVILLE, Sportswriter

I got to know a guy down at spring training who kind of cooked for Ted, this guy named Joe Lindia. He was from Cranston, Rhode Island. He told a story about one year when they were out in Scottsdale and Ted says, "Come on, I want you to meet somebody." So Joe says OK.

Joe says, "So we drive way to the far edge of Scottsdale to this seedy old motel and we drive way down the back and we knock on door #15 or something. I had no idea what Ted had in mind. He knocked on the door and this old seedy-looking guy answers the door, and Ted says, 'Joe, I want you to meet Ty Cobb.'

"They go in and they have a tremendous argument about hitting. For a couple of hours. Ty Cobb's views on hitting are diametrically opposed to Williams' views and they were really getting hot about it. They were shouting at each other and it almost looked as

> I want to have more than my toenails on the line.
>
> —Ted, on not wanting to take .3995

if they might begin to fight. Finally, Ted says, 'All right, all right. I got the answer to this. I know how we can settle this. Ty, you say one thing. I say another. Joe, what do YOU say?'

"The two greatest hitters in the history of baseball. I'm supposed to break the tie. I couldn't hit a baseball for a million dollars."

◆ ◆ ◆

MARTY MARION, Ballplayer

I hardly know Ted. The only time I remember Ted was when we played him in the All-Star Game in Fenway Park, in 1941. He hit a couple of home runs and I was playing shortstop, and as he rounded second base he looked over at me and gave me a big wink, and he says, "Kid, don't you wish you could hit like that?"

◆ ◆ ◆

VIC POWER, Ballplayer
(From They Played the Game, p. 104)

I played with some characters. Like Tony Oliva . . . Well, I was living in Minnesota. It's cold up there during the winter and I had to get up every morning to shovel snow to take my car out of the garage to drive my kids to school. I was tired of it.

I was reading in a psychology book that in life man takes advantage of other men to get ahead. Okay, I thought, let me see if this works.

Now I'm sitting in my house with Tony. I said, "Tony, you know what I just read? I was reading Ted Williams' book, and Ted said that the secret to his success was shoveling snow.

"Ted Williams was the greatest hitter—the most power, the most intelligent, the last guy to hit .400. And he said his secret is shoveling snow."

The next day Tony was at my house with a shovel. I was inside laughing, and he was outside shoveling snow. Then come October, the end of the season, and Tony Oliva was the batting champion. He said, "Vic, you were right."

And now look what happened: Kirby Puckett became the batting champion. I think he's been telling Puckett to shovel snow.

◆ ◆ ◆

BILLY CRYSTAL, Actor

Billy Crystal recalled when he met Ted Williams, one of his boyhood heroes:
"I walked up to him at a card-signing show and told him I had home movies I made of him striking out," Crystal said. He described the day of the game and the time at bat. Williams thought about it for a moment then nodded his head.
"Curveball," he said. "Low and away."

◆ ◆ ◆

Ted hands his bat to son John-Henry at an Old-Timers' game.
(Copyright David L. Pressman, M.D.)

TED WILLIAMS: THE PURSUIT OF PERFECTION

Collecting Ted

For some of us a few dog-eared baseball cards were enough. Others had to have the complete set. Some of us wrote carefully crafted letters to our favorite player, wishing all the while that we had paid more attention in Mrs. Welch's grade 6 English class. Some of us lived close enough to actually lie in wait outside the ballpark. Sometimes our heroes signed and sometimes they hurried past, but if we persevered and actually got the autograph, we had captured a piece of baseball memorabilia. Little did we know that we had also preserved a piece of our youth.

While Ted Williams is himself something of an icon around New England, these dedicated souls are engaged in a never-ending quest for inanimate objects, including the rarest and most obscure items associated with the Boston legend. Although Ted's career coincided with a somewhat less commercial era, his likeness can be found on everything from Ted's Root Beer bottles to Champ Prophylactics packages to a Norman Rockwell painting on the cover of the Saturday Evening Post. Call them the Ted Heads. They have turned the collecting of Williams artifacts from a hobby to a passion.

Opposite: Ted signing autographs in San Diego.
(Photo courtesy of San Diego Hall of Champions)

Ted Williams

One summer afternoon when I was nine years old, I spread my baseball card collection in orderly rows on the nappy green carpeting of my grandparents' rented house in Jacksonville, Illinois. My grandfather—a onetime semi-professional gambler, gone semi-legit as a Buick salesman—came home for lunch and asked me what I was doing. "Ranking guys," I said. "Ranking guys how?" Grandpa Bob asked. He stood over me, large and knowing, squinting down at me and smoking.

"By stats."

"By stats how?"

In the kitchen, my grandmother was frying something.

"Hitters by batting average," I said. "Pitchers by ERA."

He walked toward the pitcher row and, with the toe of his wingtip, nudged Tom Hilgendorf's 1970 card. "What's he doing there?" Grandpa Bob said. "On top?"

"He had a 1.50 ERA last year," I said.

"Jee-sus Christ!" said Grandpa Bob.

"Bob!" called my grandmother.

"You've got him ahead of Bob Gibson?"

I swallowed hard. "Gibson's second-best," I stammered. "His ERA was 2.18."

"Jee-sus Christ!"

"BOB!" She stood in the doorway to the kitchen. He nodded to her, put out his cigarette and sat down next to me. He explained, calmly, that Hilgendorf had pitched but six innings last year and that Gibson was the best pitcher in the National League, and what sacrilege it was to mention Hilgendorf in the same breath as Gibson.

"Let me ask you this," he said. "Who's the greatest hitter?"

"Pete Rose," I blurted.

Rose batted .348 the year before. His card topped my row. Plus, I was from Ohio and a Reds fan.

Grandpa Bob rubbed his thinning hair and looked past me, out the window, toward the vast gulf of all the things you can't make a kid understand.

"Rose is a singles hitter," he said.

"Oh," I said. I knew I hadn't better say "Johnny Bench." He wanted me to go beyond being a fan. He wanted me to think all-time. God, I loved that man.

"Babe Ruth?" I said.

He smiled just a little. And so I pushed my luck.

"Or maybe in a couple years," I said, "Hank Aaron. Aaron has a chance to break Ruth's record."

"Records?" My grandfather rubbed a hand over his face, then stood. "Jee-sus Christ."

"BOB!" She had great hearing.

"Ted Williams," he whispered down to me. "Period. You want records, he would've broken every record there was."

"Why didn't he?" I said. I was stunned. To me, Ted Williams was the guy who managed the Washington Senators. I would have never in a million years thought that the right answer to my grandfather's question was "Ted Williams." I was only nine. I had a world of things to learn.

Instead of telling me about Williams' war years, instead of telling me about the numbers he might have put up, instead of making a case for war heroism or character or brash confidence or the manly damn manliness of having fishing rods and tools named after you, my grandfather lit another cigarette.

"Listen, sport," he said. "Don't confuse a row of numbers with a man."

◆ ◆ ◆

SY BERGER, Executive, the Topps Company

I started working for Topps in '47, 50 years ago. I guess I have touched every player in Major League Baseball since 1951—and most of the minor leaguers, too. And I must confess that Ted Williams rated in my Top 3. Willie Mays and Bob Keegan, a college buddy, would be the other two. Bob Keegan? Don't laugh. We're old dear friends, since the first day of my freshman year. He pitched about six years in the majors—as a matter of fact he once pitched a no-hitter. Ted was my hero because, although I lived in the Bronx, in those days I was a Boston Red Sox fan. We often took the train up to Boston. My parents were immigrants; we rooted for underdogs.

I was involved in signing Ted to Topps in 1954. Ted's agent was Freddy Corcoran. Bowman was having players signed for them by a very sweet guy named Art Flynn. Arthur was a great friend of Freddy Corcoran. We competed with Bowman and were knocking them out of the box. I had designed a card with a little zing to it, a bigger size card with better pictures. The '52 card, which I designed and put together, was really the prototype of the modern day baseball card. In '53 we had beautiful hand-painted pictures of every player. In '54 we combined two pictures on a card—a big picture and an action picture—which had never been done. We did that again in '55.

So, in '54, after we did the hand-painted cards, I was looking for the greatest player in the game. DiMaggio was gone, and I was hating DiMaggio anyway because he was a Yankee. You couldn't like DiMaggio if you loved Williams. I always said, if Ted was in New York and DiMaggio was in Boston, Ted would have been the greatest thing that ever came along. I adored Williams and I was determined to get him. I called Corcoran up and he said, "Come on down." So I did. I was a little scared but I told him what I wanted to do. He said, "Kid, I'm going to give Ted to you." In the '54 series, Ted Williams, was card number 1 and card number 250.

At that time, we were still battling in court and we were afraid to use certain players because we didn't know who had the prior rights. But we knew Ted was clean, so I made a deal with Corcoran giving us the rights to use him on promotions and things like that. He got paid more than any other player at the time for it which, believe it or not, was $450. This was from '54-'58. The average guy in those days was getting a $125 for an exclusive contract.

In 1959 Corcoran asked if I would waive the rights to Ted because Fleer wanted to do a major series on Ted's career. They were going to give him five thousand dollars and there was a royalty. That's the reason they went broke. I know he never got a penny of royalty, but he did get his $5,000.

I am not a collector. The only thing I've got in my den that I keep is a signed 8 by 10 picture, in a Lucite frame, of Ted. He's in street clothes, waving his arm. I guess it was a farewell or something. My God, was he handsome! I remember one time I was sitting in a restaurant on 49th Street called Chandler's. Williams was at the next table and he had the most gorgeous woman I'd ever seen as his guest. She got up and went to the bathroom and he looked at me and said, "You like that, don't you, Sy?" I said, "Yeah, she's gorgeous." He said, "Aaah, you gotta see the one in Washington." Come to think of it I've noticed that my wife has one of those ball holders with a Ted Williams signed ball. And she's a terrible Yankee fan! There's Ted, a real ladies man!

◆ ◆ ◆

The first time I saw him was in the '46 Series and I've often said that when I saw him live, because I'd been saving him on the bubble gum cards, I didn't know whether to give the signal or get an autograph, I was so in awe of the man.

—Joe Garagiola

Ted's rookie card, 1939

A 1941 Play Ball card

The whole substance of them pulling the #68 card in the 1959 Fleer set of Williams' cards was that it had Bucky Harris's photograph with Ted Williams, signing his contract. Bucky was under contract with Topps. Harris was, I believe, a coach with Washington at the time. They had a contract signed by Topps, so that they had the right to show his picture. And Topps and Fleer were not gracious competitors. Topps would do whatever they could to knock Fleer out. When they found that this card #68 had Bucky Harris's name on it, they threatened to take Fleer to court unless they pulled the card. The initial run did have the number 68s in it. Two or three months afterwards, they damaged that part of the plate so they could pull it out.

In the process of refurbishing some old railroad cars in the late 1970s, they found a boxcar of the 1959 Fleer Ted Williams Cards. The printer was Milprint, out of Milwaukee, Wisconsin. They printed the cards and shipped them by boxcar. Around 1979, they come across this old boxcar on a siding someplace. Then they opened it up and found all these cases of cards.

The stuff used to be auctioned off and if my memory serves me correctly, people were getting somewhere between $25 and $30 a case for these cards. There were hundreds of these cases. The Philadelphia newspapers at the time had people advertising Ted Williams cases for sale, for anywhere between $50 and $75. There were so many of them, I wouldn't even buy them at that price.

I used to sell the complete set for $15. No one could sell them for more, even though they wanted to, because I had such a supply. I would not let anybody go over that. I would have big signs at my table at the shows that would say TED WILLIAMS CARDS FOR $15.00, and I used to sell the 68-card set at that time for around $10. I had somewhere around 20 cases. There were approximately 2300 sets. And they were all gem mint because they had never gone into gum packs.

♦ ♦ ♦

In 1955 there were 77,263,127 male American human beings. And every one of them in his heart of hearts would have given two arms, a leg, and his collection of Davy Crockett iron-ons to be Teddy Ballgame.

—From *The Great American Baseball Card Flipping, Trading and Bubble Gum Book*

JIM KAKLAMANOS, Attorney

When my son Jimmy was born in 1986, I thought it would be a great opportunity to start collecting cards again. Dragging him in a stroller, I started going to these card shows and autograph shows. It's neat to get these autographed baseballs, so I started collecting Hall of Fame autographed baseballs. It's still impersonal, so I wanted to focus in on one person. I started thinking about who was the greatest player who ever lived. Babe Ruth? Dead. OK, let's go to the next one. Who's the second greatest player to ever play the game? Gehrig. Dead. OK, let's narrow this down: who's the greatest *hitter* ever? Jeez, you know what? I think it's Ted Williams! Played in Boston, he's alive, and he's buddies with someone I knew in town. I bet you I could get an autographed photo. One autographed photo. The rest is history. I was hooked. I thought collecting Williams memorabilia would be a finite project. As we know, something new comes around the corner all the time.

♦ ♦ ♦

MAX SEITER, New Baseball Card Collector

Yup, I'm a big Ted Williams fan. I'm nine. I was born in 1987. I was about four when I first heard of Ted Williams. I really liked Babe Ruth. I said I think Babe Ruth was the best batter, but then my dad said, "Well, actually Ted Williams had a better average, with

.406." That's how I found out about him. Do you know what his lifetime OBP was? .483!! He also had a good one in 1941. I'd say his 1941 year was the best thing about Ted. Definitely! I want to collect more of his cards. I have a Ted Williams card now that's a remake, by Bowman. I'm just trying to get all the cards I can get of Ted. I only have the one card so far.

◆ ◆ ◆

ARTHUR D'ANGELO, Proprietor, Twins Souvenirs

I came to Boston from Italy the year Ted started in baseball with the Red Sox. 1939. In a way I guess you could say we started in business by selling newspapers in front of the ballpark. Then we started selling souvenirs. Baseball wasn't what it is today as far as selling things, not back in the 1940s. They only thing we really made some money on was selling Ted Williams merchandise—pennants and buttons and so forth. There were years in the 1950s that about all we could sell was Ted Williams stuff. He kept us going. We never asked his permission back then. We just went ahead and sold it. Occasionally we used to see him and he'd say, "You guys never asked me." We said, "What the hell? We're making you famous!"

◆ ◆ ◆

ED WALSH, Former Policeman, Sports Card Dealer

I grew up in Southie. I never missed a game. I met Ted back in about '55 when I was a route cop. I was in the patrol car. I noticed this guy—the minute I saw him, I said to my partner, "Ted Williams! There he goes!" He was going into the Union Oyster House; that's where he used to like to eat. We went in and introduced ourselves. He always liked cops—always. He knows it's a tough job. The working guys, that is. I was a working cop. There's other guys that couldn't find a felon in Walpole. His pal in there was Jimmy Erkstein, a real classy guy. Ted would go upstairs to the second floor and every time he'd come in, he always had a bag. I never used to look but after the second or third time, Jimmy said to me, "Look, Eddie." There were balls and bats and all kinda stuff, all going over to the Jimmy Fund. Ted paid for it all himself. He never wanted anybody to know. That's the kind of guy he was.

I was Deputy Superintendent of the Police in Boston. I started off in 1955 as a patrolman, and served for 32 years. I made so many pinches and won so many awards right away that they made me a detective and I moved right up the ladder.

I used to run the lineups at headquarters. Years ago, Ted came into headquarters and this friend of mine fixed it up for him to see the lineup. The guy was in charge of all the dignitaries. Ted stood there, and got his picture taken. Of course, he never wore the tie but the number was around his neck. Later, a guy was working Headquarters one day and he found these mug shots. He said, "Gee, if you can, I'd like to get it autographed" so I sent it down and Ted autographed one.

I used to get John-Henry into Fenway all the time. They didn't know who he was. "What the hell," I said, "His father built this place!" One time Ted threw out the first ball in a game and in the fourth inning, John-Henry came over and gave me the ball. I got it autographed by the Red Sox players and gave it to my oldest boy.

That's how I got in this baseball cards and memorabilia business. When I was a cop, everybody was always after me. "Eddie, can you get me a ball, can you get me a bat? Can you get me this? Can you get me that?" Ted went over to Jimmy's Harborside one time.

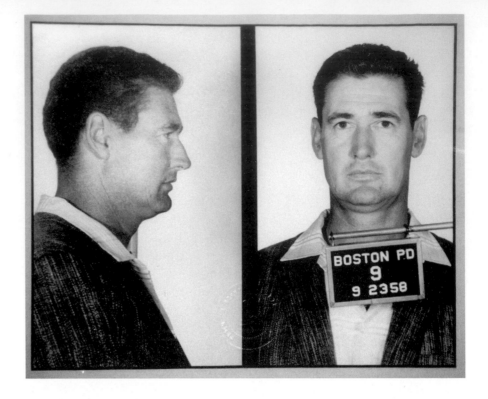

The Original Bad Boy of Boston.
(Photos courtesy of John T. Bird and the Ted Williams Museum)

You remember Newman Flanagan, the district attorney? Nice guy, good guy. He always signed the overtime checks in green. I'm coming out with John-Henry and Ted. He says, "Eddie! I've been looking for you! I've got to get an autograph from Ted Williams!" "Well," I said, "You can get one right now. Here he is." He looked up and saw Ted.

Here's what Ted did for me once! In 1989 he came in for my autograph show at Florian Hall in Boston. He showed up with his friend Louise and his Dalmatian, Slugger. What a crowd! 1782 people. The line went all the way down the street. Unbelievable. I made fifteen grand in three hours. Ted signed for three hours without stopping. I got him sodas and stuff while he's signing. He's talking to everybody. Nobody's pushing him. Finally, after three hours, he says, "How do you get to the Expressway from here?" I said, "Follow me." So he followed me, and I gave him a big high sign when he drove off. He wouldn't take a dime because I'd once helped John-Henry out. I didn't say nothing at the time but later I called up John-Henry and said, "John-Henry, I got something for you" and I gave him five grand. He was going to school at the time. And I gave the Jimmy Fund five thousand because Ted wouldn't take it. His fee at the time was $30,000 per show. He did mine for nothing.

◆ ◆ ◆

RICHARD PARKER, Executive

I was a senior in college and I decided I would go to Ted's last game. I was there with 10,000 other people and I held onto the program, very fortuitously. When Ted came to Boston for the Sportsman's Show a couple years later, I thought I would try to get in early and see if I could get him to sign the program. I ran into Rex Trailer, who was the co-star of the show, and I asked Rex where I might find Ted. He said he was in the back room drinking coffee with some of his cronies. So I went running back—this was before the show had opened up for the night—and Ted was sitting at a table there drinking coffee with a couple of guys. I went over to him and I said, "Ted, I've got the program from your last game." "LET ME SEE THAT!" So I showed it to him. Meanwhile, the police are coming in—the security has just surrounded me at this point with batons out and everything—and he hands it back to me. I said, "Ted, if I've gotta go to jail, at least let me take this with me, signed." "OH, FINE" and he signed it, and I was escorted out. That was my start in collecting Ted Williams autographs and memorabilia.

I didn't collect anything really for another 30 years, but I was asked to donate that program to the Ted Williams Museum and I went down to the opening of the Museum. That's when I got started again, and I was off and running.

◆ ◆ ◆

JOSHUA LELAND EVANS, Chairman, Leland's Auction House

In terms of interest in their memorabilia, Ted Williams is probably right now on par with DiMaggio, a step below Mantle, a step above Musial.

Easily, the best item we ever had to sell of Ted's was his 1941 uniform. It came from a salesman for one of the uniform companies. Ted was getting his new uniform and he gave the old one to the salesman, who'd become a friend of his, and it was the uniform from the '41 season. It's beautiful. A road jersey, pants and shirt. It's hanging in the All-Star Cafe in Manhattan, in the Sheen Room. It's Charlie Sheen's, sold at auction for $88,000.

◆ ◆ ◆

A 1954 baseball card advertising Kahn's wieners

BILL NOWLIN, Co-founder Rounder Records

I grew up in Greater Boston as a Williams fan. A few years ago, I decided, just for fun and a bit of nostalgia, to try and collect one of every Ted Williams card there was. I figured that he played for about 20 years, so there should be 20 or 30 of them, plus the Fleer set, and it would make a nice little wall display. I'm now over 600 items and counting. I have no wall large enough to reasonably display my collection, but I still know of at least half a dozen I haven't been able to turn up yet, and I'm sure there are others which I'm not even aware of. I keep challenging people to come up with one I don't know of.

I got started in collecting on a higher level almost by accident. I saw this Leland's auction catalog, which had an authentic game-used bat which Ted had used in his big year, 1941. I was out in Sacramento for a convention, but they said they'd phone me in my hotel room so I could join the bidding. I was lucky that day; I got it for less than half of what I was prepared to pay.

One thing led to another, and within less than a year, I had amassed a collection of game-used bats by every player in the modern era who had hit .400 or higher, another full collection of the 500 Home Run Club, and another of the Triple Crown Club—three of baseball's most exclusive "clubs." Ted Williams is the only member of all three. Those bats have been on loan to the Ted Williams Museum in Florida for the past few years.

Since then, I've acquired a complete game-used uniform of Ted's, along with a couple of game used jackets and an undershirt. I turned down a reputed game-used cap once because it was the wrong size. Everything else about it was right, and it came from a reputable dealer. The cap wasn't Ted's size, but I asked him to try it on nonetheless. It just didn't fit.

◆ ◆ ◆

Gerry Rittenberg was born in Brookline, a Massachusetts community whose border with Boston is only a long bleacher shot from Fenway Park. Even though his family moved soon after he was born, his father remains an avid Red Sox fan. Anyone born in Boston in that era was confronted, in some way, by the legend of Ted Williams. Only a few, however, were driven to re-create the excitement of that time and place. Today, Rittenberg is president of Amscan Inc., a $200 million-a-year party goods company. The company's success affords Gerry the opportunity to devote more of his time and resources to collecting.

Today Rittenberg, 45, lives in one of the bedroom communities that surround New York City. His house is filled with Ted Williams memorabilia, though the structure is so large as to make his collection seem small in comparison. Rittenberg almost certainly has the largest private collection of Ted Williams memorabilia in the world, rivaling even the Ted Williams Museum in Florida in quantity, quality, and rarity. He estimates he has somewhere between 1500 and 2000 pieces and lacks only 10 to 15 significant items.

Because he has now acquired most of the prime Williams items, Rittenberg has begun collecting original artwork, often commissioning his own paintings. A generational work by noted sports artist Ron Lewis—depicting Ted in the various stages of his life—graces one wall of his rec room. Rittenberg selected the images and worked with Lewis to create the piece. A commissioned Frank Stapleton original hangs on the wall opposite.

GERRY RITTENBERG, Executive

Back when I was seven years old, I had a baseball card collection and my 10-year-old cousin had one, too. In his stack of cards, probably 500 as compared to my 50, there was a Ted Williams. He taunted me with it. He wanted to flip, so he used the Ted Williams card as bait to get me to flip my other cards. He took the rest of my cards from me and I never did get the Ted Williams card. I guess that initially motivated me to be a collector.

About ten years ago, I went to a card show and I wanted balls signed by Ted Williams and Joe DiMaggio. I found a Joe DiMaggio ball priced at $250. I said, "That's a lot, I'll have to pass on that." I walked around the show and spotted a Ted Williams ball and I said to the lady, "How much is that?" and she said, "$30.00." I said, "Something's wrong. I was just at this first table and they wanted $250 for this Joe DiMaggio ball. How can this be $30? That doesn't make any sense. Ted Williams is a better hitter than Joe DiMaggio." She said, "In New York, they wouldn't say that." I said, "Well, the facts are the facts. If that ball's only $30, I want it." So I bought it, and then I bought every other Ted Williams ball at that show. And since then, basically, I haven't stopped.

◆ ◆ ◆

STEVE RYESON, Restaurateur

Back then, all you had was a radio. I used to go pick up the paper to see how Ted did. It was always 2 for 3, 2 for 4, 1 for 3. He always seemed to get a walk and hardly ever got five at bats. If he went 0 for 3, I had a bad day.

I first saw Ted play in 1946 when my uncle took me to Briggs Stadium in Detroit. He said, "Watch this No. 9 from Boston." After that, I used to go to the ballpark every time Boston came into town. I'd grab a bus and hop down there. One time before the game I waited out front for Ted for the longest time. This cop said he might not come in the front, sometimes he doesn't sign—trying to discourage me, you know. Finally a car pulled up and out jumped Ted Williams and he did stop and sign. First time I met him, if you could call that meeting him.

I just collected and collected. I thought I was the only screwball out there. Around '67 or '68 they started having conventions around here. I loved meeting people, and started meeting guys from around the country collecting this stuff. Here I am 60 years old, and I'm still obsessed. The guy is superhuman. When you see him, you just want to be close to him. I could listen to him talk all day long. He's everything I wanted to be, a military hero and all that. I even named my son Ted Williams Ryeson.

◆ ◆ ◆

Collector Steve Ryeson poses with No. 9.
(Photo courtesy of Steve Ryeson)

MIKE WINTER, Management Consultant

When I grew up as a rabid baseball fan in Chicago in the fifties, Ted Williams was my number one person and he remains so. I have since lost my affection for baseball, but Ted is secure in my mind forever as El Supremo.

In 1977 I got a bug in my head that LeRoy Neiman had never painted Ted. I tracked LeRoy down by mail and after a two year correspondence, he agreed to paint him. I searched for photos, which weren't easy to find, and sent LeRoy my favorites. In 1981 he finished the painting and it was, and is, sensational.

I proudly hung Neiman's work in my living room and walked on air for a few months afterward. Then one day I noticed in the Chicago papers that Ted was going to be in town at Sears headquarters. So with some persistence I found the executive with whom he was meeting, Ken Page, and made him promise to try and bring Ted over to the house to see the painting. Ken assured me that he couldn't guarantee it because this was Ted Williams, and he was used to doing only what he wanted to do.

Good fortune struck, though. Ted and Ken showed up at my door one afternoon and stayed for about three hours. Ken had tipped me off that morning and so I was prepared. I even had my sister, brother-in-law, and 17-year-old nephew—who we yanked out of school in Kenosha, 75 miles away—at my place.

Ted was delighted with the painting and surprised that someone from Chicago would have commissioned it. He thought that if anyone would have gone to the effort, it would have been a Bostonian.

We sat around the living room, basking in the glow of the painting and talked about a zillion topics. We discussed fishing, pitchers, the new Chevy Citation, Ronald Reagan, turkey hunting in Alabama, and Don the Beachcomber's—the Polynesian restaurant near my apartment where Ted had hosted a dinner the previous night and was still grousing about the $100 check! Ted and I also did a good job at consuming Jack Daniels.

We talked about two All-Star games I had seen: 1950 in Comiskey Park, where Ted had fractured his elbow making a great catch against the wall, and 1954 in Milwaukee where Willie Mays had robbed him of a double or triple on a screaming line drive to right center.

Ted Williams and Mike Winter with a LeRoy Neiman print of Ted.
(Photo courtesy of Mike Winter)

At the end of the afternoon, Ted autographed about everything in my house and posed for a thousand pictures. Ted was a delightful person—interested, intelligent, humorous, and kind.

In 1991, I received a phone call from Dick Murphy, an executive at Polaroid. Dick told me that Polaroid, a Boston company, had a process that enabled them to make high quality reproductions of paintings and that they were interested in making a limited edition replica of my painting, and selling it for $800. I told Dick that I would be honored and delighted if they would use the painting—which they did. They donated the proceeds to the Jimmy Fund, Ted's favorite charity that he has long supported and promoted.

About a year later I found myself standing in the lobby of the Dana–Farber Hospital with Ted, LeRoy, John-Henry and Claudia enjoying a terrific event. The first copy of the replica hangs today in the Dana–Farber lobby and the event and promotion generated several hundred thousand dollars for the Jimmy Fund. My recollection is that Ted and LeRoy had never met until then. It was clear that they each enjoyed that opportunity as well as the contribution that resulted from sales of the replica.

◆ ◆ ◆

MARY-ANN TIRONE SMITH, Author

My grandfather was an immigrant from Italy. He was a great Red Sox fan, and listened on the radio to every game he could, long past the time television came around. Castiglione and the other guy. I think that one of the tips he got on how to become an American was to become interested in the American game, which was baseball, and so he learned it and he just became a great fan. A diehard.

I have to tell you that when I was in the fifth grade, my class had to write an essay on the greatest living American. I wrote mine on Ted Williams. It probably had to do with his coming back from Korea, and it was very clear to me that if he had not served, his records would have just been extraordinary. My grandfather and my father just idolized him. All I remember was going home with this assignment and taking it very seriously, then coming back to school, finding out that everyone else's essay was on Eisenhower.

Whenever we would visit my grandfather in the spring, summer or fall, the Red Sox games would always be going on in the background. My father was a fan and he would take me to Fenway Park every summer. Of course, Ted Williams, the greatest hitter ever, was the icon who represented the Red Sox.

It's funny because when my son was very young—six, seven, eight years old—he would be lying in his bed, listening to Castiglione, begging us, "Let me stay up for one more inning, one more inning, one more inning." All I could think of was my grandfather, because I was hearing the same thing from my son that had I heard growing up.

Recently we heard about an Arthur Griffin photograph of Ted Williams that was being auctioned off at a dinner in Meriden, where my husband was born and raised. My husband's father had been the mayor of Meriden during JFK's term, and we often went there to visit my mother-in-law. We decided to bid on the photo. We said to ourselves, "Well, we just spent eighteen hundred dollars on these hearing aids; we'll go up to eighteen hundred dollars for the photo. It's time to buy something for ourselves!" You know, sometimes you just don't know how to do that, do something for yourself. We got the print and . . . we were delirious. It's framed, so gorgeous!

I am a writer and my last novel, *Masters of Illusion*, was based on the Hartford circus fire. In it I write a scene where the characters bring their infant daughter to see the ceremony when Ted Williams had his number retired. So I got to pay a tribute in this novel. Actually, I mention the Red Sox in every one of my novels.

◆ ◆ ◆

RICHARD YEE, Restaurant Proprietor

I came to the United States in 1952, from Hong Kong. The American Dream. I was 16. We knew that baseball was the American game but knew nothing about it. When I first came here, I remember seeing Ted Williams play on TV and then at Fenway Park. This is why I like to have the Ted Williams stuff.

I saw Ted once in 1960 in Boston near the old Statler Hilton hotel, walking along the street. I introduced myself. I asked him how he was, just normal conversation. Just a few words. I've never asked anybody for a signature. Even today, if I saw him, I wouldn't ask Ted for his signature. But I have bought many photographs of him, for the restaurant. They make good decorations and appeal to the customers. The kids like these things. The photos are an investment. And Ted's handsome! He has come to our restaurant. He likes roast duck. We've been here for a long time and many people come in. Jay Leno. Yastrzemski. Rick Middleton, Terry O'Reilly—a lot of hockey players. Once in a while, we change the photos around.

What's so good about Ted Williams? In my opinion, he was the best player in the game. He served his country.

◆ ◆ ◆

JIM WILLIAMS, Artist

I've created quite a few pieces of Ted. In my line of work, you do more artwork of the guys who have the most fans. I've always been a big Ted Williams fan, probably because my name's Williams too, and the first baseball card I ever found was one of him.

I grew up in Indiana, Connersville. One day in 1956, my mom took me and my sister to town shopping. I was about five years old. We took the shortcut from town, through the park and they had a baseball diamond there. As we were walking by, I noticed this baseball card lying under the bleachers. I picked it up, and I didn't know who it was or anything. I asked my mom, I said, "Who is this?" She said, "That's Ted Williams." This was a '54 Topps card. I don't know what I did with that card, but I've always remembered it. A couple of years ago, I made a piece for Ted, and I put that card on it for him.

I've been down to the Ted Williams Museum a few times, and I've created memorabilia bats for him, but I've never had the opportunity to meet the man personally. I've seen him at various dinners. You know how it is with those guys, everybody under the sun is trying to get into their limelight. I sort of get the feeling that these Hall of Famers . . . they appreciate it and they like it, but on the other hand, they feel, *Here's another guy who's just trying to be seen with me.* I don't like that idea. The first year I did the bats for him, they asked me to go up and have my picture taken with him. I said no. There was this line of thirty people . . . and I thought, *I'm not going to go up and stand in that line. Who knows what Ted's thinking. He might not even feel like doing this. No, I'm not interested in that, and I don't think Ted is either. If the guy wanted to see me, well, that's fine, but I'm not gonna impose.* I mean, guys like Ted Williams can't live a normal life. They can't even write checks. Things that you and me take for granted. I'd just like to talk baseball with the guy.

◆ ◆ ◆

MIKE SCHACHT, Artist

Ted Williams is my favorite subject to paint. It's a little ironic considering that I grew up in Cincinnati and was very pro National League. Back in those days, the wartime '40s, before television or even *The Game of the Week*, the lines were distinctly drawn between National and American. Our big guy was Stan the Man Musial. It was Stan we put up against Williams and DiMaggio in arguments as to which was the stronger league with greater stars.

It was later on when I really became intrigued with Ted Williams—his style, his contrariness, good looks, war record, and batting skills. I guess he became a latter-day kind of hero for me. Once I began painting again in the early 80s, and rediscovered my childhood baseball heroes as fresh subjects to recreate from all the wonderful old pictures, I painted Ted more than any of the other players. I especially like young Ted, confident, skinny, handsome, eyes wide open to his entire career ahead of him, and oh, that swing!

My challenge more and more now is to try to interpret Williams in what I call a *gesture*. In other words, to capture only the essential about him and leave out all the usual information like uniform and background details. My recent work is more like this. I prefer painting mostly in black and white with all its in-between grays, instead of using the customary ballpark colors. To me baseball is still black and white. It's the way I first learned to understand the game from pictures and newspapers. It's how I first was introduced to Ted Williams, with his classic moves and distinctive size and features.

Ted Williams will always be my painting subject of choice.

◆ ◆ ◆

BILL NOWLIN, Co-founder Rounder Records

I blew a chance to get a prime bit of Ted Williams memorabilia. I was at Fenway Park the last time Ted Williams appeared there in an "old-timers' game." The old-timers' games never draw quite the crowd of a regular game, and things are more informal in general. I was sitting right on the edge of the field, in section 29.

It was 1987. Ted was 68. He had put on a lot of weight, and I think it's a safe bet he hadn't taken an hour of batting practice prior to the event! He got up there gamely, though,

TED WILLIAMS: THE PURSUIT OF PERFECTION

and stepped into the batter's box for the last time ever. There's no really polite way to say this: it was a little pathetic. I was overcome with sadness. The years go by, and none of us are what we were.

Ted swung and missed, once or twice. Then he hit a weak little dribbler that rolled foul just past third base and just sat there on the grass at Fenway maybe 25 feet from where I sat. No one picked it up. *Ted Williams hit that ball!* I said to myself. Though Ted wouldn't like the comparison, like Castro in Saul Landau's film *Fidel*, he was granted a fourth strike. And a fifth. He never did connect. Finally, the embarrassment was over and the next batter came up. I kept looking at that ball, and wondering if they would really eject me if I ran out on the field and snagged it. I didn't really think so, but I failed to act.

A couple more batters came to the plate, and still no one touched that ball, resting nearly pure white on the green mown grass. Calling to me like a beacon. Admittedly it wasn't a bleacher shot or a game winner but it was undoubtedly The Last Ball Ted Williams Ever Hit At Fenway Park.

Then the fielders all came in and the old-timers' game was over. One of them scooped up the ball, having no idea what it represented, and tossed it into the bag with all the rest of them, to be hit again, by some mere mortal—some Yastrzemski or Boggs.

Ted Williams game-used uniform.

CURT SMITH, Broadcaster
(*Taken from* The Storytellers *by Curt Smith*)

The first big-league game I attended was August 30, 1960—Ted Williams' 42nd birthday—against the Tigers at Fenway Park. Eleven years earlier, my parents had watched a Red Sox-Indians' game at Fenway on their honeymoon. Now I saw on my father's face why Williams became John Wayne in baseball woollies for a generation of Americans . . . .

I first met Teddy Ballgame in 1966 as he and Casey Stengel were inducted at Cooperstown . . . Williams wrote an acceptance speech longhand the night before that many call the finest in Hall of Fame history. Later, Ted was besieged for autographs. "I'm not signing, you pushy kids. Learn some manners." Eclipsing voice, his roar stunned them into silence. "Know who I'm signing? Kids outside the circle who aren't rude." And, jostling pen and paper, he pushed his way toward me.

Hooked from there to eternity, I never forgot the honest outrage of this part-child and part-Gibraltar. When No. 9 retired, Ed Linn wrote, "And now Boston knows how England felt when it lost India." Pray that Gibraltar crumbles and, yes, the Rockies tumble before America forgets the seasons of The Kid.

♦ ♦ ♦

BILLY DePALMA, Toll Collector, Ted Williams Tunnel

Billy DePalma is an active Ted Williams memorabilia collector. He also works as a collector of another sort—a night-time toll collector at Boston's Ted Williams Tunnel.
He first heard of Ted as a fifth-grader, about 10 years after Ted had retired from the Red Sox.

The first time I ever heard of Ted, I was in my school auditorium watching a baseball training film he had made about hitting. At the end, my teacher came over and said, "You swing just like that guy." All I could say was 'Wow!'"

Vendor's cap, Ted's Root Beer

A lot of people from other countries drive through and say they've never heard of Ted Williams, so I tell them who he is. A guy came through a few weeks ago saying he thought Ted didn't deserve to have the tunnel named after him because he was indifferent to his fans. So I told him what a great person Ted is. He's a war hero who has been helping children with cancer for almost 60 years. He's helped about a million kids, and he's tried to do it without taking any credit for himself. Well, the driver said he had never thought of it that way before. I think I may have changed his mind, and that makes me proud.

(Courtesy of The Jimmy Fund)

◆ ◆ ◆

DAVE McCARTHY, Ted Williams Security Team

I served 26 years with the New Hampshire State Police. Dan Wheeler, Dan Florent, Eric Goodman and I all volunteer our time to provide security for Ted at special events.

I've provided security for presidents, governors and movie stars, but I've never seen anyone who generates as much excitement as Ted Williams. I remember one time I had arms locked with other security officers and this woman—she was in her 60s and wearing an evening gown—reached in between my legs with a baseball for Ted to sign! He's the only one who has this effect on people. I've seen older people cry when they see him.

When Ted came to New Hampshire to greet President Bush back in 1992, the news cameras turned away from Air Force One to focus on The Kid instead of on the President. I think the President was more excited to see Ted than Ted was excited to see the President, and Ted was pretty excited. I recall another time when Massachusetts Governor Cellucci introduced himself to me and asked, "Do you think Ted will sign a baseball for me?"

At the All-Star Game in 1999, Eric Goodman and I offered to take Matt Damon to see Ted in his hotel room. Matt couldn't believe it. He kept saying to me, 'You guys aren't kidding, are you? I'm really going to meet Ted?' He was like a little kid. I told him, 'You're Matt Damon. Trust me. We'll get you in to see Ted.'

I can tell you this, every day of my life, I tell myself I can't believe I know this guy. But it's been great. One time I was driving Nomar and Ted to dinner in Florida, and Nomar was a little in awe of Ted. Well, Ted was back-seat driving a little bit, and finally I said, "Listen, Ted, you're a great hitter—but I'm a great driver." Nomar told me later, "I can't believe you said that." But Ted loves to kid around. He's a regular guy, a regular man's man.

◆ ◆ ◆

DAVID L. PRESSMAN, M.D., Friend, Photographer, Bat Expert and Advisor

Ted knew a lot about the physics of the ball and the bat. He understood the principle of restitution. At the point of contact between the ball and the bat, both the ball and the bat compress and then re-expand. He knew that what determines the velocity of the ball coming off the bat are the speed of the pitch, bat speed, and the principle of restitution. He was one of the first players to use a lightweight bat (32 ounces) to increase bat speed. He selected narrow grain wood because the grain is the most flexible part of the wood, and the more grains lines there are per inch, the more the bat can compress and re-expand.

People used to say, when they watched him hit, that the ball would come off like an absolute rocket. Like a rocket! You cannot believe that velocity. . . . If you looked at his bats, the ball marks are right in the sweet spot. I have a lot of bats and many others, but *his* stuff is . . . right there. He knew the "sweet spot" and exactly what he was doing!

As a player myself, I recognized that on certain days the same bat would feel great and on others it would feel dead. I realized that the bats sometimes absorbed moisture. I came up with the idea of baking my bats over the embers of a coal stove before each game—even in the summer—to dry out the wood, because I had figured out that even bats with lacquer can absorb up to two ounces of moisture on a damp or humid day. I gave this tip to Ted through Tabby Ryan, who was Ted's Louisville Slugger rep.

He would weigh every bat before the game. Not that he didn't know the original weight from the factory, because he checked that when they came in. Ted modified my coal stove method by putting every bat in the clothes dryer at the ballpark with a bunch of towels. Everybody else had to wait until Ted finished with his clothes dryer. He would weigh each bat again until the bats had stopped losing weight, which then told him he had driven out all the excess moisture. He said, "Dave, don't tell anybody—but Vern Stephens and I used to put balls in there, too." They never knew. The balls became like ping pong balls. All of this easily increased the speed of the ball coming off his bat by at least 25 miles per hour. Ted hit for average as well as power. You can't catch the ball—whoosh! It was coming off the bat so fast it was past you.

Ted measured the distance of his hits using his unbaked bats and those he baked; the difference he found was 65 feet.

Fans when they watched him hit, really couldn't tell how fast the ball was coming off the bat. All they could tell is that when Ted hit it, it made a different sound. There's no question he could hit through the Boudreau shift, and he did, because the ball was coming off the bat so fast.

Things bothered Ted. Everything had to be exactly right. He was very fussy about his bats, the fit of his uniform, anything which could affect his concentration. He would often turn the bat label down, so he wouldn't be distracted by the label. So, if you see a Ted Williams bat and the hit marks are on the side you would not expect, that's consistent with an example of a Ted Williams game-used bat. He wouldn't do it all the time. Batting practice, he would go the other way. And you could also tell by the narrow grain wood.

I have Ted's uniform shirt from 1949. The neck area at the back of the shirt is composed of two layers of material and the stitching for the McAuliffe and Wilson labels and size tag were only supposed to go through the first layer. Some authenticator was looking it over and said, "There's something wrong here. That can't be. The stitching goes through both layers." I checked it out by calling Ted. He told me, "Oh, Helen Robinson put those back on for me." She was the receptionist but also the seamstress for years and years. They

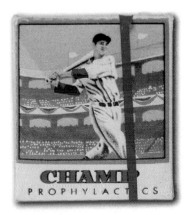

didn't have a store they went to when uniforms got ripped. She would repair them at home. Ted was bothered by the label, if the label became loose. The label was bothering him. He was going to rip it off, because it distracted him, but she sewed it back on and her stitching went all the way through. And she remembered it! I called her up and said Ted told me that you sewed these back on. "I remember that," she said. Afterwards, another authenticator confirmed this by calling Helen at Fenway. He was amazed that both Ted and Helen remembered this small detail from 50-plus years ago.

I had brought one of his old W166 bats to the first Old-Timers' game for him to autograph but didn't get to him because he was so swamped with media attention. So I called him at the Sheraton Boston after the game and got right through—it wasn't like today, with the security and ballplayers registering under a fictitious name. "Dave! Come right over!" He and John-Henry were there. He signed the 1949 uniform I had and he told me, "You should never sell it until after I die, because it'll be worth $25,000. Promise me you won't sell it, because you'll lose money if you sell it before I die." So, there he was in the Sheraton Boston with the bat, in the lobby, swinging the bat. When he got to the bat, he said, "Geez," he says, "This is great. If I'd had this today, I wouldn't have struck out. I had to use Yastrzemski's bat and it was a piece of shit." After that, I supplied him his own bats for the Old-Timers' games—two bats a game, one a 32 oz. and one 33 oz., weighed at the local post office scale and "baked" before the game in my home oven.

I had a tryout with the Red Sox a day or so after Ted came back from Korea. The team was in Chicago but he had just come back and he was catching fungos in left field [at Fenway] while I was having my tryout in center. So we got together again at that point.

When I was a Harvard student at that time, I'd get him into the Harvard cage on rainy days. Later the whole team got in. When the team came, his bats were kept separate. And he would wear a whole uniform, he was so fussy. Other people would just have the shirt on, but he would wear the whole uniform to duplicate the experience. Joe Dobson would throw batting practice. There was no catcher. Ted would make believe . . . he would make like a radio announcer: "It's 3-and-2 and Williams is up in the last of the ninth inning and there's three men on base." He would always say, "Put something on it!" He wanted a challenge. He was probably not 60 feet, 6 inches away. It was probably 50 feet away. And the stuff coming off that bat was like a laser! It was incredible. Everything had to be just like a game. "Dobson, you have to take a full windup." He'd tell him to act like there was a runner on second. Everything would be duplicated. He'd tell him to pitch inside, pitch outside. "Put something on it!" Even in the Old-Timers' game. He would bunt and he told the pitcher to "Put something on it!" Do everything like he was in the game. He wanted the challenge.

Even on his socks, he put #9 on them. Everything is exact. In the days he was playing with Pesky, he had to put a line under the 9. But the line is exact. It's precise.

I often picked him up at the airport or took him back to the airport. He would often come on these hunting trips, and he'd have these guns. Massive guns. They couldn't go in a cab. And I had to get him to the airport an hour and a half before flight time so he could clear the live ammo.

There were a couple of episodes where we'd be driving to the airport. There are many stoplights between the Sheraton Boston and the airport and he would be very visible sitting in the car. After the game, or the next day when it was sunny, people would recognize him sitting in the back of the car. He would say, "You see those people over there? They recognize me, but I don't know why they won't come over to say hello and get an autograph. Pull over! Pull over the car!" He'd go over to the person, especially if it was a kid, and say, "Hi, I'm Ted Williams. I used to play for the Red Sox. Do you play baseball? Oh, you do? Dave, get a bat from the car." He'd get out there right on Newbury Street or Boylston Street and draw this huge crowd like he did in the lobby of the hotel, swinging this bat. There he is showing the kid this upswing. He'd be teaching this Little Leaguer how to do this. By that time, there was a whole crowd. "Dave, you've got any balls?" And he would autograph the balls and give them to people on Boylston Street! Then he would ask me later, "How much did that cost, Dave?" and he would reimburse me. There aren't any players who do that! There was no publicity about this. He just liked people.

He never stayed at the Ritz-Carlton when he was in Boston, where Mrs. Yawkey lived, except once. He didn't stay there because he couldn't play this game. When he stayed at the Sheraton, he played a certain game. He said, "Watch, Dave." He would order breakfast—you wouldn't believe the huge amount of food he would order—he'd order all this stuff and he had this military wristwatch and he would push the button. "Let's see how long it takes them to get up here with the order."

Normally, if you get room service, it takes a long time. He would have a thing to see how long it took them to come. They would vie, they would compete to see who got to bring up Ted Williams' meal. They would bring stuff up for him to autograph, which he was always happy to do. At the Ritz-Carlton the kitchen staff were not allowed to do this, so Ted preferred the Sheraton.

◆ ◆ ◆

Gods Do Answer Letters

by Lawrence Baldassaro

When Ted Williams was rounding the bases after hitting a home run in his last time at bat, he had one final chance to respond to the cheers of his adoring fans. But Williams, just as he had done since his sophomore season of 1940, refused to tip his cap and ran straight into the dugout with his head bowed. In his classic essay on that final game, John Updike explained Williams' refusal to acknowledge the crowd's cheers with a simple but poignant phrase: "gods do not answer letters."

That one line—"gods do not answer letters"—seems to capture the essence of Williams' legendary indifference to his fans. The only problem is, it isn't true. Well, at least in my case it isn't. In 1982, Ted Williams did answer my letter.

It all began when we were making plans to take our five-year-old son to Disney World in March. For me, the trip also held the promise of fulfilling a childhood fantasy of my own—visiting the Red Sox spring training camp at Winter Haven, 30 miles south of Disney World.

But by chance this trip offered an even more whimsical element of wish-fulfillment. About a year earlier a faculty colleague who was editing a special issue of *The Journal of American Culture* dedicated to essays on sports had asked me to contribute a piece. I decided to write about Ted Williams, trying to explain why he had been my childhood hero. The journal was published in the fall of 1981, just as we began making plans for our Florida trip.

What followed illustrates the bizarre effects a long Wisconsin winter can have on a person's mind. Having published this essay, and knowing that Williams would be at the Red Sox training camp as a batting instructor, I thought of an idea that immediately appeared ludicrous even to me. Why not write to Williams, sending him a copy of my article, and ask to meet him at the Red Sox camp?

Sure, Ted Williams, the man who despised writers, was going to respond to some professor who happened to add to the already too deep pile of material written about him over the years. Having grown up as a Red Sox fan in Massachusetts, I knew all about Williams' attitude toward "the knights of the keyboard." But I decided to write the letter anyway, figuring that I had nothing to lose, and hoping that he would understand I was not a "real" sportswriter.

So I sent off my letter with a copy of the article, politely that I would enjoy the chance to meet him when I was in Winter Haven. That, I assumed, would be the end of it. And that's when Ted Williams proved John Updike to be wrong. Back came a letter in which he not only thanked me for the article but also wrote—this was the part I had to read several times to believe—"I'll be happy to meet you at the Red Sox camp in March." Ted Williams happy to meet someone who had written about him? The same Ted Williams who spat at the press in 1956?

(For the record, my article had not been all that flattering. I acknowledged that being a fan of Ted Williams was a bittersweet experience, given his tendency to treat his fans like the "vultures" he thought them to be. But I concluded that his work ethic and dedication to excellence made him an appropriate enough role model for youngsters.)

The letter arrived in late January and we were scheduled to go to Florida during the first week of March, which meant four weeks of anticipation, and apprehension. Granted, Williams had been polite, even cordial, in his letter, but who knew what mood he might be in when I approached him. There was plenty of evidence on record to prove that Williams could be a wrathful god, so I mentally prepared myself to face the *ira dei* that so many writers had graphically depicted during his playing days.

Finally the moment of truth arrived. Having settled my wife and son in the grandstands at Land

O'Lakes Park, I approached the Red Sox clubhouse. They players filed out—Yastrzemski, Rice, Evans, the entire team—but there was no sign of Ted Williams. Then I heard what was unmistakably his booming voice. And suddenly there he was, coming out the door, looking even bigger than I had imagined him to be, though I knew from photos that he was no longer the "Splendid Splinter." With a copy of his letter in hand for insurance, I quickly introduced myself, not knowing what response I would get from the great enigma.

More surprises. He remembered me and was as cordial in person as he had been in his letter. "What subject do you teach?", he asked, and when I told him I taught Italian his eyes lit up and he said, with obvious pride: "Yeah? My son, John-Henry, is studying French." He then asked if I had any children. When I told him that my son was in the stands he immediately said: "Go get him. I'll wait right here for you."

Was this the man that so many Boston writers had depicted as an ogre when I was a kid? The man that, according to columnist Dave "The Colonel" Egan, "had set a sorry example for a generation of kids"? Those questions crossed my mind as I hurried to find my son. A few minutes later, there I was holding Jim in my arms and standing next to Ted Williams while my wife took our picture. Mr. Updike, not only does he answer letters, he poses for snapshots.

But Williams wasn't done surprising me. He invited me to join him on the bench along the right field foul line to watch the Sox take batting practice. As he sat there fidgeting with a bat—how else could one imagine Ted Williams?—he commented in detail on each of the hitters as they took their swings. I was hearing right from the source all those well-known thoughts on the art of hitting: "You've got to be selective, hit your pitch, not the pitcher's." "Hitting a baseball is the single most difficult thing to do in sports." And on and on. What more could a Ted Williams fan ask for than to be listening to The Kid himself talk about hitting? Then what was already a fantasy became even more surreal. He turned to my son, who was standing nearby

with his mother, and asked him if he played baseball. When Jim said yes, Williams held out his bat and said: "Come here, let's take a look at your swing." With that, the greatest hitter of all time handed his Louisville Slugger to my son. Jim, who wasn't much taller than the bat, did his best to take a healthy cut, after which Williams commented: "Not bad, not bad; try to get a little more of your butt into the ball."

Not only does he answer letters and pose for pictures, he even gives batting tips to five year olds.

Ted Williams, the one-time temperamental firebrand, sat there with us for more than an hour talking in that rapid-fire, animated rhythm of his about baseball and his other great passion, fishing. Then it was time for him to head for the rookies' field to do some coaching.

Toward the end of that article I had written on Williams less than a year before meeting him, I pointed out that I did not, and probably should not, know the man behind the legend. "The reality," I wrote, "might shatter the illusion and I would have gained nothing." That day in Winter Haven no illusions were shattered and I learned that the "real" Ted Williams was more human than either John Updike or I had imagined him to be.

Ted with Larry Baldassarro and Larry's son Jim.

The Legacy of Teddy Ballgame

Ted Williams was schooled in the game of baseball. As student, he soaked up knowledge, organized it to his best advantage, and never stopped in his quest to improve upon those baseball lessons he'd learned. As teacher, he readily shared his expertise with others. For every ballplayer he might have pumped for information regarding a pitcher he hadn't yet faced, there was a struggling young hitter to whom he offered pointers. There was only one stipulation: he had to be asked.

In the end, he became what he longed to become: the greatest hitter who ever lived. From his days on a San Diego playground striking balls into the darkness, to his triumphant final swing, Ted Williams was an American legend in the making. Hall of Fame player, hero of war and children, spectacle of fans and media, sportsman, coach, perfectionist . . . individual. And always a ballplayer's ballplayer.

When he had the chance to speak out for the admission of Negro League players into the Hall of Fame, Ted used the most influential forum at his command—his own Hall of Fame induction speech—to do just that. Simply and eloquently. He spoke for the cause of honesty and fairness, things that indisputedly define him as a man. Injustice, like imperfection, required correction.

Above all, he never lost enthusiasm for his passions. Ted favored the Socratic method of instruction, forever asking questions in order to prove his points. It was only logical that Ted Williams would lend his name and talents to the next generation. For over a dozen years, the Ted Williams Baseball Camp in New England was the Harvard of hitting, the Princeton of pitching, and the Fordham of fielding. In the years following his retirement, his influence continued to be felt at the major league level. Ted spent years as a special hitting instructor in the Red Sox spring training camps, working with young, wide-eyed prospects, and served for a time as manager of the Washington Senators. His instructional book, The Science of Hitting, *became the bible of batting for the hitters of later generations.*

Opposite: Ted waiting to hit at an Old-Timers' Game.
(Copyright David L. Pressman, M.D.)

Already a hall of fame player and hall of fame fisherman, a concrete reminder of Ted's legacy was born with the formation of the Ted Williams Museum at Citrus Hills in Hernando, Florida. The Museum was conceived and created by Ted's closest friends and admirers, with artist Lewis Watkins taking the lead role. It is one of the very few such museums created to honor a living athlete.

Today, Ted continues to teach the game of baseball. He has thrown his support behind disciple Steve Ferroli to form the Ted Williams Baseball League; the hope, to stimulate a nationwide dialogue on the future of youth baseball in America. It is Ted's fervent belief that the game needs a strong foundation among young players in order to survive and flourish.

But beyond the museums and the plaques, even beyond the statistics and the on-field dramatics, Ted Williams stands for a fundamental belief: baseball is a game for young people of all backgrounds and conditions to enjoy. This may, indeed, be his most lasting legacy.

NOMAR GARCIAPARRA, Ballplayer

The first time I spoke to Ted was over the phone during my rookie year. I'll never forget it. I was renting an apartment in Boston at the time and two of my good high school buddies were visiting from California. I told them, "Tomorrow at 11:00 o'clock, we'll get a phone call and it'll be Ted Williams," and they said, "Yeah, right, whatever." Like clockwork, I get a phone call right at 11:00 and from their room I hear them yelling, "It's him! It's him! Wake up!" Just screaming! They came into my room and they were hitting me on the leg and I was like trying to brush them off to leave me alone as I was trying to talk to Ted. It was pretty funny.

We talked about hitting. I mean that's what he talked about. He grilled me! I mean he drilled me about hitting the whole time! He asked me questions. It's something he loves and he loves talking about it—and he also wants to know how much you know as a hitter. He'd seen me on TV a few times at that point, and he was just drilling me and grilling me and it was great. Did he like what he heard from me? Yeah, as a matter of fact, I remember him telling people: "Wow, I ask these questions of everybody and it's the first time I ever heard anybody answer them all right." I go, "Wow, I can't take the credit for that, I have to thank my father for that; he taught me right."

The first time I met him face to face was at the Hitters Hall of Fame in 1998. I got to talk with him and went to his house breakfast. He said, "You know I'm Mexican as well. My mother was Mexican." I said, "God, Ted, I knew I liked you." He talked hitting throughout the whole conversation. I thought to myself, "Even now he's thinking about it, even now he cares, even now he's watching closely. You know he played the game all those years, he played baseball all his professional life—most people might think well, maybe it's time I got away from it, you know? Not him! Shoot, he believes he can still hit right now. I'm sure that's what he believes and he probably could! That's his mentality and when you see that you say, "Wow, that's why he's the best!"

What a great hitter he was! For a ballplayer, reaching .400 is almost like achieving immortality! How do you reach .400? It's tough, man. And Ted's the last one to do it. That's just incredible! It tells you something. The game's changing so much and the way it's evolved makes it tougher and tougher and tougher. I'm just in awe of him doing that.

Nomar, Dave McCarthy, Ted, Bob Breitbard sit around Ted's kitchen table.
(Photo courtesy of Dave McCarthy)

When Ted called me up he just told me, "You can do it. Don't worry about it. Just keep doing what you're doing. You look great! You're doing everything right. Make sure you get a good one and just whack it like you've been doing it. Just get a good ball to hit." I laughed and said, "Aren't they all good ones?" He never gave me a hard time for swinging at the first pitch, though. He said, "I'd like to give you grief for that but, darn it, you do it so well, how can I get on you for it? Just make sure it's a good one, 'cause man you know it!"

The '99 All-Star game was special. Boston did a phenomenal job of hosting it. Seeing all those great players on the same field at one time—current all-stars, past all-stars, legends of the game. It was incredible and when Ted came out, it was like, "Oh my God!" and you're wondering, who is this one person coming on the field? It was almost like wondering who's going to light the torch at the Olympics. Who's going to light it? Who's going to light it? And then HE came out! It was like that. Oh my God! It was pretty surreal. Everyone just surrounded him and went to the middle of the mound to see him. Everybody was like, "Wow!" We were just in awe. It was a pretty special moment in baseball.

I remember going over and saying "Hi" to him. He said, "Good to see you," and actually apologized for missing a little luncheon I had earlier in the day! The greatest thing to me about meeting someone like Ted is being able to call him a friend.

I think what fascinates me about Ted more than anything is not just what he's done as a ballplayer, but just his whole life. I mean, shoot, he's been in the Marines, he's been in wars, he's been under fire, a war hero—all that's just incredible. When I was at his house . . . just looking on his wall at all the pictures, I could have been there for hours! It was like a museum to me, it was like history and I didn't want to leave. Incredible! And I was like "WOW, look at that!" You know you talk about heroes and about how there are heroes on the ball field—well, Ted's more than that. He's a real hero! You talk about the guys right now who are fighting for us. They are real heroes and he's one of them.

I'm just amazed at all he's done in his life—the war, the fishing. What a movie his life would make! But the very best thing is being able to call Ted Williams my friend.

◆ ◆ ◆

ART RUST, JR., Sports Announcer
(Taken from Confessions of a Baseball Junkie *by Art Rust, Jr.)*

Ted was not only the greatest hitter—he might be one of the greatest personalities ever. If you had to put down a list of totally unique individuals, three people that you'd select if you had a chance to invite anyone for dinner, he would be one of those. Churchill, John Kennedy, and Ted Williams.

— Bob Lobel

Sometimes you have so many idols you don't know where to worship. I cannot leave out the Splendid Splinter, the Thumper, outfielder Ted Williams, a once-in-a-generation hitter—the best in our time. What I love about the man was that he recognized his talent and knew his art and practiced it. He had a keen appreciation of the strike zone, a great eye, quick hands—and what power. If he had not gone into the military service twice (World War II and the Korean conflict), God knows how many records he would have set.

He spent a prodigious amount of time on bodybuilding and arm-developing exercises; thereby setting a pattern for players who followed.

The first time I saw Ted Williams was April of 1939. I was sitting in the right field bleachers at Yankee Stadium, and it was the Boston Red Sox's first visit to New York for the year. I was sitting with my pretend uncle Louis Mayers.

And there I saw this long lean Williams hit a double off of Yankee right-hander Charlie "Red" Ruffing. As young as I was, I could discern greatness.

They called Williams haughty and arrogant, but it has always been my contention that arrogance is applicable to the very talented who are fully aware of what they are able to produce, and I salute that. It is only ignorant or stupid arrogance that bothers me.

But there is another side to the coin. I read that Williams was a very kind and considerate person. When Ted Williams was a kid, his mother, who played the cornet in the Salvation Army Band, gave him 30 cents every morning to buy his lunch at school. However, his teachers noticed that the child seldom ate lunch and with his lean, lanky frame looked undernourished. After many inquiries the teachers found that he was giving his lunch money to boys less fortunate than he. I think admirable deeds as a child show you the measure of the man.

When Williams became eligible for a loser's share of the receipts of the 1946 World Series, a matter of $2,150.89, he thought that the Red Sox clubhouse attendant, Johnny Orlando, was deserving of a tip and gave him a check for $2,500. Williams was a madman, but he had a fine madness. The kind of madness we admire in an Albert Einstein, the Wright brothers, Margaret Sanger, Marcus Garvey, and Hannibal, who somehow got elephants over the Alps.

You could never predict what the man would do, and that was part of the beauty of the whole scheme. Williams was the man sportswriters called surly, petulant, sulking, pouting, and all those adjectives of that nature. And it was true that at various times he was all of those things.

The hell with that, he was also one of the most gifted batters in the history of baseball . . . When he arrived at Sarasota for spring training, he attracted immediate attention because of his cockiness, his promise of greatness and because he refused to wear a necktie and even missed a bus to an exhibition game; but he was just a headstrong 20-year-old. . . .

He joined the big club in 1939. He gained his greatest glory in 1941: he batted .406 and blasted one of his most memorable homers. How well do I remember July 1941. My mother was ironing in the kitchen, and I'm in my room listening to the All-Star game from Briggs Stadium in Detroit. Oh boy, was I happy. I'm a National League fan, and

Another angle of the only color photos of Ted hitting a home run.
Above, Ted is cocked and ready. Below, Ted blasts it out.
(Copyright David L. Pressman, M.D.)

they're ahead. Arky Vaughan has just hit his second home run for the National League. All of a sudden in the bottom of the ninth, up steps Ted Williams, who smacks one over the top of the roof in right field off Cub right-hander Claude Passeau. I remember sitting there in my room crying. Concerned, my mother came to me, and when I explained the situation, she laughed. Her response was, "What the hell are you getting so upset over the white man's game for anyway?" I love and adore my mother, but she did not understand the intensity of my feelings for the game.

On the final morning of the 1941 season, Williams had a batting average of .3995 and was faced with a doubleheader against the Philadelphia Athletics at Shibe Park. In the first game he banged out four hits and two in the second, six in eight tries and had the distinction of becoming the first player in the American League since 1923 to hit .400. As of yet there has been no equal.

What a career Williams went on to have. Two time triple crown winner, 1942 and 1947, and the only American Leaguer to do that. Hopefully, all of us have our great moments. Ted Williams had more than his share. . . .

When Ted Williams was inducted into the Hall of Fame in 1966, he declared, "I hope Satchel Paige and Josh Gibson [both legendary Black players who could only work for the Negro National Leagues in their time slot] will be voted into the Hall of Fame as symbols of the great Black players who are not here only because they weren't given the chance."

God, I love a human being like Williams.

I had the ultimate pleasure of meeting Ted Williams in 1969 when he was the manager of the Washington Senators. The long, lean idol that I had admired had a long paunch. Then I thought, what the hell, I know damn well I don't look like I did 20 years ago, but that does not keep me from being me. There is something about growing older that says I got over that hump, now let's try for the mountain.

Ted Williams forever.

◆ ◆ ◆

ARMAND LaMONTAGNE, Sculptor
—An interview by Bill Nowlin

Artist Armand LaMontagne reminds you of Ted: a larger than life character, with drive and passion, ready to listen and ready to learn, aware of his own talents. You can sense the relationship he and Ted have built up over the years, with LaMontagne ready to say of his subjects, "They don't dare give me a hard time, or they know I'll make their nose too big."

"I cut 'em down to size," he booms, in his studio where he is currently working on a life-size statue of Ted Williams salmon fishing, a piece which has been commissioned for the New England Sports Museum. He first attacks the 1,500- to 1,600-pound block of wood with a chain saw, then later refines with wooden mallet and chisels. "Here, watch this," he says as he approaches the work in progress with tools in hand. He taps on the chisel and takes away part of Williams' shoulder. Taking the chip off Ted's shoulder is the way Armand LaMontagne operates.

A self-described "chiseler," LaMontagne was an athlete who gave up baseball when he was granted a four-year football scholarship to Boston College. As a kid, Ted Williams was always his hero. "You can only have one childhood hero," he says.

"A work of art starts out with an emotion, preferably a positive one," he continues, explaining how he has come to work with sports and other public figures

The Lifetime Achievement Award plaque designed by Armand La Montagne. It is awarded each year at the Ted Williams Museum ceremonies.

TED WILLIAMS: THE PURSUIT OF PERFECTION

both as a sculptor and an accomplished painter. Rare these days, to have both talents. "It's all visual perception," he reflects.

On his first visit to the studio, Ted asked to see photos of the artist playing baseball. Ted looked at the shot from the Worcester Academy yearbook, and allowed that he liked how Armand had his head right on the ball. He grabbed a ruler from a nearby worktable and placed it on the photo. "You hit a ground ball." Actually, it was a triple, remembered LaMontagne, noting with pride that he himself hit about .400 that year.

A true subtractive sculptor, LaMontagne got Ted's attention that time they first met in his workshop. "Ted, you and I each swing a piece of wood for a living. The difference is that you have three chances. I've only got one." Williams thought about that, and couldn't disagree. One wrong swing of the mallet, and the sculpture becomes irreparable.

"Ted is such a ball-buster. Everyone's so frightened of this guy. He likes it, though, if you come right back at him. They're all perfectionists [talking of Ted, Larry Bird, Bobby Orr and some of the other figures of whom he has created works], which is great. Ted is thorough."

Meeting Red Sox owner Jean Yawkey in Cooperstown, LaMontagne was asked by her why he had done the sculpture of Babe Ruth. It was a commission, he replied, going on to say that, "If you boil baseball down, it distills to Babe Ruth." A silence followed, sufficiently long to make him regret letting those words come out. "I knew Babe Ruth. I admired the ball player. I did not like the man," was Mrs. Yawkey's studied comment. She had always admired Ted Williams, though, both as a hitter and a man. Soon LaMontagne had a commission to create a companion work on the Splendid Splinter.

Ted had wanted to meet the artist chosen to sculpt him. He asked Armand to show him a photo of the Ruth statue. A stickler for detail in every regard, LaMontagne had gotten Ruth's hands right on the statue—slightly off, not lined up, the way Ruth had gripped the bat. "The kid's got it right," Ted said. Williams never sat for the work, but on the first visit was photographed from almost every angle, for three hours. Ted visited the workshop four or five times while the work was in progress. He might not have wanted to admit it, but he was interested. As a perfectionist, he wanted it done right. "I know if Ted's in New England before I finish this statue, he'll be banging on the door. Nothing is too small for his attention." Whatever the area of interest, be it fly-fishing or sculpture. When Ted saw the earlier sculpture nearly completed except for the back of the head, he called LaMontagne one night about three weeks later from his fishing camp in Canada and wanted to be sure that LaMontagne kept the haircut faithful to the feathered, '50s style he had sported in the period. Equally a stickler for detail, Armand already had that down. The sculpture had been completed.

When the statue was just about done, Ted demanded that Armand show him where the center of gravity was. The sculptor pointed to a spot on the base of the statue. Ted came back asking where the center of gravity would be if you cut off the base. It would pitch over forward, LaMontagne answered. "Goddamn it, you're right," Williams said. Armand recalls feeling, "It was like God told me I'd got it right."

LaMontagne strides across the room exclaiming, "NO ONE ever asks that question—the center of gravity. Ted asks just the right questions. And he always has an opinion. Right or wrong, he has an opinion." The artist then goes off into a series of anecdotes about Ted in restaurants. "It's like E. F. Hutton talking. The whole room gets quiet, everyone listening . . ."

When it was time for the unveiling of the Williams statue, it was the first time Ted had been back to Cooperstown since his 1966 induction into the Hall. He hated the image on the plaque they made of him, had them replace it, then liked the replacement even less. He never returned. When he pulled the rope to unveil the life-size work, he was moved to tears, humbled by being one of just two figures represented, next to one of his

Ted had an imaginary little box, situated in his favorite part of the strike zone. If the pitch wasn't in Ted's box, he wouldn't swing. [When I was invited to come to the Ted Williams Museum] I turned to my wife and said "Why should I go down here to honor him? The guy ruined my life for 17 years."

—Hal Newhouser

Hitter #9 statue by British sculptors Ted Taylor and Mike Ross.

own baseball idols, Babe Ruth. *Life* magazine captured Ted's reaction in a photo essay called, "A Legendary Hitter Chokes."

LaMontagne is a painter as well as a noted sculptor, and has done a number of works on Ted Williams. He fondly remembers the time that they were both signing a limited edition series of 406 lithos. They started signing in gold ink. The first couple that Ted signed, big blotches of the gold ink pooled on the print before drying. "Ted, I want those." "What do you want those for?" Ted asked, interlaced with a bit of profanity. "It proves that Ted Williams made a mistake," shot back Armand. Ted kept rushing through the signing, then paused when he saw the way LaMontagne was signing across the bottom of the print. "You're signing those in a straight line," he noted. "Ted, I'm not rushing," Armand replied. Ted straightened his own signature out. Armand said, "He doesn't like to be outdone."

It's difficult to choose how to depict Ted in his works, LaMontagne says, "because Ted has so many looks." Ted is "the real John Wayne" but he's also got "a dozen other looks. Ted's a man of many ages, not just his own. A thinker." Working from photographs was helpful, but having the opportunity to work with Ted in person was ideal. "The camera lies," Armand says, "You gotta know where it lies. Ted said, 'I don't want those eyes going to center. I want them going to right center. I'm a pull hitter.'"

Armand LaMontagne is proud that Ted has respected his creations. "When Ted gives you a compliment," he says, "that's something!" He seems at least as pleased that one of Ted's hitting theories was hatched right in his studio, "Right there!" He points to a chest-high workbench. Armand asked Ted, since he always choked up 3/4" on his bat, why he didn't just use a 3/4" shorter bat? Ted got quiet. Sure enough, some months later there was Ted quoted in *The Sporting News*, at a MacGregor coaches clinic in Chicago, "If you took an inch off everyone's bat, you'd improve every hitter." Ted always made adjustments.

◆ ◆ ◆

DAVID WARSH, Journalist
(Taken from an article in the Boston Globe, *July 27, 1997)*

Ted Williams is one of those figures for whom baseball exists to serve as a library of types—like the Iliad, or the plays of Shakespeare. He may have had the most beautiful swing in baseball, but it was Williams' quirky, intense personality that held the real charm. He had no closer student than John Updike, who explained that Williams "was always doing something fascinating—getting injured, going off to Korea, vilifying the press, announcing his retirement, hitting .388, hitting Joe Cronin's housekeeper with a tossed bat, spitting at the stands, going fishing when he shouldn't, etc." After Williams's last game, Updike published in the *New Yorker* an essay "Hub Fans Bid Kid Adieu," that is a sportswriting landmark. He wrote, "No other player of my generation concentrated within himself so much of the sport's poignance, so assiduously refined his natural skills, so constantly brought to the plate that intensity of competence that crowds the throat with joy."

◆ ◆ ◆

EDDIE MIFFLIN, Fan
(Written by Mike Shatzkin, taken from The Ballplayers *by Mike Shatzkin)*

Ted Williams announced in a three-part article in *The Saturday Evening Post* that his retirement would follow the 1954 season. It made sense. The Red Sox slugger was 36 years old, coming off a succession of seasons interrupted by injuries and military service. The broken elbow he suffered in the 1950 All-Star Game had, he felt, permanently robbed him of his power. When he came back from the Korean War in June 1953, only a genuine need for money had compelled him to sign through the end of the 1954 season. And a broken shoulder in spring training had cemented his resolve just before the *Post* articles ran.

Near the end of the 1954 season, Eddie Mifflin encountered Williams in the Baltimore train station after a Red Sox-Orioles series. He introduced himself and said, "You're not really going to retire, are you? You can't, you know. Your numbers aren't good enough." Williams was intrigued. "What do you mean my numbers aren't good enough? I've got a lifetime batting average over .350. I've hit home runs and knocked in 100 every year of my career. How can my numbers not be good enough? Good enough for what?"

Mifflin explained. The success of Williams's career would be measured one definitive way: would he be elected to the Hall of Fame in the first year he became eligible? Williams had missed so much playing time in WWII and Korea that his career totals weren't yet impressive enough. And baseball writers were the voters for the Hall of Fame. "Ted, you barely have 350 home runs. You don't have 1,500 RBI. You don't even have 2,000 hits. And these writers hate your guts; they didn't even vote you the MVP twice when you won the Triple Crown. You needs stats that are undeniable. These aren't."

Ted arranged to meet Mifflin again in New York later in the road trip. They stayed up all night discussing Williams's lifetime stats, where he stood in relation to Ruth, Cobb, Foxx, and Gehrig. Finally, Ted said, "What do I have to do?" Said Mifflin, "You've got to hit 500 home runs. Only three guys have done it: Ruth, Foxx, and Ott. Hit 500 home runs and they'll have to put you in on the first ballot."

In May 1955 Williams rejoined the Red Sox. He went on to compile the most amazing statistics in baseball history for a hitter over 35. He won two more batting championships. And he had his new friend, Eddie Mifflin, encouraging him and marking his progress with telegrams and phone calls. "Congratulations, those two RBI yesterday moved you past Foxx."

Williams had the only off-year of his big league career in 1959. At age 41, he suffered from a painful neck throughout the season and slumped to .254. Yawkey wanted him to retire. But he finished the season with 492 home runs. Mifflin's vision for Williams was fulfilled with his triumphant final 1960 season: a .316 farewell average, soaring past Mel Ott's 511 home runs, and capping his career with the 521st in his last at-bat. And five years later, on the first ballot, Williams was elected to the Hall of Fame.

◆ ◆ ◆

ERNIE BANKS, Ballplayer, Hall of Fame

Ted Williams is one of the few great athletes to go on to manage their sport. Most athletes of his caliber would not care to step up into the role of manager like Ted did. He had a lot of courage.

In Washington, when he was a manager, he played classical music while his players took batting practice. I asked him why. "To develop rhythm," he said, "rhythm in their swings, rhythm in their movement, rhythm! You've gotta have rhythm." So when I went to instructional league I did the same thing. I was working as a coach and I put on music to play while the guys were taking batting practice and working out. They really liked it and they played better.

Ted is a Virgo, right? August 30. Virgo—he's a perfectionist. That's the key mission of an athlete, to attain perfection in their sport. We've got Jack Nicklaus, Ben Hogan, Nolan Ryan, Michael Jordan, Tiger Woods—all great athletes. As far as I'm concerned Ted

I saw him the year I went into the Hall of Fame. I was in Winter Haven, and someone came out and told me that I'd been elected to Cooperstown by the Veterans Committee. Ted Williams came out and I had a picture taken with him. A newspaperman said, "Ted, did you know that Pee Wee just made the Hall of Fame?" Ted answered, "Yes, and he should have made it the regular way."

— Pee Wee Reese

Williams was the pioneer in the art of working hard to perfect your game. Baseball is a very difficult game to play. It requires hard work in every little detail. The more natural ability you have, the harder you have to work at sustaining a career and being the best at what you do.

Ted always liked people who worked to improve their skills, in all fields of life—not just baseball. My closest contact to him was the Hall of Fame. I'd look forward to going there just to sit and listen to him talk. He'd get into hitting and I'd get into his philosophy of life. Being around him meant one thing—you have to go higher. For him success meant rising above mediocrity. Mediocrity is all around and you may choose to wallow in it but successful people get beyond it. Ted Williams got beyond it throughout his life. Now many people around him chose to talk a lot without putting much action behind their words and Ted responded to that. He always said that people who open their mouths and don't know what they're talking about wind up getting caught. Just like a fish does when it opens its mouth.

Sometimes as we mature and move on in our lives, we don't grow, we don't want to learn any more, we kind of rest on our laurels. But not Ted. He continually searches for better ways to do things, always challenging minds and questioning what people say and do.

◆ ◆ ◆

BOB COSTAS, Broadcaster
(Remarks taken from 1996 "Legends" dinner)

It's worth noting . . . some of you may know this. But on the day that he was inducted into the Baseball Hall of Fame, in 1966, Ted Williams took time out from his personal reminiscences and his thoughts about baseball to lobby for the great players from the Negro Leagues to be included in the Hall of Fame and to at least partly right a long-standing injustice. When he was an active player, and when the big leaguers used to barnstorm against the Negro League stars, Ted was always perhaps the most outspoken of all the major league stars about how the color barrier had to be broken, about the great players that he had seen and played against, and how they were as good as the top big league stars.

Only recently, I remember Larry Doby, who was the Jackie Robinson of the American League, breaking in with the Cleveland Indians and becoming the first black player in the American League, Larry Doby saying that in the lonely early days when he'd be running out onto the field at the end of a half inning and Ted Williams would be running off, Williams always made it a point to try and cross paths with Doby, just kind of flick him on the butt with his glove and say "How ya doing, kid? Everything all right? You're a good lookin' hitter. You're gonna do well." And it seems like a small thing, but the barrier was so high then and the people that were there and had prestige like Ted Williams, what they said and what they felt mattered. And Ted's been on the right side of this cause long before it became a consensus as to what the right side was. He was way ahead of it.

◆ ◆ ◆

When the greatest hitter to ever live talks hitting, he draws a crowd.
(Photo by Fred Kaplan, courtesy of Lee Kaplan)

Jackie Robinson is widely known, by folks in many lands who don't even know the rules of baseball, as the man who first broke the color barrier in the major leagues. He has even had a U. S. postage stamp issued in his honor and the 50th anniversary of Robinson's

TED WILLIAMS: THE PURSUIT OF PERFECTION

entry into Major League baseball was widely celebrated across North America in 1997.

Just 11 weeks after Robinson broke in with the Dodgers, Larry Doby became the first African-American to enter the American League, suiting up for Bill Veeck's Cleveland Indians. Doby went on to a very successful 13-year playing career. Today he serves as a special assistant to the president of the American League.

"Doby has always had to live in the shadow of Robinson," writes Larry Whiteside of the Boston Globe. *"Like Robinson, Doby heard the racial slurs and threats. He felt the same ill will from opposing fans, clubs, and even teammates." Whiteside further notes that, unlike Doby, Robinson had the benefit of a year in the minors to prepare for his baptism of fire with the Dodgers.*

The playing field at former Ted Williams Camp, Lakeville, Massachusetts. The legacy of Teddy Ballgame continues through the formation of the Ted Williams Baseball League.
(Photo by Bill Nowlin)

"Back then, segregation was the law," Doby notes, "and it didn't matter what any of us thought. If you were black in the American League or black in the National League, they treated you the same way. Jackie and I both had to accept it. People still think I had it easier because I came along 11 weeks later. Well, it didn't matter if we came along 11 weeks or two years later. The truth is that it took a long time after that for things to begin to straighten out. Remember, the situation that Jackie and I were in, we went through even before there was a civil rights movement."

A dozen more years would pass before the Civil Rights Movement began to flourish. The year Larry Doby retired (1959) was a full year before the "sit-ins" began at the Woolworth counter in Greensboro, North Carolina, and three years before the March on Washington where Rev. Martin Luther King delivered his famous "I Have A Dream" oration.

Ted Williams, on accepting a Brotherhood Award at Howard University in 1971, was quoted in Anthony J. Conner's *Baseball for the Love of It* **as saying: As I look back on my career I'm thankful that I was given the chance to play baseball: It's about the only thing I could do—and I've thought many a time, what would have happened to me if I hadn't had a chance. A chill goes up my back when I think I might have been denied this if I had been black.**

LARRY DOBY, Ballplayer, Hall of Fame

When I first got in the League in '47, Ted was one of the few people who said "Hello" and "Good luck." He and Dom DiMaggio and a fellow named Rudy York. The thing that impressed me about Ted is that . . . with some people you can feel sincerity. With other people, you can feel it was politics, or something. You could ask him a question about anything and he'd tell you what he thought.

In 1950 at the All-Star game in Chicago, Ted ran into the left field scoreboard and broke his elbow. [Luke Easter and I] went to visit him the next morning at the hospital . . . [There was some hemming and hawing a bit about a couple of black men coming to visit Ted at the hospital, and the staff were perhaps unsure of what Ted's reaction would be. Things were very different in 1950. The nurse was polite, but displayed some uncertainty or discomfort as she tried to convey that the visitors were black.] The nurse said there was two gentleman come to see you. He said, "Send 'em up!"

Jesse Owens and Howard University president Dr. James E. Cheek shake hands as Ted looks on.
(Photo courtesy of Moorland–Springarn Research Center, Howard University Archives.)

During that time you left your glove on the field, and you'd pass the outfielders on the way on & off the field. He'd just say, "Congratulations! Good luck!" He just gave me a feeling of being welcome, which was important to me, especially when you had a lot of other people not saying anything. It was not a "welcome" thing. I don't think he was that sort of person to make a spectacle of it, just a quiet kind of person, going about his business. Didn't have to make any big deal out of it. That's why I feel it was from the heart.

Ted helped other hitters a lot during the time we were playing. I'd go to the batting cage and watch him. He give out a lot of good tips. If I had a little problem swinging the bat, I'd go to him.

He is one of the good people in this world. It would be nice if we had more people like this, a person stands up for right and justice. He's a strong person. Usually if you're *good* people and you're *for* people, you have problems *with* people. When you say Liberty & Justice for all, that's how he feels. Of course some people feel Liberty & Justice for some.

◆ ◆ ◆

MONTE IRVIN, Ballplayer, Hall of Fame

Ted and I have a cordial relationship. He always has questions to ask. One time I reminded him of an old catcher named Paul Casanova who he used to manage in Washington. I said, "Ted, you're such a great teacher of baseball hitters and yet you had a catcher with the worst swing of any hitter I've ever seen! The worst!" And he said, "Well, let me tell you this. You can't remake 'em all!"

We sometimes talked about racial barriers. Ted said that there were a lot of anti-integrationists in baseball back then. Not only were there owners who felt this way but some of the players, too. He used to say, "What the hell does it matter who you play against? If you have any confidence in your abilities, you should want to play against the best." He is very articulate. He just knows how to say things.

In the Hall of Fame they have a plaque of his induction speech in which he supported Satchel Paige and Josh Gibson and other blacks for induction. Ted was supportive of those two black players in particular, and all blacks. His speech had an impact. He did change some minds. The writers picked up on it, and some of the powers-that-be up at the Hall of Fame had to kind of perk up and take notice.

Josh Gibson was the black Babe Ruth and Buck Leonard the black Ted Williams. Ted and Buck were both stylish, they had similar mannerisms. The way Leonard pushed with the bat, the way he would twist the bat around in his hands at the plate before swinging was like Ted. Even the way he would run to first base, especially when he knew he had hit a home run to win a ballgame. He would jump up and down. Now Leonard didn't study hitting like Williams, he just went up there and swung. But he was a natural.

◆ ◆ ◆

When Ted and Jim Prime released Ted Williams' Hit List *in the United States, Josh Gibson was included in Ted's ranking of the top 25 hitters of all time, this despite the fact that Gibson never played a game in the major leagues. He was excluded because of his race. Gibson is included as well in the Hitters' Hall of Fame at the Ted Williams Museum in Florida. Since it was Ted who first called for the great Negro League players such as Gibson and Satchel Paige to be brought into baseball's Hall of Fame at Cooperstown, it was only appropriate.*

JOSH GIBSON, JR., Son of Josh Gibson

Ted seems like a man who stands on his own convictions. He's very vocal. I've heard him talk on interviews at times and, though I don't know him personally, the things that he has said concerning himself and the other great ballplayers are very positive. There's no prejudice. I don't think the man has an ounce of prejudice in his body. He's a fair guy, especially when it comes to athletes and ballplayers. He understands. He tells it like it is. And he seems to be truthful in everything he says.

What he has had to say about the Negro Leagues is really inspirational. And Boston—it can be a tough town, boy. As for Ted, I just hope he lives as long as God wants him to live, and keeps on making truthful statements about baseball.

◆ ◆ ◆

PUMPSIE GREEN, Ballplayer,
First African-American to play for the Red-Sox

I came up to the majors July 21, 1959. I was at spring training with Ted and one thing he did besides hit was talk. You ask him a question, and he'll answer your question and add three or four more, five or ten minutes to it. As long as you'd listen, he'd talk to you about hitting. That's what he preferred to talk about.

He took a real interest. And if you asked him a question, he was the kind of person who might just ask you the next day what he had said. You did yourself a favor by recalling what it was. You didn't want to tell him if you forgot!

When I got there, Mr. Yawkey invited me up. I went to his box, or penthouse or whatever. It was just to say hello and to welcome me to the ballclub. If anyone had a race problem, as far as I was concerned, it was their problem not mine. My aim was always to pay attention to what I was supposed to be doing, playing the game.

◆ ◆ ◆

DICK FLAVIN, Public Speaker

I grew up in Boston, one of these lifelong Red Sox sufferers. Dom DiMaggio is my lifelong hero. I started wearing glasses in the fourth grade and I go back to the days when he was the only ballplayer in the American League who wore glasses. That's when I kind of shifted my allegiance from Ted to Dom.

I'm very interested in getting Dom DiMaggio into the Hall of Fame, and I think the only one more interested than me in doing it is Ted Williams. A couple of years ago when we made our first push to get it to happen, Ted, who's on the veteran's committee, was right out front, writing letters to newspapers, all that sort of stuff. He was chided, apparently, because once the committee met, as a member, he wasn't supposed to be campaigning for other

Williams managed the Washington Senators in 1969 and was named American League Manager of the Year.
(Photo by Fred Kaplan, courtesy of Lee Kaplan)

players. He has therefore had to pull back in his public campaigning. But he's still committed. Ted's convinced that Dom never got a fair shot for a couple of reasons: one, that he played all those years next to Ted, and, two, because he's Joe's little brother. And in all those years following World War II, the third starting outfielder in the All-Star games was . . . Dom DiMaggio. He may not have been as good as Ted or Joe, but he was better than anyone else. Ted's also spoken up for Joe Jackson. His take on that is, "Hey, Joe Jackson has been banned for life. His life was over!"

When Dom released his book, the publisher gave a party at Tavern on the Green in New York. All these crusty old New York guys were hanging around for the shrimp and everything, and all of a sudden I hear applause in the room. I'm looking around to see what happened and there in the doorway at the head of the room is Ted. He showed up for the book party. All these cynical old guys are clapping for him and Dom was way down the other end of the room, and I'm telling you, it was like the parting of the Red Sea as Ted strode through. It was an amazing sight to see the effect he had on these guys.

The publisher of the book had a post-party dinner all set at the "21." The guy said, "Oh, Ted, we'd love to have you come over for dinner with us at '21.'" Ted said, "I want to go over and have spaghetti, over there at Murray Hill. Casale played with us." There was a little restaurant that Jerry Casale—who pitched for the Red Sox—had on 34th street. The publisher said, "Well, we have this whole dinner ready for us at '21'." Ted said, "Fine. You go there, I'm going to Murray Hill." Not being a dumb guy, the publisher said, "Why don't we all go over to Murray Hill?"

A dozen of us squeezed into this little neighborhood restaurant. It was the goddamnedest thing. All of a sudden the door opens up and in walks Ted Williams. At this point, Dom is just a member of the supporting cast. It was all guys 50 years old, and the place was just in an uproar. Ted Williams has just walked into this place! People are grabbing menus and having Ted sign. Casale was in seventh heaven. Ted's effect on people is just amazing.

It's amazing to me the affection that those old guys have for each other, particularly Ted and Dominic DiMaggio and Bobby Doerr and Johnny Pesky. They go back all these years, and the relationships they have; it's really endearing to see them when they're around each other.

I'll tell you what I think one of Ted's great legacies is—it's the manner in which he is handling his current situation. He is more physically handicapped than most people realize. He has that tunnel vision and can't really see you unless you are right in front of him. He can't read because he can't control the muscles in his eyes to move from the last word on a line to the first word in the next. But he is so positive all the time. Here's a guy who is no longer able to operate by himself and his attitude is so positive, so strong. He's got courage, he's got discipline. I find it inspiring.

(Courtesy of Steve Ferroli and Ted Williams Baseball League)

◆ ◆ ◆

JIM PALMER, Ballplayer, Hall of Fame

The night that I got inducted into the Hall of Fame in 1990, both league presidents and the Commissioner of Baseball were present. They had a microphone you could pass around and they asked if anybody had anything they'd like to say. Ted got up and said, "Yeah, I'd like to say one thing. Stan Musial's not here tonight because he's suffering from some stomach problems. I just want to let everyone know how much I miss him and wish him well." I knew the Hall of Fame was a collection of the greatest players in baseball history, but for the first time I realized what a small, intimate, and caring fraternity it is. Ted changed the day of my induction from one of individual importance to me, to a

Ted takes a cut during an Old-Timers' game.
(Copyright David L. Pressman, M.D.)

feeling of being a member of this great fraternity. That's what I'll remember most about Ted.

◆ ◆ ◆

The Ted Williams Retrospective Museum and Library opened its doors on February 9, 1994.
The idea grew out of a chance remark which Ted made to Lewis Watkins. Lewis took the idea
and shepherded it into reality in a remarkably short period of time. As the Museum program for
the 1996 event indicated, "Building the Ted Williams Museum was not Ted's idea. In fact, he
wanted nothing to do with it when he was presented the idea in 1993." Watkins persisted and
enlisted Citrus Hills developers Sam Tamposi and Gerry Nash to donate land, then successfully
approached a long list of similarly generous souls who came up with building materials, display
items and funds sufficient to open the Museum debt-free within a year. It was an amazing
accomplishment, one which Ted embraced only in the hopes that it would somehow encourage
and inspire youngsters to strive towards excellence in their own lives.

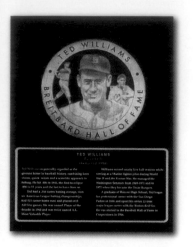

Ted's award at the San Diego Hall of Champions.
(Photo courtesy of the San Diego Hall of Champions)

Museums dedicated to living individuals are a phenomenon usually reserved for Presidents, but the Ted Williams Museum in Hernando, Florida is a fitting tribute visited annually by thousands of baseball fans. The Museum's central room is built in the shape of a baseball diamond and one moves counterclockwise around the "field" from first base towards home, he or she can follow the different stages in Ted's life. The room revolves around a bronze casting of the famous Armand LaMontagne sculpture which is featured in the National Baseball Hall of Fame in Cooperstown. The full-size casting was donated to the Museum by John Tighe. Attached to the Museum itself are two wings which were added a year later—the Hitters' Hall of Fame and a theater. Each wing is entered through one of the "dugouts." A simple design, and as it turned out, an award-winning design.

JOHN UNDERWOOD, Writer

I have a friend named Ron Frazier, who was the baseball coach at the University of Miami, won two or three national World Series championships. Real close friend of Tommy Lasorda. He asked me one time to have Ted come and talk to his players. Ted was on the Keys but he did it. Then another time, Miami made the regional finals and were on the way to Omaha and the college World Series. Ron called me on the phone and said, "Do you think you could get Ted to come up and throw out the first ball?" Ted and I used to do a lot of things like that together in those days. This was back in the '70s or maybe early '80s. Well, after he was no longer managing.

I said, "Well, I can ask him." So I called him and he said, "Well, you gonna be there?" "Yeah," I said. He said, "I'll come by your house and we can go over together." I took him out to the park appropriately early; he always wanted to be on time. Typically Ted, he was wearing his Ban-Lon shirt, his sunglasses hung from the slit down the middle. Wearing his heavy rubber-soled shoes with canvas tops, old baggy pants. Frazier came over and he said, "Ted, I appreciate you coming but I changed my mind. I'd like you to HIT the first ball." Ted kind of gave him a look, you know. Then I went up in the stands.

Ron brought him in and introduced him and announced that Ted was going to hit the first ball. The place was packed, just jam-packed. Frazier, who'd been a pitcher in the minor leagues and in college, goes out to the mound to pitch the first ball. Ted goes up to the plate, and the crowd gets hushed. You can hear the conversation. Ted has got a loud voice anyway. Frazier's warming up and Ted's standing right at the plate. He's not backed away. He's right there, so he can get a feel for the pitch. He doesn't want to embarrass himself—not in that hitting area. He might have the worst looking outfit on, and cut his own hair. He's such a good-looking man, it wouldn't have mattered what he wore. He looked like a combination John Wayne and Robert Ryan and a couple of others.

Anyway, you could hear him saying, "Throw the ball harder. Throw it harder." And Frazier's warming up, warming up. Finally Frazier gives him a nod, and Ted says, "OK, OK," and the whole crowd quiets down. And he threw Ted five pitches. Ted hit every single one of them—line drive, right field. Every single one—live drive, right field. As I recall, two of them hit the wall. None of them went out. But he was, I don't know how old he was, '60s I guess, with his potbelly and all. He wasn't the Splendid Splinter any more. He was like a museum piece had come to life, in front of all those people. It was remarkable, just remarkable, for him to be able to do that after all those years. I'm sure he hadn't swung a bat for fifteen years and here he was: line drive, right field, right field, right field.

◆ ◆ ◆

GEORGE SULLIVAN, Writer

Ted has always been an unforgettable character and he remains so. The Red Sox hadn't had old-timers games like the Yankees and other teams and I mentioned it to Mrs. Yawkey and Buddy Leroux and Haywood Sullivan the three owners. Mrs. Yawkey said, "Yes, I think it'd be a wonderful idea. One day in the winter I called Ted in Florida and explained what we wanted to do. "You know me well enough to know I always said I'd never play in one of those goddamn things and I never want to." I just held the phone out from my ear and let him rant and rave for five minutes then he said, "When do you want me there? If it's for the Yawkeys, I'll do it."

During that spring of '82, the team was on the road and I was at Fenway and I heard this CRACK! CRACK! Someone was taking batting practice. So I said, *Geez, I wonder who's taking BP*. I look out and it's Ted, the son of a bitch. He's getting ready for the old-timers game. Anyway he came and the response—mostly to Ted—was unbelievable. Even the media treated it like a World Series game and they all gathered around when he came out the runway. The place went absolutely gaga. The fans went nuts. Ted didn't get any hits but he scared the hell out of me by making a shoestring catch of a line drive hit by Mike Andrews. He couldn't brake himself and my heart was in my mouth because he broke his collarbone in Sarasota one year in spring training after being on the field for thirty seconds in a similar play where he was lunging for the ball. Luckily he didn't go down. After the game I went in the locker room and the old-timers were leisurely getting dressed and as soon as Ted—the old hawk-eye—saw me, he came over and said, "Hey, there's the son of a bitch I've been looking for! Come over here!" He grabs me and we go into manager Ralph Houk's office and I think, "Oh, oh, what's it going to be now?" He shuts the door and he says, "Listen, you remember when I told you last winter that this was the last thing I wanted to do and how I cursed you for it? When I woke up at the Sheraton this morning, the last thing I wanted to do was play baseball and I cursed you again. Then, when I got up and looked at myself in the mirror, I cursed you again. And again while I was getting ready. I want to tell you right now that this is one of the greatest days of my life." Talk about a great feeling coming from the master. It was all about him, that old-timers game.

We had another one in '84 and again he didn't get any hits. It was so ironic. In the first game it was ironic that he made the most memorable play of the game but it was with his glove and not his bat. In the second game, he didn't get one either and I knew he was bullshit about it. Hank Soar, a retired umpire, was calling the game and Ted struck out and now he was really bullshit because between the two old-timers games he was 0-6. He starts stomping back to the dugout and the crowd was oohing and awing, even for him striking out and I hear Hank Soar calling out, "Come on back, Ted, come on back! They always said we gave you four strikes anyway!"

We still had 15 minutes before the regular game started and we had time for another inning. Ted had made the last out but I said to Billy Goodman, "Let's have him lead off the inning." Billy said, "Great idea, great idea." I said, "Ask him," and he said, "Bullshit! YOU ask him." Here was Billy Goodman, a man in his sixties, and he's still afraid to ask Ted to do something. I thought that was so revealing. So I said I would and I did. I said, "Ted, you're up" He said, "I made the last out!" It was like kids in the playground. I said, "Ted, you're first up!" All of a sudden a grin broke out and he says, "Oh, okay." I'm not sure if he got a hit or not but I remember him sounding just like a kid. "But I just made the last out."

◆ ◆ ◆

WHAT I'VE LEARNED
Ted Williams
(Interviewed by Scott Rabb, Esquire *magazine, August 28, 1998)*

The bigger people are in life, the more big-league they are. That's been my experience. You meet less shits the higher up you go.

Some guys are just a little more inherently tough than the next guy. I think that's God-given genetics.

I wanted to play baseball. I don't know why, but I wanted to play. I had the opportunity, and I had desire. And talent. I heard some guy sayin', "Boy, that kid really looks good. He's quick. He's got good wrists." I said, "If that guy thinks I've got quick wrists now, wait'll the next time he sees me."

Ya gotta be ready for the fastball.

I decided I'd have a Cadillac. What the hell. I was kind of successful, and certainly it's a prestigious car. I got more tickets in that car. I figured, shit, they're just lookin' for Cadillacs so they can grab 'em for speeding.

I could have started smoking in the late twenties, but I didn't. I knew then that nicotine could attack every weakness in a person's body.

The most fun I ever had in my life was hittin' a baseball. And the best sound I ever heard in my life was a ball hit with a bat. POWWW!

Pitchers are dumb. They don't play but once every four days. They're scratchin' their ass or pickin' their nose or somethin' the rest of the time. They're pitchin', most of 'em, because they can't do anything else.

In order to be called great, ya gotta have the circumstances surrounding ya.

I was a United States Marine pilot. It was the greatest experience of my life, and the greatest people in the world that I ever met were in the Marine Corps. The two things that I'm proudest of in my life, one is that I was a Marine. The other thing is that I was lucky enough to play the game I loved.

The best? I don't really believe that. In my heart, I can't say and believe that I was any better than Lou Gehrig or Babe Ruth or Ty Cobb.

I'm not sure in my own mind that there's a supreme being. I don't have that much faith.

Rogers Hornsby was some kind of guy. Everybody thinks, oh, Hornsby—what a mean bastard. He treated me like a son, couldn't have been nicer. And he gave me the greatest single piece of advice of hitting that I ever got: Wait for a good pitch to hit.

Sixty feet six inches. If it had been two feet either way, it would have changed the whole thing.

I'm a real smart son of a bitch. I'm an old, dumb ballplayer and a real smart son of a bitch.

◆ ◆ ◆

PRESIDENT GEORGE H. W. BUSH, Former U.S. President

Let me tell you why I admire him so much. He's a first-class character. He couldn't stand phonies. His teammates adored him, rivals asked for batting tips and Ted never turned them down. Ted also faced enemies, and this is a part of his life for which I have great respect. He faced enemies in both Korea and World War II. He confronted gunfire in 39 combat missions. And never complained, never once complained about that gap . . . those 5 1/2 years out of his career in baseball to serve his country, service that deprived Ted of some statistics but made him greater in the eyes of all Americans.

[I want] not only to salute a friend, a rebel, a legend, and Gibraltar. John Wayne in a baseball uniform. Here's to the greatest hitter of them all, one of America's greatest heroes that ever lived.

◆ ◆ ◆

SPARKY ANDERSON, Manager, Hall of Fame

In spring training a while back, we played the Red Sox in Winter Haven. In batting practice before the game, a man walked up to shake my hand.

"Hi, Sparky. I'm Ted Williams," he said.

I almost fell over. I started to laugh.

"Ted, that's the funniest thing I ever head," I said.

"What do you mean?" he said.

"You telling me that you're Ted Williams," I answered. "Everybody knows you. You don't have to say who you are."

"No, Sparky, it can't be that way," he explained. "I would never want you to be embarrassed if you happened to forget who I was."

Now just imagine. This was Ted Williams. This was one of the greatest players in the history of our game making sure that I wasn't embarrassed.

That's not only success. That's class.

After that, I never meet anyone to whom I don't introduce myself before the other guy gets a chance. I always walk up with my hand out. "Hi, I'm Sparky Anderson."

◆ ◆ ◆

TED AND HIS MANY HALLS OF FAME

San Diego Hall of Champions
National Baseball Hall of Fame
Atlantic Salmon Hall of Fame
National Freshwater Fishing Hall of Fame
International Game Fish Association Hall of Fame
United States Marine Corps Sports Hall of Fame
Florida Sports Hall of Fame
Hispanic Heritage Baseball Museum Hall of Fame

At his own request, Ted has never been inducted into one prestigious Hall of Fame: the Hitters Hall of Fame at the Ted Williams Museum.

◆ ◆ ◆

FRANK DEFORD ON TED TURNING 80
A Birthday Visit to the Kid

There can be nothing more disheartening than seeing an old person who we remember for the glories of youth—a beautiful actress, say, now a faded flower. We want so much to think that people like that will always be the way they were. And now, you see, I'm going to meet with Ted Williams, Teddy Ballgame, just before he turns 80 years of age. Number 9, The Splendid Splinter, eternally The Kid. For all his names, always and forever, foremost just The Kid.

I think it was Bob Knight, the basketball coach, who said that Williams was the only person, ever, who was the best in the world at three different things: hitting a baseball, fly-casting and piloting a jet fighter plane. A young fellow named John Glenn was his wingman in Korea.

Now we're at Williams' house, where he lives on the west coast of Florida, at 9 Ted Williams Drive, which is up on what is advertised as the second-highest hill in the Sunshine State. Anyway, it looks down on his museum, an absolute gem of a place that doesn't celebrate baseball stars.

No, it celebrates baseball hitters. And just so there's no mistake, when Ted Williams means hitters—when he picks hitters for his museum—he doesn't mean those punch-and-judy choke-up guys. A hitter, according to the best hitter there ever was, is somebody who can hit for power as well as hit for average. You got that? And here comes Ted now. He's in shorts, with—yes—a Boston Red Sox cap on . . . and he's using a walker. But I will tell you something: As impossible as it seems, even with a walker, Ted Williams has a swagger. Yes, sir. Now he sits down, and boy is he . . . fun. There's a baseball encyclopedia there, which we refer to regularly.

Unlike a lot of great athletes who only play a game that comes naturally to them, Williams is an unadulterated baseball fan, a baseball expert.

"Isn't that McGwire something!" he calls out in abject joy . . . and admiration, too. There is no jealousy in the man—I suppose, because there's no insecurity if you're the best in the world at three different things. He works on the Veterans Committee to get his old lesser buddies into the Hall of Fame with him. He's also taken on the crusade of getting Shoeless Joe Jackson admitted to Cooperstown. Suddenly, in fact, Ted has an imaginary bat in his hands, and, sitting there, he's showing you how Ty Cobb swung, hands apart, pushing the ball, but then he's Shoeless Joe: smooth and full-out, like this . . . well, like Ted Williams would swing when he came along in 1939.

When Williams went into the Hall himself, he used much of his speech pumping for baseball to allow in the African-Americans from the old Negro Leagues. Now he's going to induct the great Japanese slugger, Sadaharu Oh, into his museum—and what's the matter with Cooperstown? It's baseball isn't it, not American baseball?

The energy, the enthusiasm pours out. Once Ted Williams was "controversial," so-called. Joe DiMaggio, elegant and distant, a Yankee not a Bosox, was more honored. But, in time, the appreciation for Williams, the hitter and the man, has passed DiMaggio, passed them all.

When I leave, I can only think: Damn, now this is an American.

Later that day, I see Williams again. He bursts into a crowded room where some very serious baseball fans are assembled, puts aside his walker and bellows out: "Any Marines in here?"

He'll celebrate his 80th birthday this Sunday, August 30th. Happy birthday, Kid.

Courtesy of National Public Radio's "Morning Edition."

◆ ◆ ◆

TED WILLIAMS' EDGE

by Alex Theroux

Strong opinions, in the minds of many people, is a form of bad manners. It was one of the most glaring faults held against Ted Williams all his life, a criticism most often levied, ironically enough, by some of the most opinionated dunces who ever lived, a group of envious and niggling Boston sportswriters, grudge-holding drunks for the most part, who in their willful ignorance refused Williams the very same agenda that they themselves used and abused for years in order to try and drag him down. He was supposed to have earned his way aboard, as is the belief with all longevity-mongers. He had no right to a forum, even if any moron can be an authority on sports.

Bostonians are famously parochial. It is a city of political hacks and indiscriminate freeloaders and shameless rank-pullers, a corrupt burg with more state-workers per capita than any state in the union. Real talent is as deeply resented as merit in the matter of advancement.

Hierarchy mattered even more back in 1939, when rookies were supposed to shut up and listen and walk in file. The Kid was supposed to serve a class system when he landed here, not bat .406 as he did in 1941 at the age of 23! His cockiness galled people. Old farts, fat-assed reporters, failed local columnists with the smell of breadcrumbs about them all hated him on the spot. To be a swaggering fellow from San Diego, tall, dark, handsome, and confident, was bad enough. To be a great hitter at age 21 was irksome. But for a person to be an individual? It was unforgivable.

Ted's "edge," borne of many personal difficulties, was sharpened by various setbacks. He was ashamed of his poverty when scout Eddie Collins came to visit him at the small Utah St. bungalow. "I remember being ashamed of how dirty the house was all the time," Ted once reflected. He was always highly strung and bit his nails "right down to the quick." He confesses in *My Turn At Bat* to having a "large inferiority complex."

Loud, he was also shy—one often causes the other. "Even later, when I first started signing autographs," he later wrote, "I'd hold my head down." Later, he was involved in several divorces, as well. It is obvious that his determination to succeed—to hit—grew from the raging fire of his trouble, of his inner needs, of his passion, that his grit, his greatness, came out of his pain on a thousand fronts. Deprivation informed his drive. Is this not a common pattern? In the slopped and muddied palette of Botticelli sat The Birth of Venus.

Aggression, not always lovely, is fire. With his uncompromising personality, Ted Williams, desperately loyal to his own principles, his own code of honor, his own way to do things, the private resolutions he made to himself, was a man whose temper was almost in direct proportion to his drive for perfection. Does it take much to see that, no matter what he did, he was always trying to get some of his own back? His edge was sharp because he badly yearned to be the best and strove with mad singlemindedness for exactitude.

His impatience, especially with himself, was a response to slovenliness, indifference, sloth, and the kind of ineptitude he found in others, notably in the malice of sportswriters and sometime fans. His temperament was simply not geared to anything unchallenging. Performing an act that he convincingly argued was the hardest thing in all sports, hitting a baseball, he managed to do better than anyone who ever lived. The Kid was sensitive to criticism because he was, more than anyone, his own fiercest critic.

"I have never been regarded especially as a man with great patience," he said with classic understatement. He threw bats as a younger player, frequently blew his top, kicked dugout stanchions, as he said, "would damn near kill myself." "Scream. I'd scream out of my own frustration."

Perfectionists never let up on themselves. He never tipped his hat because, as Ed Linn pointed out, "it kept him in control." His opinions on the science of batting were writ in stone, but he had opinions about everything, reporters, draft-dodgers, fighting fish, phonies, safe hitters (like Wade Boggs) who refused to swing for the fences, ballparks. Williams tied flies, flew planes, and swung baseball bats with the manic determination of a person trying almost obsessively to rectify wrongs. He hated temporizing. A lifelong Republican, he loathed politicians ("Maybe you could stretch a point and say that 1 percent of them are all right"), but he found all gladhanders whores and despised as eunuchs anyone who did things insincerely or sloppily or half-baked.

Was it any different with Beethoven, Wagner, Michelangelo, or other masters of their art? Imagine anyone approving the lie, the lunacy, of someone, anyone, saying, "I never met a man I didn't like?" Christ could even say that. No, Ted did not suffer fools gladly. And yet no man alive was ever more his own person than Ted Williams. He lived with a fire in his belly that demanded commitment, in his opinions and in his hitting. You could see it in the way he gripped his bat, when he seemed to be fist-squeezing the handle into sawdust. At the inauguration of the Hitters Hall of Fame, former President George Bush called Ted Williams "a rebel, a legend, and Gibraltar. John Wayne in a baseball uniform." John Wayne the actor, who sat out World War II, while Ted, who was once shot down, was a flying ace and hero in both World War II and Korea, prime years that would have fattened his averages and broken records and done God knows what kind of damage to big league pitching?

John Wayne wishes.

It was not only Ted Williams' impatient and exasperated exclusion of the idiot world that has always made him seem so intractable but also his vision, for he was, before all else, a man always trying to matriculate within himself, to school himself literally to be the best that he could be. He had a dream of what he wanted to be and never relinquished it. He had no humor for those of us who are simply getting by with a buck-and-wing, the fakes, the phonies, the freebooters. In a very real sense, he was the last man.

◆ ◆ ◆

JOHN KRISTON, Executive Director, Ted Williams Museum

Nine, that's a good number, don't you think? The Ted Williams Museum has really evolved over its first nine years. It's no longer just a dream some of Ted's friends Ted had, an idea they talked him into accepting. It's no longer a rookie; it's become a seasoned veteran, and we're proud to say that for several years it's been one of the leading tourist attractions in Citrus County, Florida.

It's a marvel to work here. It seems like every day I learn something more about this man, and I remain in awe. It's really cementing Ted's life story. I can't tell you the number of people who come into the Museum and have no idea that Ted Williams was a Marine Corps pilot who fought for our country, let alone that he crash-landed his jet coming back from a mission. We had one guy the other day just amazed, "Wow! I didn't know Ted was a fighter pilot." He'd thought Ted Williams being a Marine was little more than a series of public relations appearances.

I first got to know Ted while working at the Department of Transportation in Massachusetts. Governor Bill Weld decided to dedicate the harbor tunnel as the Ted Williams Tunnel and I became the primary liaison with the Williams family. I got to know Ted and his son John-Henry fairly well and we stayed in contact after the tunnel was completed. John-Henry would call when he was in Boston, sometimes with Dad, and we'd always have dinner. A few years later, they began to look for someone to take the Museum to the

Pennant designating the opening of Ted Williams Tunnel in Boston.

next level, and decided to offer me the job. I was really stunned, because I never expected it, but was thrilled and honored to become part of Ted's team.

I really value getting to know Ted's family. I assure you no one has a deeper love for his father than John-Henry. For over a full year now, following Ted's heart operation, John-Henry has absolutely been by his father's side all the time, and Ted always comes first. And I'm so pleased that Claudia has become more involved with the Museum. I know how Ted feels about her and she hit a grand slam when she helped to host the 2001 induction weekend. She'd been around her dad and his friends many times before that, but that weekend she really got to know what deep feelings all these people had for her father and what he really meant to them. She was profoundly moved. She's just an incredible lady.

I've never had a conversation with Ted where he didn't want to know more about the subject matter. Ted does not engage in much small talk. We never just talk about the weather. Things that interest him, he has a passion to know more about them. It stimulates Ted. Even before a meal was served, he'd ask the chef, "How're you making that, now? Why don't we do this, or that?"

Tunnel workers outside of the Ted Williams tunnel in Boston.
(Photo by Bill Nowlin)

Ted is also an extremely caring man. We had Mike Hampton Day [Hampton was a local Citrus County pitcher who led the National League in wins in 1999] here at the Museum a couple of years ago, in the fall. Ted almost drove me nuts worrying about the guests. Obviously we were going to take great care of Mike and his family, but Ted wanted to know just what was being done for the fans. "What about the people who are going to be here? The kids? They could be hungry." He wanted to make sure everybody was going to be comfortable. Especially the kids—always the kids. He had this real concern for detail, and doing everything right for the people around him. It's truly genuine.

One of the highlights for me each year is the time Ted and I spend talking about the hitters and ballplayers who are inducted at our annual February legends weekend. Just to have the opportunity to discuss these incredible ballplayers with Ted and to hear how he feels about them, well, it's simply priceless. Legends like Kaline, Berra, Yastrzemski and current award-winners like Cal Ripken, Jr., Jason Giambi and Nomar Garciaparra. It's a star-studded weekend here in Hernando.

We're really proud to have opened up a charter of the Ted Williams League a couple of years ago. Now we have a very active group of kids working hard at baseball right here on the Museum grounds. We really want to do all we can to forward the mission we have set for ourselves.

[Note: check out both the Ted Williams League and the Museum itself at www.tedwilliamsmuseum.com.]

◆ ◆ ◆

JIM PRIME, Fan

Almost immediately after the Ted Williams Museum opened, the decision was made to add another dimension: the Hitters Hall of Fame. The direct inspiration was the book Ted coauthored with Jim Prime, Ted Williams' Hit List, *which ranked Ted's choices of the top hitters of all time—and those hitters were the initial inductees into the Hitters Hall of Fame.*

I first met Ted in September of 1981. Responding to a combination fan letter and interview request, he and his friend Louise Kaufman had invited me to spend a couple of days as their guest at his fishing lodge in New Brunswick, Canada. Louise and I hit it off and with her help, I managed to obtain an invitation to Ted's salmon lodge each of the next several summers.

With John Underwood, Ted had written *My Turn At Bat,* a brilliant autobiography. Underwood and Williams also collaborated on *The Science of Hitting,* still the definitive how-to book on hitting. One vital component of a logical Williams baseball trilogy was missing. Ted had never formalized his opinions on the great hitters of all time. He had spoken often—but never written—about the raw power of Foxx and Mantle, the style and grace of DiMaggio and Musial, the greatness of Babe Ruth. I urged Ted to let me work with him on the book which became *Ted Williams' Hit List.*

Over the course of several visits to his Miramichi River retreat, and in dozens of letters, I pressed my case. There are people out there who actually think Pete Rose is the greatest hitter of all time, I goaded.

Millions of fans don't know anything about Rogers Hornsby's place in the hierarchy of hitters, I pleaded. I drove home the point by actually showing him books on the great hitters composed by . . . writers! One had even placed Reggie Jackson before Foxx, Greenberg and Joe Jackson. Another had placed Aaron and Mays ahead of DiMaggio. This got his attention. I could see his blood start to boil and his teeth clench. He began to warm to the idea. I (apparently) naively asked him if he felt that Carl Yastrzemski was as good a hitter as he was. He gave me a five minute explanation—completely lacking in both false modesty and egotism—that left no room for further doubt on the subject.

One day on the pickup truck on the way to a salmon pool downstream from his camp, he abruptly turned to me and demanded: "When you hit the ball on the ground, are you generally late or early?" In the split second that it took for me to absorb the question, I was instinctively aware that my answer might have implications beyond our casual conversation. "Early!," I stammered instinctively. Ted was pleased. "That's right! That's right! Some of today's hitters are still trying to figure that out." The subject was quickly dropped but I had a feeling that my stock with Ted Williams had just gone up a notch.

Later, back at the lodge, with a cold drink in our hands, I again asked Ted to collaborate on the book. Instead he warned: "Remember one thing. I don't want to make a f------ career out of this book." I knew that I had him. He had agreed to participate, and in doing so he gave me one of the highest compliments I have received from anyone: "You are the most persistent son of a bitch I ever met." With that blessing, we were on our way.

Not surprisingly, Ted soon became passionate about the project. He said that he "wanted to contribute something to the lore of baseball." I almost laughed in his face, knowing full well that he has contributed more to the lore of this game than all the writers in all the press boxes in all the ballparks in America. He opined about the steady decline in hitting skills over the past 35-40 years. He was especially critical of those hitters who did not get the most out of their abilities. Improper thinking at the plate was inexcusable to this hitting scientist.

I would talk hitting with Ted while he tied flies for the next day's fishing. I sat on the shore while he was waist deep in the Miramichi River. I would sit with him and his guide Roy Curtis on his front porch, overlooking the dark, inscrutable river, as they dissected the details of that day's fishing. When the fishing anecdotes were finally exhausted, I was able to cautiously nudge the conversation toward baseball. Any doubt that Ted Williams is a perfectionist were put to rest immediately. He insisted that the statistics support our arguments. He insisted that power and average were vastly superior to even a very high average. Volume of hits did not impress Ted unless the accomplishment was done in a superior "per time at bat" manner. He was a walking encyclopedia and a living legend rolled into one. He talked about player's "baseballic intelligence" and he talked about intricacies of hitting so obscure and minute that they seemed trivial to a mere mortal. He talked about temperature affecting hitting, about poor hitting backgrounds, about the impact of the slider (considerable), rabbit balls (significant) and corked bats (negligible). He extolled the virtues of lighter bats and decried the lack of patience in today's hitters.

One thing was certain: Ted Williams knew about hitting a baseball. He talked about the lineage of hitting. He told me how Babe Ruth had modeled his swing on that of Shoeless Joe Jackson, and how one of the biggest compliments he had ever received was having Eddie Collins compare his swing to Shoeless Joe's. He talked about learning from Cobb and Hornsby and Terry and Heilmann and Cronin and Collins.

He knew the frustration inherent in seeking hitting perfection. "In hitting," he told me, "a .700 futility percentage is a much coveted goal. The fans are willing to accept and appreciate such apparent mediocrity because they know the degree of difficulty involved in hitting a baseball." He called the players on his list "the aristocracy of hitting."

He wanted to include Joe Jackson in his rankings even though he knew that such recognition would rile the "powers that be" in baseball. He talked of the purity of Jackson's swing and the unfairness of his exile from baseball. He confessed that he preferred Jackson's hitting style to Ty Cobb's, even though the statistics compelled him to rank Cobb sixth and Shoeless Joe eighth. He resisted every suggestion that we include Ted Williams in the rankings. "I'll leave that to others," he said, no doubt aware that the numbers speak eloquently in his behalf.

He brought his perfectionist's eye to the project. He attacked it and pursued it and honed it and embraced it. He peppered me with research requests. "We need to be able to substantiate our choices," he said.

When the Ted Williams Hitters' Hall of Fame, an adjunct to the Ted Williams Museum opened its doors in, I took some considerable pride in having planted the idea in Ted's fertile brain. As the 25 members of *Ted Williams' Hit List* were inducted one by one, I took inordinate pride in each selection. If I hadn't been such a persistent son of a bitch, I thought, this may never have happened. Of course, if Ted hadn't been such a persistent son of a bitch himself, baseball would have a much poorer history.

◆ ◆ ◆

DICK FLAVIN, Public Speaker
The Ultimate Road Trip

The year 2001 was a depressing year for Ted and his friends. Ted had been feeling poorly the previous year, when he'd had a pacemaker installed. It really hadn't worked as well as the doctors had hoped and he needed a more extensive, riskier procedure. A nine-hour-long heart operation took a lot out of The Kid. He had the operation in January, but didn't get home until his 83rd birthday at the end of August. Even then, he was frail and facing months of recovery. Still, it was good to be home.

In 1942, when Johnny Pesky joined the Red Sox, firm bonds of friendship brought together four men from the West, all Red Sox players, all fairly close in age: Johnny Pesky, Bobby Doerr, Dom DiMaggio and Ted Williams. They all saw World War II come and go, then reunited for those wonderful Red Sox teams of the late 1940s. Those were the years when teams were teams and teammates felt like teammates. Sixty years later, the four remain close friends with the most special of relationships.

Dom DiMaggio was heading south for the winter, planning to drive from his Massachusetts home to his place in Florida. Dick Flavin offered to drive with him, and Dom thought to invite Johnny Pesky as well. They figured they'd drop in on Ted and pay him a visit. The three hopped in DiMaggio's car and headed for Hernando, Florida.

Dick Flavin tells the story of what Dan Shaughnessy dubbed "the ultimate road trip."

"Got a call about a year ago," Curt Gowdy says. "Seven A.M. I was sound asleep. I heard this gruff voice, 'Gowdy, it's Teddy Ballgame. Wake up. I want to ask you something. Where in the hell are those golden years?' And then he hung up."

Maureen Cronin tells a story about another time Ted pursued perfection.

She was at an event at Fenway Park in the 1970s, and afterwards everyone lined up to get Ted's autograph. A striking, sophisticated woman with long blonde hair was in line with a baseball and after she secured Ted's signature, Maureen noticed that the woman looked at her prize and started laughing. "Why are you laughing?" she asked her. Ted had signed the ball "Ted Williams, Room 303, Somerset Hotel."

When Dom and Johnny pulled up in front of the house in Citrus Hills with the big number 9 emblazoned on the wrought iron gate to the property, they were an excited as little kids. To get there the 80-something kids had driven 1,400 miles, but they knew their adventure has just begun. After hand shakes, hugs, and perhaps a tear or two, the three old buddies settled in for a three-day visit. One thing was immediately apparent: Ted Williams, for all he has been through, is still Ted Williams. He is feisty, charismatic, inquisitive and—something he has always been but is not as well known for—full of affection for his old teammates.

The conversation had not been going on for long when Ted, as challenging as ever, posed a quiz: Who was the most underrated clutch hitter they had played against? Was it Tommy Henrich, someone asked. No, but he was a left-handed hitter. Another hint: he played for Cleveland as well as for some other teams. Mickey Vernon? No. Larry Doby? No. Finally someone asked, "Was it Eddie Robinson?" "That's the guy!" Ted boomed. His voice is raspy now, but the inflection is unmistakable and, when he wants to, he can still crank up the volume.

His old teammates found Ted to be thinner even that in the Splendid Splinter years of his early career, but that could change soon. His appetite is as hearty as ever and he visibly gained strength each day they were there.

They talked of Tommy Lasorda and the Yankees' Paul O'Neill, both of whom Ted admires, and of Slugger, his beloved Dalmatian who died a few years ago. Every now and then Ted would look across at his old friends, a big smile would cross his face, and he'd say, "Gee, it's great to see you guys!"

At one point Dom decided to serenade his friend of more than sixty years. In a rich baritone voice he sang an Italian aria which, to Ted's delight, he then translated as being about two best friends, one of whom has a girlfriend with whom the other is madly in love. A visitor then decided to balance the ledger with an Irish song, and there at Ted's kitchen table, broke into a full-throated if poorly executed version of "I'll Take You Home Again, Kathleen." [The visitor was, as you might imagine, Dick Flavin.] The two serenaders then finished the mini-concert with a duet, a Ted Lewis-like rendition of "Me and My Shadow." Through it all Ted laughed, smiled and even applauded, proof that he has indeed mellowed with age.

When the visit was over, Dom and Johnny both agreed that the visit had been a great tonic for Ted. He got stronger, more animated and more feisty as it went along. But an observer could not fail to see that it had an uplifting effect on his visitors, as well. It made all three of them young again.

Johnny Pesky said it was the best road trip he'd ever had—and he spent most of his years since the late 1930s on the road with baseball. "They wouldn't let me drive," Johnny laughed. "So I just sat back and enjoyed the ride. I didn't smoke a single cigar for three days straight. That's one way I helped out. It was almost like a circus. We laughed and talked all the way to Florida.

"When I first saw Ted, though, I damn near cried. He was so very thin. But he's tough—and he was sharp. We talked about pitchers we'd faced. That was Ted again, talking about hitting. I had worried that I'd never see him again, but there he is, still fighting and with that old sparkle in his eye. He'll never give up. He showed me that again.

"It made me feel great. Bobby couldn't make it. He's taking care of Monica, his wife. But there we were—Ted, Dom and me. It really was like we were kids all over again."

◆ ◆ ◆

"A HERO IS FOREVER"
by Mike Barnicle
(Taken from article in Boston Globe, May 19, 1991)

When the old man swung the imaginary bat through the fresh air of a clear, sunlit afternoon, the weight and dust of all the years fell away like marbles toppling off the edge of a three-legged table. Adults clapped. Little kids hung from the rail and sat stop a parent's shoulder. Some men and women, of a certain age, and with a certain look to them, even cried.

The swing was still smooth as tap water tumbling from a faucet on the hottest of August days. The hips turned perfectly and the huge hitter's hands rolled right over. The bulk of seven decades didn't even show through the old man's sports jacket because all anybody really saw was the number 9.

It seems odd, maybe even sacrilegious, to call him an old man because he lives beyond any calendar. Birthdays do not matter. When you are Ted Williams, nobody adds up the years.

I first saw Ted Williams in 1951. He was part of a pretty good team that could never quite catch the Yankees. When I shut my eyes, his swing at Fenway Park Sunday is the same swing I recall across all the vanished decades.

I first met Ted Williams in 1953. It was the year he returned from Korea. He did not have posttraumatic stress disorder. He did have 13 home runs and, once in awhile, if you waited long enough, you could catch him behind the old Somerset Hotel on Commonwealth Avenue.

In those days, I had very little idea what he might be doing inside the Somerset. Eating there? Living there? Who knew? All I knew was that rumor was the currency of youth and if there was even a whisper that Ted was around the hotel, the stakeout for autographs would begin.

There was no television then. Drugs and guns were unheard of to us, perhaps preposterous myths to older people. The few gangs that did exist were a collection of unemployed guys with duck-tail haircuts and pegged pants. Parents let kids ride trains, buses and trolleys around town with not a second thought given to safety.

We would go to the ballpark in clumps. Sometimes we'd go to Braves Field, but more likely it was Fenway because that's where the greatest hitter in the history of the game lived.

And Fenway became our church. Just as there was a downstairs 8 o'clock children's Mass each Sunday in the parish, there was mandatory seating at the park: As close as you could get to the sloping left field rail where no. 9 prowled below.

He was then—and is now—larger than life. Unlike so many others—politicians, actors, statesmen, teachers, scientists, war heroes—time has not shrunk or sullied Ted Williams.

And Sunday, when they commemorated the fact that it is 50 summers since he hit .406 (and since Joe DiMaggio hit safely in 56 straight baseball games), you could hear the ballpark talk. Oh yes, ballparks do have voices, and they're filled with memory and emotion.

I heard it, I think a lot of others did, too. And I'm sure Ted Williams heard it because it nearly caused him to cry in full view of all those strangers.

The ballpark spoke about The Kid from San Diego who hit .400 in that year of lost innocence. We were on the threshold of a war that would change America forever but, back then, baseball was our best seller, a story people bought and talked about every day, a tale from radios perched on a thousand windowsills as a million men, women and children gathered on stoops and porches, following the action.

*Ted Williams display,
San Diego Hall of
Champions.*
(*Courtesy of San Diego Hall of
Champions*)

Ted Williams is that time. Ted Williams is that country. Other heroes have come and gone. The violence of the brutal years defeated a lot of dreams, but Ted Williams remains. Still looking like . . . well, Ted Williams.

Why has he survived? Simple: He could do whatever it was that needed to be done. You need a guy to hit .388 with 38 home runs? No problem. You need a man to sit in the cockpit of a fighter plane and protect democracy? You need someone to make sure John Glenn doesn't get killed in Korea before he flies into outer space? Are you looking for a straight-talking, truth-telling, uncomplicated, no bee-essing, get-it-done, old fashioned, can-do, American kind of guy? Meet No. 9.

Baseball is a funny thing. It's bigger than just a game. It has all these memories and stories attached to it, which makes it truly unique. Who tells football or basketball stories? What kid really has an indelible hockey memory?

Sunday, you could see—really see—through the fog of those long-gone summers. And you could hear —absolutely hear—the ballpark talk when Ted Williams stepped to the microphone, The Kid come home.

Then he took that swing. Spoke a few words. Tipped his cap. Glances around, eyes repelling years of current gratitude and nostalgic regret. There he was, legend married to magic: Ted Williams, up there for all the kids who ever were. He is the man who made summer last forever.

TED WILLIAMS
by Mark Schraf

Splintered

distilled American
singular stud
master of sticks
ash
reel or
flight control
alone not lonely in
box
stream or
miles high

now
wheeled like a 70's
reliever
never left
yet so

alone

(*"Ted Williams" is from Mark Schraf's book,* Cooperstown Verses:
Poems About Each Hall Of Famer, *published by McFarland and Co., Inc., 2001*)

Index

Permissions

MIKE BARNICLE
From "A Hero is Forever" first published in *The Boston Globe*, May 19, 1991. Reprinted courtesy of *The Boston Globe*.

WADE BOGGS & DAVID BRISSON
Excerpt from *The Techniques of Modern Hitting*, copyright 1990 by CSMG Productions, Inc. Reprinted by permission of The Putnam Publishing Group.

BOB CAIRNS
Excerpt from *Pen Men*, copyright 1992 by Bob Cairns. Reprinted by permission of St. Martin's Press, Inc.

GENE CARNEY
"The Kid" from *Romancing the Horsehide: Baseball Poems on Players and the Game*, copyright 1993 by Gene Carney. Reprinted by permission of McFarland & Company, Inc. Publishers.

JOSEPH CARRIERI
Excerpt from *Searching for Heroes*, copyright 1995 by Carolyn Productions. Reprinted by permission of author.

DAVID CATANEO
Excerpts from *Peanuts and Crackerjack*, copyright 1991 by David Cataneo. Reprinted by permission of Rutledge Hill Press.

JOCKO CONLAN & ROBERT CREAMER
Excerpts from *Jocko*, copyright 1967 by Time, Inc. Reprinted by permission of the University of Nebraska Press.

GREGORY CORSO
"Dream of a Baseball Star" from *The Happy Birthday of Death*, copyright 1960 by New Directions Publishing Corp. Reprinted by permission of New Directions Publishing Corp.

ARTHUR DALEY
Excerpt from All the Home Run Kings copyright 1972 by Arthur Daley. Reprinted by permission of G. P. Putnam's Sons.

DON DRYSDALE WITH BOB VERDI
Excerpt from *Once a Bum, Always a Dodger* copyright 1990 by Don Drysdale and Bob Verdi. Reprinted by permission of St. Martin's Press, Inc.

DAVID JAMES DUNCAN
Excerpt from *Brothers K*, copyright 1992 by David James Duncan. Reprinted by permission of Doubleday, a division of Bantam Doubleday Dell Publishing Group, Inc.

LARRY R. GERLACH
Excerpts from *The Men in Blue*, copyright 1980 by Larry R. Gerlach. Reprinted by permission of the University of Nebraska Press.

PETER GOLENBOCK
Excerpts from *Fenway*, copyright 1992 by Peter Golenbock. Reprinted by permission of Benay Enterprises, Inc.

LEE HEIMAN, DAVE WEINER, & BILL GUTMAN
Excerpt from *When the Cheering Stops*, copyright 1990 by Lee Heiman, Dave Weiner, and Bill Gutman. Reprinted by permission of Macmillan General Reference USA, a Simon & Schuster Macmillan Co.

TOMMY HENRICH
Excerpt from *Five O'clock Lightning*, copyright 1992 by Tommy Henrich. Reprinted by permission of Carol Publishing Group, a Birch Lane Press book.

JOHN HOLWAY
Excerpts from *The Last .400 Hitter*, copyright 1991 by John Holway. Reprinted by permission of author.

DONALD HONIG
Excerpt from *The Power Hitters*, copyright 1989. Reprinted by permission of The Sporting News.

NEIL D. ISAACS
Excerpts from *Innocence and Wonder*, copyright 1994 by Neil D. Isaacs. Reprinted by permission of Masters Press.

MARVIN KONER
"Ted Williams—Still a Major Leaguer" first published in *Collier's* magazine, July 18, 1953. Reprinted by permission of Sylvia Koner.

MICKEY MANTLE
Excerpt from *The Education of a Baseball Player*, copyright 1967 by Mickey Mantle. Reprinted by permission of Simon & Schuster.

LARRY MOFFI
Excerpts from *This Side of Cooperstown: An Oral History of Major League Baseball in the 1950's*, copyright 1996 by Larry Moffi. Reprinted by permission of the University of Iowa Press.

BILL NOWLIN
"Ted Williams: His Photos Are Real Find After 50 Years" first published in *Red Sox Official Scorebook Magazine*, Fifth Edition, 1996. Reprinted by permission of author.

GRANTLAND RICE
"Open Letter to Ted Williams" from *SPORT* magazine, copyright 1957. Reprinted courtesy of *SPORT* magazine.

ART RUST, JR.
Excerpt from *Confessions of a Baseball Junkie*, copyright 1985 by Art Rust, Jr. Reprinted by permission of William Morrow & Co.

MARK SCHRAF
"Ted Williams" is from Mark Schraf's book, *Cooperstown Verses: Poems About Each Hall of Famer*, published by McFarland and Co., Inc., 2001. Reprinted by permission of the author.

MIKE SCHACHT
Excerpts from *Mudville Diaries*, copyright 1996 by *Fan Magazine*. Reprinted by permission of William Morrow & Co.

MIKE SHANNON
"Ted Williams in His Hotel Room" from *The Day Satchel Paige and the Pittsburgh Crawfords Came to Hertford, N.C.*, copyright 1992 by Mike Shannon. Reprinted by permission of McFarland & Company, Inc. Publishers.

MIKE SHATZKIN
Excerpt from *The Ballplayers* copyright 1990 by Mike Shatzkin. Reprinted by permission of author.

CURT SMITH
Excerpts from *The Storytellers*, copyright 1995 by Curt Smith. Reprinted by permission of Macmillan General Reference USA, a Simon & Schuster Macmillan Co.

GEORGE SULLIVAN
Excerpts from *The Picture History of the Boston Red Sox*, copyright 1979 by George Sullivan. Reprinted by permission of author.

ALEX THEROUX
"Ted Williams' Edge" was written for this book.

DENNIS TUTTLE
Excerpt from manuscript in progress titled *Still Slingin': The Sammy Baugh Story*, copyright by Dennis Tuttle. Reprinted by permission of author.

JOHN UNDERWOOD WITH TED WILLIAMS
Excerpts taken from *Fishing "The Big Three"*, copyright 1982 by John Underwood and Ted Williams. Reprinted by permission of Simon & Schuster.

DAN VALENTI
Excerpt from *From Florida to Fenway*, copyright 1982 by Dan Valenti. Reprinted by permission of author.

DAVID WARSH
From "Weld's Turn at Bat" first published in *The Boston Globe*, July 27, 1997. Reprinted courtesy of *The Boston Globe*.

SHELBY WHITFIELD
Excerpts from *Kiss It Goodbye*, copyright 1973 by Shelby Whitfield. Reprinted by permission of author.

DICK WIMMER
Excerpt from manuscript in progress titled *Teddy Ballgame* copyright by Dick Wimmer. Reprinted by permission of author.

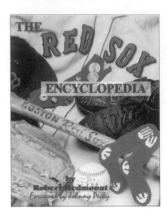
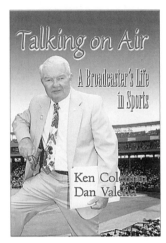
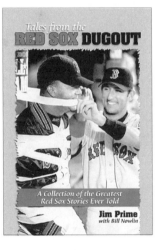